Weight equivalents

IMPERIAL	METRIC	IMPERIAL	METRIC
½oz	15g	5½oz	150g
¾oz	20g	6oz	175g
1oz	30g	7oz	200g
1½oz	45g	8oz	225g
1¾oz	50g	9oz	250g
2oz	60g	10oz	300g
2½oz	75g	1lb	450g
3oz	85g	1lb 2oz	500g
3½oz	100g	1½lb	675g
4oz	115g	2lb	900g
4½oz	125g	2¼lb	1kg
5oz	140g	3lb 3oz	1.5kg

Cake pan equivalents

ROUND PAN	SQUARE PAN
6in (15cm)	5in (12cm)
7in (18cm)	6in (15cm)
7½in (19cm)	6½in (16cm)
8in (20cm)	7in (18cm)
9in (23cm)	8in (20cm)
10in (25cm)	9in (23cm)

Yeast equivalents

1 tsp dried yeast = ⅕oz / 5g fresh yeast

1 cake fresh yeast = 3 tsp dried yeast = ½oz / 15g fresh yeast

Calculating pastry quantities

For basic shortcrust pastry use half the amount of fat to flour.

SIZE OF TART PAN	QUANTITY OF FLOUR
6in (15cm)	4oz (115g)
7in (18cm)	5oz (140g)
7½in (19cm)	5½oz (150g)
8in (20cm)	6oz (175g)
9in (23cm)	7oz (200g)
10in (25cm)	8oz (225g)

ILLUSTRATED STEP-BY-STEP
Baking

ILLUSTRATED STEP-BY-STEP
Baking

Caroline Bretherton

LONDON, NEW YORK,
MUNICH, MELBOURNE, DELHI

Senior Editor Alastair Laing
Project Art Editor Kathryn Wilding
US Editor Rebecca Warren
Managing Editor Dawn Henderson
Managing Art Editor Christine Keilty
Senior Jacket Creative Nicola Powling
Senior Production Editor Maria Elia
Senior Production Controller Alice Holloway
Creative Technical Support Sonia Charbonnier
Photographers Howard Shooter, Michael Hart

DK INDIA
Project Editor Charis Bhagianathan
Senior Art Editor Neha Ahuja
Project Designer Divya PR
Assistant Art Editor Mansi Nagdev
Managing Editor Glenda Fernandes
Managing Art Editor Navidita Thapa
DTP Manager Sunil Sharma
Production Manager Pankaj Sharma
DTP Operators Neeraj Bhatia,
Sourabh Challariya, Arjinder Singh

First American Edition, 2011
Published in the United States by
DK Publishing, 375 Hudson Street
New York, New York 10014

11 12 13 10 9 8 7 6 5 4 3 2 1
001 – 181842 – Sept/2011

A catalog record for this book is available from
the Library of Congress.

ISBN 978-0-7566-8679-6

Color reproduction by Alta Image
Printed and bound by L-Rex, China

DK books are available at special discounts when
purchased in bulk for sales promotions, premiums,
fund-raising, or educational use. For details, contact:
DK Publishing Special Markets, 375 Hudson Street,
New York, New York 10014 or SpecialSales@dk.com

Discover more at www.dk.com

Contents

Introduction

My first introduction to baking was at my first birthday party, when family history has it that I launched myself into a cream-laden gâteau head first, a moment carefully preserved forever by my mother's polaroid camera. Years later I have a similarly enthusiastic response to baked goods, albeit tempered by a lifetime of experience.

Getting It Right: Be Patient, Be Precise

Baking is something most people approach with caution, speaking of fallen sponges, soggy bottoms, and crumbling pastry. Yet it is, above all, a science. With a tried-and-tested recipe (as all the recipes in this book are) and careful application to quantities, timing, and temperature, there is little that cannot be achieved by the home baker. The key to competent baking is patience and precision. Read the recipe carefully, follow it unwaveringly, and you will rarely fail.

Must-have Equipment

Having said that, there are a few items of equipment that will help you along the way. Digital scales are an absolute must. Weighing ingredients carefully is vital to most baking. Unlike everyday cooking, where we can rely on taste and personal preference, the correct balance of fat to flour to eggs is always required to make a cake rise.

Beyond the scales a simple set of baking equipment should include: a set of quality, non-stick cake and tart pans, and baking sheets. A large mixing bowl, a set of measuring spoons, a spatula, a balloon whisk, electric mixer, and some wooden spoons. Many of the recipes in this book can be achieved with little else, but if you love to bake and would like to attempt the more complex recipes, I would recommend a standing mixer with dough hook. This takes a lot of the hard work out of bread making, for example, and well kneaded dough will always produce better bread.

Finally, an oven thermometer. It may seem strange when your oven has a temperature display on it, but the temperature inside some ovens differs significantly from the dial setting. For a small outlay you can buy a simple thermometer that hangs from the oven shelf and accurately reads the temperature inside your oven.

My Essential Tips

Once you have your equipment in place the best thing to do is practice. Carefully follow a new recipe the first couple of times you attempt it and you will soon find your confidence growing. You will start to understand how ingredients respond and work together so that, with time, you will be able to create your own alternative versions.

Cakes should mostly be light and airy. Barring the heavier fruit varieties, most cakes rely on air being whisked into the mixture then carefully preserved by a light touch when folding in the flour, before cooking. Although butter gives a richer taste to the finished cake, baking margarine will produce a lovely, light result too.

Meringues need a scrupulously clean bowl and not a trace of yolk in the egg whites, or they will not whisk well. A long, slow cook always helps. My oven is always too hot to produce a pure white meringue, so I counteract this by propping the door open slightly with the handle of a wooden spoon to allow the temperature to drop. Meringues that are cooled in the oven tend to crack less, too.

Pastry is often seen as more challenging than it should be. "Pastry hands" are basically just cool hands, helpful in preventing the fat from softening too much when preparing and rolling the pastry, which can cause it to end up greasy. If you're a little too warm-blooded, minimize contact by using a food processor to produce pastry crumbs, and even to bind the dough; also try to work in a cool kitchen and with chilled equipment. The real secret to making good pastry, however, is to use good-quality butter and egg yolks (and a little water if necessary) to bind it together. Other than that, pastry must be rested in a cool place before rolling, as this allows the glutens in the flour to relax; otherwise they become springy and cause the pastry to shrink and crack when baked. Do not over-flour the board, or the pastry will absorb too much flour. And handle pastry as little as possible, or it will become tough. Simple!

Bread making is the thing that has the average home baker running scared. Many of us rely on a bread maker, but using your hands and really getting to know your dough is the only way to produce top-quality bread at home. Yeast is a living organism and learning how it responds to time and temperature is a revelation. With thoughtful practice you could be producing quality artisan breads and saving yourself a fortune. If something goes wrong, try and work out why—did you under or over knead the dough? Did it have enough time to rise the first time? Did it rise too quickly? Was it too warm? Was the loaf sufficiently proofed before it went into the oven? Was the oven hot enough? These are all questions that may provide the answers to why a loaf came out less than perfect.

Strangely enough, my most common fault is one that is easily rectified. I always want to cut into my loaves as soon as possible. If they have just come out of the oven, the steam created inside them will be continuing to cook the loaf from the inside. Cut into the bread too early and all this steam will escape. The loaf will be compressed by the cutting action, and the crumb will feel damp on first eating, only to go dry and hard afterward. After all your patience in the process of making the loaf, surely it's worth waiting a little longer to produce a perfect crust and crumb?

About the Recipes

I have divided the recipes into classics, step-by-steps, and variations. The classics are of the "must have" variety, loved by bakers everywhere. The step-by-step spreads will help even the first-time baker get it right, and the variations are exactly that: variations on the theme of the step-by-step recipes, so that once you have mastered the main recipe you can try alternative versions, adding your own touches and developing new variations, to take your baking onto the next level.

Each recipe starts with information about quantity of servings, how long the recipe takes to prepare (including chilling, rising, and proofing times), cooking time, and whether it is possible to freeze the finished bake or freeze at an earlier stage of preparation. At the end of recipes, I provide information about whether the baked goods will store well and for how long, and steps you can take to prepare ahead if you are pressed for time or planning a party. I have also included some crucial nuggets of advice from my baking experience in the form of Baker's Tips.

Caroline

Traditional Afternoon Tea

Currant Scones
page 142

15–20 MINS 12–15 MINS

Fondant Fancies
page 120

20–25 MINS 25 MINS

Carrot Cake
page 42

20 MINS 45 MINS

Shortbread
page 220

15 MINS 35–40 MINS

Light Fruit Cake
page 87

25 MINS 1¾ HOURS

English Muffins
page 444

25–30 MINS 13–16 MINS

Chocolate Éclairs
page 165

30 MINS 25–30 MINS

Coffee and Walnut Cake
page 30

20 MINS 20–25 MINS

Bara Brith
page 78

40 MINS 25–40 MINS

Chelsea Buns
page 160

🥣 30 MINS 🔥 30 MINS

Chocolate Cake
page 54

🥣 30 MINS 🔥 25–30 MINS

Pecan and Cranberry Loaf Cake page 76

🥣 30 MINS 🔥 50–60 MINS

Cherry and Almond Cake
page 71

🥣 20 MINS 🔥 1½–1¾ HOURS

Crumpets
page 516

🥣 10 MINS 🔥 20–26 MINS

Strawberry Shortcakes
page 143

🥣 15–20 MINS 🔥 12–15 MINS

White Loaf
page 402

🥣 20 MINS 🔥 40–45 MINS

Victoria Sponge Cake
page 28

🥣 30 MINS 🔥 20–25 MINS

Scones
page 140

🥣 15–20 MINS 🔥 12–15 MINS

Weekend Brunch

Waffles
page 532

10 MINS 20–25 MINS

English Muffins
page 444

25–30 MINS 13–16 MINS

Zweibelkuchen
page 368

30 MINS 60–65 MINS

Almond Crescents
page 156

30 MINS 15–20 MINS

Pão de queijo
page 410

10 MINS 30 MINS

Brioche Nanterre
page 101

30 MINS 30 MINS

Multi-grain Breakfast Bread
page 416

45–50 MINS 40–45 MINS

Buttermilk Biscuits
page 514

10 MINS 15 MINS

Croissants
page 150

1 HOUR 15–20 MINS

Banana, Yogurt, and Honey Pancake Stack page 512

10 MINS | 15–20 MINS

Jam Doughnuts page 182

30 MINS | 5–10 MINS

Hazelnut and Raisin Rye Bread page 464

25 MINS | 40–50 MINS

Danish Pastries page 154

30 MINS | 15–20 MINS

Staffordshire Oatcakes page 522

10 MINS | 15 MINS

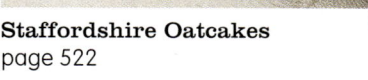

Crumpets page 516

10 MINS | 20–26 MINS

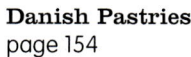

Buckwheat Galettes page 520

25 MINS | 25–30 MINS

Bagels page 434

40 MINS | 20–25 MINS

Skillet Bread page 498

5–10 MINS | 30–40 MINS

Picnic Basket

Feta Filo Pie
page 386

30 MINS   35-40 MINS

Chicken and Ham Raised Pie
page 378

50-60 MINS   1½ HOURS

Cornish Pasties
page 392

20 MINS   40-45 MINS

Forfar Bridie
page 395

15 MINS   20-25 MINS

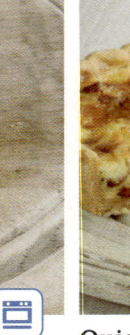

Spinach and Goat Cheese Tart
page 365

20 MINS   55-65 MINS

Quiche Lorraine
page 363

35 MINS   47-52 MINS

Walnut and Rosemary Loaf
page 403

20 MINS   30-40 MINS

Individual Pork Pies
page 380

40 MINS   1 HOUR

Spiced Lamb Pies
page 482

40-45 MINS   10-15 MINS

Fougasse
page 423

30–35 MINS | 15 MINS

Sausage Rolls
page 384

30 MINS | 10–12 MINS

Chocolate and Hazelnut Brownies page 228

25 MINS | 12–15 MINS

Pissaladière
page 478

20 MINS | 85 MINS

Whole wheat Fennel Seed Rolls page 409

20 MINS | 25–35 MINS

Pistachio and Cranberry Oat Cookies page 190

20 MINS | 10–15 MINS

Strawberry Tart
page 292

40 MINS | 25 MINS

Apple and Almond Galettes
page 172

25–30 MINS | 20–30 MINS

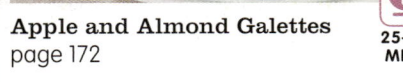

Almond and Peach Tart
page 289

20 MINS | 30 MINS

Sweet Party Bites

Whoopie Pies
page 126

40 MINS | 12 MINS

Mince Pies
page 336

20 MINS | 10–12 MINS

Raspberry Cream Meringues
page 242

10 MINS | 1 HOUR

Strawberries and Cream Macarons page 246

30 MINS | 18–20 MINS

Baklava
page 346

50–55 MINS | 1¼–1½ HOURS

Blackberry Focaccia
page 422

30–35 MINS | 15–20 MINS

Fruit Tartlets
page 297

40–45 MINS | 11–13 MINS

Raspberry Macarons
page 251

30 MINS | 18–20 MINS

Cinnamon Palmiers
page 178

45 MINS | 25–30 MINS

Savory Party Bites

Ciabatta Crostini
page 426

15 MINS | 10 MINS

Blinis
page 524

20 MINS | 15 MINS

Prawn and Guacamole Tortilla Stacks page 493

15 MINS | 10–15 MINS

Pizza Bianca
page 477

25 MINS | 20 MINS

Pane di patate
page 404

50–55 MINS | 40–45 MINS

Spanish Picos
page 432

40–45 MINS | 18–20 MINS

Pita Crisps
page 483

10 MINS | 7–8 MINS

Parma Ham-wrapped Canapés page 433

45 MINS | 15–18 MINS

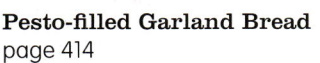

Parmesan and Rosemary Thins page 236

10 MINS | 15 MINS

Pesto-filled Garland Bread
page 414

35–40 MINS | 30–35 MINS

Chocolate Fix

Profiteroles
page 162

30 MINS | 22 MINS

Marbled Millionaire's Shortbread page 223

45 MINS | 35–40 MINS

Devil's Food Cake
page 58

30 MINS | 30–35 MINS

Pains au chocolat
page 152

1 HOUR | 15–20 MINS

Chocolate Cupcakes
page 118

20 MINS | 20–25 MINS

White Chocolate and Coconut Snowballs page 125

40 MINS | 25 MINS

Chocolate Fondants
page 132

20 MINS | 5–15 MINS

Chocolate Muffins
page 136

10 MINS | 15 MINS

Chocolate Millefeuilles
page 170

2 HOURS | 25–30 MINS

Raspberry Tart with Chocolate Cream
page 296

40 MINS · 20–25 MINS

Chocolate and Brazil Nut Cake page 50

25 MINS · 45–50 MINS

Chocolate Palmiers
page 180

45 MINS · 25–30 MINS

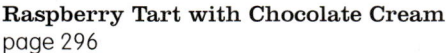

White Chocolate and Macadamia Nut Cookies page 191

25 MINS · 10–15 MINS

Sour Cherry and Chocolate Brownies page 232

15 MINS · 20–25 MINS

Chocolate and Pear Meringue Roulade page 262

25 MINS · 15 MINS

Chocolate Marble Cheesecake
page 274

35–40 MINS · 50–60 MINS

Chocolate Chestnut Roulade
page 104

50–55 MINS · 5–7 MINS

Chocolate Walnut Truffle Tart
page 326

45–50 MINS · 35–40 MINS

Children's Parties

Fondant Fancies
page 120

20–25 MINS · 25 MINS

Vanilla Cream Cupcakes
page 114

20 MINS · 20–25 MINS

Swiss Roll
page 36

20 MINS · 12–15 MINS

Sausage Rolls
page 384

30 MINS · 10–12 MINS

Chocolate Fudge Cake Balls
page 122

35 MINS · 25 MINS

Tarta di nata
page 317

30 MINS · 20–25 MINS

Hot Dog Pretzels
page 442

30 MINS · 15 MINS

Mini Bagels
page 436

45 MINS · 15–20 MINS

Spiced Carrot Cake
page 45

20 MINS · 30 MINS

Children's Bake Time

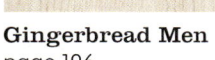

Gingerbread Men
page 196
20 MINS | 10-12 MINS

Banana Bread
page 74
20-25 MINS | 35-40 MINS

Rock Cakes
page 146
15 MINS | 15-20 MINS

Four Seasons Pizza
page 472
40 MINS | 40 MINS

Blueberry Cobbler
page 348
15 MINS | 30 MINS

**Hazelnut and Raisin
Oat Cookies** page 188
20 MINS | 10-15 MINS

Butter Cookies
page 192
15 MINS | 10-15 MINS

Quick Pumpkin Bread
page 500
20 MINS | 50 MINS

Cinnamon and Plum Crumble
page 352
10 MINS | 30-40 MINS

Flapjacks
page 224
15 MINS | 40 MINS

Prepare Ahead

Tropical Fruit Pavlova
page 255

15 MINS   65–80 MINS

Pistachio and Orange Biscotti
page 214

15 MINS   40–45 MINS

Dried Fruit Strudel
page 344

45–50 MINS   30–40 MINS

Black Forest Gâteau
page 108

55 MINS   40 MINS

Giant Pistachio Meringues
page 244

15 MINS   1½ HOURS

Ginger Cheesecake
page 275

40–45 MINS   50–60 MINS

Sticky Toffee Puddings
page 52

20 MINS   20–25 MINS

Individual Stuffed Panettones
page 93

1 HOUR   30–35 MINS

Tarte aux pommes
page 298

20 MINS 50–55 MINS

Cinnamon Rolls
page 158

40 MINS 25–30 MINS

Apple Jalousie
page 174

1¼–1½ HOURS 30–40 MINS

Rich Fruit Cake
page 82

25 MINS 2½ HOURS

Sourdough Rolls
page 456

45–50 MINS 25–30 MINS

Flamiche
page 366

20 MINS 40–45 MINS

Beef and Ale Cobbler
page 374

40 MINS 2½–3¼ HOURS

**Chicken Pot Pies
with Herb Crust** page 376

25–35 MINS 22–25 MINS

Anadama Cornbread
page 418

25 MINS 45–50 MINS

Salmon En Croûte
page 385

25 MINS 30 MINS

Fast and Fabulous

Brandy Snaps
page 218

15 MINS | 6–8 MINS

Apple Brown Betty
page 354

15 MINS | 35–45 MINS

Welsh Cakes
page 144

20 MINS | 16–24 MINS

Orange Soufflés
page 264

20 MINS | 12–15 MINS

Lemon Cheesecake
page 278

30 MINS

Madeleines
page 138

15–20 MINS | 10 MINS

Swedish Spice Cookies
page 198

20 MINS | 10 MINS

Génoise Cake with Raspberries and Cream
page 34

30 MINS | 25–30 MINS

Pear and Chocolate Cake
page 57

15 MINS 30 MINS

Swedish Pancake Stack Cake
page 521

10 MINS 15 MINS

Macaroons
page 202

10 MINS 12–15 MINS

American Blueberry Pancakes page 508

10 MINS 15–20 MINS

Chocolate Amaretti Roulade
page 106

25–30 MINS 20 MINS

Apple Muffins
page 137

10 MINS 20–25 MINS

Churros
page 185

10 MINS 5–10 MINS

Parsnip and Parmesan Bread
page 503

20 MINS 50 MINS

Southern US-style Cornbread
page 506

10–15 MINS 25–35 MINS

Stilton and Walnut Biscuits
page 234

10 MINS 20 MINS

everyday
cakes

Victoria Sponge Cake

Probably the most iconic British cake, a good Victoria sponge should be well-risen, moist, and as light as air.

SERVES 6–8　**30 MINS**　**20–25 MINS**　**4 WEEKS, UNFILLED**

Special equipment
2 x 8in (20cm) round cake pans

Ingredients
1 stick, plus 4 tbsp unsalted butter, softened, plus extra for greasing
¾ cup sugar
3 large eggs, at room temperature
1 tsp pure vanilla extract
1¼ cups all-purpose flour
1 tsp baking powder
½ tsp salt

For the filling
4 tbsp unsalted butter, softened
⅓ cup confectioner's sugar, plus more to serve
1 tsp pure vanilla extract
⅓ cup good-quality seedless raspberry jam

1 Preheat the oven to 350°F (180°C). Grease the cake pans and line with parchment paper.

2 Cream the butter and sugar with an electric mixer until fluffy, about 2 minutes.

3 Add the eggs one at a time, being sure to mix well between additions to avoid curdling.

4 Add the vanilla extract, and beat briefly until it is well blended through the batter.

5 Beat the mixture for a further 2 minutes until bubbles start to appear on the surface.

6 Remove the beaters, then sift the flour, baking powder, and salt into the bowl.

7 With a spoon, gently fold in the flour until just smooth. You can also mix in on low.

8 Divide the batter evenly between the pans, and smooth the tops with a palette knife.

9 Cook for 20 minutes or until golden brown and springy to the touch.

10 Test the sponges by inserting a skewer. If it comes out clean, the cakes are cooked.

11 Leave for a few minutes in the pans, then turn out on to a wire rack. Let cool completely.

12 For the filling, beat the butter, confectioner's sugar, and vanilla extract until smooth.

13 Spread the buttercream evenly onto the flat side of one sponge, using a palette knife.

14 Spread the raspberry jam in an even layer over the buttercream, right to the edges.

15 Top with the other sponge, flat sides together. Serve dusted with sifted confectioner's sugar.

STORE The filled cake will keep in an airtight container for 2 days. Unfilled, the sponges will keep for up to 3 days.

Victoria Sponge Cake variations

Coffee and Walnut Cake

A slice of coffee and walnut cake is the perfect accompaniment to morning coffee. Here the cake is made in smaller pans than the classic Victoria sponge to give it extra height and impact.

| SERVES 8 | 20 MINS | 20–25 MINS | 8 WEEKS, UNFILLED |

Special equipment
2 x 6¾in (17cm) round cake pans

Ingredients
1 stick, plus 4 tbsp unsalted butter, softened
1 cup light brown sugar
3 large eggs, at room temperature
1 tsp pure vanilla extract
1¼ cups all-purpose flour, plus extra for dusting
1 tsp baking powder
½ tsp salt
1 tbsp instant coffee mixed with 2 tbsp boiling water and cooled

For the frosting
7 tbsp unsalted butter, softened
1 cup confectioner's sugar
9 walnut halves

Method

1 Preheat the oven to 350°F (180°C). Grease the cake pans and dust with flour.

2 Cream the butter and sugar in an electric mixer or with an electric hand mixer until fluffy, about 2 minutes. Add the eggs one at a time, beating well between additions. Add the vanilla extract, and beat for a further 2 minutes until bubbles appear on the surface. Sift in the flour, baking powder, and salt.

3 Mix the flour on low until just smooth; try to keep the batter light. Fold in half the coffee mixture. Divide the batter evenly between the prepared pans, and smooth the tops with a palette knife.

4 Cook for 20–25 minutes or until golden and springy to the touch of a finger. Test the cakes by inserting a thin skewer. If it comes out clean, the cakes are cooked. Leave the cakes in the pans for a few minutes, then turn out on to a wire rack to cool completely.

5 To make the filling, beat the butter and confectioner's sugar together until smooth. Beat in the remaining coffee mixture. Spread half the buttercream evenly on to the flat side of one of the cakes. Top with the second cake, flat sides together, and spread with the remaining buttercream. Decorate with the walnut halves.

STORE The cake will keep in an airtight container in a cool place for 3 days.

Madeira Cake

In this simple cake, the flavors of lemon and butter shine through.

SERVES 8–10 | **20 MINS** | **50–60 MINS** | **UP TO 8 WEEKS**

Special equipment
8in (20cm) springform round cake pan

Ingredients
12 tbsp unsalted butter, softened
1½ cups all-purpose flour, plus extra for dusting
¾ cup sugar
3 large eggs, at room temperature
1½ tsp baking powder
½ tsp salt
finely grated zest of 1 lemon

Method
1 Preheat the oven to 350°F (180°C). Butter the cake pan and dust with flour.

2 Cream the butter and sugar in an electric mixer or with an electric hand mixer until fluffy, about 2 minutes. Add the eggs one at a time, mixing very well between additions.

3 Whisk for 2 minutes until bubbles appear on the surface. Sift in the flour, baking powder, and salt. Add the lemon zest. Mix in the flour mixture and zest on low until just smooth.

4 Spoon into the pan. Bake for 50–60 minutes or until a thin skewer comes out clean. Leave the cake in the pan for a couple of minutes, then turn out on to a wire rack to cool.

STORE The cake will keep in an airtight container for 3 days.

Marble Loaf Cake

For a twist on a classic sponge mixture, divide the batter in two and flavor half with cocoa before mixing them together for a wonderful marbled effect.

SERVES 8–10 | **25 MINS** | **40–50 MINS** | **UP TO 8 WEEKS**

Special equipment
9 x 5in (23 x 12cm) loaf pan

Ingredients
12 tbsp unsalted butter, softened, plus extra for greasing
1 cup all-purpose flour, plus more for dusting
¾ cup sugar
3 large eggs, at room temperature
1 tsp pure vanilla extract
1 tsp baking powder
½ tsp salt
¼ cup cocoa powder

Method
1 Preheat the oven to 350°F (180°C). Grease the loaf pan and dust with flour.

2 Cream the butter and sugar in an electric mixer or with an electric hand mixer until fluffy, about 2 minutes. Add the eggs one at a time, beating very well between additions. Add the vanilla extract, and beat for another 2 minutes until bubbles appear on the surface. Sift in the flour, baking powder, and salt. Mix on low just until smooth.

3 Divide the batter evenly between 2 bowls. Sift the cocoa powder into 1 of the bowls and fold in gently. Pour the vanilla cake batter into the loaf pan, then top with the chocolate batter. Using the end of a wooden spoon, a knife, or a skewer, swirl the 2 mixtures together, creating a marbled effect.

4 Cook for 45–50 minutes. Leave to cool slightly, then turn out on to a wire rack.

STORE The cake will keep in an airtight container for 3 days.

Angel Food Cake

This cake is as light as air. It contains no fat, so does not keep well, and is best enjoyed on the day of baking.

SERVES 8–12 | **30 MINS** | **35–45 MINS**

Special equipment
10in (25cm) tube pan with removable bottom
candy thermometer

Ingredients

For the cake
1¼ cups all-purpose flour
¾ cup confectioner's sugar

8 large egg whites
pinch of cream of tartar
1 cup sugar
few drops of almond or pure vanilla extract
fresh mixed berries, to serve

For the frosting
⅔ cup sugar
1 large egg white

Method

1 Preheat the oven to 350°F (180°C). Sift the flour and confectioner's sugar into a bowl.

2 Whisk the egg whites and cream of tartar until stiff, then whisk in the sugar, 1 tablespoon at a time. Gradually sift in the flour mixture, folding in with a metal spoon. Fold in the almond or pure vanilla extract.

3 Spoon the mixture gently into the tube pan, and level the surface with a palette knife. Place the pan on a baking sheet, and bake for 35-45 minutes, or until just firm to the touch.

4 Remove the cake from the oven, and invert the pan on to a wire rack. Leave the cake to cool completely, then run a knife around the edge and remove the bottom of the pan. Run the knife around the tube and the base to remove the cake from the pan.

5 To make the frosting, place the sugar in a saucepan with 4 tablespoons of water. Heat gently, stirring, until the sugar dissolves. Boil until the syrup reaches

soft-ball stage (238–245°F/114–118°C), or until a little of the syrup forms a soft ball when dropped into very cold water.

6 Meanwhile, whisk the egg white until stiff. As soon as the sugar syrup reaches the correct temperature, plunge the base of the pan into cold water to stop the syrup from getting any hotter, then pour slowly into the egg whites, still whisking, until the frosting forms stiff peaks.

7 Working quickly, because the frosting will set, spread it over the cake with a palette knife, swirling the surface to give texture. Serve with mixed berries.

STORE Angel food cake does not keep well, and the texture will change even on the second day, so avoid storing.

BAKER'S TIP
Sifting the flour twice produces a very light cake. For best results, try to lift the sieve high above the bowl, allowing the flour to come into contact with as much air as possible as it floats down. For an even lighter cake, sift the flour twice before sifting again into the egg mixture.

Genoise Cake with Raspberries and Cream

This delicate, whisked cake makes an impressive dessert, but is also ideal as the centerpiece for an afternoon picnic on a sunny summer's day.

SERVES 8–10 | **30 MINS** | **40 MINS** | **4 WEEKS, UNFILLED**

Special equipment
9in (20cm) springform cake pan

Ingredients

For the cake
3 tbsp unsalted butter, melted and cooled, plus extra for greasing

1 cup all-purpose flour, plus extra for dusting
4 large eggs
½ cup sugar
1 tsp pure vanilla extract
finely grated zest of 1 lemon

For the filling
2 cups heavy cream
11oz (325g) raspberries
1 tbsp confectioner's sugar, plus extra to serve

Method

1 Preheat the oven to 350°F (180°C). Grease the cake pan and dust with flour.

2 In an electric mixer with whisk attachment, or using a large bowl and a hand mixer, whisk together the eggs and sugar for at least 5 minutes, until they are thick, pale, and at least doubled in volume.

3 Sift the flour and carefully fold it into the mixture. Fold in the vanilla, lemon zest, and butter.

4 Put the batter into the cake pan and bake immediately for 40 minutes, or until the top is springy and a skewer inserted into the middle of the cake comes out clean.

5 Leave the cake to cool in the pan for a few minutes, then turn out and leave to cool completely on a wire rack.

6 When the cake is cold, cut it very carefully horizontally into three equal pieces, using a serrated bread knife.

7 In a large bowl, whip the cream until stiff. Crush the raspberries lightly with the confectioner's sugar and fold into the cream, leaving behind any juice so that the cream is not too wet.

8 Spread half the cream and raspberry mixture onto one piece of the cake, and top with a second piece. Spread the remaining cream mixture on to the second layer of cake and top with the final layer. Dust the cake with confectioner's sugar and serve immediately.

PREPARE AHEAD The cake will keep, unfilled, in an airtight container for one day.

BAKER'S TIP
This is a classic Italian cake that uses very little fat, and only a little melted butter, for flavor. These cakes are infinitely adaptable, and can be filled with anything you like, but should ideally be eaten within 24 hours of baking, because the lack of fat means they do not store as well as other cakes.

Swiss Roll

There is a trick to rolling up a Swiss roll—follow these simple steps and yours will come out perfectly every time.

SERVES 8–10 | **20 MINS** | **12–15 MINS** | **8 WEEKS, UNFILLED**

Special equipment
17 x 11in (43 x 28cm) jelly roll pan

Ingredients
3 large eggs
½ cup sugar, plus more to sprinkle
1 tsp pure vanilla extract
pinch of salt
½ cup all-purpose flour
½ tsp baking powder
6 tbsp strawberry jam, raspberry
    jam, or chocolate-hazelnut spread

1 Preheat the oven to 400°F (200°C). Line the jelly roll pan with parchment paper.

2 Set a bowl over a pan of simmering water; the base of the bowl shouldn't touch the water.

3 Whisk the eggs, sugar, vanilla, and salt with a hand mixer or whisk for 5 minutes, until thick.

4 Test the mixture is ready: drips from the beaters should stay formed for a few seconds.

5 Remove the bowl from the pan. Place it on a work surface. Whisk for 1–2 minutes until cool.

6 Sift in the flour, baking powder, and salt over the egg mixture and fold in very gently.

7 Pour onto the pan and level into the corners, smoothing the top with a palette knife.

8 Bake for 10-12 minutes, until firm and springy to the touch of a finger.

9 Check that the cake has shrunk away from the sides of the pan; this shows it is ready.

10 Sprinkle a large sheet of parchment paper evenly with a thin layer of sugar.

11 Carefully turn the Swiss roll out of its pan onto the sugar, so it lies upside down.

12 Leave to cool for 5 minutes, then carefully peel the parchment from the cake.

13 If the jam is too thick to spread, warm it gently in a small pan.

14 Spread the jam evenly over the top of the cake, being sure to reach all the edges.

15 Make an indent with the back of a knife along one short side, ¾in (2cm) from the edge.

16 With the indented side facing you, carefully start to roll the cake up, being gentle but firm.

17 Use the parchment paper to keep the cake tightly rolled and in shape. Leave to cool.

18 Peel off the parchment and place the cake, seam-side down, on a serving plate. Sprinkle with sugar. **STORE** It will keep in an airtight container for 2 days.

Swiss Roll variations

Orange and Pistachio Swiss Roll

Using the delicate flavors of pistachio nuts and orange flower water gives this classic recipe a slightly more modern twist. It is easily portioned and makes an ideal dessert for large parties and buffets.

| SERVES 8 | 20 MINS | 15 MINS | 8 WEEKS, UNFILLED |

EVERYDAY CAKES

Special equipment
17 x 11in (43 x 28cm) jelly roll pan

Ingredients
3 large eggs
½ cup sugar, plus more to sprinkle
½ cup all-purpose flour
½ tsp baking powder
pinch of salt
finely grated zest of 2 oranges and 3 tbsp juice
2 tsp orange flower water (optional)
confectioner's sugar, to dust
¾ cup heavy cream
2½ oz (75g) unsalted shelled pistachio nuts

Method
1 Preheat the oven to 400°F (200°C). Line the pan with paper. Combine eggs and sugar in a glass or metal bowl set over simmering water; the base should not touch the water.

2 Whisk the mixture with an electric hand mixer or balloon whisk for 5 minutes, or until thick and creamy. Drips from the beaters should briefly sit on the surface.

3 Remove the bowl from the pan. Whisk for 1-2 minutes until cool. Sift in the flour, baking powder, and salt over the egg mixture, and add half the zest and 1 tablespoon orange juice. Fold together.

4 Pour onto the pan and level into corners, smoothing with a palette knife. Bake for 10-12 minutes, or until firm to the touch and the cake has shrunk away from the sides.

5 Sprinkle a large sheet of parchment paper evenly with sugar. Carefully turn the cake onto the sugar. Leave to cool for 5 minutes, then carefully peel the parchment from the cake. Sprinkle with orange water.

6 Make an indent with the back of a knife along one short side, about ¾in (2cm) from the edge. With this side facing you, carefully roll the cake up, using the parchment to keep the cake in shape. Leave to cool.

7 For the filling, chop the nuts and set aside. Whip the cream, and fold in the nuts, remaining zest, and juice. Unroll the cake and spread with cream. Discard the parchment and carefully place the cake, seam-side down, on a serving plate or cake stand, and dust with confectioner's sugar. Serve immediately.

BAKER'S TIP
If a recipe requires a Swiss roll to be completely cool before filling, the cake will need to be rolled into shape while still warm, and then unrolled. Roll the cake around a fresh sheet of parchment paper. This will prevent the layers from sticking and allow the cake to be rolled tightly for a neat shape, and easily unrolled.

Spanish Rolled Sponge Cake

In this sophisticated Spanish take on Swiss roll, a tangy lemon sponge is rolled around a smooth filling of chocolate-rum ganache, forming a pretty spiral for slicing. Impressive as a dinner party dessert. ▶

| SERVES 8–10 | 40–45 MINS | 7–9 MINS | 8 WEEKS, UNFILLED |

Chilling time
6 hours

Ingredients
butter, for greasing
⅔ cup sugar
5 eggs, separated
finely grated zest of 2 lemons
⅓ cup all-purpose flour, sifted
pinch of salt
½ cup confectioner's sugar
1 tsp ground cinnamon
candied lemon zest, to serve (optional)

For the ganache
4½oz (125g) dark chocolate, coarsely chopped
⅔ cup heavy cream
½ tsp ground cinnamon
1½ tbsp dark rum

Method
1 Preheat the oven to 425°F (220°C). Grease and line a baking sheet with parchment paper. Mix ½ cup sugar with the egg yolks and zest. With an electric mixer, beat for 3–5 minutes until thick. In a metal bowl, whisk the egg whites until stiff. Sprinkle in the remaining sugar and whisk until glossy. Add salt to the yolk mix, then sift and fold in the flour, and the egg whites.

2 Pour the mixture on to the prepared baking sheet and spread it almost to the edges. Bake near the bottom of the oven for 7–9 minutes, until firm and golden brown. Remove cake from the oven, remove the parchment, and roll cake up. Let cool.

3 For the ganache, put the chocolate in a large bowl. Heat the cream with the cinnamon in a small saucepan until almost boiling. Add to the chocolate and stir until melted. Let cool and add the rum. Beat the ganache with an electric whisk for 5–10 minutes, until thick and fluffy.

4 Mix half the confectioner's sugar with cinnamon in a small sieve. Sprinkle the mixture evenly over a large sheet of parchment paper. Place the cake on the sugared paper and gently unroll it. Spread the ganache evenly over the cake. Carefully roll up the filled cake as before and chill for about 6 hours, or until the filling is firm. Unwrap the cake, trim each end, sift over the remaining confectioner's sugar, and scatter with candied lemon zest (if using).

Ginger Cake

Deeply flavored with preserved ginger, this rich and moist ginger cake is a firm favorite, and keeps well for up to a week—should it last that long!

| SERVES 12 | 20 MINS | 35–45 MINS | UP TO 8 WEEKS |

Special equipment
8in (20cm) square cake pan

Ingredients
8 tbsp unsalted butter, softened, plus extra for greasing
1 cup corn syrup
½ cup dark brown sugar
¾ cup milk
4 tbsp syrup from preserved ginger jar
finely grated zest of 1 orange
1½ cups all-purpose flour
1 tsp baking powder
¼ tsp salt
1 tsp baking soda
1 tsp pumpkin pie spice
1 tsp cinnamon
2 tsp ground ginger
4 pieces of preserved ginger, finely chopped and tossed in 1 tbsp all-purpose flour
1 large egg, lightly beaten

Method

1 Preheat the oven to 340°F (170°C). Grease the cake pan and line the base with parchment paper.

2 In a saucepan, gently heat the corn syrup, sugar, butter, milk, and ginger syrup until the butter has melted. Add the orange zest and leave to cool for 5 minutes.

3 In a large mixing bowl, sift together the flour, baking powder, salt, baking soda, and ground spices. Pour the warm liquid ingredients into the dry ingredients and beat them well, using a balloon whisk. Stir in the preserved ginger and egg.

4 Pour the batter into the pan and cook for 35–45 minutes, until a skewer inserted into the middle of the cake comes out clean. Leave to cool in the pan for at least 1 hour before turning out to cool on a wire rack. Remove the parchment paper before serving.

STORE This cake is very moist and keeps well in an airtight container for up to 1 week.

BAKER'S TIP
The use of corn syrup and dark brown sugar here gives a dense, moist cake that keeps very well. If the cake is beginning to get a little dry with age, try slicing it and spreading with butter as a breakfast snack, or even turning it into a rich version of Bread and Butter Pudding (see page 92).

Carrot Cake

For a more luxurious cake, double the frosting, slice the cake in two, and fill the middle as well.

| SERVES 8–10 | 20 MINS | 45 MINS | UP TO 8 WEEKS |

Special equipment
9in (22cm) round springform cake pan
zester

Ingredients
1 cup (4oz) walnuts
¾ cup sunflower or vegetable oil, plus extra for greasing
3 large eggs
1 tsp pure vanilla extract
1¼ cup light brown sugar
2 cups packed, coarsely grated carrots (about 3 small carrots)
⅔ cup (3oz) golden raisins
1½ cups all-purpose flour, plus extra for dusting
½ cup whole wheat flour
2 tsp baking powder
½ tsp salt
1 tsp cinnamon
1 tsp ground ginger
about ¼ tsp finely grated nutmeg
finely grated zest of 1 orange

For the cream cheese frosting
4 tbsp unsalted butter, softened
⅓ cup cream cheese, room temp
1½ cups confectioner's sugar
½ tsp pure vanilla extract
finely grated zest of ½ an orange

1 Preheat the oven to 350°F (180°C). Bake the walnuts for 5 minutes, until lightly browned.

2 Put the nuts into a clean kitchen towel and rub them to remove excess skin.

3 Pour the oil and eggs into a large bowl, add the vanilla, and pour in the sugar.

4 Using an electric hand mixer, beat the oil mixture until it appears lighter and thickened.

5 Squeeze the grated carrot very well in a clean kitchen towel to remove excess liquid.

6 Gently fold the carrot into the cake batter, ensuring it is evenly blended throughout.

7 By now, the walnuts should be cool. Roughly chop them, leaving some large pieces.

8 Add the walnuts to the mixture, along with the raisins, and gently fold them in.

9 Sift over the two types of flour and baking powder, then add in any bran left in the sieve.

10 Add the salt, spices, and orange zest, and fold all the ingredients together to combine.

11 Oil the base and sides of the cake pan and dust with flour. Pour the cake batter into pan.

12 Bake for 45 minutes. Test by inserting a skewer into the cake; it should come out clean.

13 If not, bake for a few more minutes and test again. Transfer to a wire rack to cool.

14 Combine the butter, cream cheese, vanilla, and confectioner's sugar, then grate in zest.

15 Using an electric mixer, cream together ingredients until smooth, paler, and fluffy.

16 Using a palette knife, spread the frosting over the cake. Make swirls for texture.

17 For additional decoration, zest the remaining orange using a zester tool.

18 Carefully place the finished cake on a serving plate or cake stand. Decorate the cake with the strands of orange zest. **STORE** The cake will keep in an airtight container for 3 days.

Carrot Cake variations

Zucchini Cake

This intriguing alternative to carrot cake is a true favorite.

SERVES 8–10 | 20 MINS | 45 MINS | UP TO 2 MONTHS

Special equipment
9in (22cm) round springform cake pan

Ingredients
¾ cup (4oz) hazelnuts
1 cup sunflower oil, plus extra for greasing
3 large eggs
1 tsp pure vanilla extract
1 cup sugar
1½ cups coarsely grated zucchini (1 small)
1½ cups all-purpose flour, plus more for dusting
½ cup whole wheat flour
2 tsp baking powder
1 tsp cinnamon
½ tsp salt
finely grated zest of 1 lemon

Method

1 Preheat the oven to 350°F (180°C). Oil the base and sides of the pan and dust with flour. Spread hazelnuts on a baking sheet and cook for 5 minutes, until lightly browned. Put the nuts on a clean kitchen towel and rub them to get rid of excess skin. Roughly chop and set aside.

2 Pour the oil and eggs into a bowl, add the vanilla, and pour in the sugar. Mix the oil mixture until lighter and thickened. Squeeze moisture from the zucchini and fold in with the nuts. Sift over the flour, add in any bran left in the sieve. Add the salt, cinnamon, and lemon zest, and fold.

3 Pour the batter into the pan. Bake for 45 minutes, or until springy to the touch. Turn out to cool completely on a wire rack.

STORE The cake will keep in an airtight container for 3 days.

BAKER'S TIP
Don't be put off by the unusual inclusion of zucchini. Zucchini are less sweet than carrots, but add moisture and a fresh flavor. The lack of frosting makes this cake healthier, too.

Quick Carrot Cake

Carrot cakes are perfect for novice bakers because they do not require lengthy whisking or delicate folding. This popular variation is very moist and will disappear fast.

SERVES 8 · **15 MINS** · **20–25 MINS** · **UP TO 8 WEEKS**

Special equipment
8in (20cm) round cake pan

Ingredients

For the cake
¾ cup vegetable oil, plus some extra for greasing
1 cup all-purpose flour, plus some extra for dusting
½ tsp ground allspice
1 tsp baking powder
½ tsp ground ginger
¼ tsp salt
2 carrots (about 1 heaping cup), coarsely grated
½ cup light brown sugar
⅓ cup (2oz) golden raisins
2 eggs, beaten
1 tbsp fresh orange juice

For the frosting
½ cup cream cheese, at room temperature
2 tbsp unsalted butter, softened
⅔ cup confectioner's sugar
2 tbsp fresh orange juice
lemon zest, to decorate

Method

1 Preheat the oven to 375°F (190°C). Grease the cake pan and dust with flour. Sift the flour, allspice, baking powder, ginger, and salt into a large bowl. Add the carrots, sugar, and golden raisins, then stir to mix.

2 Add the eggs, 1 tbsp of orange juice, and the oil. Stir together until well blended.

3 Pour in the cake mixture, and level the surface using a palette knife. Bake for 20 minutes, or until skewer inserted into the center comes out clean. Let stand in the pan for 10 minutes, to cool.

4 Run a knife around the sides, invert onto a wire rack, and leave to cool completely.

5 Meanwhile, beat the cream cheese with the rest of the orange juice and the confectioner's sugar. Spread the frosting over the top of the cake and decorate with lemon zest.

STORE The cake will keep in an airtight container for 3 days.

Spiced Carrot and Orange Cake

A fabulous cake for winter, with hints of warming spice and zesty orange. Baking it in a square pan allows the cake to be cut into bite-sized pieces, perfect for a party. **PICTURED OVERLEAF**

MAKES 16 SQUARES · **20 MINS** · **30 MINS** · **UP TO 8 WEEKS**

Special equipment
8in (20cm) square cake pan

Ingredients

For the cake
1 ½ cups all-purpose flour, plus extra for dusting
1 tsp ground cinnamon
1 tsp pumpkin pie spice
1 ½ tsp baking soda
½ tsp salt
½ cup brown sugar
⅔ cup sunflower oil or light olive oil, plus extra for greasing
2 large eggs
⅓ cup corn syrup
1 packed cup coarsely grated carrots (2 carrots)
finely grated zest of 1 orange

For the frosting
½ cup confectioner's sugar
⅓ cup cream cheese, at room temperature
1–2 tbsp orange juice
finely grated zest of 1 orange, plus extra to decorate (optional)
finely grated zest of 1 orange, plus extra to decorate (optional)

Method

1 Preheat the oven to 350°F (180°C). Grease the cake pan and dust with flour. In a large bowl, mix together the flour, spices, baking soda, salt, and sugar.

2 In another bowl, mix the oil, eggs, and syrup, then combine with the dry ingredients. Stir in the carrot and zest, transfer to the pan, and level the top.

3 Bake for 30 minutes, or until firm to the touch. Leave in the pan for a few minutes, then turn out to cool completely on a wire rack.

4 For the frosting, sift the confectioner's sugar into a bowl, add the cream cheese, orange juice, and orange zest, and beat with an electric hand mixer until thick and spreadable. Spread the frosting over the cake. Decorate with extra orange zest (if using), and cut into squares.

STORE The cake will keep in an airtight container for 3 days.

Lemon Polenta Cake

One of the few wheat-free cakes that work just as well as those made from wheat flour.

    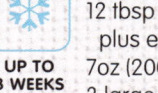

SERVES 6–8 | **30 MINS** | **50–60 MINS** | **UP TO 8 WEEKS**

Special equipment
9in (22cm) round springform pan

Ingredients
12 tbsp unsalted butter, softened, plus extra for greasing
7oz (200g) sugar
3 large eggs
½ cup polenta or coarse-ground cornmeal
1⅓ cups (6oz) ground almonds
finely grated zest and juice of 2 lemons
1 tsp gluten-free baking powder

1 Preheat the oven to 325°F (160°C). Grease the pan and line the base with parchment paper.

2 By hand, or in an electric mixer, cream the butter and 6oz (175g) of the sugar until fluffy.

3 Whisk the eggs and gradually beat them into the creamed mixture.

4 Fold in the polenta and almonds, or gently pulse-blend in a processor until well blended.

5 Finally mix in the lemon zest and baking powder well. The batter will seem stiff.

6 Scrape the mixture into the prepared pan and smooth the surface with a palette knife.

7 Bake the cake for 50–60 minutes, until springy to the touch. It will not rise much.

8 Check that the cake is cooked by inserting a skewer. The skewer should emerge clean.

9 Leave the cake in the pan for a few minutes, until cool enough to handle.

10 Meanwhile, put the lemon juice and the remaining sugar in a small saucepan.

11 Heat the juice over medium heat until the sugar has completely dissolved.

12 Turn the cake out on to a wire rack, baked side up, peeling off the parchment paper.

13 Using a thin skewer or toothpick, poke holes in the top of the cake while still warm.

14 Pour the hot lemon syrup a little at a time over the surface of the cake.

15 Only once the syrup has soaked into the cake, pour more on, until it is all used up.

16 Once cooled, serve the cake at room temperature on its own or with heavy cream or whipped cream. **STORE** The cake will keep in an airtight container for 3 days.

Wheat-free Cake variations

Chocolate and Brazil Nut Cake

This unusual wheat-free cake uses Brazil nuts instead of the typical almond and chocolate combination, to give a moist, rich finish to the cake.

SERVES 6–8 | **25 MINS** | **45–50 MINS** | **UP TO 4 WEEKS**

Special equipment
8in (20cm) round springform cake pan
food processor

Ingredients
5 tbsp unsalted butter, cubed,
  plus extra for greasing
3½oz (100g) good-quality dark chocolate,
  chopped
5½oz (150g) Brazil nuts
½ cup sugar
4 large eggs, separated
cocoa powder or confectioner's sugar, to serve

Method
1 Preheat the oven to 350°F (180°C). Grease the cake pan and line the base with parchment paper. Melt the chocolate in a bowl over a little simmering water (don't let the base of the bowl touch the water).

2 In a food processor, grind the Brazil nuts and sugar as finely as possible. Add the butter and pulse just until blended in. Continue to blend while adding the egg yolks one at a time. Add the melted chocolate and blend in thoroughly.

3 In a separate bowl, whisk the egg whites to stiff peaks. Turn the chocolate mixture into a large bowl and beat in a few tablespoons of the egg whites to loosen the mixture. Now carefully fold in the remaining egg whites.

4 Scrape into the pan and bake for 45–50 minutes, until the surface is springy and a skewer inserted into the middle of the cake comes out clean. Allow to cool in the pan for a few minutes, then turn out to cool completely on a wire rack. Remove the parchment paper. Sift over the cocoa powder or confectioner's sugar and serve with whipped cream.

STORE The cake will keep in an airtight container for 3 days.

BAKER'S TIP
This cake is a delicious dessert with thick cream. Be careful to pulse the butter into the nut and sugar mixture in short bursts—prolonged blending will release the oils in the nuts and give the finished cake an oily flavor.

Torta margherita

This Italian classic is made with potato flour and is as light as air.

SERVES 6–8 | **20 MINS** | **25–30 MINS** | **UP TO 8 WEEKS**

Special equipment
8in (20cm) round springform cake pan

Ingredients
2 tbsp unsalted butter, melted and cooled, plus
  extra for greasing
2 large eggs, plus 1 egg yolk
½ cup sugar
½ tsp pure vanilla extract
½ cup potato flour, sifted
½ tsp baking powder
finely grated zest of ½ lemon
confectioner's sugar, for dusting

Method
1 Preheat the oven to 350°F (180°C). Grease the pan and line the base with parchment paper.

2 In a large bowl, using an electric hand mixer, or an electric mixer with a whisk attachment, whisk the eggs, egg yolk, sugar, and vanilla extract together for at least 5 minutes, until thick, pale, and at least doubled in size. Gently fold in the potato flour, baking powder, and lemon zest, then fold in the butter.

3 Scrape the batter into the prepared pan and bake for 25–30 minutes, until the surface is golden brown and springy to the touch, and a skewer inserted into the middle comes out clean.

4 Leave the cake to cool for 10 minutes in its pan, then turn out to cool completely on a wire rack. Remove the parchment. Dust with confectioner's sugar to serve.

STORE The torta will keep in an airtight container for 2 days.

Castagnaccio

A traditional cake with a dense, moist texture.

SERVES 6–8 **25 MINS** **50–60 MINS**

Special equipment
8in (20cm) round springform cake pan

Ingredients
1 tbsp olive oil, plus extra for greasing
⅓ cup (2oz) raisins
¼ cup (scant 1oz) sliced almonds
¼ cup (scant 1oz) pine nuts
3 cups chestnut flour
2 tbsp sugar
pinch of salt
1¾ cup milk or water
1 tbsp finely chopped rosemary leaves
zest of 1 orange

Method

1 Preheat the oven to 350°F (180°C). Grease the cake pan and line the base with parchment paper. Cover the raisins in warm water and leave for 5 minutes to plump them up. Drain.

2 Put the almonds and pine nuts on a baking sheet and toast gently for 5–10 minutes, until lightly browned. Sift the chestnut flour into a large mixing bowl. Add the sugar and salt.

3 Using a balloon whisk, gradually whisk in the milk or water to produce a thick, smooth batter. Whisk in the olive oil and pour the batter into the pan. Scatter over the raisins, rosemary, zest, and nuts.

4 Bake at the center of the oven for 50–60 minutes until the surface is dry and cracked and the edges slightly browned. The cake will not really rise. Leave in the pan for 10 minutes, then carefully turn it out and leave it to cool completely on a wire rack. Remove the parchment paper.

STORE The Castagnaccio will keep in an airtight container for 3 days.

NOTE Chestnut flour is available from Italian delicatessens.

Sticky Toffee Puddings

This new British classic is said to have been invented in the Lake District in the 1960s. This recipe gets the balance of sweetness just right.

MAKES 8	20 MINS	20–25 MINS	UP TO 8 WEEKS

Special equipment
8 x (7oz/200g) ramekins

Ingredients

For the pudding
9 tbsp unsalted butter, at room temperature,
  plus extra for greasing
7oz (200g) pitted dates (Medjool are best)

2 tsp baking soda
2 cups all-purpose flour
1 cup brown sugar
1 tsp salt
3 large eggs

For the toffee sauce
¾ cup brown sugar
5 tbsp unsalted butter, cubed
⅔ cup heavy cream
pinch of salt
half-and-half, to serve (optional)

Method

1 Preheat the oven to 375°F (190°C). Butter the 8 ramekins well, getting into all the corners.

2 In a small pan, simmer the dates with the baking soda and 1 cup water for 5 minutes until softened. Purée with the cooking liquid in a blender.

3 Sift the flour into a mixing bowl, or into the bowl of an electric mixer, add the butter, sugar, salt, and eggs, and whisk with an electric hand mixer until well combined, then mix in the date purée. Pour the mixture into the ramekins, then place them on a baking sheet.

4 Bake for 20–25 minutes, or until firm to the touch. Meanwhile, make the toffee sauce. Melt the sugar, butter, and cream together in a pan until smooth and combined. Stir in the salt and allow to boil for a few minutes. Serve the warm puddings with the hot toffee sauce and some half-and-half, if you like.

PREPARE AHEAD The puddings and sauce can be made up to 2 days ahead and reheated. Place the puddings on a baking tray and warm through in an oven preheated to 350°F (180°C) for 15–20 minutes, and gently warm the sauce in a small pan. They can also be frozen and reheated in the same way after defrosting.

BAKER'S TIP
This recipe can also be used to make one large pudding. Add a few of the simmered dates, coarsely chopped, to the bottom of a 9 x 13in (23 x 33cm) baking dish before topping with the cake mixture, and bake for 40–45 minutes, until it is firm to the touch. Turn out onto a plate and drizzle with the toffee sauce.

Chocolate Cake with Buttercream

Everyone loves a classic chocolate cake, and in this version the yogurt in the mix makes it extra moist.

SERVES 6–8 · **30 MINS** · **20–25 MINS** · **8 WEEKS, UNFILLED**

Special equipment
2 x 6¾in (17cm) round cake pans

Ingredients
14 tbsp unsalted butter, softened, plus extra for greasing
¾ cup light brown sugar
3 large eggs
⅔ cup all-purpose flour
½ cup cocoa powder, plus extra for dusting
1 tsp baking powder
¼ tsp salt
¼ cup Greek, or thick plain yogurt

For the chocolate buttercream
4 tbsp unsalted butter, softened
⅔ cup confectioner's sugar, sifted, plus extra to serve
¼ cup cocoa powder
a little milk, if necessary

1 Preheat the oven to 350°F (180°C). Grease the pans with butter and dust with cocoa powder.

2 Place the butter and sugar into a large bowl, or in the bowl of an electric mixer.

3 With an electric hand mixer, or in the electric mixer, cream the mixture until light and fluffy.

4 Beat in the eggs one at a time, beating well after each addition, until well mixed.

5 In a separate bowl, sift together the flour, cocoa powder, baking powder, and salt.

6 Fold the flour mixture into the cake batter until well blended, trying to keep volume.

7 Gently fold through the thick yogurt. This will help to make the cake moist.

8 Divide the mixture between the 2 cake pans, smoothing the surfaces with a palette knife.

9 Bake in the middle of the oven for 20–25 minutes until risen and springy to the touch.

10 Test each cake by inserting a skewer into the middle; it should come out clean.

11 Leave the cakes in their pans for a few minutes then turn out on to a wire rack to cool.

12 For buttercream, put butter, confectioner's sugar, and cocoa powder into a large bowl.

13 With an electric hand mixer, blend mixture for 5 minutes, or until light and fluffy.

14 If the cream is stiff, add milk, 1 teaspoon at a time, until it reaches a spreading consistency.

15 Spread the flat base of one sponge with the buttercream, then top with the other sponge.

16 Place on a serving plate and sift confectioner's sugar evenly over the cake.
STORE The cake will keep in an airtight container for 2 days.

Chocolate Cake variations

Chocolate Almond Cake

A moist cake with a rich ganache topping. Use the best dark chocolate you can find—it will make all the difference.

| SERVES 6–8 | 30 MINS | 25 MINS | UP TO 4 WEEKS |

Special equipment
7in (18cm) round springform cake pan

Ingredients
12 tbsp unsalted butter, softened, plus extra for greasing
all-purpose flour, for dusting
8oz (250g) good-quality dark chocolate
²⁄₃ cup sugar
3 large eggs, separated
½ cup (2oz) ground almonds
¼ cup (1oz) white bread crumbs
½ tsp baking powder
1 tsp almond extract
1 tbsp brandy or rum (optional)

Method
1 Preheat the oven to 350°F (180°C). Grease the cake pan with a little butter, line with parchment paper, and sprinkle in some flour, tapping out any excess.

2 Break chocolate into pieces, and melt 4oz (115g) in a bowl over a pan of simmering water. Let cool. In a separate bowl, beat 8 tablespoons of the butter and sugar until creamy. Add the egg yolks one at a time, and beat well. Beat in the chocolate. Fold in the other ingredients with a rubber spatula.

3 Whisk the egg whites until soft peaks form. Fold into mixture, spoon into the pan, and bake for 25 minutes. Remove and cool on a wire rack. Melt the remaining chocolate and butter in a bowl over a pan of simmering water. Cool and spread over the cake.

STORE The cake will keep for 3 days.

BAKER'S TIP
Choose chocolate with a minimum of 60 percent cocoa solids for a richer taste. Do not melt this kind of chocolate in a microwave as the cocoa solids cause it to burn easily.

Fudge-Frosted Chocolate Cake

Always a crowd-pleaser, this cake is a must for your repertoire.

| SERVES 8–12 | 20 MINS | 40 MINS | UP TO 8 WEEKS |

Special equipment
8in (2 x 20cm) round cake pans

Ingredients
16 tbsp unsalted butter, plus extra for greasing
1½ cups all-purpose flour
¼ cups cocoa powder, plus extra for dusting
4 large eggs
1 cup sugar
1 tsp pure vanilla extract
1 tsp baking powder

For the chocolate fudge frosting
⅓ cup cocoa powder
1¼ cups confectioner's sugar
3 tbsp unsalted butter, melted
3 tbsp milk, plus extra to thin the mixture

Method
1 Preheat the oven to 350°F (180°C). Grease the pans, then dust with flour and cocoa powder. Sift the flour and cocoa powder into a bowl, and add all the other cake ingredients. Mix together with an electric hand mixer for a few minutes until well combined. Whisk in 2 tablespoons of warm water so the mixture is soft. Divide evenly between the pans, and smooth the tops.

2 Bake for 35–40 minutes, or until risen and firm to the touch. Leave to cool in the pans for a few minutes before turning out onto wire racks to cool completely.

3 For the frosting, sift the cocoa powder and sugar into a bowl, add the butter and milk, and mix with an electric hand mixer until smooth and well combined. Add a little extra milk if the mixture is too thick; you need to be able to spread it easily. Spread over the tops of the cooled cakes, then sandwich together.

STORE The cake will keep for 2 days in an airtight container.

Pear and Chocolate Cake

This rich, luscious cake is a good choice when you want to impress.

SERVES 6–8   **15 MINS**   **30 MINS**

Special equipment
8in (20cm) round springform cake pan

Ingredients
2 cups all-purpose flour, sifted
½ cup cocoa powder, sifted, plus more for dusting
2 tsp baking powder
1 tsp salt
9 tbsp unsalted butter, plus extra for greasing
¾ cup sugar
4 large eggs, lightly beaten
2oz (50g) dark chocolate, chopped (see Baker's Tip)
2 pears, peeled, cored, and chopped
⅔ cup milk
confectioner's sugar, for dusting

Method

1 Preheat the oven to 350°F (180°C). Grease the pan with butter and dust with cocoa powder. Sift flour, cocoa powder, baking powder, and salt into a medium bowl.

2 Cream the butter with the sugar using a wooden spoon or an electric hand mixer until pale and creamy. Beat in the eggs. Then add flour mixture gradually, add a little of the milk each time until all of it is combined. Fold in the chopped chocolate and pears.

3 Pour the cake mixture into the prepared pan, put it in the oven, and bake for 30–45 minutes, or until firm and springy to the touch. Allow to cool in the pan for 15 minutes, then remove from the pan, and transfer the cake to a wire rack to cool completely. Sift over confectioner's sugar before serving.

STORE The cake will keep in an airtight container for 2 days.

Devil's Food Cake

This American classic uses the flavor of coffee to enhance the richness of the chocolate, adding a wonderful depth to the finished cake.

SERVES 8–10	30 MINS	30–35 MINS	8 WEEKS, UNFILLED

Special equipment
2 x 8in (20cm) cake pans

Ingredients
7 tbsp unsalted butter, softened, plus extra
 for greasing
⅔ cup cocoa powder, plus more for dusting
1¼ cups sugar
2 large eggs, at room temperature

1½ cups all-purpose flour
1½ tsp baking powder
½ tsp salt
½ cup strong cold coffee
½ cup milk
1 tsp pure vanilla extract

For the frosting
1 stick unsalted butter, diced
¼ cup cocoa powder
¾ cup confectioner's sugar
2–3 tbsp milk
chocolate, for the shavings

Method

1 Preheat the oven to 350°F (180°C). Grease the cake pans and dust them with cocoa powder. By hand, or in an electric mixer, cream together the butter and sugar until light and fluffy.

2 Beat in the eggs one at a time, beating well after each addition, until well mixed. In a separate bowl, sift together the flour, cocoa powder, baking powder, and salt. In another bowl, mix together the cooled coffee, milk, and vanilla extract.

3 Next, beat alternate spoonfuls of the dry and liquid ingredients into the cake batter. Once the mixture is well blended, divide it between the pans.

4 Bake for 30–35 minutes, until the cake is springy to the touch and a skewer inserted into the middle comes out clean. Leave to cool in the pans for a few minutes, then turn out to cool completely on a wire rack.

5 For the frosting, melt the butter in a saucepan over low heat. Add the cocoa powder and continue to cook for a minute or two, stirring frequently. Allow the mixture to cool slightly.

6 Sift in the confectioner's sugar, beating thoroughly to combine. Blend, adding the milk 1 tablespoon at a time, until smooth and glossy. Allow to cool (it will thicken), then use half to sandwich the cakes together and the remainder to decorate the top and sides of the cake. Finally, use a vegetable peeler to create chocolate shavings and scatter them evenly over the top of the cake.

STORE This cake will keep in an airtight container in a cool place for 5 days.

BAKER'S TIP
Don't be put off by the inclusion of coffee in this recipe. Even if you don't normally like coffee-flavored cakes, use it here, as its inclusion gives a deep, dark fudgy texture to the chocolate cake, and also subtly enhances the chocolate flavor, rather than an overt coffee taste.

Chocolate Fudge Cake

Everyone should have a chocolate fudge cake recipe, and this one is a winner. The oil and syrup keeps it moist, and the frosting is a classic.

SERVES 6–8 | **40 MINS** | **30 MINS** | **8 WEEKS, UNFILLED**

Special equipment
2 x 8in (20cm) cake pans

Ingredients
⅔ cup sunflower oil, plus extra for greasing
1¼ cups all-purpose flour
¼ cup cocoa powder, plus extra for dusting
1 tsp baking powder
½ tsp salt
¾ cup light brown sugar
2 large eggs, at room temperature
⅔ cup milk
3 tbsp corn syrup

For the frosting
1 stick unsalted butter, at room temperature
¼ cup cocoa powder
¾ cup confectioner's sugar
2 tbsp milk, if necessary

Method

1 Preheat the oven to 350°F (180°C). Grease the pans and dust with cocoa powder. In a large bowl, sift together the flour, cocoa, baking powder, and salt. Mix in the sugar.

2 Gently heat the corn syrup until runny and leave to cool. In a separate bowl, using an electric hand mixer or balloon whisk, beat together the eggs, sunflower oil, and milk.

3 Whisk the egg mixture into the flour mixture until well combined. Gently add the syrup and divide the batter between the pans.

4 Bake the cakes in the middle of the oven for about 30 minutes, until springy to the touch, and a skewer inserted into the middle comes out clean. Leave to cool in the pans for a few minutes, then turn out to cool completely on a wire rack.

5 To make the frosting, melt the butter over low heat. Stir in the cocoa powder and cook gently for a minute or two, then leave to cool. Sift the confectioner's sugar into a bowl.

6 Pour the cooled melted butter and cocoa into the confectioner's sugar and beat to combine. If the mixture seems dry add the milk, 1 tablespoon at a time, until you have a smooth, glossy frosting. Leave to cool for up to 30 minutes. It will thicken as it cools.

7 When thick, use half the frosting to fill the cake and the other half to top it.

STORE This cake will keep in an airtight container for 3 days.

BAKER'S TIP

The frosting used here is a real staple in my kitchen, and can be used to finish so many chocolate recipes. Any cake that is slightly old can be heated for 30 seconds in a microwave, where the frosting will melt into a rich sauce, and can be served with vanilla ice cream for a delicious, quick dessert.

Baked Chocolate Mousse

Classic, but very easy to make, even for a novice. Slice the moist, fragile mousse with a sharp knife dipped in hot water, and wipe between cuts.

SERVES 8–12   **20 MINS**   **1 HOUR**

Special equipment
9in (23cm) round springform cake pan

Ingredients

2 sticks, plus 2 tbsp unsalted butter, cubed
12oz (350g) dark chocolate, broken into pieces
1½ cups light brown sugar
5 large eggs, at room temperature, separated
pinch of salt
cocoa powder or confectioner's sugar, for dusting

Method

1 Preheat the oven to 350°F (180°C). Line the base of the pan with parchment paper. In a heatproof bowl set over a pan of simmering water, melt the butter and chocolate together until smooth and glossy, stirring now and again (make sure the base of the bowl does not touch the water).

2 Remove from the pan and allow to cool slightly, then stir in the sugar, followed by the egg yolks, one at a time.

3 Put the egg whites in a mixing bowl with the salt and whisk with an electric hand whisk until soft peaks form. Gradually fold into the chocolate mixture, then pour into the cake pan and smooth the top.

4 Bake for 1 hour, or until the top is firm but the middle still wobbles slightly when you shake the pan. Leave to cool completely in the pan. Remove the parchment paper. Dust with cocoa powder or confectioner's sugar before serving.

BAKER'S TIP

To give a deliciously moist, almost gooey finish to this recipe, be sure not to overcook the cake. The center should be only just set when it is taken out of the oven, and when pressed gently with a finger it should hold the impression and not spring back. Serve with whipped cream.

German Apple Cake

This simple apple cake is transformed into something special with a delicious, crumbly streusel topping.

SERVES 6–8 | **30 MINS** | **45–50 MINS**

Chilling time
30 mins

Special equipment
8in (20cm) springform cake pan

Ingredients

1 stick, plus 4 tbsp unsalted butter, softened, plus extra for greasing
1 cup light brown sugar
finely grated zest of 1 lemon
3 large eggs, lightly beaten
1¼ cups all-purpose flour, plus extra for dusting
1 tsp baking powder
½ tsp salt
3 tbsp milk
2 tart apples, peeled, cored, and cut into even, slim wedges

For the streusel topping
1 cup all-purpose flour
½ cup light brown sugar
2 tsp ground cinnamon
6 tbsp unsalted butter, diced

1 To make the topping, put the flour, sugar, and cinnamon in a mixing bowl.

2 Rub in the butter gently with your fingertips to form a crumbly ball of dough.

3 Wrap the streusel dough in plastic wrap and chill in the refrigerator for 30 minutes.

4 Preheat the oven to 375°F (190°C). Grease the cake pan and line with parchment paper.

5 Cream the butter and sugar with an electric mixer until pale and creamy.

6 Add the lemon zest and beat slowly until well dispersed through the batter.

7 Beat in the eggs, a little at a time, beating well after each addition to avoid curdling.

8 Sift the flour, baking powder, and salt into the bowl, then mix in to the batter.

9 Finally, add the milk to the batter, and gently mix it in.

10 Spread half the mixture in the prepared pan, and smooth the surface.

11 Arrange half the apple wedges over the batter, reserving the best pieces for the top.

12 Spread the rest of the batter over the apples, and smooth once more with a knife.

13 Arrange the remaining apple wedges on top of the cake in an attractive pattern.

14 Remove the streusel dough from the refrigerator and coarsely grate it.

15 Sprinkle the grated streusel evenly over the top of the cake.

16 Bake in the center of the oven for 50–60 minutes. Insert a skewer into the center.

17 If the skewer emerges coated in batter, cook for a few minutes more and test again.

18 Leave the cake in the pan for 10 minutes, then carefully remove from the pan, always keeping the streusel on top, and cool on a wire rack. Serve warm.

Apple Cake variations

Apple, Raisin, and Pecan Cake

Sometimes I like a healthier cake. This cake uses little fat and is stuffed full of fruit and nuts, making it a virtuous yet delicious choice.

SERVES 10–12 | **25 MINS** | **30–35 MINS**

Special equipment
9in (23cm) round springform cake pan

Ingredients
butter, for greasing
2 cups all-purpose flour, plus more for dusting
⅓ cup (2oz) shelled pecans
1⅔ (7oz) cups peeled, cored, diced apples
¾ cup light brown sugar
2 tsp baking powder
2 tsp cinnamon
1 tsp salt
¼ cup sunflower oil
¼ cup milk, plus extra if necessary
2 large eggs, at room temperature
1 tsp pure vanilla extract
⅓ cup golden raisins
whipped cream, or confectioner's sugar, to serve

Method
1 Preheat the oven to 350°F (180°C). Grease the pan and dust with flour. Place the pecans on a baking sheet and toast in the oven for 5 minutes until crisp. Cool and coarsely chop.

2 In a large bowl, mix together the apples and sugar. Sift over the flour, baking powder, cinnamon, and salt, and fold in gently. In a bowl, whisk together the oil, milk, eggs, and vanilla extract.

3 Pour the milk mixture over the flour mixture and stir until well combined. Add more milk if needed to create a dropping consistency. Fold in the nuts and raisins and pour into the pan.

4 Bake in the center of the oven for 30–35 minutes, until golden and well risen. The cake is ready when the surface is springy to the touch. Leave to cool for a few minutes in the pan, then turn out on to a wire rack. Serve warm with whipped cream, or cold and dusted with confectioner's sugar.

STORE The cake will keep in an airtight container for 3 days.

Torta di mela

A firm dessert apple is best for this moist, dense Italian cake.

SERVES 8 | **20–25 MINS** | **1¼–1½ HOURS** | **UP TO 8 WEEKS**

Special equipment
9–10in (23–25cm) round springform cake pan

Ingredients
12 tbsp unsalted butter, softened
1¼ cups all-purpose flour, plus extra for dusting
½ tsp salt
1 tsp baking powder
1lb 6oz (630g) apples (about 3 medium apples)
finely grated zest and juice of 1 lemon
1 cup sugar, plus ¼ cup for glazing
2 large eggs, at room temperature
¼ cup milk

Method
1 Preheat the oven to 350°F (180°C). Grease the pan, and sprinkle with a little flour. Sift the flour with the salt and baking powder. Peel, core, and thinly slice the apples. Squeeze the lemon juice over the apples and toss well.

2 With an electric mixer, beat the butter until creamy. Add the sugar and zest, and beat until light and crumbly. Add the eggs one by one, beating well after each addition. Slowly beat in the milk until the batter is smooth.

3 Sift over the flour mixture and mix in gently. Stir in half the apple slices. Spoon the batter into the pan and smooth the top. Arrange the remaining apple slices in concentric circles on top. Bake for 1¼–1½ hours.

4 Meanwhile, make the glaze: Heat 4 tablespoons water with the sugar in a small saucepan over low heat until the sugar has dissolved. Bring to a boil and simmer for 2 minutes, without stirring, then let cool.

5 The cake is done when it shrinks slightly from the sides of the pan. Brush the sugar glaze on top of the cake, and let the cake cool in the pan. Transfer to a serving plate.

STORE The cake will keep in an airtight container for 2 days.

Toffee Apple Cake

Caramelizing the apples in this cake gives them a wonderful toffee apple taste, and soaking the cake in the buttery cooking juices after baking makes it especially moist and flavorful.

| SERVES 8–10 | 40 MINS | 40–45 MINS | UP TO 4 WEEKS |

Special equipment

9in (22cm) round springform cake pan

Ingredients

1 stick, plus 6 tbsp unsalted butter, softened, plus extra for greasing

¼ cup sugar

1⅔ cups (9oz) peeled, cored, and diced apples (about 1 large apple)

¾ cup light brown sugar

3 large eggs, at room temperature

1 cup all-purpose flour

1 tsp baking powder

½ tsp salt

confectioner's sugar, sifted, or whipped cream, to serve

Method

1 Preheat the oven to 350°F (180°C). Grease the cake pan and line the base with parchment paper. In a large frying pan, slowly melt 3 tablespoons of the butter and the sugar until the mixture is golden brown. Add the apples and fry gently for 7–8 minutes until they start to soften, brown, and take on a caramelized appearance.

2 By hand, or in an electric mixer, cream together the remaining butter and brown sugar until light and fluffy. Beat in the eggs one at a time, beating well between each addition. Sift the flour, baking powder, and salt together and fold into the egg mixture.

3 Remove the apples from the pan with a slotted spoon and set aside the pan with the juices to use later. Scatter the apples over the base of the pan. Spoon the batter on top, then place the pan on a baking tray, with sides to catch any drips, and bake in the center of the oven for 40–45 minutes. Leave to cool slightly, then transfer to a wire rack.

4 Put the frying pan with the leftover juices back on low heat, and heat gently until fully liquid. With a skewer, make holes over the surface of the cake. Put the cake on a plate and pour over the apple syrup, letting it soak in. Serve warm with whipped cream, or cooled and dusted with confectioner's sugar.

STORE The cake will keep in an airtight container for 3 days.

Rhubarb and Ginger Upside Down Cake

Young rhubarb is cooked into a simple upside down cake to give a modern twist on a classic dessert.

SERVES 6–8	40 MINS	40–45 MINS

Special equipment
9in (22cm) round springform cake pan

Ingredients

1 stick, plus 3 tbsp unsalted butter, softened, plus extra for greasing
1lb 2oz (500g) young, pink rhubarb
¾ cup dark brown sugar
4 tbsp finely chopped preserved ginger in syrup
3 large eggs, at room temperature
1 cup all-purpose flour

2 tsp ground ginger
1¼ tsp baking powder
½ tsp salt
heavy cream, whipped, or crème fraîche, to serve

1 Preheat the oven to 350°F (180°C). Grease the cake pan with the softened butter.

2 Line the base and sides of the cake pan with parchment paper.

3 Wash the rhubarb, removing discolored pieces and the dry ends of the stalks.

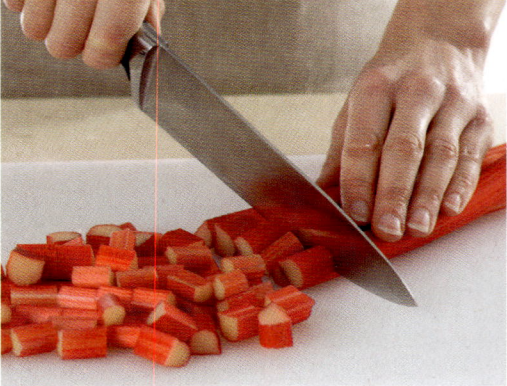

4 Cut the rhubarb into even-sized ¾in (2cm) lengths with a sharp knife.

5 Scatter a little of the sugar evenly over the base of the cake pan.

6 Now scatter half the chopped ginger evenly over the base of the pan.

7 Lay the rhubarb in the pan, tightly packed, making sure the base is well covered.

8 Place the butter and remaining sugar into a large bowl.

9 With an electric mixer, cream the butter and sugar until light and fluffy, about 2 minutes.

10 Beat in the eggs one at a time, beating as much air as possible into the mixture.

11 Gently mix the remaining chopped ginger into the cake batter, until well dispersed.

12 Sift the flour, ground ginger, baking powder, and salt into a separate large bowl.

13 Add the sifted ingredients to the bowl containing the cake batter.

14 Gently mix the sifted dry ingredients into the wet ingredients, keeping the batter's volume.

15 Spoon the cake batter over the rhubarb base, being careful not to disturb the rhubarb.

16 Bake the cake in the center of the oven for 45 minutes until the surface is springy.

17 Leave the cake to cool in its pan for 20–30 minutes, before carefully turning it out.

18 Serve warm as a dessert with whipped cream or crème fraîche. **STORE** The cake is also good cold and will keep in a cool place in an airtight container for 2 days.

Fresh Fruit Cake variations

Blueberry Upside Down Cake

This is an unusual yet delicious way of turning a basket of blueberries and a few pantry essentials into a quick and delicious dessert for a crowd.

SERVES 8–10 | 15 MINS | 40 MINS

Special equipment
9in (22cm) round springform cake pan

Ingredients
1 stick, plus 3tbsp unsalted butter, softened, plus extra for greasing
2/3 cup sugar
3 large eggs, at room temperature
1 tsp pure vanilla extract
3/4 cup all-purpose flour
1 tsp baking powder
1/2 tsp salt
1/3 cup ground almonds
2 1/4 cups (9oz) fresh or frozen blueberries
confectioner's sugar, to serve

Method
1 Preheat the oven to 350°F (180°C) and place a baking sheet inside. Grease the cake pan and line the base with parchment paper. By hand, or in an electric mixer, cream together the butter and sugar until light and fluffy.

2 Gradually beat in the eggs and vanilla extract, beating well between each addition, until well combined. Sift over the flour, baking powder, and salt and mix it in gently. Gently mix in the ground almonds.

3 Place the blueberries into the bottom of the prepared cake pan, ensuring there is an even layer. Spread the batter over the berries, taking care not to dislodge them.

4 Bake the cake on the baking sheet in the center of the oven for 40-50 minutes until golden brown and springy to the touch; a skewer inserted into the middle of the cake should come out clean. Leave to cool in the pan for a few minutes, before loosening the sides and gently lifting off the pan base and parchment paper.

5 Place the cake on a serving plate. Dust with confectioner's sugar and serve cold, or serve warm as a dessert with heavy cream or light vanilla custard.

STORE The cake will keep for 2 days in an airtight container.

Pear Cake

Fresh pear, yogurt, and almonds make this a very moist cake.

SERVES 6–8 | 40 MINS | 45–50 MINS | UP TO 8 WEEKS

Special equipment
8in (20cm) round springform cake pan

Ingredients
7 tbsp unsalted butter, softened
1/3 cup light brown sugar
1 egg, at room temperature, lightly beaten
3/4 cup all-purpose flour, plus extra for dusting
1 tsp baking powder
1/2 tsp ground ginger
1/2 tsp cinnamon
1/2 tsp salt
finely grated zest and juice of 1/2 orange
1/4 cup Greek yogurt, or sour cream
1/4 cup ground almonds
1 large pear, peeled, cored, and finely sliced
confectioner's sugar, to dust

For the topping
2 tbsp flaked almonds, lightly toasted
2 tbsp demerara sugar

Method
1 Preheat the oven to 350°F (180°C). Grease the cake pan and dust with flour. Cream the butter and sugar with an electric mixer or by hand until fluffy. Beat the egg into the creamed mixture.

2 Sift together the flour, baking powder, ground ginger, cinnamon, and salt and mix into the creamed mixture. Mix in the orange zest and juice, and yogurt or sour cream, then the almonds. Spread half the cake batter into the pan. Top with the pears and cover with the other half of the batter.

3 In a small bowl, toss together the flaked almonds and demerara sugar. Sprinkle the mixture over the top of the cake and bake in the center of the oven for 45–50 minutes.

4 Leave the cake to cool in its pan for about 10 minutes, then turn it out to cool on a wire rack. Serve warm or at room temperature.

STORE The cake will keep in a cool place in an airtight container for 3 days.

Cherry and Almond Cake

A classic combination of flavors, always popular with guests.

SERVES 8–10 · **20 MINS** · **1½–1¾ HOURS** · **UP TO 4 WEEKS**

Special equipment
8in (20cm) deep round springform cake pan

Ingredients
1 stick, plus 3tbsp unsalted butter, softened
²⁄₃ cup sugar
2 large eggs, at room temperature, lightly beaten
1¾ cups all-purpose flour, sifted
2 tsps baking powder
1 tsp salt
1⅓ cups (6oz) ground almonds
1 tsp pure vanilla extract
⅓ cup whole milk
14oz (400g) pitted cherries
¼ cup (scant 1oz) whole blanched almonds, chopped (lengthways looks pretty)

Method

1 Preheat the oven to 350°F (180°C). Lightly grease the cake pan and dust with flour. In a bowl, beat the butter and sugar with an electric hand mixer until creamy. Beat in the eggs one at a time, adding 1 tablespoon of the flour before adding the second egg.

2 Mix in the remaining flour, the baking powder, salt, ground almonds, and vanilla extract. Stir in the milk; and mix in half the cherries, then spoon the mixture into the pan and smooth the top. Scatter the remaining cherries over the surface, followed by the almonds.

3 Bake for 1½–1¾ hours, or until golden and firm to the touch. The exact cooking time will depend on how juicy the cherries are. If the surface of the cake starts to brown too much before it is fully cooked, cover with foil. When cooked, cool in the pan for a few minutes and transfer to a wire rack to cool completely before serving.

STORE This cake will keep in an airtight container for 2 days.

Bavarian Plum Cake

Bavaria is famous for its sweet baking. This unusual cake is a cross between a sweet bread and a custard fruit tart.

SERVES 8–10 | 35–40 MINS | 50–55 MINS | UP TO 4 WEEKS

Rising and proofing time
2–2¾ hrs

Special equipment
11in (28cm) tart pan

Ingredients

For the brioche dough
1½ tsp dried yeast
vegetable oil, for greasing

2¾ cups all-purpose flour
2 tbsp sugar
1 tsp salt
3 large eggs, at room temperature
1 stick, plus 1 tbsp unsalted butter, plus extra for greasing

For the filling
2 tbsp dried breadcrumbs
1lb 12½oz (875g) purple plums, stoned and quartered
2 large egg yolks
½ cup sugar
¼ cup heavy cream

Method

1 Sprinkle yeast over ¼ cup lukewarm water in a small bowl. Let stand for 5 minutes, until dissolved. Lightly oil another bowl. Sift the flour on to a work surface. Make a well in the center and add the sugar, salt, yeast mixture, and eggs.

2 Work in the flour to form a soft dough; adding more flour if it is very sticky. Knead on a floured work surface for 10 minutes, until very elastic. Work in more flour as needed so that the dough is slightly sticky but peels easily from the work surface.

3 Pound the butter with a rolling pin to soften it. Add the butter to the dough; pinch and squeeze to mix it in, then knead until smooth. Shape into a ball and put it into the oiled bowl. Cover, and let rise in the refrigerator for 1½–2 hours, or overnight, until doubled in bulk.

4 Grease the tart pan. Knead the chilled brioche dough lightly to knock out the air. Flour the work surface; roll out the dough into a 13in (32cm) round. Wrap the dough around the rolling pin and loosely drape it over the dish. Press the dough into the dish,

and cut off any excess. Sprinkle the breadcrumbs over the dough. Preheat the oven to 425°F (220°C). Put a baking sheet in the oven to heat.

5 Arrange the plum wedges, cut side up, in concentric circles on the brioche shell. Let stand at room temperature for 30–45 minutes, until the dough is puffed.

6 Put the egg yolks and two-thirds of the sugar into a bowl. Pour in the heavy cream, whisk together, and set aside.

7 Sprinkle the plum wedges with the remaining sugar and bake the tart on the baking sheet for 5 minutes. Reduce the heat to 350°F (180°C). Ladle the custard mixture over the fruit, return the tart to the oven, and continue baking for 45–50 minutes longer, until the dough is browned, the fruit tender, and the custard just set. Let cool on a wire rack. Serve warm or at room temperature.

STORE The tart will keep in an airtight container in the fridge for 2 days.

BAKER'S TIP

Baked custard should never be completely set when it is taken from the oven; instead, there should always be a slight wobble at the center when the pan is shaken, or the custard will be rubbery and hard rather than unctuous and yielding.

Banana Bread

Ripe bananas are delicious baked in this sweet quick bread. Spices and nuts add flavor and crunch.

MAKES 2 LOAVES **20–25 MINS** **35–40 MINS** **UP TO 8 WEEKS**

Special equipment
2 x 8½ x 4½ x 2½in (1lb) loaf pans

Ingredients
unsalted butter, for greasing
2¾ cups all-purpose flour,
  plus extra for dusting
2 tsp baking powder
2 tsp cinnamon
1 tsp salt
1 cup (4 oz) walnut pieces,
  coarsely chopped

3 large eggs, at room temperature
3 ripe bananas, peeled
  and chopped
finely grated zest and juice
  of 1 lemon
½ cup vegetable oil
1 cup sugar
½ cup brown sugar
2 tsp pure vanilla extract

EVERYDAY CAKES

1 Preheat the oven to 350°F (180°C). Grease each of the loaf pans thoroughly.

2 Sprinkle 2–3 tablespoons flour into each pan and turn to coat, then tap to remove excess.

3 Sift the flour, baking powder, cinnamon, and salt into a large bowl. Mix in the walnuts.

4 Make a well in the center of the flour mixture for the wet ingredients.

5 With a fork, beat the eggs in a separate bowl just until mixed.

6 Mash the bananas in another bowl with a fork, until they form a smooth paste.

7 Stir the bananas into the egg until well blended. Add the lemon zest and mix well.

8 Add the oil, both sugars, vanilla, and lemon juice. Stir until thoroughly combined.

9 Pour ¾ of the banana mixture into the well in the flour, and stir well.

10 Gradually draw in the dry ingredients, adding the remaining banana mixture.

11 Stir until just smooth; if the batter is over-mixed, the banana bread will be tough.

12 Spoon the batter into the prepared pans. The pans should be about half full.

13 Bake for 35–40 minutes, until the loaves start to shrink from the sides of the pans.

14 Test the loaves with a metal skewer inserted in the center; it should come out clean.

15 Let the loaves cool slightly, then transfer to a wire rack to cool completely.

16 Serve the banana bread sliced and spread with cream cheese, or toasted and buttered.
STORE Banana bread will keep in an airtight container for 3–4 days.

Loaf Cake variations

Apple Loaf Cake

Here, apples and whole wheat flour make for a healthier cake.

MAKES 1 LOAF | 30 MINS | 40–50 MINS | UP TO 8 WEEKS

Special equipment
9 x 5in (23 x 12cm) loaf pan

Ingredients
8 tbsp unsalted butter, softened, plus extra for greasing
½ cup all-purpose flour, plus extra for dusting
⅓ cup light brown sugar
¼ cup sugar
2 large eggs
1 tsp pure vanilla extract
½ cup whole wheat flour
1 tsp baking powder
¼ tsp salt
2 tsp cinnamon
2 apples, peeled, cored, and diced

Method
1 Preheat the oven to 350°F (180°C). Grease the pan and dust the base with flour. In a bowl, whisk together the butter and the sugars.

2 Beat in the eggs, one at a time. Add the vanilla extract. In a separate bowl, sift together the flours, baking powder, salt, and cinnamon. Fold the dry ingredients into the batter, mixing well.

3 Toss the apples in a little all-purpose flour, then fold them into the batter. Pour the mixture into the pan. Bake in the center of the oven for 40–50 minutes, until the cake is golden brown. Leave to cool slightly then turn out onto a wire rack.

STORE The cake will keep in an airtight container for 3 days.

BAKER'S TIP
When baking with any dried or fresh fruit, toss it lightly in flour before adding it to the wet ingredients. This floury coating will help stop the fruit from sinking to the bottom of the cake while cooking, ensuring it stays evenly distributed throughout.

Pecan and Cranberry Loaf Cake

Dried cranberries make a novel alternative to the more commonly used raisins, adding sweet and sharp notes to this wholesome cake. ▶

MAKES 1 LOAF | 30 MINS | 50–60 MINS | UP TO 4 WEEKS

Special equipment
9 x 5in (23 x 12cm) loaf pan

Ingredients
7 tbsp unsalted butter, plus extra for greasing
1¾ cups all-purpose flour, plus extra for dusting
½ cup light brown sugar
½ cup dried cranberries, coarsely chopped
⅓ cup pecans, coarsely chopped
finely grated zest and juice of 1 orange
2 large eggs, at room temperature
½ cup milk
2 tsp baking powder
1 tsp salt
½ tsp cinnamon
¾ cup confectioner's sugar, sifted

Method
1 Preheat the oven to 350°F (180°C). Grease the loaf pan and dust with flour. In a saucepan, melt the butter. Leave to cool slightly, then stir in the sugar, cranberries, pecans, and zest of 1 orange. Whisk together the eggs and milk, then stir them in as well.

2 In a separate bowl, sift together the flour, baking powder, salt, and cinnamon. Fold into the batter, mixing well. Pour into the pan, then bake in the center of the oven for 50–60 minutes. Leave to cool slightly, then turn out.

3 Mix the confectioner's sugar and remaining zest. Add enough orange juice for a drizzling consistency. Drizzle the icing over the cooled cake and let dry before slicing.

STORE Will keep in a container for 3 days.

Sweet Potato Bread

Savory sounding, this is very much a sweet cake and similar to a banana bread in looks and texture.

MAKES 1 LOAF | 10 MINS | 1 HOUR | UP TO 4 WEEKS

Special equipment
9 x 5in (23 x 12cm) loaf pan

Ingredients
7 tbsp unsalted butter, softened, plus extra for greasing
1½ cups all-purpose flour, plus more for dusting
6oz (175g) sweet potatoes, peeled and diced
2 tsp baking powder
pinch of salt
½ tsp pumpkin pie spice
½ tsp cinnamon
⅔ cup sugar
½ cup pecans, coarsely chopped
½ cup chopped dates
2 large eggs
½ cup sunflower or vegetable oil

Method
1 Grease the pan and dust with flour, knocking out any excess. Place the sweet potatoes in a saucepan, cover with water, and bring to a boil. Simmer for 10 minutes, until tender. Mash and set aside to cool.

2 Preheat the oven to 335°F (170°C). In a large bowl, sift together the flour, baking powder, salt, spices, and sugar. Add the pecans and dates and mix in thoroughly. Make a well in the center.

3 In a large measuring cup, whisk the eggs with the oil until emulsified. Stir in the potatoes until smooth. Pour into the flour mix and stir until well combined with no lumps.

4 Pour the batter into the loaf pan and smooth the top with a palette knife. Bake in the center of the oven for 1 hour, until well risen and a skewer comes out clean. Leave to cool for 5 minutes before turning out.

STORE The cake will keep in an airtight container for 3 days.

Bara Brith

This sweet Welsh "speckled bread" is at its best eaten the same day it is made, ideally while still warm and spread with butter.

MAKES 2 LOAVES | 40 MINS | 25–40 MINS | UP TO 8 WEEKS

Rising and proofing time
3–4 hrs

Special equipment
2 loaf pans (optional), 9 x 5½in (23 x 13cm)

Ingredients
1 (¼oz/10g) package yeast
1 cup warm milk
¼ cup sugar, plus 2 tbsp for sprinkling
1 small egg, plus a little more, beaten, for glazing
3¾ cups bread flour, plus extra for dusting
1 tsp salt
4 tbsp unsalted butter, softened and diced
1 tsp pumpkin pie spice
oil, for greasing
1½ cups dried mixed fruit (raisins, golden raisins, and mixed citrus peel)

Method

1 Whisk the yeast into the milk with 1 teaspoon of the sugar, cover with a towel, and leave in a warm place for 10 minutes until the mixture froths. Beat in the egg.

2 By hand, or in an electric mixer with a whisk attachment, rub the flour, salt, and butter together until the mixture resembles fine bread crumbs. Stir in the pumpkin pie spice and remaining sugar.

3 Make a well in the center of the dry ingredients. Pour in the milk mixture and bring it together with your hands to form a sticky dough. Turn out on to a lightly floured work surface and knead for up to 10 minutes. (If using an electric mixer, change to a dough hook and knead for 5 minutes.)

4 You should now have a soft, pliable dough. It should be quite sticky, but if it is not balling up into a single piece of dough, add a little more flour, 1 tablespoon at a time.

5 Place the dough in a lightly oiled bowl and cover with plastic wrap. Leave it to rise in a warm place for 1½–2 hours until doubled in size. Turn out on to a lightly floured work surface and stretch it gently out to a sheet around ¾in (2cm) thick.

6 Scatter the dried fruit over the dough and bring it together from the sides into the middle to form a ball again. Knead lightly for a couple of minutes until the fruit is well incorporated into the dough.

7 Shape the dough into your desired shape, or halve and put into the loaf pans. Cover with plastic wrap and a clean kitchen towel and leave in a warm place to rise for another 1½–2 hours, until again doubled in size.

8 Meanwhile, preheat the oven to 375°F (190°C). Brush the bread with a little egg wash and sprinkle it with 1 tablespoon of sugar. Bake for 25–30 minutes for loaf pans, or 35–40 minutes for a large freeform loaf. Cover halfway through cooking time with foil if it browns too much.

9 The bread is done when it is golden brown and firm and the bottom is hollow when tapped. Leave to cool for a good 20 minutes before cutting, as it will continue to cook after being removed from the oven. Cutting too early causes the steam to escape and the loaf to harden.

STORE The bread will keep in an airtight container for 2 days (see Baker's Tip).

BAKER'S TIP

As with most breads, baking two loaves and freezing one of them makes good sense when there is lengthy rising. Leftover bread can be toasted for a couple of days after baking, or sliced and used in Bread and Butter Pudding (see page 92).

celebration cakes

Rich Fruit Cake

This recipe makes a wonderfully moist, rich fruit cake, ideal for Christmas, weddings, christenings, or birthdays.

SERVES 16   **25 MINS**   **2½ HOURS**

Soaking time
overnight

Special equipment
Deep 8–10in (20–25cm) cake pan

Ingredients
- 1¼ cups (7oz) golden raisins
- 2½ cups (14oz) raisins
- 2 cups (12oz) prunes, chopped
- 2½ cups (12 oz) glacé cherries
- 2 small apples, peeled, cored, and finely chopped
- 2 cups cider
- 4 tsp pumpkin pie spice
- 1 stick, plus 6 tbsp unsalted butter, softened
- 1 cup dark brown sugar
- 3 large eggs, beaten
- 1⅓ cups (6oz) ground almonds
- 2 cups all-purpose flour
- 2 tsp baking powder
- 14oz (400g) store-bought marzipan
- 2–3 tbsp apricot jam
- 4 cups confectioner's sugar, plus extra for dusting
- 3 large egg whites

1 Place the golden raisins, raisins, prunes, cherries, apple, cider, and spice in a saucepan.

2 Bring slowly to a simmer over a medium-low heat, cover, and simmer for 20 minutes.

3 Remove from the heat. Leave overnight at room temperature; the fruits will absorb liquid.

4 Preheat the oven to 325°F (160°C). Double-line the cake pan with parchment paper.

5 Cream the butter and sugar with an electric mixer until fluffy, about 2 minutes.

6 Add the eggs, a little at a time, beating very well after each addition to avoid curdling.

7 Gently mix in the fruit and ground almonds, trying to keep the volume in the batter.

8 Sift the flour and baking powder into a large bowl, and mix into the batter.

9 Spoon the batter into the prepared pan, cover with foil, and bake for 2½ hours.

10 Test the cake is ready: a skewer inserted into the center should come out clean.

11 Leave to cool, then turn out on a wire rack to cool completely. Remove the parchment paper.

12 Trim the cake to level it. Transfer to a stand and hold in place with some marzipan.

13 Warm the jam and brush thickly over the whole cake. This will help the marzipan stick.

14 On a lightly floured surface, knead the remaining marzipan until softened.

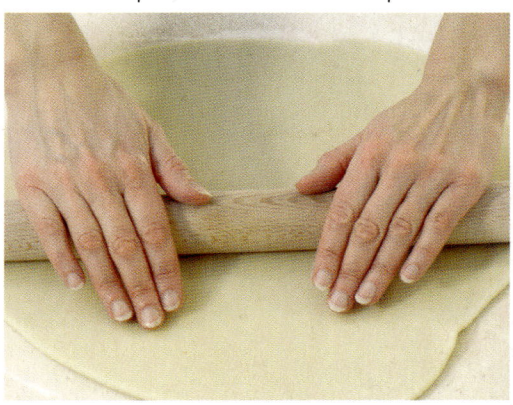

15 Roll out the softened marzipan until wide enough to cover the cake.

16 Wrap the marzipan around the rolling pin, and drape it over the cold fruit cake.

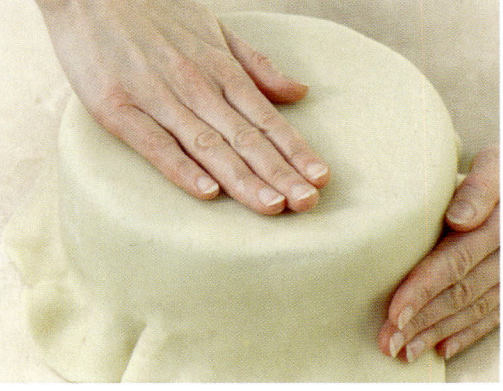

17 Gently, with your hands, ease the marzipan into place, smoothing out any bumps.

18 With a small, sharp knife, cut away any excess marzipan from the base of the cake.

19 Place the egg whites in a bowl and sift in the confectioner's sugar. Stir well to combine.

20 With an electric mixer, beat the sugar mixture for 10 minutes until stiff.

21 Spread the icing with a palette knife. **STORE** Will keep, un-iced, for 8 weeks.

Fruit Cake variations

Prune Chocolate Dessert Cake

Soaked prunes give this rich, dark cake a warming depth of flavor, making it a perfect dessert for the winter months.

SERVES 8–10 | **30 MINS** | **40–45 MINS** | **UP TO 8 WEEKS**

Soaking time
overnight

Special equipment
9in (22cm) round springform cake pan

Ingredients
½ cup (4oz) prunes, roughly chopped
½ cup brandy, or cold black tea
1 stick, plus 1 tbsp unsalted butter, diced, plus extra for greasing
9oz (250g) good-quality dark chocolate, at least 60% cocoa solids
3 large eggs, at room temperature, separated
⅔ cup sugar
1 cup (4oz) ground almonds
cocoa powder, sifted, to dust

Method

1 Soak the prunes in the brandy or tea overnight. When ready to bake, preheat the oven to 350°F (180°C). Grease the pan and line the base with parchment paper.

2 Melt the chocolate and butter over a pan of gently simmering water; do not let the base of the bowl touch the water. Cool. Whisk together the egg yolks and sugar with an electric hand mixer. Whisk the egg whites separately to soft peaks.

3 Mix the cooled chocolate into the egg yolk mixture. Fold in the ground almonds, prunes, and their soaking liquid, and mix until well combined. Beat 2 tablespoons of the egg whites into the cake batter. Gently fold in the remaining egg whites.

4 Pour the mixture into the pan, smooth the top, and bake in the center of the oven for 40–45 minutes. The center will still be slightly soft. Leave the cake to cool for a few minutes in its pan, then turn it out on to a wire rack.

5 Serve the cake upside down. Dust with cocoa powder and serve with cream.

STORE This will keep in an airtight container for 5 days.

Tea Bread

A simple recipe; don't forget to use the soaking water as well as the fruit.

SERVES 8–10 | **20 MINS** | **1 HOUR** | **UP TO 4 WEEKS**

Soaking time
overnight

Special equipment
9 x 5½in loaf pan

Ingredients
1¾ cups (9oz) mixed dried fruit (golden raisins, raisins, currants, and mixed citrus peel)
½ cup light brown sugar
1 cup cold black tea
unsalted butter, for greasing
½ cup (2oz) walnuts or hazelnuts, roughly chopped
1 large egg, beaten
1½ cups all-purpose flour, plus more for dusting
1½ tsp baking powder
½ tsp salt

Method

1 Mix the dried fruit and sugar together and leave to soak in the cold tea overnight. When ready to bake, preheat the oven to 350°F (180°C). Grease the loaf pan and dust with flour.

2 Add the nuts and the egg to the fruit mixture, and mix well to combine. Sift over the flour, baking powder, and salt, and mix in thoroughly.

3 Bake in the center of the oven for about 1 hour, until the top is dark golden brown and springy to the touch, and a skewer inserted into the center comes out clean.

4 Leave to cool for a few minutes in the pan, then turn out to cool completely on a wire rack. This is best served sliced or toasted with butter.

STORE The bread will keep in an airtight container for 5 days.

Light Fruit Cake

Not everyone enjoys a classic rich fruit cake, especially after a hearty celebration meal. This lighter version is a quick and easy alternative that's less heavy on the fruit.

SERVES 8–12   **25 MINS**   **1¾ HOURS**   **UP TO 8 WEEKS**

Special equipment
Deep 8in (20cm) round cake pan

Ingredients
1 stick, plus 4 tbsp unsalted butter, softened
1 cup light brown sugar
3 large eggs, at room temperature
1¾ cups all-purpose flour, sifted
2 tsp baking powder
1 tsp salt
2–3 tbsp milk
2 cups (10 oz) mixed dried fruit such as figs, pineapple, cherries if possible

Method
1 Preheat the oven to 350°F (180°C). Line the base and sides of the pan with parchment paper. In a bowl, beat the butter and sugar together with an electric hand mixer until creamy, then beat in the eggs, one at a time, adding a little of the flour after each. Mix in the remaining flour, baking powder, salt, and the milk; the mixture should drop easily from the beaters. Add the dried fruit and mix in until well combined.

2 Spoon the mixture into the pan, level the top, and bake for 1½–1¾ hours, or until firm to the touch and a skewer inserted into the middle of the cake comes out clean. Leave in the pan to cool completely. Remove the parchment paper.

STORE This will keep in an airtight container for 3 days.

Plum Pudding

So-named because it contains prunes, this is a classic Christmas dish, here using butter instead of the traditional beef suet.

SERVES 8–10 | **45 MINS** | **8–10 HOURS** | **UP TO 1 YEAR**

Soaking time
overnight

Special equipment
2¼lb (1kg) pudding bowl or 1 quart bowl

Ingredients
½ cup (3oz) raisins
½ cup (2oz) currants
⅔ cup (4oz) golden raisins
¼ cup (2oz) mixed citrus peel, chopped
1 cup (4oz) mixed dried fruit, such as figs, dates, and cherries, chopped
⅔ cup beer
1 tbsp whisky or brandy
finely grated zest and juice of 1 orange
finely grated zest and juice of 1 lemon
½ cup pitted prunes, chopped
⅔ cup cold black tea
1 apple, grated
8 tbsp unsalted butter, melted, plus extra for greasing
1 cup dark brown sugar
1 tbsp unsulfured light molasses
2 large eggs, at room temperature, beaten
½ cup all-purpose flour
1 tsp pumpkin pie spice
½ tsp baking powder
¼ tsp salt
1 cup fresh white bread crumbs
⅓ cup chopped almonds

Method

1 Put the first 9 ingredients into a large bowl and mix well. Put the prunes in a small bowl and pour in the tea. Cover the bowls, then leave to soak overnight.

2 Drain the prunes and discard any remaining tea. Add the prunes and the apple to the rest of the fruit, followed by the butter, sugar, molasses, and eggs. Stir well.

3 Sift in the flour with the pumpkin pie spice, baking powder, and salt, then stir the bread crumbs and almonds into the mixture. Mix together well until all the ingredients are thoroughly combined.

4 Grease the pudding bowl and pour in the mixture. Cover with 2 layers of parchment paper and 1 layer of foil. Tie the layers to the bowl with string, then put the bowl on a rack in a large deep pan of simmering water that comes at least halfway up the side. Cover tightly and steam for 8–10 hours.

5 Check regularly to make sure that the water level does not drop too low. Serve with brandy butter, cream, or custard.

STORE If well sealed, the pudding will keep for up to 1 year in a cool place.

BAKER'S TIP
When steaming a pudding for an extended time, it is very important that the water level in the pan should not drop too low. There are a couple of easy ways to avoid this. Either set a timer every hour, to remind you to check the water level, or put a marble in the pan so it rattles when the water level drops.

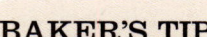

Panettone

A sweet bread eaten all over Italy at Christmas. Making one is not as hard as it seems, and the results are delicious.

SERVES 8 | **30 MINS** | **40–45 MINS** | **UP TO 4 WEEKS**

Rising and proofing time
4 hrs

Special equipment
High-sided panettone mold or 8in (20cm) springform cake pan

Ingredients
1½ tsp dried yeast
1 cup milk
¼ cup sugar
3¼ cups bread flour, plus extra for dusting
½ tsp salt
5 tbsp unsalted butter, melted
2 large eggs, plus 1 small egg at room temperature, beaten
1 tsp pure vanilla extract
1 cup mixed dried fruit (cranberries, apricots, golden raisins, and mixed citrus peel), chopped
finely grated zest of 1 orange
vegetable oil, for greasing
confectioner's sugar, for dusting

1 Add the yeast to the warm milk in a jug. Mix the sugar, flour, and salt in a large bowl.

2 Once the yeasted milk is frothy (5 minutes), whisk in the butter, large eggs, and vanilla.

3 Mix the liquid and dry ingredients to form a soft dough; it will be stickier than bread dough.

4 On a lightly floured surface, knead the dough for about 10 minutes until elastic.

5 Form the dough into a loose ball and stretch it out flat onto a floured work surface.

6 Scatter the dried fruit and orange zest on top and knead again until well combined.

7 Form the dough into a loose ball and put it in a lightly oiled bowl.

8 Cover the bowl with a damp, clean kitchen towel or place inside a large plastic bag.

9 Leave the dough to rise in a warm place for up to 2 hours, until doubled in size.

10 Line the pan with a double layer of parchment paper, or a layer of silicone paper.

11 If using a cake pan, form a collar with the paper, 2–4in (5–10cm) higher than the pan.

12 Knock the air out of the dough with your fist and turn out onto a lightly floured surface.

13 Knead the dough into a round ball just big enough to fit into the pan.

14 Put it into the pan, cover, and leave to rise for another 2 hours, until doubled in size.

15 Preheat the oven to 375°F (190°C). Brush the top of the dough with egg wash.

16 Bake in the middle of the oven for 40–45 minutes. If it's browning fast, cover with foil.

17 The bottom will sound hollow when ready. Leave to cool for 5 minutes, then turn out.

18 Remove the parchment paper, and cool completely on a wire rack before dusting with confectioner's sugar to serve. **STORE** The panettone will keep in an airtight container for 2 days.

Panettone variations

Chocolate and Hazelnut Panettone

This variation of the classic panettone is a surefire winner with any children and any leftovers make a particularly delicious Bread and Butter Pudding (see recipe below).

SERVES 8 | 30 MINS | 45–50 MINS | UP TO 4 WEEKS

Rising and proofing time
3 hrs

Special equipment
High-sided panettone mold or 8in (20cm) springform cake pan

Ingredients
3¼ cups bread flour, plus extra for dusting
¼ cup sugar
1½ tsp dried yeast
½ tsp salt
5 tbsp unsalted butter, melted
2 large eggs, at room temperature
½ cup milk
1 tsp pure vanilla extract
⅔ cup hazelnuts, coarsely chopped
finely grated zest of 1 orange
vegetable oil, for greasing
½ cup dark chocolate chips, or dark chocolate chunks, coarsely chopped
1 small egg, for glazing
confectioner's sugar, for dusting

Method

1 Combine the flour, sugar, yeast, and salt in a mixing bowl. Whisk together the butter, eggs, milk, and vanilla extract in a bowl.

2 Add the liquid to the dry ingredients and bring them together to make a soft, sticky dough. Knead for about 10 minutes by hand, until it forms a smooth, elastic dough.

3 Form the dough into a loose ball and stretch it out on a floured work surface. Scatter the hazelnuts and orange zest on top and knead the dough again until well incorporated. Form the dough into a loose ball and put it in a lightly oiled bowl.

4 Put the bowl inside a large plastic bag and leave it to proof to rise in a warm place for up to 2 hours, until doubled. Meanwhile, line the mold with silicone paper or double thickness parchment paper. If using a springform pan, make a ring of paper that forms a collar around the sides of the pan, finishing higher than the edge of the pan by 2-4in (5-10cm).

5 When the dough has doubled in size, knock it back and stretch it out again as in step 3. Scatter the chocolate over the surface and bring together, lightly kneading it before shaping it into a round ball just big enough to fit into the mold. Put it into the mold, cover it, and leave it to rise for another 2 hours.

6 When ready to bake, preheat the oven to 375°F (190°C). Brush the top with beaten egg, then bake in the middle of the oven for 45–50 minutes, covering with parchment paper after 20 minutes to prevent the top from browning.

7 Let the panettone cool in the mold for a few minutes before turning out to cool on a wire rack. Remove the parchment paper. Dust with confectioner's sugar to serve.

STORE The panettone will keep in an airtight container for 2 days.

Panettone Bread and Butter Pudding

Any leftover panettone can be turned into this quick and easy dessert. Try introducing different flavors such as orange zest, chocolate, or dried cherries to the dish before baking.

SERVES 4–6 | 10 MINS | 30–40 MINS

Ingredients
4 tbsp unsalted butter, softened
9oz (250g) panettone
1½ cups half-and-half, or a mixture of half heavy cream and half milk
2 large eggs
¼ cup sugar
1 tsp pure vanilla extract

Method

1 Preheat the oven to 350°F (180°C). Use a little softened butter to grease a medium sized, shallow baking dish.

2 Slice the panettone into ½in (1cm) thick slices. Butter each slice and lay them, overlapping slightly, into the baking dish. Whisk together the half-and-half, or cream and milk, eggs, sugar, and vanilla extract. Pour the liquid over the panettone and then gently press down on top to make sure it has all been soaked in the liquid.

3 Bake in the center of the oven for 30–40 minutes until it is just set, golden brown, and puffed up. Serve warm.

ALSO TRY...
Festive Panettone Pudding Plain panettone can also be spread with a little marmalade and the cream enriched with 1–2 tbsp whiskey and a grating of orange zest and nutmeg.

CELEBRATION CAKES

Individual Stuffed Panettones

Try these as an alternative dessert at a Christmas meal.

SERVES 6   **1 HOUR**   **30–35 MINS**

Rising, proofing, and chilling time
3 hrs proofing and minimum 3 hrs chilling

Special equipment
6 x 8oz (225g) ramekins

Ingredients
butter, for greasing
1 x panettone dough, see page 90, steps 1–9
7oz (200g) mascarpone cheese
7oz (200g) crème fraîche
1 tbsp Kirsch or other fruit liqueur (optional)
12 glacé cherries, quartered
4 tbsp pistachio nuts, coarsely chopped
confectioner's sugar, for dusting

Method

1 Grease the ramekins, then line them with parchment paper. The paper should stand about 2in (5cm) taller than the ramekins.

2 Cut the panettone dough into six, and place 1 piece in each ramekin. Cover, and leave to rise for 1 hour, or until doubled in size. Preheat the oven to 375°F (190°C).

3 Bake for 30–35 minutes. The panettones will be golden-brown. Remove 1 from its ramekin and tap the base. It should sound hollow. If it doesn't, remove all the panettones from their ramekins, place on a baking sheet, and bake for 5 minutes. Place on a wire rack and leave to cool completely.

4 Cut a disk from the bottom of each panettone, leaving a rim of around ½in (1cm). Use a gentle sawing action to lever the disk of bread out in 1 piece. Set aside.

5 Cut along the insides of the rim nearly to the bottom of the upside down panettone. Cut all around, then use your fingers to pull and scrape as much of the interior out as possible, leaving an intact shell.

6 Put the extracted pieces into a mini food processor and reduce to fine bread crumbs.

In a bowl, cream together the mascarpone and crème fraîche with the liqueur, if using.

7 Mix in the panettone crumbs and beat well. Fold through the cherries and pistachios. Pile the mixture back into the panettone shells and replace the disk of panettone you had set aside.

8 Wrap and refrigerate for at least 3 hours or overnight before unwrapping and dusting with confectioner's sugar to serve.

PREPARE AHEAD These will keep overnight in the refrigerator.

BAKER'S TIP
Panettone is an Italian sweet bread traditionally baked for Christmas. Although the process is lengthy, the time taken is mostly for the bread to rise twice. It is not complicated to make, and gives a marvelously light result unlike a store-bought panettone.

Stollen

This rich, fruity sweet bread, originally from Germany, is traditionally served at Christmas and makes a great alternative to Christmas cakes or pies.

SERVES 12 | **30 MINS** | **50 MINS** | **UP TO 4 WEEKS**

Soaking time
overnight

Rising and proofing time
2–3 hours

Ingredients
1¼ cup (7oz) raisins
¾ cup (4oz) currants
½ cup rum
3 cups all-purpose flour, plus extra for dusting
1 (¼oz/10g) package dried yeast
¼ cup sugar
½ cup milk
few drops of pure vanilla extract
pinch of salt
½ tsp pumpkin pie spice
2 large eggs, at room temperature
12 tbsp unsalted butter, softened
7oz (200g) mixed candied citrus peel
1 cup (4oz) ground almonds
confectioner's sugar, for dusting

Method

1 Put the raisins and currants into a medium bowl, pour in the rum, and leave the ingredients to soak overnight.

2 The following day, sift the flour into a large bowl, make a well in the center, sprinkle in the yeast, and add 1 teaspoon of the sugar. Gently heat the milk until lukewarm and pour on top of the yeast. Let stand at room temperature for 15 minutes, or until frothy.

3 Add the rest of the sugar, the vanilla extract, salt, pumpkin pie spice, eggs, and butter. Using a wooden spoon, or electric mixer with a dough hook, mix, then knead the ingredients together for 5 minutes, or until they form a smooth dough.

4 Transfer to a lightly floured work surface. Add the candied peel, soaked raisins and currants, and almonds, kneading for a few minutes until incorporated. Return the dough to the bowl, cover with plastic wrap, and let rise in a warm place until doubled in size.

5 Preheat the oven to 325°F (160°C). Line a baking sheet with parchment paper. On a floured surface, roll out the dough to make a 12 x 10in (30 x 25cm) rectangle. Fold 1 long side over, just beyond the middle, then fold over the other long side to overlap the first, curling it over slightly on top to create the stollen shape. Transfer to the baking sheet, and put in a warm place to rise again until doubled in size.

6 Bake in the oven for 50 minutes, or until risen and pale golden. Transfer to a wire rack to cool completely, then generously dust with confectioner's sugar. Serve cut into thick slices, with or without butter.

STORE The stollen will keep in an airtight container for 4 days.

BAKER'S TIP
Stollen can be made with any combination of dried fruits. It can be plain, as in this recipe, or stuffed with a marzipan or frangipane layer. Any leftovers are great for breakfast, lightly toasted, with butter.

Bienenstich

The name of this German recipe translates as "bee sting cake". Legend has it that the honey attracts bees that sting the baker!

SERVES 8-10 | **20 MINS** | **20–25 MINS**

Rising and proofing time
1 hr 5 mins–1 hr 20 mins

Special equipment
8in (20cm) round cake pan

Ingredients
¾ cup all-purpose flour, plus extra for dusting
1 tbsp unsalted butter, softened and diced, plus extra for greasing
2 tsp sugar
1 tsp dried yeast
pinch of salt
1 large egg
oil, for greasing

For the glaze
2 tbsp butter
2 tbsp sugar
1 tbsp honey
1 tbsp heavy cream
⅓ cup (1oz) slivered almonds
1 tsp lemon juice

For the crème pâtissière
1 cup whole milk
1 tbsp cornstarch
2 vanilla beans, split and seeded
¼ cup sugar
3 large egg yolks
2 tbsp unsalted butter, diced

Method

1 Sift the flour into a bowl. Quickly rub in the butter, then add the sugar, yeast, and salt and mix well. Beat in the egg and add enough water to make a soft dough.

2 Knead on a floured surface for 5–10 minutes, or until smooth, elastic, and shiny. Put in a clean, oiled bowl, cover with plastic wrap, and leave to rise in a warm place for 45–60 minutes, or until doubled in size.

3 Grease the cake pan and dust with flour. Knock back the dough and roll it out into a circle, so that it fits the pan. Push it into the pan and cover with plastic wrap. Leave to rise for 20 minutes.

4 To make the glaze, melt the butter in a small pan, then add the sugar, honey, and cream. Cook over low heat until the sugar has dissolved, then increase the heat and bring to the boil. Allow to simmer for 3 minutes, then remove the pan from the heat and add the almonds and lemon juice. Allow to cool.

5 Preheat the oven to 375°F (190°C). Carefully spread the glaze over the dough, leave to rise for a further 10 minutes, then bake for 20–25 minutes, ensuring it doesn't get too dark on the top. Allow to cool in the pan for 30 minutes, then carefully transfer to a wire rack.

6 Now, make the crème pâtissière. Pour the milk into a heavy saucepan and add the cornstarch, vanilla seeds and beans, and half the sugar. Place over low heat. Meanwhile, whisk the egg yolks with the remaining sugar in a bowl. Continue whisking and slowly pour in the hot milk. Transfer to the pan and whisk until it just comes to a boil, then remove from the heat.

7 Immediately place the whole saucepan into a bowl of iced water and remove the vanilla beans. Once the sauce has cooled, add the butter and briskly whisk into the sauce until it is smooth and glossy.

8 Slice the cake in half. Spread a thick layer of crème pâtissière on the bottom half, then place the almond layer on top. Transfer to a serving plate.

BAKER'S TIP
This German recipe is traditionally filled with crème pâtissière, as in this recipe. It makes a smooth, luxurious filling, which, these days, is a real treat. However, if you are pressed for time, an easier option would be to fill the cake with whipped heavy cream, lightly scented with vanilla extract.

Brioche des Rois

This French bread is usually eaten for the Epiphany, January 6th. The *fève* represents the gifts of the Three Kings.

SERVES 10–12 **25 MINS** **25–30 MINS** **UP TO 4 WEEKS**

Rising and proofing time
4–6 hrs

Special equipment
10in (25cm) ring mold (optional)
fève porcelain or metal trinket

Ingredients

For the brioche
1 (¼oz/10g) package dried yeast
2 tbsp sugar
5 large eggs, beaten

2¾ cups bread flour, extra for dusting
1½ tsp salt
oil, for greasing
12 tbsp unsalted butter,
cubed and softened

For the topping
1 large egg, lightly beaten
⅓ cup (2oz) mixed candied fruit
(orange and lemon zest, glacé
cherries, and angelica), chopped
¼ cup coarse sugar crystals

1 Whisk yeast, 1 teaspoon sugar, 2 tablespoons warm water. Leave for 10 minutes. Add eggs.

2 In a large bowl, sift together the flour and salt, and add the remaining sugar.

3 Make a well in the flour and pour in the eggs and yeast mixture.

4 Bring the dough together with a fork, then your hands, to form a sticky dough.

5 Turn out the dough on to a floured work surface.

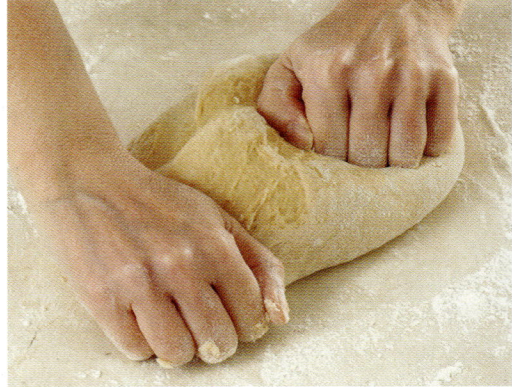

6 Knead the dough for 10 minutes until elastic but still sticky.

7 Put in an oiled bowl and cover with plastic wrap. Leave in a warm place for 2–3 hours.

8 Gently knock the dough back on a lightly floured work surface.

9 Scatter one-third of the cubed butter over the surface of the dough.

CELEBRATION CAKES

10 Fold the dough over the butter and knead gently for 5 minutes until all butter is used.

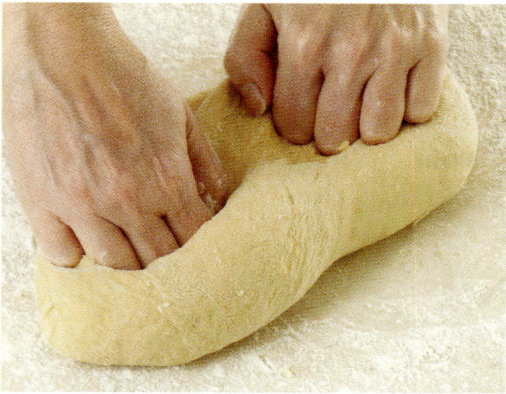

11 Repeat until all the butter is absorbed. Keep kneading until no streaks of butter show.

12 Form into a round and work it into a ring. Bury the *fève*, if using (see Baker's Tip, page 101).

13 Transfer to an oiled baking sheet or fill an oiled ring mold, if using.

14 If you don't have a ring mold, use a ramekin to keep the shape of the hole.

15 Cover with plastic wrap and a kitchen towel and let rise for 2–3 hours until doubled in size.

16 Brush the brioche with beaten egg. Sprinkle over candied fruit, and sugar crystals if using.

17 Preheat the oven to 400°F (200°C). Bake for 25–30 minutes until golden brown.

18 Leave in the pan for a few minutes, then turn out to cool on a wire rack, without dislodging the toppings. **STORE** This will keep in an airtight container for 3 days.

Brioche variations

Brioche Buns

These bite-sized little buns are known in French as brioche *à tête*, for obvious reasons.

MAKES 10 BUNS | 45–50 MINS | 15–20 MINS | UP TO 8 WEEKS

Rising and proofing time
1½–2 hrs

Special equipment
10 x 3in (7.5cm) brioche molds

Ingredients
butter, melted, for greasing
1 quantity brioche dough,
  see pages 98–99, steps 1–11
flour, for dusting
1 egg, beaten, for glazing
½ tsp salt, for glazing

Method

1 Grease the molds and set on a baking sheet. Divide the dough in half. Roll one piece into a cylinder 2in (5cm) in diameter. Cut the cylinder into 5 pieces. Repeat with the remaining dough. Flour the work surface, then roll the dough so it forms a smooth ball.

2 Pinch ¼ of each ball between your thumb and forefinger, almost dividing it from the remaining dough, to form the head. Lower each ball into a mold, twisting the head on to the base of the brioche. Cover and let rise for 30 minutes, until the molds are full.

3 Preheat the oven to 425°F (220°C). Brush with the egg glaze, and bake for 15–20 minutes, until puffed and brown. Unmold and transfer to a wire rack to cool.

STORE The buns will keep in an airtight container for 3 days.

Rum Babas

Rum soaked versions of brioche—perfect for a dinner party.

MAKES 4 BABAS | 20 MINS | 20 MINS

Rising time
30 mins

Special equipment
4 individual baba molds

Ingredients
¾ cup bread flour
¼ cup (2oz) raisins
1½ tsp dried yeast
2 tbsp sugar
pinch of salt
2 large eggs, at room temperature, lightly beaten
¼ cup milk, warmed
4 tbsp butter, melted, plus extra for greasing
vegetable oil, for greasing
½ cup sugar
3 tbsp rum
1¼ cups heavy whipping cream
2 tbsp confectioner's sugar
grated chocolate, to garnish

Method

1 Place the flour in a bowl and stir in the raisins, yeast, sugar, and salt. Beat together the egg and milk and add to the flour mixture. Stir in the melted butter. Beat well for 3–4 minutes then pour the mixture into well-greased baba molds to half fill them.

2 Place the molds on a baking sheet and cover with a sheet of oiled plastic wrap. Let rise in a warm place for 30 minutes. Preheat the oven to 400°F (200°C). Bake for 10–15 minutes, until golden and just firm to the touch. Let cool for a few minutes, then turn out on to a wire rack to cool completely.

3 Pour ½ cup of water into a saucepan and add the sugar. Stir constantly over low heat until the sugar dissolves. Increase the heat and boil rapidly for 2 minutes. Remove from the heat and leave to cool. Stir in the rum.

4 Dip the babas in the syrup. Whisk the cream and confectioner's sugar together until it forms soft peaks. Pipe a swirl of cream in the center of each baba. Sprinkle a little chocolate over the cream, and serve.

Brioche Nanterre

Basic brioche dough can be baked into rings, buns, or loaves. This classic brioche loaf is best for slicing and fantastic toasted.

MAKES 1 LOAF	30 MINS	25–30 MINS	UP TO 4 WEEKS

Rising and proofing time
4–6 hrs

Special equipment
9 x 5½in (23 x 13cm) loaf pan

Ingredients
1 quantity brioche dough,
  see pages 94–95, steps 1–11
1 egg, beaten, for glazing

Method

1 Line the bottom and sides of the pan with parchment paper. Put a double layer on the base. Divide the dough into 8 pieces, and roll them up to form small balls. They should fit in pairs, side by side, in the base of the prepared pan.

2 Cover with plastic wrap and a kitchen towel, and let rise for another 2–3 hours until the dough has again doubled in size.

3 Preheat the oven to 400°F (200°C). Brush the top of the brioche loaf with a little beaten egg, and bake near the top of the oven for 30 minutes, or until the bottom of the loaf sounds hollow when tapped. Check the loaf after 20 minutes and cover the top with a piece of loose-fitting parchment paper if it is in danger of becoming too brown.

4 Leave to cool in the pan for a few minutes, then turn out to cool on a wire rack. This brioche is delicious toasted and buttered.

STORE The loaf will keep in an airtight container for 3 days.

BAKER'S TIP
Brioche originates from France, and was often made to celebrate Epiphany on January 6. Traditionally a *fève* is hidden in the dough, and the finder is guaranteed luck for the coming year. In the past a dried bean (*fève*) was used, but these days small decorative ceramic figures are more common.

Kugelhopf

Dark raisins and chopped almonds are baked into this classic kugelhopf, an Alsatian favorite. A dusting of confectioner's sugar hints at the sweet filling.

MAKES 1 RING — **45–50 MINS** — **45–50 MINS** — **UP TO 8 WEEKS**

Rising and proofing time
2–2½ hrs

Special equipment
10 cup kugelhopf or ring mold, or see page 99, steps 12–14, for how to shape without a mold

Ingredients

⅔ cup milk
2 tbsp sugar
11 tbsp unsalted butter, diced,
  plus extra for greasing
1 tbsp dried yeast
3¾ cups bread flour
1 tsp salt
3 large eggs (at room temperature), beaten
½ cup (3oz) raisins
⅓ cup (2oz) blanched almonds, chopped,
  plus 7 whole blanched almonds
confectioner's sugar, for dusting

Method

1 Bring the milk just to a boil in a saucepan, pour ¼ cup of it into a bowl, and let cool to lukewarm. Add the sugar and butter to the milk in the pan and stir until melted. Let cool.

2 Sprinkle the yeast over the ¼ cup milk and let stand for 5 minutes until dissolved, stirring once. Sift the flour and salt into the bowl of an electric mixer fitted with a dough hook. Add the dissolved yeast, eggs, and the butter mixture.

3 Gradually draw in the flour and work it into the other ingredients to form a smooth dough. Knead for 5–7 minutes, until very elastic. It should be very sticky. Cover with a damp kitchen towel and let rise in a warm place for 1–1½ hours, until doubled in bulk.

4 Meanwhile, grease the mold with butter. Freeze the mold until the butter is hard (about 10 minutes) then butter it again. Pour boiling water over the raisins and allow to plump up.

5 Knock back the dough lightly with your hand to push out the air. Drain the raisins, reserving 7 of them, and knead the rest into the dough with the chopped almonds. Arrange the reserved raisins and whole almonds in the bottom of the mold.

6 Drop the dough into the mold, cover with a kitchen towel, and let rise in a warm place until it comes just above the top of the mold. It should take about 30–40 minutes. Preheat the oven to 375°F (190°C) when the bread has risen.

7 Bake the kugelhopf until puffed and brown, and the bread starts to shrink from the side of the mold, 45–50 minutes. Let it cool slightly. Turn out on to a wire rack and let cool completely. Just before serving, sift over the confectioner's sugar.

STORE The kugelhopf will keep in an airtight container for 3 days.

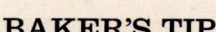

BAKER'S TIP

This dough is very sticky. It is natural to want to add more flour, in order to make it look more like a conventional dough. However, this would be a mistake, as it would make the kugelhopf tough.

Chocolate Chestnut Roulade

Perfect for a winter celebration, this rolled sponge is filled with a rich chestnut purée mixed with whipped cream.

SERVES 8–10 | **50–55 MINS** | **5–7 MINS** | **8 WEEKS, UNFILLED**

Special equipment
17 x 11in (43 x 28cm) baking sheet
piping bag and star nozzle

Ingredients
butter, for greasing
¼ cup cocoa powder
1 tbsp all-purpose flour
pinch of salt
5 large eggs, separated
⅔ cup sugar

For the filling
⅔ cup heavy cream
4oz (125g) chestnut purée
2 tbsp dark rum
1oz (30g) dark chocolate, finely chopped
sugar to taste (optional)

To finish and decorate
¼ cup sugar
2 tbsp dark rum
½ cup heavy cream
2oz (50g) dark chocolate, grated

1 Preheat the oven to 425°F (220°C). Grease a baking sheet. Line with parchment paper.

2 Sift the cocoa powder, flour, and salt into a large bowl and set aside.

3 Beat the egg yolks with ⅔ of the sugar; it should leave a ribbon trail.

4 Whisk the egg whites until stiff. Sprinkle in the remaining sugar and whisk again until glossy.

5 Sift ⅓ of the cocoa mixture over the yolk mixture. Add ⅓ of the egg whites.

6 Fold together lightly. Add the remaining cocoa mixture and egg white in 2 batches.

7 Pour the batter onto the prepared baking sheet. Spread the batter almost to the edges.

8 Bake in the bottom of the oven for 5–7 minutes. The cake will be risen and just firm.

9 Remove the cake from the oven, invert onto a damp towel, and peel off the parchment paper.

10 Tightly roll up the cake around the damp kitchen towel and leave to cool.

11 Put the chestnut purée in a bowl with the rum. Whip the cream until it forms soft peaks.

12 Melt the chocolate in a bowl over a pot of simmering water. Stir into the chestnut mixture.

13 Fold the chocolate and chestnut mixture into the whipped cream. Add sugar to taste.

14 To finish, simmer half the sugar in ¼ cup of water for 1 minute. Cool and stir in the rum.

15 Unroll the cake on fresh parchment paper. Brush with syrup and spread the chestnut mix.

16 Using the parchment underneath, carefully roll up the filled cake as tightly as possible.

17 Whip the cream and remaining sugar until stiff. Fill the piping bag with the cream.

18 With a serrated knife, trim each end of the cake diagonally. Transfer to a serving plate. Decorate with the whipped cream and chocolate shavings. Best eaten on the day it is made.

Chocolate Roulade variations

Chocolate Log

A roulade with the classic pairing of dark chocolate and raspberry.

SERVES 10	30 MINS	15 MINS	UP TO 24 WEEKS

Special equipment
8 x 12in (20 x 30cm) jelly roll pan

Ingredients
3 large eggs, at room temperature
⅓ cup sugar
½ cup all-purpose flour
3 tbsp cocoa powder
½ tsp baking powder
¾ cup heavy cream
5oz (140g) dark chocolate, chopped
3 tbsp raspberry jam
confectioner's sugar, for dusting

Method

1 Preheat the oven to 350°F (180°C). Line the pan with parchment paper.

2 In a bowl, whisk the eggs with the sugar and 1 tablespoon water for 5 minutes, until light; the mixture should hold a trail. Sift the flour, cocoa powder, and baking powder over the beaten eggs, then quickly fold in.

3 Pour the cake mixture into the lined pan and bake for 12 minutes. Turn it out on to a new piece of parchment paper. Peel the paper from the base of the cake and discard. Roll the cake up, while still hot, keeping the paper inside. Leave to cool.

4 Meanwhile, to make the frosting, pour the cream into a saucepan, bring to a boil, then remove from the heat. Add the chopped chocolate and leave it to melt, stirring occasionally, so it cools and thickens.

5 Carefully unroll the cake and spread raspberry jam over the surface. Spread ⅓ of the frosting over the raspberry jam, and roll it up again. Place the roll on a board, seam-side down. Spread the rest of the frosting over the the cake. Transfer to a serving plate. Just before serving, dust with confectioner's sugar.

STORE The cake will keep, chilled, for 2 days.

Chocolate Amaretti Roulade

Crushed Amaretti cookies add texture and crunch to this beautiful and indulgent roulade. ▶

SERVES 6–8	25–30 MINS	20 MINS	8 WEEKS, UNFILLED

Special equipment
8 x 12in (20 x 30cm) jelly roll pan

Ingredients
6 large eggs (at room temperature), separated
⅔ cup sugar
½ cup cocoa powder
confectioner's sugar, for dusting
1¼ cup heavy whipping cream
2–3 tbsp Amaretto or brandy
20 Amaretti cookies, crushed, plus 2 for topping
2oz (50g) dark chocolate

Method

1 Preheat the oven to 350°F (180°C). Line the pan with parchment paper. Put the egg yolks and sugar in a large bowl set over a pan of simmering water and whisk vigorously with a balloon whisk or an electric hand mixer until pale, thick, and creamy. This will take about 10 minutes. Remove from the heat.

2 Put the egg whites in a large bowl and whisk until soft peaks form. Sift the cocoa powder into the egg yolk mixture and fold in along with the egg whites. Pour into the pan and bake for 20 minutes, or until just firm to the touch. Allow the pan to cool slightly before turning the cake out face down on to a sheet of parchment paper dusted with confectioner's sugar. Remove the pan, but leave the parchment. Let cool for 30 minutes.

3 Whisk the cream with an electric hand mixer until soft peaks form. Peel the parchment paper from the cake and place it underneath. Trim the sides, then drizzle with the Amaretto or brandy. Spread with the cream, scatter with the crushed cookies, and grate most of the chocolate over the top.

4 Starting from one of the short sides, roll the roulade up. Place on a serving plate with the seam underneath. Crumble over the extra cookies, grate with the remaining chocolate, and dust with confectioner's sugar.

Chocolate and Buttercream Roll

This chocolatey variation on a Swiss roll is simple to make and always a hit with kids—perfect for a children's party.

SERVES 8–10	20–25 MINS	10 MINS

Special equipment
8 x 12in (20 x 30cm) jelly roll pan

Ingredients
3 large eggs, at room temperature
⅓ cup sugar
¼ cup all-purpose flour
¼ cup cocoa powder, plus extra to dust
5 tbsp butter, softened
1 cup confectioner's sugar

Method

1 Preheat the oven to 400°F (200°C) and line the pan with parchment paper. Sit a bowl over a pot of simmering water, add the eggs and sugar, and whisk for 5–10 minutes, until thick and creamy. Remove from the heat, sift in the flour and cocoa, and fold in.

2 Pour into the pan and bake for 10 minutes, or until springy to the touch. Cover with a damp kitchen towel and let cool. Turn the cake out, face down, onto a sheet of parchment paper dusted with cocoa powder. Peel off the parchment paper it was baked on.

3 Whisk the butter until creamy. Beat in the confectioner's sugar, a little at a time, then spread the mixture over the cake. Using the parchment paper to help you, roll the cake up, starting from one of the ends. Dust with more cocoa powder, if needed, and serve.

STORE The cake will keep, chilled, for 3 days.

Black Forest Gâteau

Newly resurrected to its glorious best, this classic German cake deserves its place on a celebration table.

SERVES 8 | **55 MINS** | **40 MINS** | **UP TO 4 WEEKS**

Special equipment
9in (23cm) springform cake pan
piping bag with star-shaped nozzle

Ingredients
6 tbsp butter, melted
6 large eggs, at room temperature
¾ cup sugar
¾ cup all-purpose flour
½ cup cocoa powder,
  plus more for dusting
1 tsp pure vanilla extract

For the filling and decoration
2 x 14oz (425g) can pitted black cherries,
  drained, 6 tbsp juice reserved and
  cherries from 1 can roughly chopped
4 tbsp Kirsch
2 cups heavy cream
6oz (150g) dark chocolate, grated

1 Preheat the oven to 350°F (180°C). Grease and line the pan with parchment paper.

2 Put the eggs and sugar into a large heatproof bowl that will fit over a saucepan.

3 Place the bowl over a pot of simmering water. Don't let the bowl touch the water.

4 Whisk until the mixture is pale and thick, and will hold a trail from the beaters.

5 Remove from the heat and whisk for another 5 minutes, or until cooled slightly.

6 Sift the flour and cocoa together, and gently fold into the egg mixture using a spatula.

7 Fold in the vanilla and butter. Transfer to the prepared pan and level the surface.

8 Bake in the oven for 40 minutes, or until risen and just shrinking away from the sides.

9 Turn out on to a wire rack, discard the paper, and cover with a clean cloth. Let it cool.

CELEBRATION CAKES

108

10 Carefully cut the cake into 3 layers. Use a serrated knife and long sweeping strokes.

11 Combine the reserved cherry juice with the Kirsch, and drizzle a third over each layer.

12 Whip the cream in a separate bowl until it just holds its shape; it should not be stiff.

13 Place a layer of cake on a plate. Spread with cream and half the chopped cherries.

14 Repeat with the second sponge. Top with the final sponge, baked side up. Press down.

15 Cover with a thin layer of cream. Transfer the remaining cream to the piping bag.

16 Press grated chocolate onto the creamy sides with a palette knife.

17 Pipe a ring of cream swirls around the cake and place the whole cherries inside.

18 Sprinkle any remaining chocolate evenly over the peaks of piped cream, to serve.
STORE The cake can be covered and chilled for up to 3 days.

Gâteau variations

German Cream Cheese Torte

This German dessert is a cross between a cheesecake and a sponge cake. It makes a good party dessert as it can be made in advance.

SERVES 8–10 · **40 MINS** · **30 MINS**

Chilling time
3 hrs, or overnight

Special equipment
9in (22cm) springform pan

Ingredients
11 tbsp unsalted butter, softened,
  or soft margarine, plus extra for greasing
1 cup sugar
3 large eggs
1 cup all-purpose flour
1 tsp baking powder
1 tbsp unflavored powdered gelatin
juice of 2 lemons and finely grated zest of 1
1 cup heavy cream
1 cup (9oz) quark, or see Baker's Tip
confectioner's sugar, for dusting

Method

1 Preheat the oven to 350°F (180°C). Grease the pan and dust with flour.

2 Cream the butter or margarine and ⅔ cup sugar together. Beat in the eggs, one at a time, until the mixture is smooth and creamy. Sift together the flour and baking powder, and fold into the batter with the zest. Spoon into the pan and bake for 30 minutes, or until well risen. Turn the cake out onto a wire rack. Slice it in half horizontally with a serrated knife. Allow it to cool completely.

3 To make the filling, heat the lemon juice in a small pan, then remove from heat. Add the gelatin to the lemon juice. Stir until dissolved, then let cool.

4 Whisk the cream until firm. Beat together the quark, zest, and the remaining sugar, then beat in the lemon juice and gelatin. Fold in the cream.

5 Spoon the filling onto one cake half. Slice the second half into eight pieces and arrange on top of the filling; pre-cutting the top layer makes it easier to serve. Chill for at least 3 hours, or overnight. Sift over confectioner's sugar and sprinkle with lemon zest.

PREPARE AHEAD Can be made up to 3 days ahead and kept in the refrigerator.

BAKER'S TIP
If you cannot find any quark it can easily be substituted with low-fat cottage cheese, processed to a paste in a food processor with blade attachment.

Bavarian Raspberry Gâteau

When raspberries are not in season, you can use frozen berries.

SERVES 8 | 55–60 MINS | 20–25 MINS

Chilling time
4 hrs

Special equipment
9in (22cm) springform pan
blender

Ingredients
4 tbsp unsalted butter, plus extra for greasing
1 cup all-purpose flour, plus extra for dusting
pinch of salt
4 large eggs, beaten
⅔ cup sugar
2 tbsp Kirsch

For the raspberry cream
1lb 2oz (500g) raspberries
3 tbsp Kirsch
1 cup sugar
1 cup heavy cream
4 cups milk
1 vanilla bean, split, or 2 tsp pure vanilla extract
10 large egg yolks
3 tbsp cornstarch
1 tbsp unflavored powdered gelatin

Method

1 Preheat the oven to 425°F (220°C). Grease the pan with butter and line the base with buttered parchment paper. Sprinkle in 2–3 tablespoons flour. Melt the butter and let it cool. Sift the flour and salt into a bowl. Put the eggs in a bowl and beat in the sugar, using an electric hand mixer, for 5 minutes.

2 Sift one-third of the flour mixture over the egg mixture and fold in. Add the remaining flour in 2 batches. Fold in the butter. Pour into the pan and bake for 20–25 minutes, until the cake has risen.

3 Turn out the cake onto a wire rack. Let cool. Remove the parchment. Trim the top and bottom so that they are flat. Cut the cake horizontally in half. Clean, dry, and re-grease the pan. Put a cake round in the pan and sprinkle it with 1 tablespoon of the Kirsch.

4 Purée three-quarters of the berries in a blender, then work through a sieve to remove the seeds. Stir in 1 tablespoon of the Kirsch with ½ cup of the sugar. Whip the cream until it forms soft peaks.

5 Put the milk in a pan. Add the vanilla bean, if using. Bring to a boil. Remove the pan from the heat, cover, and let stand in a warm place for 10–15 minutes. Remove the bean. Set aside one-quarter of the milk. Stir the remaining sugar into the milk in the pan.

6 Beat the egg yolks and cornstarch in a bowl. Add the hot milk and whisk until smooth. Pour the yolk mixture back into the pan and cook over medium heat, stirring, until the custard comes to a boil. Stir in the reserved milk and the vanilla extract, if using.

7 Strain the custard equally into 2 bowls. Let cool. Stir 2 tablespoons of Kirsch into one half. Set this custard aside to serve with the finished dessert. Sprinkle the gelatin over 4 tablespoons of water in a small pan and let soften for 5 minutes. Heat until the

gelatin is melted and pourable. Stir into the bowl of unflavored custard, along with the raspberry purée.

8 Set the bowl in a pan of iced water. Stir the mixture until it thickens. Remove the bowl from the water. Fold the raspberry custard into the whipped cream. Pour half into the cake pan. Sprinkle with a few reserved raspberries. Pour the remaining Bavarian cream on the berries. Sprinkle with 1 tablespoon of Kirsch over the second cake round.

9 Lightly press the cake round, sprinkled-side down, on the cream. Cover with plastic wrap and refrigerate for at least 4 hours, until firm. To serve, remove the side of the pan and place on a serving plate. Decorate the top of the cake with the reserved raspberries, and serve the Kirsch custard sauce separately.

PREPARE AHEAD Can be made up to 2 days ahead and kept in the refrigerator; remove 1 hour before serving.

small cakes

Vanilla Cream Cupcakes

A cupcake is quite dense in consistency, which allows it to carry more elaborate types of frosting.

MAKES 24 | **20 MINS** | **20–25 MINS** | **4 WEEKS, UN-ICED**

Special equipment
2 x 12-hole cupcake pans
piping bag and star nozzle (optional)

Ingredients
1⅓ cups all-purpose flour
2 tsp baking powder
1 cup sugar
½ tsp salt
7 tbsp unsalted butter, softened
3 large eggs, at room temperature
⅔ cup milk
1 tsp pure vanilla extract

For the frosting
1 cup confectioner's sugar
1 tsp pure vanilla extract
7 tbsp unsalted butter, softened
cupcake sprinkles (optional)

1 Preheat the oven to 350°F (180°C). Place the first 5 ingredients in a bowl.

2 Mix together with your fingertips until it resembles fine bread crumbs.

3 In another bowl, whisk the eggs, milk, and vanilla extract together until well blended.

4 Slowly pour the egg mixture into the dry ingredients, whisking all the time.

5 Whisk gently until smooth, being careful not to over-mix. Too much beating toughens cakes.

6 Pour all the cake batter into a large measuring cup to make it easier to handle.

7 Place the cupcake paper liners into the holes in the cupcake pans.

8 Carefully pour the cake mixture into the liners, filling each one only half full.

9 Bake for around 20 minutes, until lightly colored, firm, and springy to the touch.

10 Test the cakes are done by inserting a skewer into the center of one cupcake.

11 If traces of cake batter remain on the skewer, cook for a minute more, then test again.

12 Leave for a few minutes, then transfer the cupcakes to a wire rack to cool completely.

13 For the frosting, combine the confectioner's sugar, vanilla extract, and butter in a bowl.

14 Beat with an electric hand mixer until very light and fluffy; this will take about 5 minutes.

15 Check the cakes are completely cool to the touch, or they will begin to melt the frosting.

16 If frosting by hand, add a spoonful of the frosting mix to the top of each cake.

17 Then use the back of a spoon dipped in warm water to smooth the surface.

18 For a more professional result, transfer the frosting to the piping bag.

19 Pipe by squeezing out the frosting with one hand, while holding the cake with the other.

20 Starting from the edge, pipe a spiral of frosting that comes to a peak in the center.

21 Decorate with sprinkles. **STORE** Will keep in an airtight container for 3 days.

Cupcake variations

Chocolate Cupcakes

Classic chocolate cupcakes are another must-have recipe. A guaranteed winner for children's parties!

MAKES 24 | 20 MINS | 20–25 MINS | 4 WEEKS, UN-ICED

Special equipment
2 x 12-hole cupcake pans
piping bag and star nozzle (optional)

Ingredients
1⅓ cups all-purpose flour
2 tsp baking powder
4 tbsp cocoa powder
1 cup sugar
½ tsp salt
7 tbsp unsalted butter, softened
3 large eggs, at room temperature
⅔ cup milk
1 tsp pure vanilla extract
1 tbsp Greek yogurt

For the frosting
1 cup confectioner's sugar
¼ cup cocoa powder
7 tbsp softened butter

Method

1 Preheat the oven to 350°F (180°C). Sift the flour, baking powder, and cocoa into a bowl. Add the sugar, salt, and butter. Mix until it resembles fine breadcrumbs. In a bowl, whisk the eggs, milk, vanilla extract, and yogurt together until well blended.

2 Slowly pour in the egg mixture to combine. Mix gently until smooth. Place the cupcake paper liners into the holes in the cupcake pans. Spoon the mixture into the liners, filling each one only half full.

3 Bake for around 20 minutes, until lightly colored, firm, and springy to the touch. Leave for a few minutes, then transfer the cupcakes to a wire rack to cool completely.

4 For the frosting, beat the confectioner's sugar, cocoa powder, and butter until smooth.

5 Frost by hand, using the back of a spoon dipped in warm water to smooth the surface, or transfer the frosting to the piping bag and pipe on to the cakes.

STORE These cupcakes keep in an airtight container for 3 days.

Lemon Cupcakes

For a delicate taste, try flavoring the basic cupcake batter with lemon.

MAKES 24 | 20 MINS | 20–25 MINS | 4 WEEKS, UN-ICED

Special equipment
2 x 12-hole cupcake pans
piping bag and star nozzle (optional)

Ingredients
1⅓ cups all-purpose flour
2 tsp baking powder
1 cup sugar
½ tsp salt
7 tbsp unsalted butter, softened
3 large eggs, at room temperature
⅔ cup milk
finely grated zest and juice of 1 lemon

For the frosting
7 tbsp unsalted butter, softened
1 cup confectioner's sugar

Method

1 Preheat the oven to 350°F (180°C). Sift the flour and baking powder into a bowl. Add the sugar, salt, and butter. Mix until it resembles fine breadcrumbs. In a bowl, whisk the eggs and milk until well blended.

2 Pour in the egg mixture to combine. Add half the lemon zest and all the lemon juice. Mix gently until smooth. Place the cupcake paper liners into the cupcake pans. Spoon the mixture into the papers, filling each one only half full. Bake for 20–25 minutes, until springy. Cool completely on a wire rack.

3 To make the frosting, beat the butter, confectioner's sugar, and remaining lemon zest until smooth. Frost by hand, using the back of a spoon, or with the piping bag.

STORE These cupcakes keep in an airtight container for 3 days.

BAKER'S TIP
Due to their fairly dense texture, these classic cupcakes will keep well for a few days. If you prefer them well risen, replace the all-purpose flour with self-rising flour but reduce the baking powder to 1 teaspoon, accordingly.

Coffee and Walnut Cupcakes

Definitely one for adults, coffee and nuts add depth to these cupcakes.

| MAKES 24 | 20 MINS | 20–25 MINS | 4 WEEKS, UN-ICED |

Special equipment
2 x 12-hole cupcake pans
piping bag and star nozzle (optional)

Ingredients
1⅓ cups all-purpose flour, plus more for dusting
2 tsp baking powder
1 cup sugar
½ tsp salt
7 tbsp unsalted butter, softened
3 large eggs, room temperature
⅔ cup milk
1 tbsp instant coffee and 1 tbsp boiling water, combined and cooled, or 1 cooled expresso
1 cup (4oz) halved walnuts, plus extra to decorate

For the frosting
7 tbsp unsalted butter, softened
1 cup confectioner's sugar
1 tsp pure vanilla extract

Method
1 Preheat the oven to 350°F (180°C). Sift the flour and baking powder into a bowl. Add the sugar, salt, and butter. Mix until it resembles fine breadcrumbs. In a bowl, whisk the eggs and milk until well blended.

2 Pour in the egg mixture, add half the coffee, and mix until smooth. Roughly chop the walnuts and toss them in a bowl with a little flour, then fold them into the batter. Place the cupcake liners in the trays. Spoon the mixture into the liners, filling each one only half full. Bake for 20–25 minutes until springy, then cool completely on a wire rack.

3 To make the frosting, beat the butter, confectioner's sugar, vanilla extract, and remaining coffee until smooth. Frost by hand, with the back of a spoon, or with the piping bag. Top each cake with a walnut half.

STORE These cupcakes keep in an airtight container for 3 days.

Fondant Fancies

Dainty in size, gorgeous to look at, and delectable to eat, these little cakes are perfect for a party or as a special teatime treat.

MAKES 16 | 20–25 MINS | 25 MINS

Special equipment
8in (20cm) square cake pan

Ingredients
1⅓ cups all-purpose flour, plus extra for dusting
1½ tsp baking powder
½ tsp salt
1 stick, plus 4 tbsp unsalted butter
¾ cup sugar

3 large eggs, at room temperature
1 tsp pure vanilla extract
2 tbsp milk
2–3 tbsp raspberry or red cherry conserve

For the buttercream
5 tbsp unsalted butter, at room temperature
¾ cup confectioner's sugar

For the frosting
juice of ½ lemon
3⅔ cup confectioner's sugar
1–2 drops natural pink food coloring
icing flowers, to decorate (optional)

Method

1 Preheat the oven to 375 °F (190°C). Grease the cake pan and dust with flour. Sift flour, baking powder, and salt into a bowl. Place the butter and sugar in a large bowl, or the bowl of an electric mixer, and beat until pale and fluffy. Set aside.

2 Lightly beat the eggs and vanilla extract in another large bowl. Add about ¼ of the egg mixture and 1 tablespoon of the flour mixture to the butter mixture and beat well, then add the rest of the egg, a little at a time, beating as you go. Add the rest of the flour mixture and the milk, and mix in gently.

3 Transfer the mixture to the prepared pan and bake in the middle of the oven for about 25 minutes, or until lightly golden and springy to the touch. Remove from the oven, leave to cool in the pan for about 10 minutes, then remove from the pan and cool upside down on a wire rack.

4 To make the buttercream, beat the butter with the confectioner's sugar until smooth. Set aside. Slice the cake horizontally and

spread the fruit conserve on one half and the buttercream on the other. Sandwich together, then cut into 16 equal squares.

5 To make the frosting, put the lemon juice in a measuring cup and fill it up to a ¼ cup with hot water. Mix this with the confectioner's sugar, stirring continuously and adding more hot water as required until the mixture is smooth. Add the pink food coloring and stir well.

6 Use a palette knife to transfer the cakes to a wire rack placed over a board or plate (to catch the drips), then drizzle with the icing to cover the cakes completely, or just cover the tops of the cakes and allow the icing to drip down the sides so the sponge layers are visible. Decorate with icing flowers (if using), then leave to set for about 15 minutes. Use a clean palette knife to transfer each cake carefully to a paper liner.

STORE These fancies will keep in the refrigerator for 1 day.

BAKER'S TIP
These little fancies are beautiful, but for a chocolate version, chill the filled squares well, then pierce each with a cocktail stick. Holding the stick, dip each cake into a bowl of dark melted chocolate, then set on a wire rack. Once set, drizzle with melted white chocolate for a contrasting pattern.

Chocolate Fudge Cake Balls

These are the new "it" cakes. Deceptively simple to make, packet or leftover cake can also be used.

MAKES 20–25 | **35 MINS** | **25 MINS** | **4 WEEKS, UNDIPPED**

Chilling time
3 hours, or 30 mins freezing

Special equipment
8in (20cm) cake pan

Ingredients
7 tbsp unsalted butter, softened, or soft margarine, plus extra for greasing
½ cup sugar
2 large eggs, at room temperature
⅔ cup all-purpose flour,
¼ cup cocoa powder, plus more for dusting
1 tsp baking powder
¼ tsp salt
5 tbsp milk, plus extra if needed
½ cup (6oz) store-bought chocolate fudge frosting (or use recipe for Chocolate Fudge Cake frosting, page 60)
10oz (250g) chocolate coating bark
2oz (50g) white chocolate

1 Preheat the oven to 350°F (180°C). Grease the pan and line with parchment paper.

2 With an electric hand mixer, cream the butter and sugar until fluffy.

3 Beat in the eggs one at a time, beating well in between each, until smooth and creamy.

4 Sift together the flour, cocoa, baking powder, and salt and mix into the cake batter.

5 Mix in enough milk to loosen the batter to a dropping consistency.

6 Pour into the pan, and bake for 25-30 minutes, until the top is springy to the touch.

7 Check the cake is cooked; a skewer inserted should emerge clean. Turn on to a wire rack.

8 When the cake is cool, process it in a food processor until it resembles breadcrumbs.

9 Add the frosting and blend together to a smooth, uniform color.

10 Using dry hands, roll the cake mix into balls, each the size of a walnut.

11 Put the balls on a plate and refrigerate for 3 hours or freeze for 30 minutes until quite firm.

12 Line 2 trays with parchment paper. Melt the chocolate coating bark.

13 Take a few cake balls at a time. Put them, one by one, into the molten chocolate mixture.

14 Using 2 forks, turn the balls in the chocolate until covered. Remove, allowing excess to drip.

15 Transfer the coated cake balls to the baking sheets to dry. Continue to coat all the cakes.

16 Melt the white chocolate in a bowl over a saucepan of simmering water.

17 Drizzle the white chocolate over the cakes with a spoon, to decorate.

18 Leave the white chocolate to dry completely before transferring to a serving plate.
STORE The cakes can be kept in an airtight container for 3 days.

Cake Ball variations

Strawberries and Cream Cake Pops

These are a fantastically impressive treat to serve at a children's party. You could even decorate a whole birthday cake with them.

| MAKES 20–25 | 20 MINS | 25 MINS | 4 WEEKS, UNDIPPED |

Chilling time
3 hrs, or 30 mins freezing

Special equipment
8in (20cm) round cake pan
food processor
25 pieces of bamboo skewer, cut to
   approximately 4in (10cm) lengths,
   to resemble lollipop sticks

Ingredients
7 tbsp unsalted butter, softened, plus extra
¾ cup all-purpose flour, plus extra for dusting
½ cup sugar
2 large eggs, at room temperature
1 tsp baking powder
¼ tsp salt
½ cup store-bought buttercream frosting, (or see
   vanilla buttercream frosting, page 127)
2 tbsp good quality, smooth strawberry jam
10oz (300g) white chocolate coating bark

Method

1 Preheat the oven to 350°F (180°C). Grease the cake pan and dust with flour. Cream together the butter and sugar. Beat in the eggs one at a time, until the mixture is smooth and creamy. Sift together the flour, baking powder, and salt and mix into the cake batter.

2 Pour the batter into the pan and bake for 20–30 minutes, until the surface is springy to the touch. Turn out to cool on a wire rack.

3 When the cake is cool, process it until it resembles bread crumbs. Weigh out 2¾ cups and place in a bowl. Add the frosting and the jam and mix thoroughly. Using dry hands, roll the mix into balls the size of a walnut. Put the balls on a plate and stick a skewer into each. Refrigerate for 3 hours or freeze for 30 minutes. Line a baking sheet with parchment paper.

4 Melt the coating bark in a bowl set over barely simmering water. Dip the chilled balls one at a time into the molten chocolate, turning until completely covered, right up to the stick.

5 Gently take them out of the chocolate mixture and allow any excess to drip back into the bowl before transferring them to the baking sheets to dry. The pops should be eaten on the same day.

BAKER'S TIP
To ensure a smooth, round finish to cake pops, cut an apple in half and place the halves cut side down on the lined baking sheet. Dip the cake pops, then stick their bamboo skewers into the apple. This will help the cake pops dry without any marks on the surface.

Fruit Cake Balls

I love to serve these cute little cakes at Christmas parties. An easy and delicious way to use up leftover fruit cake.

| MAKES 15–20 | 20 MINS | 25 MINS | 4 WEEKS, UNDIPPED |

Chilling time
3 hrs, or 30 mins freezing

Special equipment
food processor

Ingredients
2 cups leftover Fruit Cake (see recipe, page 82)
6oz (150g) dark chocolate coating bark
2oz (50g) white chocolate coating bark
glacé cherries and candied angelica (optional)

Method

1 Pulse the cold fruit cake in a food processor until thoroughly broken up. Using dry hands, roll the fruit cake into balls about the size of a walnut. Put the balls on a plate and refrigerate them for 3 hours or freeze for 30 minutes until quite firm.

2 Line 2 baking sheets with wax paper. In a small, microwave-proof bowl, heat the dark chocolate coating bark in bursts of 30 seconds until it is melted, but not too hot. Or, melt it in a small heatproof bowl over a saucepan of barely simmering water.

3 Take the cake balls out of the refrigerator a few at a time. Dip them, one at a time, into the molten chocolate mixture, turning them quickly with 2 forks until covered in chocolate. Take them out of the chocolate mixture and allow any excess chocolate to drip back into the bowl. Transfer them to the lined baking sheets to dry. Continue the process until all of the balls are coated. You will have to work quickly, as the chocolate

can harden very fast, and the cake balls can disintegrate if left in the warm chocolate for too long.

4 Melt the white chocolate coating bark as above. Using a teaspoon, drop a little of the white chocolate mixture on to the top of the hardened fruit cake balls, so that it looks as if they have been drizzled with icing, or snow. The white chocolate should drip down the sides a little bit.

5 If you are feeling ambitious, small slivers of glacé cherries and candied angelica can be cut to resemble holly leaves and berries and stuck to the still molten white chocolate. Leave the cake balls to rest until the white chocolate is quite hard.

STORE Will keep in the refrigerator for 5 days.

White Chocolate and Coconut Snowballs

These coconut balls are sophisticated enough to serve as canapés.

MAKES 25–30 | **40 MINS** | **25 MINS** | **4 WEEKS, UNDIPPED**

Chilling time
3 hrs, or 30 mins freezing

Special equipment
8in (20cm) cake pan
food processor

Ingredients
7 tbsp unsalted butter, softened, plus extra for greasing
½ cup sugar
2 large eggs, at room temperature
1 cup all-purpose flour, plus more for dusting
1 tsp baking powder
1¼ cups store-bought buttercream frosting, (or see vanilla buttercream frosting, page 127)
8oz (225g) unsweetened, shredded coconut
10oz (300g) white chocolate coating bark

Method

1 Preheat the oven to 350°F (180°C). Grease the pan and line the base with parchment paper. Cream the butter and sugar until pale and fluffy. Beat in the eggs one at a time, beating well between each addition. Sift together the flour and baking powder, and mix into the cake batter.

2 Pour the batter into the pan and bake for 25 minutes. Turn out to cool on a wire rack. Remove the baking parchment.

3 When the cake is cool, process until it resembles fine bread crumbs. Weigh out 2¾ cups of the crumbs and put them in a bowl. Add the frosting and 3oz (75g) of the coconut and cream the mixture together

4 Using dry hands, roll the mix into balls the size of a walnut. Refrigerate for 3 hours or freeze for 30 minutes. Line a baking sheet with parchment paper and put the remaining coconut on a plate.

5 Melt the coating bark in a heatproof bowl over a saucepan of barely simmering water. Place the chilled cake balls, one at a time, into the melted chocolate mixture, using two forks to turn them until covered.

6 Transfer them to the plate of coconut. Roll them around in the coconut, then transfer to the baking sheet to dry. You will have to work fast, as the chocolate can harden quickly, and the balls start to disintegrate if they are left in the chocolate too long.

STORE The cake balls will keep in a cool place in an airtight container for 2 days.

Whoopie Pies

Fast becoming a modern classic, whoopie pies are a quick and easy way to please a crowd.

**MAKES
10 PIES** **40
MINS** **12
MINS** **4 WEEKS,
UNFILLED**

Ingredients
1 stick, plus 4 tbsp unsalted butter, softened
¾ cup light brown sugar
1 large egg, at room temperature
1 tsp pure vanilla extract
1¾ cups all-purpose flour
⅔ cup cocoa powder
2 tsp baking powder

1 tsp salt
⅔ cup whole milk
2 tbsp Greek yogurt

For the vanilla buttercream
7 tbsp unsalted butter, softened
1 cup confectioner's sugar
2 tsp pure vanilla extract
2 tsp milk, plus extra if necessary

To decorate
white and dark chocolate
7oz (200g) confectioner's sugar

1 Preheat the oven to 350°F (180°C). Line several baking sheets with parchment paper.

2 With an electric hand mixer, cream together the butter and sugar until light and fluffy.

3 Add the egg and vanilla extract to the creamed mixture and beat in.

4 Beat the egg in well to avoid curdling. The cake batter should look as shown above.

5 In a separate large bowl, sift together the flour, cocoa powder, baking powder, and salt.

6 Gently fold a spoonful of the dry ingredients into the cake batter.

7 Add a little of the milk and gently mix in. Repeat until everything is combined.

8 Blend in the yogurt, folding gently, until very well combined; this will moisten the pies.

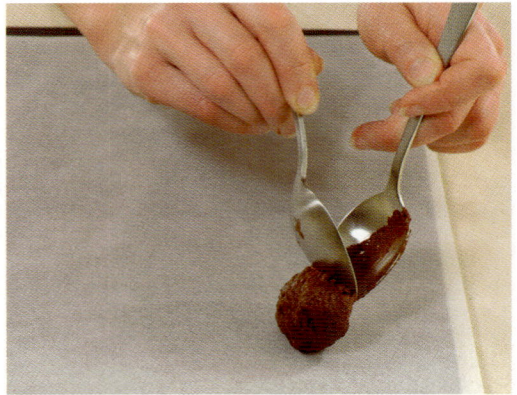

9 Place 20 heaped tablespoons of mixture on the lined baking sheets.

10 Leave space for the mixture to spread out; each half will spread to 3in (8cm).

11 Dip a clean tablespoon in warm water and use it to smooth the surface of the balls.

12 Bake for around 12 minutes, until a skewer comes out clean. Cool on a wire rack.

13 Mix together the buttercream ingredients, except the mik, with a wooden spoon initially.

14 Add the milk, change to a mixer, and beat the mix for 5 minutes, until light and fluffy.

15 If the mixture seems stiff, loosen with extra milk to make the buttercream spreadable.

16 Spread a tablespoon of the buttercream onto the flat sides of half the cakes.

17 Sandwich together the iced with the un-iced halves to form the pies, pressing gently.

18 To decorate, use a vegetable peeler to produce white and dark chocolate shavings.

19 Place the confectioner's sugar in a bowl and add water to form a thick paste.

20 Spoon the frosting onto the top each pie, spreading it out for an even covering.

21 Lightly press the chocolate shavings onto the wet icing. **STORE** Will keep for 2 days.

Whoopie Pie variations

Peanut Butter Whoopie Pies

Sweet, salty, and creamy, these whoopie pies are addictive.

MAKES 20 PIES | 40 MINS | 12 MINS | 4 WEEKS, UNFILLED

Ingredients
1 stick, plus 4 tbsp unsalted butter, softened
¾ cup light brown sugar
1 large egg, at room temperature
1 tsp pure vanilla extract
2 cups all-purpose flour
⅔ cup cocoa powder
2 tsp baking powder
1 tsp salt
⅔ cup whole milk
2 tbsp Greek yogurt or thick plain yogurt
2oz cream cheese, at room temperature
¼ cup smooth peanut butter
1 cup confectioner's sugar, sifted
2 tsp milk, plus extra if necessary

Method
1 Preheat the oven to 350°F (180°C). Line several baking sheets with parchment paper. Place the butter and sugar into the bowl of an electric mixer. Cream together until fluffy. Beat in the egg and vanilla.

2 In a separate bowl, sift the flour, cocoa powder, baking powder, and salt. Mix the dry ingredients and milk into the batter by turns, a spoonful at a time. Fold in the yogurt.

3 Put heaped tablespoons of the batter on the baking sheets, leaving space for the mixture to spread. Roll into smooth balls with wet hands, then press down gently. Bake for 12 minutes. Turn out on a wire rack.

4 Beat together the cream cheese and peanut butter until smooth. Cream in the confectioner's sugar, adding a little milk if needed. Spread the frosting on to the flat sides of half the cakes. Sandwich together with the un-iced cakes to make the pies.

STORE The whoopie pies will keep in the refrigerator for 1 day.

Chocolate Orange Whoopie Pies

Rich, dark chocolate combined with the zesty tang of orange is a classic combination, used here to full advantage in these delicious little cakes.

MAKES 20 PIES | 40 MINS | 12 MINS | 4 WEEKS, UNFILLED

Ingredients
2 sticks plus 2 tbsp unsalted butter, softened
¾ cup soft light brown sugar
1 large egg
2 tsp pure vanilla extract
finely grated zest and juice of 1 orange
1½ cups all-purpose flour
½ tsp baking powder
½ tsp salt
⅔ cup cocoa powder
⅔ cup whole milk or buttermilk
2 tbsp Greek yogurt or thick plain yogurt
1⅔ cups confectioner's sugar

Method
1 Preheat the oven to 350°F (180°C). Line several baking sheets with parchment paper. Cream 12 tablespoons butter and the brown sugar. Beat in the egg and 1 teaspoon vanilla, and add the zest. In a bowl, sift the flour, cocoa, baking powder, and salt. Mix the dry ingredients and the milk into the batter, in alternate spoonfuls. Fold in the yogurt.

2 Place heaped tablespoons onto the baking sheets, leaving space between them. Roll into smooth balls with wet hands, then press down gently onto the baking sheets. Bake for 12 minutes, until risen. Leave to cool slightly, then transfer to a wire rack.

3 For the frosting, blend the remaining butter, confectioner's sugar, 1 teaspoon vanilla, and orange juice, loosening with a little water. Spread 1 tablespoon of the filling onto the flat side of each cake half, and sandwich together with the remaining halves.

STORE The whoopie pies will keep for 2 days.

Coconut Whoopie Pies

This simple yet delicious variation uses the natural affinity between coconut and chocolate to great effect.

MAKES 20 PIES | 40 MINS | 12 MINS | 4 WEEKS, UNFILLED

Ingredients
1 stick, plus 4 tbsp unsalted butter, softened
¾ cup light brown sugar
1 large egg, at room temperature
1 tsp pure vanilla extract
2 cups all-purpose flour
⅔ cup cocoa powder
2 tsp baking powder
1 tsp salt
⅔ cup whole milk
2 tbsp Greek yogurt or thick plain yogurt

For the coconut frosting
7 tbsp unsalted butter, softened
1 cup confectioner's sugar
1 tsp pure vanilla extract
2 tsp whole milk
5 tbsp unsweetened, flaked coconut

Method
1 Preheat the oven to 350°F (180°C). Line several baking sheets with parchment paper. Cream together the butter and sugar until fluffy. Beat in the egg and vanilla. In a separate bowl, sift together the flour, cocoa powder, baking powder, and salt. Mix the dry ingredients and the milk into the batter by turns, a spoonful at a time. Fold in the yogurt.

2 Put tablespoons of batter onto the sheets. Roll into smooth balls with wet hands, then press down gently onto the baking sheets. Bake for 12 minutes, until risen. Leave to cool slightly, then transfer to a wire rack. Soak the coconut for 10 minutes in a little milk. Drain.

3 For the frosting, whisk the butter, confectioner's sugar, vanilla, and milk until fluffy. Beat in the coconut. Spread on half the cakes. Sandwich with the remaining halves.

Black Forest Whoopie Pies

A modern imitation of the famous gâteau, using tinned cherries.

MAKES 20 PIES | **40 MINS** | **12 MINS** | **4 WEEKS, UNFILLED**

Ingredients

12 tbsp unsalted butter, softened
¾ cup soft light brown sugar
1 large egg
1 tsp pure vanilla extract
1½ cups all-purpose flour
½ tsp baking powder
½ tsp salt
⅔ cup cocoa powder
⅔ cup whole milk or buttermilk
2 tbsp Greek yogurt or thick plain yogurt
8oz (225g) canned black cherries, drained, or use frozen, defrosted
9oz (250g) mascarpone
2 tbsp sugar

Method

1 Preheat the oven to 350°F (180°C). Line several baking sheets with parchment. Cream 12 tablespoons butter and brown sugar until fluffy. Beat in the egg and vanilla.

2 In a bowl, sift the flour, cocoa, baking powder, and salt. Mix the dry ingredients and the milk into the batter, in alternate spoonfuls. Fold in the yogurt. Chop 4oz (100g) of the cherries and fold these in, too.

3 Place heaped tablespoons onto the baking sheets, leaving space between them. Roll into smooth balls with wet hands, then press down gently onto the baking sheets. Bake for 12 minutes. Transfer to a wire rack.

4 Purée the remaining cherries until smooth. Mix the blended cherries and sugar into the mascarpone until well mixed; alternatively, leave a ripple effect in the filling. Spread 1 tablespoon of the filling onto the flat side of each cooled cake half, and sandwich together with the remaining halves.

STORE Best eaten the day of baking but can be stored for 1 day in the refrigerator.

Strawberries and Cream Whoopie Pies

Best served immediately, these strawberry layered whoopie pies make a lovely addition to a traditional afternoon tea.

MAKES 20 PIES | **40 MINS** | **12 MINS** | **4 WEEKS, UNFILLED**

Ingredients

1 stick, plus 4 tbsp unsalted butter, softened
¾ cup light brown sugar
1 large egg, at room temperature
1 tsp pure vanilla extract
1¾ cups all-purpose flour
½ cup cocoa powder
2 tsp baking powder
1 tsp salt
⅔ cup whole milk
2 tbsp Greek yogurt or thick plain yogurt
⅔ cup heavy cream, whipped
9oz (250g) strawberries, sliced
confectioner's sugar, for dusting

Method

1 Preheat the oven to 350°F (180°C). Line several baking sheets with parchment paper.

Cream together the butter and sugar until fluffy. Beat in the egg and vanilla. In a separate bowl, sift together the flour, cocoa powder, baking powder, and salt. Mix the dry ingredients and the milk into the batter by turns, a spoonful at a time. Fold in the yogurt.

2 Put heaped tablespoons of the batter onto the baking sheets, leaving space for the mixture to spread. Roll into smooth balls with wet hands, then press down gently onto the baking sheets.

3 Bake for 12 minutes, until well risen. Leave the pies for a few minutes, then turn out to cool completely on a wire rack.

4 Spread the whipped cream on half the cakes. Top with a layer of sliced strawberries and a second cake. Dust with confectioner's sugar and serve immediately.

Chocolate Fondants

Usually thought of as a restaurant dessert, chocolate fondants are really surprisingly easy to prepare at home.

SERVES 4 | **20 MINS** | **5–15 MINS** | **1 WEEK, UNBAKED**

Special equipment
4 x 5fl oz (150ml) dariole molds
  or 4in (10cm) ramekins

Ingredients
11 tbsp unsalted butter, cubed,
  plus extra for greasing

1 heaping tbsp all-purpose flour,
  plus extra for sprinkling
6oz (150g) good-quality dark chocolate,
  minimum 60% cocoa solids
3 large eggs, at room temperature
⅓ cup sugar
cocoa powder or confectioner's sugar, for dusting
ice cream, to serve

Method

1 Preheat the oven to 400°F (200°C). Thoroughly grease the ramekins with butter and sprinkle with a little flour, then turn it around in the dish until the butter is covered with a thin layer of flour. Tap out the excess.

2 Line the bases of the ramekins with small disks of parchment paper. In a heatproof bowl over simmering water, gently melt together the chocolate and butter, stirring all the time. Make sure the base of the bowl does not touch the water. Cool slightly.

3 In a separate bowl, whisk together the eggs and sugar. Once the chocolate mixture has cooled slightly, beat it into the eggs and sugar until thoroughly amalgamated. Sift the flour over the top and blend it in.

4 Divide the mixture between the molds or ramekins, making sure that the mixture does not come right up to the top. At this stage the fondants can be refrigerated for up to 12 hours, as long as they are brought back to room temperature before cooking.

5 Cook the fondants in the middle of the oven for 5–6 minutes if using molds, 12–15 minutes for ramekins. The sides should be firm, but the middles soft to the touch. Run a sharp knife around the edge of the molds or ramekins. Turn the fondants out on to individual serving plates by placing a plate on top and inverting the whole thing. Gently remove the mold or ramekin and peel off the parchment paper.

6 Dust with cocoa powder or confectioner's sugar if desired and serve immediately with ice cream. The middle should be completely liquid.

PREPARE AHEAD The uncooked mixture in the molds or ramekins can be refrigerated overnight (see Baker's Tip).

BAKER'S TIP

Chocolate fondants are surprisingly simple to get right. They can be prepared up to a day in advance, which makes them a great dinner party dessert. Bring them back to room temperature before they go into the oven (and do the same after defrosting), or they may need cooking for slightly longer.

Lemon and Blueberry Muffins

These featherlight muffins are glazed with lemon juice for an extra burst of flavor. Best served warm.

MAKES 12 | **20–25 MINS** | **15–20 MINS** | **UP TO 4 WEEKS**

Special equipment
12-hole muffin pan

Ingredients
4 tbsp unsalted butter
2 cups all-purpose flour
1 tbsp baking powder
½ tsp salt
½ cup sugar
1 large egg, at room temperature

finely grated zest and juice of
 1 lemon
1 tsp pure vanilla extract
1 cup milk
2¼ cups blueberries

1 Preheat the oven to 425°F (220°C). Melt the butter in a saucepan over medium-low heat.

2 Sift the flour, baking powder, and salt into a bowl (do not make muffins in an electric mixer).

3 Set 2 tablespoons sugar aside and stir the rest into the flour. Make a well in the center.

4 In a separate bowl, beat the egg lightly until just broken down and mixed together.

5 Add the melted butter, lemon zest, vanilla, and milk. Beat the egg mixture until foamy.

6 In a slow, steady stream, pour the egg mixture into the well in the flour.

7 Stir with a rubber spatula, gradually drawing in the dry ingredients to make a smooth batter.

8 Gently fold in all the blueberries, taking care not to bruise any of the fruits.

9 Do not over-mix, or the muffins will be tough. Stop when the ingredients are blended.

10 Place the muffin liners in the pan. Spoon in the batter, filling to three-quarters full.

11 Bake for 15–20 minutes, until a skewer inserted in the center comes out clean.

12 Let the muffins cool slightly, then transfer them to a wire rack.

13 In a small bowl, stir the reserved sugar with the lemon juice until the sugar dissolves.

14 While the muffins are warm, dip the crown of each into the sugar and lemon mixture.

15 Set the muffins upright back on the wire rack and brush with any remaining glaze.

16 The warm muffins will absorb the maximum amount of the lemony glaze.
STORE Best served warm, but will keep in an airtight container for 2 days.

Muffin variations

Chocolate Muffins

These muffins will fix chocolate cravings, and the buttermilk lends a delicious lightness.

MAKES 12 · 10 MINS · 15 MINS · UP TO 8 WEEKS

Special equipment
12-hole muffin pan

Ingredients
1¾ cups all-purpose flour
⅔ cup cocoa powder
1 tbsp baking powder
pinch of salt
½ cup light brown sugar
¾ cups chocolate chips
1 cup buttermilk
6 tbsp sunflower oil
½ tsp pure vanilla extract
2 large eggs, at room temperature

Method
1 Preheat the oven to 400°F (200°C). Line the muffin pan with paper muffin liners and set aside. Sift the flour, cocoa powder, baking powder, and salt into a large bowl. Stir in the sugar and chocolate chips, then make a well in the center of the dry ingredients.

2 Beat together the buttermilk, oil, vanilla, and eggs and pour the mixture into the center of the dry ingredients. Mix together lightly to make a lumpy batter. Spoon the mixture into the paper liners, filling each ¾ of the way full.

3 Bake for 15 minutes, or until well risen and firm to the touch. Immediately transfer the muffins to a wire rack and leave to cool.

STORE The muffins will keep in an airtight container for 2 days.

BAKER'S TIP
The use of liquid in these muffins, whether sour cream, buttermilk, or oil, will ensure a moist, longer lasting cake. If a recipe calls for oil, make sure that you use a light, flavorless one such as sunflower or vegetable, to ensure that the delicious flavors of the muffins are not masked by the taste of the oil.

Lemon Poppy-seed Muffins

The poppy seeds add a pleasing crunch to these delicate muffins.

MAKES 12 · 20–25 MINS · 15–20 MINS · UP TO 4 WEEKS

Special equipment
12-hole muffin pan

Ingredients
4 tbsp unsalted butter
1¾ cups all-purpose flour
1 tbsp baking powder
½ tsp salt
½ cup sugar, plus 2 tsp for sprinkling
1 large egg, (room temperature), beaten
1 tsp pure vanilla extract
1 cup milk
2 tbsp poppy seeds
finely grated zest and juice of 1 lemon

Method
1 Preheat the oven to 425°F (220°C). Melt the butter in a saucepan over medium-low heat, then leave to cool slightly. Sift the flour, baking powder, and salt into a large bowl (do not make muffins in an electric mixer). Stir in the sugar. Make a well in the center of the dry ingredients.

2 Put the egg in a separate bowl; add the melted butter, vanilla, and milk. Beat the egg mixture until foamy. Stir in the poppy seeds, and the lemon zest and juice.

3 In a slow, steady stream, pour the egg mixture into the well in the flour. Stir to make a smooth batter, but do not over-mix, or the muffins will be tough. Stop as soon as the ingredients are blended.

4 Place the muffin liners in the muffin pan. Spoon the batter evenly between the liners. Sprinkle evenly with 2 teaspoons of sugar.

5 Bake for 15–20 minutes. Let the muffins cool slightly, then transfer them to a wire rack to cool completely.

STORE The muffins will keep in an airtight container for 2 days.

Apple Muffins

These healthier muffins are best served straight from the oven.

MAKES 12   10 MINS   20–25 MINS   UP TO 8 WEEKS

Special equipment
12-hole muffin pan

Ingredients
1 Golden Delicious apple, peeled and chopped
2 tsp lemon juice
½ cup light brown sugar, plus extra for sprinkling
1½ cups all-purpose flour
⅔ cup whole-wheat flour
4 tsp baking powder
1 tbsp ground pumpkin pie spice
½ tsp salt
⅓ cup (2oz) pecans, chopped
1 cup milk
¼ cup sunflower oil
1 large egg (room temperature), beaten

Method

1 Preheat the oven to 400°F (200°C). Line the muffin pan with the paper liners and set aside. Put the apple in a bowl, add the lemon juice, and toss. Add 4 tbsp of the sugar and set aside for 5 minutes.

2 Meanwhile, sift both flours, baking powder, pumpkin pie spice, and salt into a large bowl, adding in any bran left in the sieve. Stir in the remaining sugar and pecans, then make a well in the center of the dry ingredients.

3 Beat together the milk, oil, and egg, then add the apple. Pour the wet ingredients into the center of the dry ingredients and mix together lightly to make a lumpy batter.

4 Spoon the mixture into the paper liners, filling each liner ¾ of the way full. Bake the muffins for 20–25 minutes, or until the tops are peaked and brown. Transfer the muffins to a wire rack and sprinkle with extra sugar. Eat warm or cooled.

STORE The muffins will keep in an airtight container for 2 days.

Madeleines

These elegant treats were made famous by French writer Marcel Proust, who took a bite and was transported back to his childhood.

| MAKES 12 | 15–20 MINS | 10 MINS | UP TO 4 WEEKS |

Special equipment
Madeleine pan, or 12-hole mini muffin pan

Ingredients

4 tbsp unsalted butter, melted and cooled
⅓ cup all-purpose flour, sifted, plus extra
   for dusting
⅓ cup sugar
2 large eggs, at room temperature
1 tsp pure vanilla extract
¼ tsp baking powder
confectioner's sugar, to dust

Method

1 Preheat the oven to 350°F (180°C). Liberally brush the pan with melted butter and dust with flour. Invert the pan and tap to remove excess flour.

2 Put the sugar, eggs, and vanilla into a mixing bowl and whisk until the mixture is pale, thick, and will hold a trail. This should take 5 minutes with an electric hand mixer, or a bit longer if you are whisking by hand.

3 Sift the flour over the top and pour the melted butter down the side of the mixture. Using a large spatula, fold them in quickly, being careful not to knock out any air.

4 Fill the molds with the mixture and bake in the oven for 15 minutes or until golden brown around the edges and springy to the touch. Remove from the oven and transfer to a wire rack to cool before dusting with confectioner's sugar.

STORE The madeleines will keep in an airtight container for 1 day.

BAKER'S TIP

These delightful little treats are meant to be as light as air. Care should be taken to incorporate as much air as possible into the batter at the whisking stage, and to lose as little volume from the batter when folding in the flour. Best eaten the same day.

Scones

Homemade scones are one of the simplest and best teatime treats. Buttermilk makes the lightest scones.

MAKES 6–8 | 15–20 MINS | 12–15 MINS | UP TO 4 WEEKS

Special equipment
3in (7cm) pastry cutter

Ingredients
4 tbsp unsalted butter,
 chilled and cut into pieces,
 plus extra for greasing
1¾ cups all-purpose flour,
 plus extra for dusting
2 tsp baking powder
½ tsp salt
⅔ cup buttermilk

1 Preheat the oven to 425°F (220°C). Line a baking sheet with parchment and grease.

2 Sift the flour, baking powder, and salt into a large chilled bowl.

3 Put the butter in the bowl, keeping all ingredients as cold as possible.

4 Rub with your fingertips until it forms fine crumbs, working quickly, lifting to aerate it.

5 Make a well in the mixture and in a slow, steady stream, pour the buttermilk into it.

6 Quickly toss the flour mixture and buttermilk with a fork. Do not over-mix.

7 Stir the mixture till the crumbs form a dough. Add a little more buttermilk if it seems dry.

8 Turn onto a floured surface and knead for a few seconds. Keep it rough, not smooth.

9 Pat the dough out to a round ½in (1cm) thick, keeping it as cool and unworked as you can.

10 Cut out rounds with the pastry cutter; see Baker's Tip, page 142.

11 Pat out the trimmings and cut additional rounds until all the dough has been used.

12 Arrange the scones so they are about 2in (5cm) apart on the prepared baking sheet.

13 Bake in the preheated oven for 12–15 minutes, until lightly browned and risen. Scones should be eaten the day they are baked, ideally still warm from the oven, and spread with butter, jam, and clotted cream.

Scone variations

Currant Scones

Serve these currant-studded scones straight from the oven, spread with butter or clotted cream.

MAKES 6 | 15–20 MINS | 12–15 MINS | UP TO 4 WEEKS

Ingredients

4 tbsp unsalted butter, chilled and diced, plus extra for greasing
1 large egg yolk, for glazing
2/3 cup buttermilk, plus 1 tbsp for glazing
1¾ cups all-purpose flour, plus extra for dusting
2 tsp baking powder
½ tsp salt
¼ tsp baking soda
2 tsp sugar
2 tbsp currants

Method

1 Preheat the oven to 425°F (220°C), and grease a baking sheet with butter. Beat the egg yolk and the 1 tbsp buttermilk together, and set aside.

2 Sift the flour, baking powder, salt, and baking soda into a bowl, and add the sugar. Add the butter and rub the mixture with your fingertips until it forms fine crumbs. Stir in the currants. Pour in the buttermilk and quickly toss the mixture with a fork to form crumbs. Stir just until the crumbs hold together and form a dough.

3 Transfer the dough to a floured work surface. Cut it in half and pat each half into a 6in (15cm) round, about ½in (1cm) thick. With a sharp knife, cut each round into 4 wedges. Arrange the wedges about 2in (5cm) apart on the prepared baking sheet. Brush them with the glaze.

4 Bake the scones in the heated oven until lightly browned, 12–15 minutes. Leave for a few minutes on the baking sheet, then transfer to a wire rack to cool.

BAKER'S TIP

One of the secrets to well-risen scones is in the way they are cut. It is best to use a sharp pastry cutter or knife, as here, preferably made of metal. They should be cut with a strong downward motion, and the cutter should not be twisted at all when cutting. This ensures a high, even rise on cooking.

Cheese and Parsley Scones

Basic scone mix is easily adapted for a tasty savory variation.

20 SMALL OR 6 BIG | 20 MINS | 8–10 MINS | UP TO 12 WEEKS

Special equipment

1½in (4cm) pastry cutter for mini scones, or 2½in (6cm) pastry cutter for large scones

Ingredients

oil, for greasing
1¾ cups all-purpose flour, sifted, plus extra for dusting
1 tsp baking powder
pinch of salt
4 tbsp unsalted butter, chilled and cubed
1 tsp dried parsley
1 tsp black peppercorns, crushed
2oz (50g) aged Cheddar cheese, grated
½ cup milk

Method

1 Preheat the oven to 425°F (220°C). Lightly oil a medium-sized baking sheet. In a large bowl, mix together the flour, baking powder, and salt. Add the butter and, using your fingertips, rub it in until the mixture resembles fine breadcrumbs.

2 Stir in the parsley, pepper, and half the cheese, then add enough milk to bind and make the dough come together (reserve the rest for brushing on the top of the scones). Mix into a soft dough.

3 Roll out the dough on a lightly floured board to a thickness of about ¾in (2cm). Using your chosen pastry cutter, cut out rounds. Set them on the prepared baking sheet, brush with the remaining milk, and sprinkle over the remaining cheese.

4 Bake on the top shelf of the oven for 8–10 minutes until golden. Leave on the baking sheet for a couple of minutes to cool a little, then either serve warm or cool completely on a wire rack.

Strawberry Shortcakes

These shortcakes are perfect served as a light summer dessert.

| MAKES 6 | 15–20 MINS | 12–15 MINS | 4 WEEKS, UNFILLED |

Special equipment
3in (8cm) pastry cutter

Ingredients
4 tbsp unsalted butter, cut into pieces
1¾ cups all-purpose flour, plus extra for dusting
1 tbsp baking powder
½ tsp salt
¼ cup sugar
⅔ cup heavy cream, plus extra if needed

For the coulis
1lb 2oz (500g) strawberries, hulled
2–3 tbsp confectioner's sugar
2 tbsp Kirsch (optional)

For the filling
1lb 2oz (500g) strawberries, hulled and sliced
¼ cup sugar, plus 2–3 tbsp
1 cup heavy cream
1 tsp pure vanilla extract

Method

1 Preheat the oven to 425°F (220°C). Butter a baking sheet. Sift the flour into a bowl with the baking powder, and salt, and stir in the sugar. Rub to form crumbs. Add cream, tossing; add more, if dry. Add the butter and rub in with your fingertips to form crumbs.

2 Press the crumbs together to form a ball of dough. On a floured surface, lightly knead the dough. Pat out a round, ½in (1cm) thick, and cut out 6 rounds with the cutter (see Baker's Tip). Transfer to the baking sheet, and bake for 12–15 minutes. Cool on a wire rack.

3 For the coulis, purée the strawberries, then stir in the confectioner's sugar and Kirsch.

4 For the filling, mix the strawberries and sugar. Whip the cream until soft peaks form. Add 2–3 tablespoons of sugar and the vanilla. Whip until stiff. Cut the cakes in half. Put the strawberries on the bottom halves, followed by the cream. Top each with its lid. Pour the coulis around. Serve immediately.

Welsh Cakes

These traditional small cakes from Wales take minutes to prepare and cook, and you don't even have to remember to preheat the oven.

24 SMALL CAKES   **20 MINS**   **16–24 MINS**   **UP TO 4 WEEKS**

Special equipment
2in (5cm) pastry cutter

Ingredients
1⅓ cups all-purpose flour, plus extra for dusting
1½ tsp baking powder
½ tsp salt
7 tbsp unsalted butter, chilled and diced
⅓ cup sugar, plus extra for dusting
½ cup (4oz) golden raisins
1 large egg (room temperature), beaten
a little milk, if needed

Method

1 Sift the flour, baking powder, and salt into a large bowl. Rub the butter into the flour until the mixture resembles fine breadcrumbs. Mix in the sugar and the golden raisins. Pour in the egg.

2 Mix the ingredients together, bringing the mixture into a ball using your hands. This should be firm enough to roll out, but if it seems too stiff you can add a little milk.

3 On a floured work surface, gently roll out the dough to about ¼in (5mm) thick, and cut disks out of the dough, using the pastry cutter. Heat a large, heavy based frying pan, cast iron skillet, or flat griddle over medium-low heat.

4 Fry the cakes, in batches, in a little melted butter for 2–3 minutes each side, until they puff up, are golden brown, and are cooked through. While still warm, dust the cakes with a little sugar before serving. (Note that Welsh cakes are best eaten immediately. If you freeze them, be sure to reheat in the oven after defrosting.)

BAKER'S TIP
These are a delightfully easy afternoon treat, and can be ready to eat within minutes of starting. The secret is to cook them over a fairly low heat, and to be extremely careful when turning them over to cook on the second side. Delicious eaten immediately with butter.

Rock Cakes

It's high time these classic British buns enjoyed a renaissance. Correctly cooked, they are light, crumbly, and incredibly simple to make.

MAKES 12 · **15 MINS** · **15–20 MINS** · **UP TO 4 WEEKS**

Ingredients

1½ cups all-purpose flour
1½ tsp baking powder
½ tsp salt
7 tbsp unsalted butter, chilled and diced
⅓ cup sugar
¾ cup (4oz) mixed dried fruit (raisins, golden raisins, and mixed peel)
2 large eggs
2 tbsp milk, plus extra if needed
½ tsp pure vanilla extract

Method

1 Preheat the oven to 375°F (190°C). In a large bowl, rub together the flour, baking powder, salt, and butter until the mixture resembles fine bread crumbs. Mix in the sugar. Add the dried fruit to the bowl and mix together throughly.

2 In a bowl, whisk together the eggs, milk, and vanilla extract. Make a well in the center of the flour mixture and pour the egg mixture into the middle. Mix thoroughly to combine, producing a firm mixture. Use a little more milk if the mixture seems too stiff.

3 Line 2 baking sheets with parchment paper. Place large tablespoons of the mixture on to the baking sheets, leaving plenty of space for the cakes to spread. Bake the cakes in the center of the oven for 15–20 minutes until they are golden brown. Remove to a wire rack to cool slightly.

4 Serve warm, split, and spread with butter or jam. Rock cakes should be eaten the day they are baked as they do not store well.

BAKER'S TIP

Easy-to-make rock cakes are named after their classic, rugged shape, rather than their texture! Make sure that the mixture is piled at least 2–3in (5–7cm) high on the baking sheet, which will ensure the classic rough edges even after they have spread out on baking.

patisserie

Croissants

These may take some time to make, but the final result is well worth the effort. Start a day ahead.

MAKES 12 | **1 HOUR** | **15–20 MINS** | **4 WEEKS, UNBAKED**

Chilling time
5 hrs, plus overnight

Rising time
1 hr

Ingredients
2¼ cups plus 2 tbsp all-purpose flour, plus extra for dusting
½ tsp salt
2 tbsp sugar
1 (¼oz) package dried yeast

1 cup milk, at room temperature
vegetable oil, for greasing
2 sticks, plus 2 tbsp unsalted butter, chilled, cut into ½-inch thick slices
1 large egg, beaten

1 Place the flour, salt, sugar, and yeast in a large bowl, and stir to blend well.

2 Using a butter knife, mix in enough warm water, a little at a time, to form a soft dough.

3 Knead on a lightly floured surface until it becomes elastic under your hands.

4 Place back in the bowl, cover with lightly oiled plastic wrap, and chill for 1 hour.

5 Roll the dough out into a rectangle that measures 10 x 17in (25 x 43cm).

6 Squash the chilled butter with a rolling pin, keeping the pat shape, until ½in (1cm) thick.

7 Place the butter in the center of the dough. Fold the dough over it. Chill for 1 hour.

8 Roll out the dough on a lightly floured surface to a 24 x 14in (61 x 36cm) rectangle.

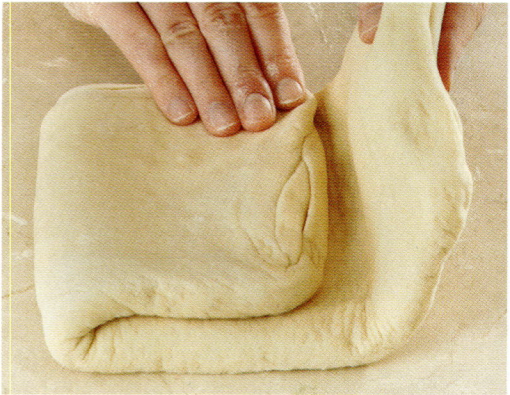

9 Fold the right third to the center, then the left third over the top. Chill for 1 hour, until firm.

PATISSERIE

10 Repeat the rolling, folding, and chilling twice. Wrap in plastic wrap and chill overnight.

11 Cut the dough in half, and roll out one half to a 5 x 14½in (12 x 36cm) rectangle.

12 Cut into 1 x 5in (3 x 12cm) squares, then cut diagonally to make 6 triangles. Repeat.

13 Holding the ends of the longest side, roll it toward you. Curve into crescent shapes.

14 Place on baking sheets lined with parchment paper, leaving space between each.

15 Cover with lightly oiled plastic wrap. Leave for 1 hour until doubled in size. Remove the film.

16 Preheat the oven to 425°F (220°C). Brush them with egg, then bake for 10 minutes.

17 Reduce the temperature to 375°F (190°C) and bake for another 5–10 minutes.

STORE The croissants are best served when still warm, with butter and jam, but will keep in an airtight container for 2 days; gently reheat to serve.

Croissant variations

Pains au chocolat

Fresh pains au chocolat, still warm from the oven and oozing with melted chocolate, make the ultimate weekend breakfast treat.

MAKES 8 | 1 HOUR | 15–20 MINS | UP TO 4 WEEKS

Chilling time
5 hrs, plus overnight

Rising time
1 hr

Ingredients
1 quantity croissant dough,
  see pages 150–151, steps 1–10
7oz (200g) dark chocolate
1 large egg, beaten

Method

1 Divide the dough into 4 equal pieces and roll each out into a rectangle, about 4 x 16in (10 x 40cm). Cut each piece in half, to give 8 rectangles approximately 4 x 8in (10 x 20cm).

2 Cut the chocolate into 16 even-sized pieces. If you buy two 4oz (115g) bars, they normally divide naturally into 8 pieces each. Mark each piece of pastry along the long edge at one-third and two-thirds.

3 Put a piece of chocolate at the one-third mark, and fold the short end of the dough over it to the two-thirds mark. Now place a second piece of chocolate on top of the folded edge at the two-thirds mark, brush the dough next to it with beaten egg, and fold the other side of the dough into the center, making a three-layered parcel with pieces of chocolate tucked in on either side. Seal all the edges together to prevent the chocolate from oozing out while cooking.

4 Line a baking sheet with parchment paper, place the pastries on it, cover, and leave to rise in a warm place for 1 hour, until puffed up and soft. Preheat the oven to 425°F (220°C). Brush the pastries with beaten egg and bake in the oven for 10 minutes, then reduce the oven temperature to 375°F (190°C). Bake for another 5–10 minutes, or until golden brown.

STORE These will keep in an airtight container for 1 day.

Cheese and Ham Croissants

Ham combined with tangy cheese is used here to great effect.

MAKES 8 | 1 HOUR | 15–20 MINS | UP TO 4 WEEKS

Chilling time
5 hrs, plus overnight

Rising time
1 hr

Ingredients
1 quantity croissant dough,
  see pages 150–151, steps 1–10
8 slices ham, prosciutto, or Spanish chorizo
8 slices cheese, such as Emmental
  or Jarlsberg
1 large egg, beaten

Method

1 Divide the dough into 4 equal pieces and roll each out into a rectangle, about 4 x 16in (10 x 40cm). Cut each piece in half, to get 8 rectangles about 4 x 8in (10 x 20cm).

2 Place a slice of ham or slices of chorizo on the middle of each croissant and fold one side over it. Place a slice of cheese on the folded over piece, brush with beaten egg, and fold the remaining side over it. Seal all the edges. Cover and place in a warm place for 1 hour or until spongy and soft. Preheat the oven to 425°F (220°C).

3 Brush the pastries with egg and bake for 10 minutes, then reduce the temperature to 375°F (190°C). Bake for another 5–10 minutes, or until golden brown.

STORE Keep in an airtight container for 1 day.

BAKER'S TIP
These pastries are endlessly adaptable and can be made with a variety of fillings. Ham and cheese is the most common, but try using a layer of smoked ham and a layer of overlapped chorizo, and sprinkling with smoked paprika, for a more piquant flavor.

Croissants aux amandes

These frangipane-stuffed pastries are light and delicious.

MAKES 12 | **1 HOUR** | **15–20 MINS** | **UP TO 4 WEEKS**

Chilling time
5 hrs, plus overnight

Rising time
1 hr

Ingredients
1 quantity croissant dough,
  see pages 150–151, steps 1–10
1 large egg, beaten
½ cup (2oz) sliced almonds
confectioner's sugar, to serve
2 tbsp unsalted butter, softened
⅓ cup sugar
¾ cup (3oz) ground almonds
2–3 tbsp milk, if needed

Method

1 For the almond paste, cream the butter and sugar, using an electric hand mixer. Mix in the almonds, adding milk if too thick.

2 Cut the dough into 2 and roll half out on a floured surface to a 5 x 14½in (12 x 36cm) rectangle. Cut into 3 x 5in (12cm) squares, then cut diagonally to make 6 triangles. Repeat with remaining dough.

3 Spread 1 tablespoon of the paste onto each triangle, leaving a ¾in (2cm) border along the 2 longest sides. Brush the borders with egg. Roll the croissant up carefully from the longest side toward the opposite point.

4 Line 2 baking sheets with parchment paper and put the croissants on them. Cover and put in a warm place for 1 hour, until soft and spongy. Preheat oven to 425°F (220°C).

5 Brush the croissants with egg. Sprinkle with sliced almonds. Bake for 10 minutes, then reduce the temperature to 375°F (190°C). Bake for 5–10 minutes, or until golden. Cool. Dust with confectioner's sugar to serve.

STORE Keep in an airtight container for 1 day.

Danish Pastries

Although these deliciously buttery pastries take time to prepare, the home-baked taste is incomparable.

**MAKES
18**

**30
MINS**

**15–20
MINS**

**UP TO 4
WEEKS**

Chilling time
1 hr

Rising time
50 mins

Ingredients

⅔ cup warm milk
2 tsp dried yeast
2 tbsp sugar
2 large eggs, plus 1 for glazing,
  at room temperature
3½ cups all-purpose flour, sifted,
  plus extra for dusting
½ tsp salt

vegetable oil, for greasing
2 sticks, plus 2 tbsp chilled butter
¾ cup good-quality cherry,
  strawberry, or apricot jam
  or compote

1 Mix the milk, yeast, and 1 tablespoon sugar. Cover for 20 minutes, then beat in the eggs.

2 Place the flour, salt, and remaining sugar in a bowl. Make a well and pour in the yeast mix.

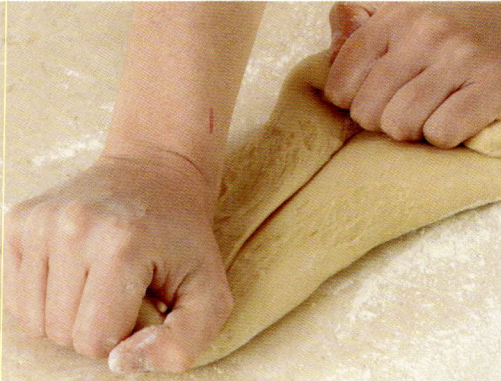

3 Mix the ingredients into a soft dough. Knead for 15 minutes on a floured surface until soft.

4 Place the dough in a lightly oiled bowl, cover with plastic wrap and refrigerate for 15 minutes.

5 On a lightly floured surface, roll the dough out to a square, about 10 x 10in (25 x 25cm).

6 Cut the butter into 3–4 slices, each about 5 x 2½ x ½in (12 x 6 x 1cm).

7 Lay the butter slices on one half of the dough, leaving a border of ½–¾in (1–2cm).

8 Fold the other half of the dough over the top, pressing the edges with a rolling pin to seal.

9 Generously flour and roll it into a rectangle 3 times as long as it is wide, and ½in (1cm) thick.

10 Fold the top third down into the middle, then the bottom third back over it.

11 Wrap and chill for 15 minutes. Repeat steps 9–10 twice, chilling for 15 minutes each time.

12 Roll on a floured surface to ¼-½in (5mm–1cm) thick. Cut to 4 x 4in (10 x 10cm) squares.

13 With a sharp knife, make diagonal cuts from each corner to within ½in (1cm) of the center.

14 Put a teaspoon of jam in the center of each square and fold each corner into the center.

15 Spoon jam on the center, place on a lined baking sheet, and cover with a kitchen towel.

16 Keep for 30 minutes in a warm place until risen. Preheat the oven to 400°F (200°C).

17 Brush with egg wash and bake at the top of the oven for 15–20 minutes, until golden.

18 Leave to cool slighty then transfer to a wire rack. **STORE** These will keep in an airtight container for 2 days. **PREPARE AHEAD** Make up to end of step 11 and refrigerate overnight.

DANISH PASTRIES

Danish Pastry variations

Almond Crescents

Butter, sugar, and ground almonds are combined here to make a delicious filling for these light and flaky, crescent-shaped Danish pastries. The pastry can be prepared the night before, ready for rolling.

MAKES 18 | 30 MINS | 15–20 MINS | UP TO 4 WEEKS

Chilling time
1 hr

Rising time
30 mins

Ingredients
1 quantity danish pastry dough, see pages 154–155, steps 1–11
1 large egg, beaten, for glazing
confectioner's sugar, to serve

For almond paste
2 tbsp unsalted butter, softened
⅓ cup sugar
¾ cup ground almonds

Method

1 Preheat the oven to 400°F (200°C). Roll half the dough out on a floured surface to a 12in (30cm) square. Trim the edges and cut out 9 x 4in (10cm) squares. Repeat with the remaining dough. Beat the butter and sugar until creamed, then beat in the ground almonds until smooth.

2 Divide the almond paste into 18 small balls. Roll them into sausage shapes a little shorter than the length of the squares. Place a roll of the almond paste at one edge of the square, leaving a gap of ¾in (2cm) between it and the edge. Press it down.

3 Brush the clear edge with egg and fold the pastry over the paste, pressing it down. Use a knife to make 4 cuts into the folded edge to within ½–¾in (1½–2cm) of the sealed edge.

Transfer to lined baking sheets, cover, and leave in a warm place for 30 minutes, or until puffed. Bend the edges in.

4 Brush with egg and bake in the top third of the oven for 15–20 minutes, until golden brown. Cool. Dust confectioner's sugar over to serve.

STORE The pastries will keep in an airtight container for 2 days.

BAKER'S TIP

Danish pastry recipes often call for the butter to be rolled out between pieces of parchment paper—or bashed with a rolling pin to render it pliable. This takes a lot of time. Use sliced chilled butter instead, for a fuss-free result.

PATISSERIE

Cinnamon and Pecan Pinwheels

Try substituting hazelnuts or walnuts here if pecans are unavailable.

MAKES 16 | 30 MINS | 15–20 MINS | UP TO 4 WEEKS

Chilling time
1 hr

Rising time
50 mins

Ingredients
1 cup (4oz) pecan nuts, chopped
½ cup light brown sugar
2 tbsp cinnamon
1 quantity danish pastry dough,
  see pages 154–155, steps 1–11
1 large egg, beaten, for glazing
2 tbsp unsalted butter, melted

Method

1 To make the filling, mix the pecans, sugar, and cinnamon. Roll half the dough out on a floured work surface to an 8in (20cm) square. Trim the edges, brush the surface with half the butter, and scatter half the pecan mixture over the top, leaving a ½in (1cm) border at the long side that is farthest from you. Brush the border with a little egg.

2 Press the sugar mixture with the palm of your hand to ensure it sticks to the dough. Roll the dough up, starting with the long side and working toward the border. Turn seam-side down. Repeat.

3 Trim the ends and cut each into 8 slices. Turn over and press them to allow the edges to stick. Secure the ends of the dough with a cocktail stick. Line 4 baking sheets with parchment paper. Place 4 pastries on each sheet. Cover and leave in a warm place for 30 minutes, until well puffed up.

4 Preheat the oven to 400°F (200°C). Brush with egg and bake in the top third of oven for 15–20 minutes, until golden brown.

STORE The pastries will keep in an airtight container for 2 days.

Apricot Pastries

The pastry can be prepared the night before, so that 30 minutes of rising in the morning and a quick bake will give you fresh pastries in time for coffee.

MAKES 18 | 30 MINS | 15–20 MINS | UP TO 4 WEEKS

Chilling time
1 hr

Rising time
50 mins

Ingredients
1 quantity danish pastry dough,
  see pages 154–155, steps 1–11
½ cup apricot jam
2 x 14oz (400g) cans apricot halves

Method.

1 Roll half the dough out on a well floured work surface to a 12in (30cm) square. Trim the edges and cut out 9 x 4in (10cm) squares. Repeat with the remaining dough.

2 If the apricot jam has lumps, purée it until smooth. Take 1 tablespoon of jam and, using the back of the spoon, spread it all over a square, leaving a border of about ½in (1cm). Take 2 apricot halves and trim a little off their bottoms if too chunky. Place an apricot half in 2 opposite corners of the square.

3 Take the 2 corners without apricots and fold them into the middle. They should only partially cover the apricot halves. Repeat to fill all the pastries. Place on lined baking sheets, cover, and leave to rise in a warm place for 30 minutes until puffed up. Preheat the oven to 400°F (200°C).

4 Brush the pastries with egg and bake in the top third of the oven for 15–20 minutes, until golden. Melt the remaining jam and brush over the pastries, to glaze. Cool for 5 minutes then transfer to a wire rack to cool.

STORE The pastries will keep in an airtight container for 2 days.

Cinnamon Rolls

If you prefer, leave the rolls to prove overnight in the fridge (after step 15) and bake in time for a breakfast treat.

MAKES 10–12 | 40 MINS | 25–30 MINS | UP TO 4 WEEKS

Rising and proofing time
3–4 hrs or overnight

Special equipment
12in (30cm) springform cake pan

Ingredients
½ cup milk
7 tbsp unsalted butter, plus extra for greasing
1 (¼oz) package dried yeast
¼ cup sugar
4¼ cup flour, sifted, plus more for dusting
1 tsp salt

1 large egg plus 2 large egg yolks, at room temperature
vegetable oil, for greasing

For the filling and glaze
2 tbsp cinnamon
½ cup light brown sugar
2 tbsp unsalted butter, melted
1 large egg, lightly beaten

1 In a pan, heat ½ cup water, the milk, and butter until just melted. Let it cool slightly.

2 When just warm, whisk in the yeast and a tablespoon of sugar. Cover for 10 minutes.

3 Place the flour, salt, and remaining sugar in a large bowl.

4 Make a well in center of the dry ingredients and pour in the warm milk mixture.

5 Whisk the eggs and egg yolks, and add to the mixture. Combine to form a rough dough.

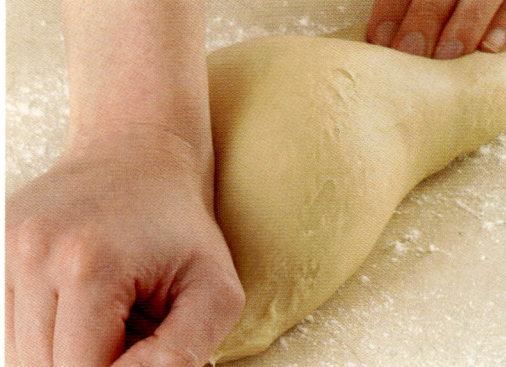

6 Place on a floured surface and knead for 10 minutes. Add extra flour if it's too sticky.

7 Put in an oiled bowl, cover with plastic, and keep in a wam place for 2 hours till well risen.

8 Prepare the filling by mixing 2 tablespoons of cinnamon with the brown sugar.

9 When the dough has risen, turn it onto a floured work surface, and gently knock it back.

10 Roll it out into a rectangle about 16 x 12in (40 x 30cm). Brush with the melted butter.

11 Scatter with the cinnamon. Leave a ½in (1cm) border on one side and brush it with the egg.

12 Press the sugar mixture with the palm of your hand to ensure it sticks to the dough.

13 Roll the dough up, working toward the border. Do not roll too tightly.

14 Cut into 10–12 equal pieces with a serrated knife, being careful not to squash the roll.

15 Grease and line the pan. Pack in the rolls. Cover and proof for 1–2 hours until well risen.

16 Preheat the oven to 350°F (180°C). Brush with egg and bake for 25–30 minutes.

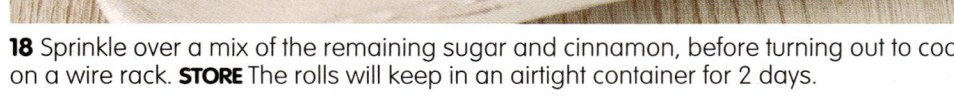

17 Heat 3 tablespoons water and 2 of sugar until dissolved. Brush the glaze on the rolls.

18 Sprinkle over a mix of the remaining sugar and cinnamon, before turning out to cool on a wire rack. **STORE** The rolls will keep in an airtight container for 2 days.

Sweet Roll variations

Chelsea Buns

These sweet and spicy buns were invented in the 18th century at The Bun House in Chelsea, London, where they proved a hit with royalty.

| MAKES 9 | 30 MINS | 30 MINS | UP TO 4 WEEKS |

Rising and proofing time
2 hrs

Special equipment
9in (23cm) square cake pan

Ingredients
2¼ cups bread flour, sifted, plus extra for dusting
½ tsp salt
2 tbsp sugar
1 tsp dried yeast
3 tbsp butter, plus extra for greasing
1 large egg, lightly beaten
½ cup warm milk
vegetable oil, for greasing
1 cup (4oz) mixed dried fruit
⅓ cup light brown sugar
1 tsp pumpkin pie spice
honey, for glazing

Method
1 Mix the flour, salt, sugar, and yeast in a mixing bowl. Rub in 1 tablespooon of the butter. Pour in the egg, then the milk. Mix to form a soft dough. Knead for 5 minutes. Place in a lightly oiled bowl and cover with oiled plastic wrap. Leave in a warm place for 1 hour, or until doubled in size.

2 Grease the pan. Put the dough on a lightly floured surface and knead. Roll out to a 12 x 9in (30 x 23cm) rectangle. Melt the rest of the butter in a saucepan over low heat, then brush over the surface of the dough, leaving a border along the long edges.

3 Mix the fruit, brown sugar, and spice together and scatter over the butter. Roll up the dough from the long edge like a Swiss roll, sealing the end with a little water. Cut the dough into 9 pieces. Put the pieces in the pan and cover with plastic wrap. Leave to rise for 1 hour until doubled. Preheat the oven to 375°F (190°C). Bake for 30 minutes, then brush with honey and cool before transferring to a wire rack.

STORE The buns will keep in an airtight container for 2 days.

Spiced Fruit Buns

These delicious sweetened rolls make a perfect afternoon snack.

| MAKES 12 | 30 MINS | 15 MINS | UP TO 4 WEEKS |

Rising and proofing time
1½ hrs

Ingredients
1 cup tepid milk
1 (¼oz/7.5g) package dried yeast
3¾ cups bread flour, sifted, plus extra for dusting
1 tsp pumpkin pie spice
½ tsp ground nutmeg
1 tsp salt
6 tbsp sugar
4 tbsp unsalted butter, diced, plus extra for greasing
vegetable oil, for greasing
1½ cups (6oz) mixed dried fruit
2 tbsp confectioner's sugar
¼ tsp pure vanilla extract

Method
1 Warm the milk until tepid, stir in the yeast, cover, and leave for 10 minutes until frothy. Place the flour, spices, salt, and sugar in a bowl. Rub in the butter. Add the yeasted milk to form a soft dough. Knead well for 10 minutes. Shape into a ball, then place in a lightly oiled bowl and cover loosely. Leave in a warm place for 1 hour until risen.

2 Place the dough onto a lightly floured work surface and knead in the dried fruit. Divide the dough into 12 pieces, roll into balls, and place, well spaced, on lightly greased baking sheets. Cover loosely and leave in a warm place for 30 minutes, until doubled. Preheat the oven to 400°F (200°C).

3 Bake for 15 minutes, or until the buns sound hollow when tapped on the base. Transfer to a wire rack to cool. While the buns are still hot, combine the confectioner's sugar, vanilla extract, and 1 tablespoon of cold water, and brush over the top of the buns to glaze.

STORE Keep in an airtight container for 2 days.

Hot Cross Buns

These sweet buns are too delicious to have just for Easter.

| MAKES 10–12 | 30 MINS | 15–20 MINS | UP TO 4 WEEKS |

Rising and proofing time
2–4 hrs

Special equipment
piping bag with thin nozzle

Ingredients
¾ cup milk
4 tbsp unsalted butter
1 tsp pure vanilla extract
1 (¼oz/10g) package dried yeast
½ cup sugar
3¾ cups bread flour, sifted,
  plus extra for dusting
1 tsp salt
2 tsp pumpkin pie spice
1 tsp ground cinnamon
1½ cups (6oz) mixed dried fruit (raisins, golden
  raisins, and mixed peel)
1 large egg, beaten, plus 1 extra for glazing
vegetable oil, for greasing

For the paste
1 tbsp all-purpose flour
1 tbsp sugar

Method

1 Heat the milk, butter, and vanilla in a pan until the butter is just melted. Cool until tepid. Whisk in the yeast and 1 tablespoon of sugar. Cover for 10 minutes until it froths.

2 Put the remaining sugar, flour, salt, and spices into a bowl. Mix in the egg. Add the milk mixture and form a dough. Knead for 10 minutes on a floured surface. Press the dough out into a rectangle, scatter over the dried fruit, and knead briefly to combine.

3 Place the dough in an oiled bowl, cover with plastic wrap, and leave in a warm place for 1–2 hours until doubled. Turn the dough out onto a floured surface, knock it back, and divide into 10–12 balls. Place them on lined baking sheets. Cover with plastic wrap and a kitchen towel and leave for 1–2 hours.

4 Preheat the oven to 425°F (220°C). Brush the buns with the beaten egg. For the paste,

mix the flour and sugar with water to make it spreadable. Put it into the piping bag and pipe crosses on the buns. Bake in the top of the oven for 15–20 minutes. Remove to a wire rack and allow to cool for 15 minutes.

STORE The buns will keep in an airtight container for 2 days.

BAKER'S TIP
These traditional Easter buns are very different and far superior to their bland store-bought namesakes. They have a delicate, crispy exterior surface and a light, moist, fragrant crumb with authentically assertive levels of fruit and spice. They are delicious still warm from the oven, spread with plentiful cold butter.

Profiteroles

These cream-filled choux pastry buns, drizzled with chocolate sauce, make a deliciously decadent dessert.

SERVES 4 | **30 MINS** | **22 MINS** | **12 WEEKS, UNFILLED**

Special equipment
2 piping bags with a ½in (1cm) plain nozzle and ¼in (5mm) star nozzle

Ingredients

For the choux buns
½ cup all-purpose flour
4 tbsp unsalted butter
2 large eggs, beaten

For the filling and topping
1¾ cup heavy cream
7oz (200g) good-quality dark
 chocolate, broken into pieces
2 tbsp butter
2 tbsp corn syrup

1 Preheat the oven to 425°F (220°C). Line 2 large baking sheets with parchment paper.

2 Sift the flour into a large bowl, holding the sieve up high to aerate the flour.

3 Put the butter and ⅔ cup water into a small saucepan and heat gently until melted.

4 Bring to a boil, remove from the heat, and add in the flour all at once.

5 Beat with a wooden spoon until smooth; the mixture should form a ball. Cool for 10 minutes.

6 Gradually add the eggs, beating very well after each addition to incorporate.

7 Carry on adding the egg, little by little, to form a stiff, smooth, and shiny paste.

8 Spoon the mixture into a piping bag fitted with a ½in (1cm) plain nozzle.

9 Pipe walnut-sized rounds, set well apart. Bake for 20 minutes until risen and golden.

10 Remove from the oven and slit the side of each bun to allow the steam to escape.

11 Return to the oven for 2 minutes, to crisp, then transfer to a wire rack to cool completely.

12 Before serving, pour ½ cup cream into a saucepan and whip the rest until just peaking.

13 Add the chocolate, butter, and syrup to the cream in the pan and heat gently until melted.

14 Pile the whipped cream into a piping bag fitted with a ¼in (5mm) star nozzle.

15 Pipe cream into each choux bun and arrange onto a serving plate or cake stand.

16 Stir the sauce well, pour it over the buns, and serve immediately.
PREPARE AHEAD The unfilled buns will keep in an airtight container for 2 days.

Choux Pastry variations

Chocolate Orange Profiteroles

A delicious twist on the original, heightened by sharp orange zest and liqueur. Try to use dark chocolate that is at least 60 percent cocoa solids for a bitter chocolate orange taste.

| SERVES 6 | 20 MINS | 30–35 MINS | 12 WEEKS, UNFILLED |

Special equipment
2 piping bags with a ½in (1cm) plain nozzle and ¼in (5mm) star nozzle

Ingredients

For the choux buns
4 tbsp unsalted butter, plus extra for greasing
¾ cup all-purpose flour, sifted
2 large eggs, beaten

For the chocolate sauce
6oz (150g) good-quality dark chocolate, broken into pieces
1¼ cups half-and-half
2 tbsp corn syrup
1 tbsp Grand Marnier

For the filling
2 cups heavy whipping cream
finely grated zest of 1 large orange
2 tbsp Grand Marnier

Method

1 Preheat the oven to 425°F (220°C). Grease 2 baking sheets. To make the choux pastry, melt the butter with 1¼ cups water in a pan, then bring to a boil. As soon as the mixture comes to a boil, remove from the heat and add the flour. Beat hard with a wooden spoon until the mixture is thick and glossy and comes away from the sides of the pan. Gradually beat in the egg a little at a time until the mixture is smooth, thick, and shiny; it should drop easily off the spoon.

2 Fit the piping bag with the plain nozzle and pipe walnut-sized rounds, well spaced apart on the baking sheets. Bake for 10–15 minutes, or until puffed up, then reduce the heat to 375°F (190°C) and bake for another 20 minutes, or until crisp and golden. Remove from the oven and make slits in the sides for the air to escape. Return to the oven for a few minutes so that the centers dry out. Cool completely on a wire rack.

3 To make the filling, whisk the cream, orange zest, and Grand Marnier in a bowl until just thicker than soft peaks. Fill the profiteroles with the cream using the piping bag with star nozzle.

4 To make the chocolate sauce, melt the chocolate, cream, syrup, and Grand Marnier together in a small pan, whisking until the sauce is smooth and glossy. Serve the profiteroles with the hot sauce spooned over.

PREPARE AHEAD The unfilled buns will keep in an airtight container for 2 days.

BAKER'S TIP
Immediately after removing choux pastries from the oven, it is vital to create a slit in each to allow the steam to escape. This will result in an open-textured, dry, and crisp pastry. If you do not slit the pastries, the steam will remain inside and the buns will be soggy.

Cheese Gougères with Smoked Salmon

These savory choux pastry puffs are a traditional dish of the Burgundy region of France, where they are displayed in almost every bakery window. Stuffed with smoked salmon, they make sophisticated canapés.

| SERVES 8 | 40–45 MINS | 30–35 MINS |

Ingredients
5 tbsp unsalted butter, diced, extra for greasing
1¼ tsp salt
1 cup all-purpose flour, sifted
5–6 large eggs
5oz (125g) Gruyère cheese, coarsely grated

For the smoked salmon filling
salt and pepper
2¼lb (1kg) fresh spinach, trimmed and washed
2 tbsp unsalted butter
1 onion, finely chopped
4 garlic cloves, finely chopped
pinch of ground nutmeg
1 cup cream cheese
6oz (175g) smoked salmon, sliced into strips
4 tbsp milk

Method

1 Preheat the oven to 375°F (190°C). Grease 2 baking sheets. Melt the butter in a pan with 1 cup water and ¾ teaspoon of salt. Bring to a boil. Remove from the heat and add the flour. Beat until the mixture is smooth. Return the pan to the stove and beat over low heat for 30 seconds to dry out the dough.

2 Remove from the heat. Add 4 eggs, 1 at a time, beating after each. Beat the fifth egg in a separate bowl and add gradually until the dough is shiny and soft. Stir in half the cheese. Place 8 x 2½in (6cm) mounds of dough on the baking sheets, leaving room for the dough to spread as it bakes. Beat the remaining egg and salt. Brush over each of the puffs.

3 Bring a saucepan of salted water to a boil. Add the spinach and wilt for 1–2 minutes. Drain. When cool, squeeze to remove any water, then finely chop. Melt the butter in a frying pan. Add the onion and cook until soft. Add the garlic, nutmeg, salt, and pepper to taste, and the spinach. Keep cooking, stirring, until any liquid has evaporated. Add the cream cheese and stir until the mixture is thoroughly combined. Remove from the heat.

4 Add two-thirds of the smoked salmon, pour in the milk, and stir. Mound 2–3 tablespoons of filling into each cheese puff. Put the rest of the salmon on top. Rest the lid against the side of each puff and serve.

Chocolate Éclairs

These cousins of the profiterole can be easily adapted: try the chocolate orange topping and orange cream filling (see opposite), or filling with crème pâtissière (see page 166) or chocolate crème pâtissière (see page 296).

MAKES 30 | **30 MINS** | **25–30 MINS** | **12 WEEKS, UNFILLED**

Special equipment
piping bag with ½in (1cm) plain nozzle

Ingredients
5 tbsp unsalted butter
1 cup all-purpose flour, sifted
3 large eggs
2 cups whipping cream
6oz (150g) good-quality dark chocolate

Method

1 Preheat the oven to 400°F (200°C). Melt the butter in a pan with ¾ cup cold water, then bring to the boil, remove from the heat, and stir in the flour. Beat with a wooden spoon until well combined.

2 Lightly beat the eggs and add to the flour and butter mixture a little at a time, whisking constantly. Continue whisking until the mixture is smooth and glossy and comes away easily from the sides of the pan. Transfer to the piping bag.

3 Pipe 4in (10cm) lengths of the mixture on to 2 baking sheets lined with parchment paper, cutting the end of the length of pastry from the bag with a wet knife. You should have around 30 in all. Bake for 20–25 minutes or until golden brown, then remove from the oven and make a slit down the side of each. Return to the oven for 5 minutes for the insides to cook through. Then remove and leave to cool.

4 Put the cream in a mixing bowl and whisk until soft peaks form. Spoon or pipe into each éclair. Break the chocolate into pieces and place in a heatproof bowl. Sit the bowl over a pan of simmering water (make sure the bowl does not touch the water) and stir until the chocolate is melted and smooth. Spoon over the éclairs and serve.

PREPARE AHEAD The unfilled éclairs will keep in an airtight container for 2 days.

Chestnut Millefeuilles

Sure to impress, this dessert is actually quite easy to make and can be prepared up to 6 hours ahead and chilled.

SERVES 8 | **2 HOURS** | **25–30 MINUTES**

Chilling time
1 hr

Ingredients

1½ cups milk
4 large egg yolks
¼ cup sugar
3 tbsp all-purpose flour, sifted
2 tbsp dark rum

1lb 5oz (600g) all-butter puff pastry, store-bought, or see pages 174–5, steps 1–10
1 cup heavy cream
1lb 2oz (500g) marrons glacés (candied chestnuts), crumbled
⅓ cup confectioner's sugar, plus extra if needed

1 Heat the milk in a pan over medium heat until it just comes to a boil. Take off heat.

2 Whisk the egg yolks and sugar for 2–3 minutes until thick. Whisk in the flour.

3 Gradually whisk the milk into the egg mixture until smooth. Return to a clean pan.

4 Bring to a boil, whisking, until thickened. Reduce heat to low and whisk for 2 minutes.

5 If lumps form in the pastry cream, remove from the heat and whisk until smooth again.

6 Let cool, then stir in rum. Transfer to a bowl, cover with plastic wrap, and chill for 1 hour.

7 Preheat the oven to 400°F (200°C). Sprinkle a baking sheet evenly with cold water.

8 Roll out the pastry to a rectangle a little larger than the baking sheet, about ⅛in (3mm) thick.

9 Roll the dough around a rolling pin. Unroll it onto the baking sheet. Let the edges overhang.

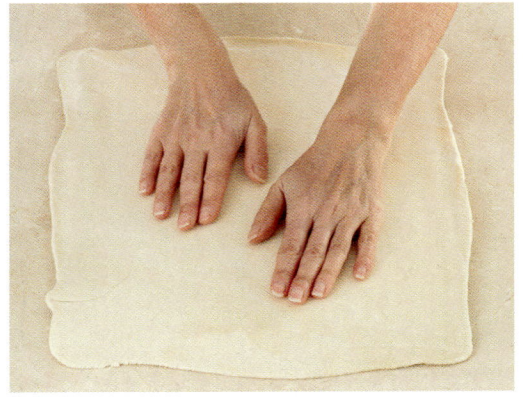

10 Press the dough down lightly on the baking sheet, then chill for about 15 minutes.

11 Prick the dough all over with a fork. Cover with parchment paper. Set a wire rack on top.

12 Bake for 15–20 minutes. Remove from the oven, grip the sheet and rack, invert the pastry.

13 Slide the baking sheet back under the pastry and bake for a further 10 minutes.

14 Remove from the oven and carefully slide the pastry onto a cutting board.

15 While still warm, trim around the edges with a large, sharp knife to neaten.

16 Cut the trimmed sheet lengthwise into 3 equal strips. Allow to cool.

17 Pour the cream into a bowl and whip until fairly firm.

18 Using a large metal spoon, fold the whipped cream into the chilled pastry cream.

19 With a palette knife, spread half the cream mixture evenly over one pastry strip.

20 Sprinkle with half the chestnuts. Repeat to make 2 layers and top with the last strip.

21 Sift over confectioner's sugar and divide into portions with a serrated knife.

Millefeuilles variations

Chocolate Millefeuilles

A decadent and mouth-watering millefeuilles, filled with dark chocolate cream and decorated with white chocolate drizzles.

SERVES 8 | **2 HOURS** | **25–30 MINS**

PATISSERIE

Chilling time
1 hr

Ingredients
1 quantity pastry cream, see page 166, steps 1–5
2 tbsp brandy
1lb 5oz (600g) all-butter puff pastry, store-bought, or see pages 174–175, steps 1–10
2oz (50g) dark chocolate, melted and cooled
1½ cups heavy cream
1oz (30g) white chocolate, melted and cooled

Method

1 Stir the brandy into the cream, cover with plastic wrap, and chill for 1 hour.

2 Preheat the oven to 400°F (200°C). Sprinkle a baking sheet with cold water. Roll out the pastry to a rectangle larger than the baking sheet. Transfer to the sheet, letting the edges overhang. Press the dough down. Chill for 15 minutes. Prick all over with a fork. Cover with parchment paper, then set a wire rack on top. Bake for 15–20 minutes, until it just begins to brown.

Gripping the sheet and rack, invert the pastry, slide the baking sheet back under and continue baking for 10 minutes, until both sides are browned. Remove from the oven and slide the pastry onto a cutting board. While still warm, trim the edges then cut lengthwise into 3 equal strips. Let cool.

3 Whip the heavy cream until stiff. Stir it into the pastry cream with two-thirds of the melted dark chocolate. Cover and chill. Spread the remaining melted chocolate over one of the pastry strips to cover it. Let it set.

4 Put another pastry strip on a plate, spread with half the cream, top with the remaining strip, and spread with the rest of the cream. Cover with the chocolate-coated strip.

5 Put the white chocolate into one corner of a plastic bag. Twist the bag to enclose the chocolate and snip off the tip of the corner. Pipe trails of chocolate over the millefeuilles.

PREPARE AHEAD The dish can be made ahead and chilled for up to 6 hours.

Vanilla Slices

Classic pastries sandwiched with thick custard and sweet, luscious jam.

MAKES 6 | **2 HOURS** | **25–30 MINS**

Chilling time
1 hr

Special equipment
small piping bag with thin nozzle

Ingredients
1½ cups heavy cream
1 quantity pastry cream, see page 166, steps 1–5
1lb 5oz (600g) all-butter puff pastry, store-bought, or see pages 174–175, steps 1–10
¾ cup confectioner's sugar
1 tsp cocoa powder
½ jar smooth strawberry or raspberry jam

Method

1 Whip the heavy cream until stiff peaks form. Fold it into the pastry cream and chill. Preheat the oven to 400°F (200°C). Sprinkle a baking sheet with cold water. Roll out the pastry to a rectangle larger than the baking sheet, then transfer to the sheet, letting the edges overhang. Press the dough down. Chill for 15 minutes.

2 Prick the dough with a fork. Cover with parchment paper, then set a wire rack on top. Bake for 15–20 minutes, until it just begins to brown. Hold the sheet and rack and invert the pastry. Slide the baking sheet back under and bake for 10 more minutes, until both sides are browned. Remove from the oven and slide the pastry onto a cutting board. While still warm, cut it into 2 x 4in (5 x 10cm) rectangles, in multiples of 3.

3 Put the confectioner's sugar in a bowl and add 1–1½ tablespoons cold water. Take 2 tablespoons out and mix with the cocoa to make a small amount of chocolate icing. Place the chocolate icing in a piping bag with a thin nozzle. Take a third of the pastry pieces and spread them with the white icing. While the icing is wet, pipe horizontal lines across them using the chocolate icing, then drag a skewer through the lines vertically to produce a striped effect. Allow to dry.

4 Spread the remaining pastry pieces with a thin layer of the jam. Spread a ½in (1cm) layer of pastry cream on top of the jam, and clean up the edges with a knife.

5 To assemble the vanilla slices, take a piece of pastry with jam and pastry cream, and place another gently on top. Press down lightly before topping with a third iced piece of pastry.

PREPARE AHEAD The dish can be made ahead and chilled for up to 6 hours.

Summer Fruit Millefeuilles

Beautiful and appetizing on a buffet table, or at a garden tea party. ▶

SERVES 8   **2 HOURS**   **25–30 MINS**

Chilling time
1 hr

Ingredients
1 quantity pastry cream, see page 166, steps 1–5
1lb 5oz (600g) all-butter puff pastry, store-bought, or see pages 174–175, steps 1–10
1 cup heavy cream
14oz (400g) mixed summer fruits, such as strawberries, diced, and raspberries
confectioner's sugar, for dusting

Method
1 Preheat the oven to 400°F (200°C). Sprinkle a baking sheet evenly with cold water. Roll out the pastry to a rectangle larger than the baking sheet, and about ⅛in (3mm) thick. Roll the dough around a rolling pin, then unroll it onto the baking sheet, letting the edges overhang. Press the dough down. Chill for about 15 minutes.

2 Prick the dough with a fork. Cover with parchment paper, then set a wire rack on top. Bake for 15–20 minutes, until it just begins to brown. Gripping the sheet and rack, invert the pastry. Slide the baking sheet back under and bake for 10 more minutes, until both sides are browned.

Remove from the oven and slide the pastry onto a cutting board. While still warm, trim the edges then cut lengthwise into 3 equal strips. Let cool.

3 Whip the heavy cream until firm. Fold into the pastry cream. Spread half the pastry cream filling over 1 pastry strip. Sprinkle with half the fruit. Repeat with another strip, to make 2 layers. Put the last pastry strip on top, and press down. Sift the confectioner's sugar thickly over the millefeuilles.

PREPARE AHEAD The dish can be made ahead and chilled for up to 6 hours.

BAKER'S TIP
Once you have mastered the art of assembling the pastry, millefeuilles can be made in endless variations. Large, for an impressive buffet centerpiece, or in individual portions for an indulgent afternoon tea, sandwiched together with whatever filling you prefer.

Apple and Almond Galettes

This elegant dessert is deceptively simple to make. A sprinkling of sugar caramelizes on the apple slices to form the only decoration necessary.

MAKES 8   25–30 MINS   20–30 MINS

Ingredients

1lb 5oz (600g) puff pastry (store-bought, or see pages 174–175, steps 1–10)
all-purpose flour, for dusting
8oz (215g) marzipan
1 lemon
8 small, tart apples
¼ cup sugar

Method

1 Lightly flour a work surface. Roll out half the pastry to a 14in (35cm) square, about ⅛in (3mm) thick. Using a 6in (15cm) plate as a guide, cut out 4 rounds.

2 Sprinkle 2 baking sheets with water. Set the rounds on 1 baking sheet, and prick each with a fork, avoiding the edge. Repeat with the remaining dough. Chill for 15 minutes. Divide the marzipan into 8 portions, and roll each into a ball.

3 Spread a sheet of parchment paper on the work surface. Set 1 ball of marzipan on the parchment, and cover with another sheet. Roll out the marzipan to a 5in (12.5cm) round between the sheets. Set on top of a pastry dough round, leaving a ½in (1cm) border. Repeat with the remaining marzipan and pastry bases. Chill, until ready to bake.

4 Cut the lemon in half, and squeeze the juice from 1 half into a small bowl. Peel, halve, and core the apples; then cut into thin slices. Drop the slices into the lemon juice as you work, and toss to prevent discoloration (see Baker's Tip).

5 Preheat the oven to 425°F (220°C). Arrange the apple slices, overlapping them slightly, in a ring on the marzipan rounds, covering them completely. Leave a thin border of puff pastry dough around the edge.

6 Bake the galettes for 15–20 minutes, until the pastry edges have risen around the marzipan, and are light golden. Sprinkle the apples evenly with the sugar.

7 Return to the oven, and continue baking for 5–10 minutes, or until the apples are golden brown, caramelized around the edges, and just tender when tested with the tip of a small knife. Transfer to warmed serving plates, and serve at once.

PREPARE AHEAD Roll out the puff pastry rounds and top them with the marzipan not more than 2 hours in advance. Prepare the apples, finish and bake the galettes just before serving.

BAKER'S TIP

When working with apples or pears, coating the slices with lemon juice will prevent discoloration. On contact with the air, both fruits will turn unattractively brown, which also makes the texture soften. If you are worried that the lemon juice will affect the flavor, it can be diluted in a bowl of water.

PATISSERIE

Apple Jalousie

In France, a *jalousie* is a shuttered window. This pastry is slashed to look like a shutter, revealing the apple inside.

SERVES 6–8 | 1¼–1½ HOURS | 30–40 MINS | UP TO 4 WEEKS

Chilling time
1¼ hrs

Ingredients

For the puff pastry
18 tbsp cold unsalted butter, frozen for 30 mins
1⅓ cups all-purpose flour, sifted, plus extra for dusting
1 tsp salt
1 tsp lemon juice

For the filling
1 tbsp unsalted butter
2¼lb (1kg) tart apples, peeled, cored, and diced
1in (2.5cm) fresh ginger, finely chopped
½ cup sugar
1 large egg white, beaten
½ cup superfine sugar
1 egg white, beaten

1 Coarsely grate the butter into a bowl. Sift with the flour and salt. Rub together until crumbly.

2 Pour in ⅓ cup water and the lemon juice. Form a rough dough.

3 Turn the dough out onto a floured surface. Work into a ball, then flatten it slightly.

4 Place the dough into a plastic bag and chill in the refrigerator for 20 minutes.

5 On a floured surface, thinly roll it out to a long rectangle, short sides 10in (25cm).

6 Take a third of the pastry and fold it into the middle. Fold over the remaining third.

7 Turn it over so the ends are easily sealed when it is re-rolled. Give it a quarter turn.

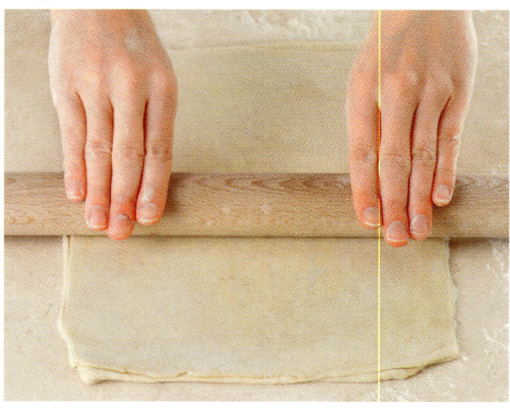

8 Roll out again to a similar size as the original rectangle. Keep the short sides even in size.

9 Repeat the folding, turning, and rolling. Put back in the bag, and chill for 20 minutes.

10 Roll, fold, and turn the pastry twice more, then chill for a final 20 minutes.

11 In a pan, melt the butter. Add the apples, ginger, and all but 2 tablespoons of the sugar.

12 Sauté and stir for 15–20 minutes, until the apples are tender and caramelized. Let cool.

13 Roll out the pastry on a floured surface to 11 x 13in (28 x 32cm). Cut lengthways in half.

14 Fold one half lengthways, and cut across the fold at ¼in (5mm) gaps, leaving a border.

15 Put the uncut dough on a non-stick baking sheet and spoon the apple along the center.

16 Top with the cut dough. Chill for 15 minutes. Preheat the oven to 425°F (220°C).

17 Bake for 20–25 minutes. Brush with the egg white and sprinkle over the remaining sugar.

18 Return to the oven and continue baking for 10–15 minutes. Serve the slices warm or at room temperature. **PREPARE AHEAD** The jalousie can be frozen at step 16.

Jalousie variations

Banana Shuttles

These miniature jalousies get their name from their resemblance to the shuttle tools traditionally used by weavers at the loom. Bananas and rum add a Caribbean spin.

| MAKES 6–8 | 1¼–1½ HOURS | 30–40 MINS | 4 WEEKS, UNBAKED |

Chilling time
1 hr

Ingredients
¼ cup sugar, plus 2 tbsp for sprinkling
¼ tsp cloves
¼ tsp cinnamon
3 tbsp dark rum
3 bananas
1lb 5oz (600g) puff pastry, store-bought or see pages 174–175, steps 1–10
1 egg white, beaten, for glazing

Method

1 Mix the sugar, cloves, and cinnamon. Pour the rum into another dish. Peel the bananas and cut each in half. Dip in the rum and coat with the sugar mixture.

2 Sprinkle a baking sheet with water. Roll out the puff pastry dough and trim it to a 12–15in (30–37cm) rectangle. Cut the dough into twelve 3–5in (7.5–12cm) rectangles. Fold 6 of the rectangles in half lengthwise, and make three ½in (1cm) cuts across the fold of each. Set the remaining rectangles on the baking sheet, pressing lightly.

3 Cut each banana half into thin slices; then set the slices in the center of each puff pastry rectangle, leaving a ½in (1cm) border around the edge. Brush the borders with cold water.

4 Line up and unfold the slashed rectangles over the filled bases. Press the edges with to seal. Trim one end of each rectangle to a blunt point. Scallop the edges of the shuttles with the back of a small knife.

5 Chill the shuttles for 15 minutes. Preheat the oven to 425°F (220°C). Bake for 15–20 minutes. Brush with the egg white, and sprinkle over the remaining sugar. Return to the oven for 10–15 minutes, until crisp and golden. Transfer to a wire rack and let cool. Serve warm or at room temperature.

PREPARE AHEAD The shuttles can be frozen at the chilling stage, step 5.

BAKER'S TIP
There is nothing wrong with buying ready-made puff pastry. However, do try to find pastry made only from butter, and not other fats. Some commercial pastries contain unhealthy trans fats. In any case, non-butter puff pastry will never taste as good, can have unwelcome trace flavors, and can be oily.

Chicken Jalousie

Although it looks impressive, this dish is quick to make.

SERVES	25	25	4 WEEKS,
4	MINS	MINS	UNBAKED

Ingredients
2 tbsp unsalted butter
2 leeks, thinly sliced
1 tsp chopped thyme
1 tsp all-purpose flour, plus extra for dusting
⅓ cup chicken stock
1 tsp lemon juice
1lb 5oz (600g) puff pastry, store-bought
  or see pages 174–175, steps 1–10
10oz (300g) skinless, boneless cooked chicken,
  chopped
salt and freshly ground black pepper
1 egg, beaten, for glazing

Method
1 Melt the butter in a pan. Add the leeks and cook over low heat, stirring, for 5 minutes, or until fairly soft. Stir in the thyme, then sprinkle with the flour and stir in. Gradually blend in the stock and bring to a boil, stirring until thickened. Remove from the heat, stir in the lemon juice, and leave to cool.

Preheat the oven to 425°F (220°C). Roll out just under half the pastry on a lightly floured work surface to a 10 x 6in (25 x 15cm) rectangle. Lay the pastry on a dampened baking sheet. Roll out the remaining pastry to a 10 x 7in (25 x 18cm) rectangle, lightly dust with flour, then fold in half lengthwise. Make cuts ½in (1cm) apart along the folded edge to within 1in (2.5cm) of the outer edge.

2 Stir the chicken into the leek mixture and season. Spoon over the pastry base, leaving a 1in (2.5cm) border. Dampen the edges of the pastry with water. Place the second piece of pastry on top and press the edges together to seal; trim off excess. Brush the top with beaten egg and bake for 25 minutes, or until golden brown and crisp. Let cool for a few minutes before serving.

PREPARE AHEAD Freeze after sealing and trimming excess.

Pear and Mincemeat Pie

Mincemeat is flattered by the subtle-tasting pear perhaps more than by its more usual apple accompaniment.

SERVES	15	40	8 WEEKS,
8–10	MINS	MINS	UNBAKED

Ingredients
unsalted butter, for greasing
1lb 5oz (600g) puff pastry, store-bought
  or see pages 174–175, steps 1–10
all-purpose flour, for dusting
14oz (400g) mincemeat
1 tbsp brandy
finely grated zest of 1 orange
¼ cup ground almonds
1 ripe pear, peeled, cored, and thinly sliced
beaten egg, to glaze

Method
1 Preheat the oven to 400°F (200°C). Lightly grease a baking sheet. Roll the puff pastry out on a lightly floured work surface into 2 sheets, each 11 x 8in (28 x 20cm).

2 Mix the mincemeat with the brandy and orange zest. Lay 1 sheet of pastry on the sheet, then scatter over the almonds, leaving a ¾in (2cm) border around the edges. Spoon the mincemeat mixture over the ground almonds, top with the pear, then brush the border with beaten egg.

3 Carefully place the second sheet of pastry on top of the first. Press the edges together, pinching the sides with your finger and thumb to decorate them. Make a few slashes on the top with a knife for the steam to escape.

4 Brush the pastry with beaten egg and bake for 30–40 minutes, or until golden brown and cooked through.

PREPARE AHEAD The pie can be frozen at the end of the step 4.

Cinnamon Palmiers

Grating frozen butter is a great shortcut when making puff pastry—or use store-bought pastry if pressed for time.

MAKES 24 | **45 MINS** | **25–30 MINS** | **8 WEEKS, UNBAKED**

Chilling time
1 hr 10 mins

Ingredients

For the puff pastry
18 tbsp unsalted butter, frozen for 30 minutes
1⅓ cups all-purpose flour, plus extra for dusting
1 tsp salt
1 large egg, lightly beaten

For the filling
7 tbsp unsalted butter, softened
½ cup light brown sugar
4–5 tsp cinnamon, to taste

1 Coarsely grate the butter into a bowl. Sift over the flour and salt. Rub together until crumbly.

2 Pour in 3–3½fl oz (90–100ml) water. Use a fork, then your hands to form a rough dough.

3 Place the dough into a plastic bag and chill in the refrigerator for 20 minutes.

4 On a floured surface, thinly roll it out to a long rectangle, short sides 10in (25cm).

5 Take a third of the pastry and fold into the middle. Fold over the remaining third.

6 Turn it over so the joins are easily sealed when it is re-rolled. Give it a quarter turn.

7 Roll out again to a similar size as the original rectangle. Keep the short sides even in size.

8 Repeat the folding, turning, and rolling. Put back in the bag, and chill for 20 minutes.

9 Roll, fold, and turn the pastry twice more, then chill for a final 20 minutes.

10 Meanwhile, make the filling by beating together the butter, sugar, and cinnamon.

11 Preheat the oven to 400°F (200°C). Line 2 baking sheets with parchment paper.

12 Roll the dough out once again. Trim the edges. Spread the filling thinly over the surface.

13 Loosely roll one of the long sides into the middle, and repeat with the other side.

14 Brush with egg wash, press together, then turn over and chill for 10 minutes.

15 Carefully cut into ¾in (2cm) pieces and turn the palmiers face up.

16 Squeeze them to form an oval, and press down lightly with your palm to flatten slightly.

17 Brush with egg wash and bake the palmiers for 25–30 minutes.

18 They are ready when golden brown, puffed up, and crisp in the center. Remove to a wire rack to cool. **STORE** The palmiers will keep in an airtight container for 3 days.

Palmiers variations

Chocolate Palmiers

Once the pastry is prepared, palmiers are quick and tasty snacks that are portable enough to take on a picnic.

| MAKES 24 | 45 MINS | 25–30 MINS | 8 WEEKS |

Chilling time
1 hr 10 mins, plus overnight (optional)

Ingredients
1 quantity puff pastry, see page 178, steps 1–9
1 egg, beaten, for glazing

For the filling
6oz (150g) dark chocolate, broken up

Method

1 Make the filling by melting the chocolate in a bowl set over a pan of simmering water. Set aside to cool. Preheat the oven to 400°F (200°C). Line 2 baking sheets with parchment paper.

2 Roll the dough to a rectangle ¼in (5mm) thick. Spread the filling over. Roll up one of the long sides of the pastry nearly into the middle, and repeat with the other side. Brush the sides with egg and roll them together. Turn over and chill for 10 minutes.

3 Trim the ends of the roll and cut it into ¾in (2cm) pieces. Turn the pastries face up, press them together to form an oval shape and press down to bring the roll together.

4 Transfer to the baking sheets, brush with a little beaten egg, and bake at the top of the oven for 25–30 minutes. They are ready when golden brown, puffed up, and crisp in the center. Remove to a wire rack to cool.

ALSO TRY... Substitute Nutella or another chocolate and hazelnut spread, straight from the jar, for a quicker filling.

STORE The palmiers will keep in an airtight container for 3 days.

BAKER'S TIP
The secret to rolling a pinwheel shape with any type of dough or pastry is to make sure that it is rolled up evenly, but not too tightly. Over-tight rolls will result in the center of the palmiers rising up as they cook, leaving an uneven finish to the pastries.

Tapenade Palmiers

Use a ready-made tapenade, if you like, for an even quicker filling.

| MAKES 24 | 55 MINS | 25–30 MINS | 8 WEEKS |

Chilling time
1 hr 10 mins

Special equipment
food processor

Ingredients
1 quantity puff pastry, see page 178, steps 1–9
1 egg, beaten, for glazing

For the tapenade
5oz (140g) pitted black olives
2 garlic cloves, crushed
¼ cup roughly chopped flat-leaf parsley
3–4 tbsp extra virgin olive oil, plus extra if needed
2 anchovy fillets (optional)
freshly ground black pepper

Method

1 Combine all the ingredients for the tapenade in a food processor and process to a coarse, spreadable paste, adding a little extra oil if necessary. Preheat the oven to 400°F (200°C). Line 2 baking sheets with parchment paper.

2 Roll the dough to a rectangle. Trim any irregular edges. Take the filling and spread it thinly over the surface of the pastry.

3 Roll the 2 long sides of pastry nearly into the middle. Brush with beaten egg and roll them together to form the palmier. Turn the roll over and chill for 10 minutes.

4 Trim the ends of the roll and cut it into ¾in (2cm) pieces. Turn the pastries face up, press them together to form an oval shape and press down to bring the roll together.

5 Transfer to the baking sheets, brush with egg, and bake at the top of the oven for 25–30 minutes, until puffed up and crisp.

STORE The palmiers will keep in an airtight container for 3 days.

Parmesan Smoked Paprika Palmiers

A perfect snack to serve with pre-dinner drinks when entertaining.

MAKES 24	45 MINS	25–30 MINS	8 WEEKS

Chilling time
1 hr 10 mins, plus overnight (optional)

Ingredients
1 quantity puff pastry, see page 178, steps 1–9
1 egg, beaten, for glazing

For the filling
2oz (50g) Parmesan cheese, finely grated
1 tsp smoked paprika
4 tbsp unsalted butter, softened

Method

1 Make the filling by tossing the Parmesan and the paprika together, then mixing with the butter until combined. Preheat the oven to 400°F (200°C). Line 2 baking sheets with parchment paper.

2 Roll the dough out to a rectangle. Trim any irregular edges. Spread the filling carefully over the surface of the pastry.

3 Roll up one of the long sides of the pastry nearly into the middle, and repeat with the other side. Brush the sides with egg and roll together. Turn the roll of pastry over and chill for 10 minutes to allow the sides to attach.

4 Trim the ends of the roll and cut it into ¾in (2cm) pieces. Turn the pastries face up, gently squeeze them together to form a more oval shape, and press down lightly to bring the roll together.

5 Transfer to the baking sheets, brush with a little beaten egg, and bake at the top of the oven for 25–30 minutes. They are ready when golden brown, puffed up, and crisp in the center. Transfer to a wire rack to cool.

STORE The palmiers will keep in an airtight container for 3 days.

Jam Doughnuts

Doughnuts are simple to make. These are light, airy, and taste far nicer than any store-bought varieties.

MAKES 12
30 MINS
5–10 MINS

Rising and proofing time
3–4 hrs

Special equipment
oil thermometer
piping bag with thin nozzle

Ingredients
⅔ cup milk
5 tbsp unsalted butter
½ tsp pure vanilla extract
1 (¼oz/10g) package dried yeast
⅓ cup sugar

2 large eggs, beaten
2¼ cups all-purpose flour,
  plus extra for dusting
½ tsp salt
1 quart (1 liter) sunflower oil or
  vegetable oil, for deep-frying, plus
  extra for greasing

For the coating and filling
sugar, for dusting
¾ cup jam (raspberry, strawberry,
  or cherry), processed until smooth

1 Heat the milk, butter, and vanilla in a pan until the butter melts. Cool until tepid.

2 Whisk in yeast and 1 tablespoon of sugar. Cover and leave for 10 minutes. Mix in the eggs.

3 Sift the flour and salt into a large bowl. Stir in the remaining sugar.

4 Make a well in the flour and add the milk mixture. Bring together to form a rough dough.

5 Turn the dough onto a floured surface and knead for 10 minutes until soft and pliable.

6 Put in an oiled bowl and cover with plastic wrap. Keep it warm until doubled; about 2 hours.

7 On a floured surface, knock back the dough and divide into 12 equal pieces.

8 Roll them between your palms to form balls. Place on baking sheets, spaced well apart.

9 Cover with plastic wrap and a towel. Leave in a warm place for 1–2 hours until doubled.

PATISSERIE

10 Heat a 4in (10cm) depth of oil to 340–350°F (170–180°C), keeping a lid nearby for safety.

11 Slide the doughnuts off the sheets. Do not worry if they are flatter on one side.

12 Carefully lower into the hot oil 3 at a time, rounded side down. Turn after 1 minute.

13 Remove with a slotted spoon when golden brown all over. Switch off the heat.

14 Drain on paper towels, then, while still hot, toss them in sugar. Cool before filling.

15 Put the jam in the piping bag. Pierce each doughnut on the side and insert the nozzle.

16 Gently squirt in about 1 tablespoon of jam, until it almost starts to spill out. Dust the hole with a little more sugar, and serve. **STORE** These will keep in an airtight container for 1 day.

Doughnut variations

Ring Doughnuts

Doughnuts are surprisingly easy to make, and home-cooked ones taste delicious. Don't waste the cut-out middles, just fry them separately for a bonus bite-sized treat.

MAKES 12 · **35 MINS** · **5–10 MINS**

Rising and proofing time
3–4 hrs

Special equipment
oil thermometer
1½in (4cm) round pastry cutter

Ingredients
1 quantity doughnut dough,
  see page 182, steps 1–6
1 quart (1 liter) sunflower oil or vegetable oil, for
  deep-frying, plus extra for greasing
sugar, for coating

Method

1 Turn the dough out onto a lightly floured work surface. Gently knock it back and divide into 12 balls.

2 Place the balls on baking sheets, spacing them well apart to allow room for spreading. Cover with plastic wrap and a paper towels, and leave in a warm place for about 1–2 hours until doubled in size.

3 Take a rolling pin and gently flatten the doughnuts to around 1¼in (3cm) in height. Oil the pastry cutter. Cut the centers out and set aside.

4 Pour the oil into a large saucepan to a depth of at least 4in (10cm) and heat it to 340–350°F (170–180°C). Keep the saucepan lid near and do not leave the hot oil unattended. Keep the temperature even, or the doughnuts will burn.

5 Slide the doughnuts off the baking sheets using a metal spatula. Don't worry if they are flat on one side; they will puff up on cooking. Add them, rounded-side down, into the hot oil and cook 3 at a time for about 1 minute, turning when the underside is golden brown. When golden brown all over, remove from the oil with a slotted spoon and drain them on paper towels. If you like, fry the cut-out centers in a similar way—these are very popular with younger children! Turn off the heat when finished frying.

6 While still hot, toss them in sugar and leave to cool a little before eating.

STORE These will keep in an airtight container for 1 day.

Custard Doughnuts

Custard is my favorite filling for doughnuts. Use good-quality, store-bought custard here—one that is made with real eggs and plenty of cream.

MAKES 12 · **30 MINS** · **5–10 MINS**

Rising and proofing time
3–4 hrs

Special equipment
oil thermometer
piping bag with thin metal nozzle

Ingredients
1 quantity doughnut dough,
  see page 182, steps 1–6
1 quart (1 liter) sunflower oil or vegetable oil, for
  deep-frying, plus extra for greasing
sugar, for dusting

For the coating and filling
sugar, for coating
1 cup ready-made custard

Method

1 Turn the dough out onto a lightly floured work surface. Gently knock it back and divide into 12 balls.

2 Place the balls on baking sheets, spacing them well apart to allow room for spreading. Cover lightly with plastic wrap and a paper towels, and leave in a warm place for 1–2 hours until almost doubled in size.

3 Pour the oil into a large, heavy-bottomed saucepan to a depth of at least 4in (10cm) and heat it to 340–350°F (170–180°C). Keep the saucepan lid nearby and never leave the hot oil unattended. Regulate the temperature, making sure it remains even, or the doughnuts will burn.

4 Slide the risen doughnuts off the baking sheets using a metal spatula. Do not worry if they are flatter on one side; they will puff up when cooking. Place them rounded-side down into the hot oil and cook 3 at a time for about 1 minute, turning as soon as the underside is golden brown. When golden brown on all sides, remove the doughnuts from the oil with a slotted spoon and drain them on paper towels. Turn off the heat when finished frying.

5 While hot, toss them in sugar and leave to cool. To fill the doughnuts, place the custard in the piping bag and pierce the doughnut on the side, where there is a perceptible mark, if possible. Make sure the nozzle goes into the center of the doughnut. Squirt 1 tablespoon of custard into the doughnut, until it almost starts to spill out. Dust the hole with sugar to disguise it. Serve.

STORE Keep in an airtight container for 1 day.

Churros

These cinnamon- and sugar-sprinkled Spanish snacks take minutes to make and will be devoured just as quickly. Try them dipped in hot chocolate.

SERVES 2–4 | **10 MINS** | **5–10 MINS**

Special equipment
oil thermometer
piping bag with ¾in (2cm) nozzle

Ingredients
2 tbsp unsalted butter
1½ cups all-purpose flour
¼ cup sugar
1 tsp baking powder
1 quart (1 liter) sunflower or vegetable oil, for frying
1 tsp cinnamon

Method

1 Measure ¾ cup boiling water into a bowl. Add the butter and stir until it melts. Sift together the flour, 2 tablespoons of the sugar, and the baking powder into a bowl.

2 Make a well in the center of the flour mixture and slowly pour in the hot butter mixture, beating, until you have a thick paste (you may not need all the liquid). Leave the mixture to cool and rest for 5 minutes.

3 Pour the oil into a large, heavy-bottomed saucepan to a depth of at least 4in (10cm) and heat it to 340–350°F (170–180°C). Keep the saucepan lid nearby and never leave the hot oil unattended. Regulate the temperature, making sure it remains even, or the churros will burn.

4 Place the cooled mixture into the piping bag. Pipe scant 3in (7cm) lengths of the dough into the hot oil, using a pair of scissors to snip off the ends. Do not crowd the pan, or the temperature of the oil will go down. Cook the churros for 1–2 minutes on each side, turning them when they are golden brown.

5 When done, remove from the oil with a slotted spoon and drain on paper towels. Turn off the heat when finished frying.

6 Mix the remaining sugar and the cinnamon together on a plate and toss the churros in the mixture while still hot. Leave to cool for 5–10 minutes before serving while still warm.

STORE These will keep in an airtight container for 1 day.

BAKER'S TIP

Churros are an almost instant treat, and can be made in only a few minutes. The batter can be enriched with egg yolk, butter, or milk, but the basic quantities of liquid to dry ingredients should be maintained. The thinner the batter, the lighter the results, but frying with a liquid batter takes a little practice.

DOUGHNUT VARIATIONS

185

cookies
& slices

Hazelnut and Raisin Oat Cookies

These cookies are an ideal cookie jar staple—tasty enough to please the kids and healthy enough for the adults.

MAKES 18 | **20 MINS** | **10–15 MINS** | **UP TO 8 WEEKS**

Ingredients

¾ cup (4oz) hazelnuts
7 tbsp unsalted butter, softened
1¼ cup light brown sugar
1 large egg (room temperature), beaten
1 tsp pure vanilla extract

1 tbsp honey
¾ cup all-purpose flour, sifted
½ tsp baking powder
1½ cups oats
¼ tsp salt
⅔ cup raisins
a little milk, if needed

1 Preheat the oven to 375°F (190°C). Toast the hazelnuts on a baking sheet for 5 minutes.

2 Once toasted, rub with a clean tea towel to remove most of the skins.

3 Roughly chop the hazelnuts and then set aside.

4 In a bowl, cream together the butter and sugar with an electric hand mixer until smooth.

5 Add the egg, vanilla extract, and honey, and beat well until smooth once more.

6 Combine the flour, baking soda, oats, and salt in a separate large bowl, and stir to mix.

7 Stir the flour mixture into the creamed mixture and beat until very well combined.

8 Add the chopped nuts and raisins, and mix until evenly distributed throughout the dough.

9 If the mixture is too stiff to work with easily, add a little milk until it becomes pliable.

10 Line 2 or 3 baking sheets with parchment paper. Roll the dough into walnut-sized balls.

11 Flatten each ball slightly, leaving plenty of space between them.

12 Bake in batches for 10–15 minutes until golden. Cool slightly, then move to a wire rack.

13 Leave to cool completely before serving. **STORE** The cookies will keep in an airtight container for 5 days, so if you make a batch on Sunday night they will last the school and working week.

Cookie variations

Pistachio and Cranberry Oat Cookies

The jewel colors of the pistachios and cranberries gleam out from these slightly more grown up versions of the classic fruit and nut cookies.

MAKES 24   **20 MINS**   **10–15 MINS**   **UP TO 8 WEEKS**

Ingredients

1 cup (4oz) pistachio nuts
7 tbsp unsalted butter, softened
1¼ cups light brown sugar
1 large egg
1 tsp pure vanilla extract
1 tbsp honey
¾ cup all-purpose flour, sifted
½ tsp baking soda
1½ cups oats
¼ tsp of salt
¾ cup (4oz) dried cranberries, roughly chopped
2-3 tbsp milk, if needed

Method

1 Preheat the oven to 375°F (190°C). Place the pistachio nuts on a baking sheet and toast them in the oven for 5 minutes, then remove and roughly chop.

2 Combine the butter and sugar in a bowl and cream with an electric hand mixer until smooth. Add the egg, vanilla extract, and honey and beat well until smooth.

3 Stir in the flour, baking soda, oats, and salt to combine. Add the chopped nuts and cranberries, mixing them into the cookie dough with your hands, if necessary. If the mixture is too stiff, add a little milk.

4 Take walnut-sized pieces and roll them into a ball between your palms. Flatten them slightly and place on 2 or 3 non-stick baking sheets, leaving space for the cookies to spread. Bake for 10–15 minutes until golden brown (you may need to do this in batches). Leave on the sheets for a couple of minutes before transferring to a wire rack to cool completely.

STORE The cookies will keep in an airtight container for 5 days.

BAKER'S TIP

Once you have mastered the recipe for oatmeal cookies, try experimenting with different combinations of fresh or dried fruit and nuts, or adding seeds such as sunflower seeds and pumpkin seeds into the mix.

Apple and Cinnamon Oat Cookies

Adding grated apple to the dough makes these cookies soft and chewy.

MAKES 24   **20 MINS**   **10–15 MINS**   **UP TO 8 WEEKS**

Ingredients

7 tbsp unsalted butter, softened
1¼ cups light brown sugar
1 large egg
1 tsp pure vanilla extract
1 tbsp honey
¾ cup all-purposed flour, sifted
½ tsp baking powder
1½ cups oats
2 tsp cinnamon
¼ tsp of salt
2 apples, peeled, cored, and coarsely grated
a little milk, if needed

Method

1 Preheat the oven to 375°F (190°C). Combine the butter and sugar in a bowl and cream together with an electric hand mixer until smooth. Add the egg, vanilla extract, and honey, and beat well until smooth.

2 Stir the flour, baking soda, oats, cinnamon, and salt into the creamed mixture to combine. Mix in the apple. If the mixture seems a bit too stiff, add a little milk. Take walnut-sized pieces of dough and roll them into a ball between your palms.

3 Flatten them slightly and place on 2 or 3 non-stick baking sheets, leaving space for the cookies to spread. Bake for 10–15 minutes until golden brown. Leave on the sheets for a couple of minutes before transferring them to a wire rack to cool completely.

STORE The cookies will keep in an airtight container for 5 days.

White Chocolate and Macadamia Nut Cookies

Here classic chocolate cookies are given a sophisticated twist.

| MAKES 24 | 25 MINS | 10–15 MINS | UP TO 4 WEEKS |

Chilling time
30 mins

Ingredients
6oz (150g) dark chocolate, broken into pieces
¾ cup all-purpose flour
¼ cup cocoa powder
½ tsp baking powder
¼ tsp salt
5 tbsp unsalted butter, softened
1 cup light brown sugar
1 large egg, beaten
1 tsp pure vanilla extract
⅓ cup (2oz) macadamia nuts, chopped
1¾oz (50g) white chocolate chunks

Method

1 Preheat the oven to 350°F (180°C). Melt the dark chocolate in a heatproof bowl set over a pan of simmering water. The bowl should not touch the water. Set aside to cool. Sift the flour, cocoa powder, baking powder, and salt together.

2 In a large bowl, cream together the butter and sugar with an electric hand mixer until light and fluffy. Beat in the egg and vanilla extract. Mix in the flour mixture. Add the chocolate and mix thoroughly. Finally, stir in the nuts and white chocolate chunks, wrap in plastic wrap, and chill for 30 minutes.

3 Place tablespoons of the chilled cookie dough on non-stick baking sheets, at least 2in (5cm) apart, as they will spread.

4 Bake in the top third of the oven for 10–15 minutes until cooked through but still soft in the middle. Leave on the sheets for a few minutes, then transfer to a wire rack to cool.

STORE The cookies will keep in an airtight container for 3 days.

Butter Cookies

These thin, elegant cookies are one of my favorite recipes. They are quick, simple, and decidedly moreish.

MAKES 30 | **15 MINS** | **10–15 MINS** | **UP TO 8 WEEKS**

Special equipment
2¾in (7cm) round cookie cutter
food processor with blade
attachment (optional)

Ingredients
11 tbsp unsalted butter, softened
  and diced
½ cup sugar
1½ cups all-purpose flour, sifted,
  plus extra for dusting
1 large egg yolk
1 tsp pure vanilla extract

1 Preheat the oven to 350°F (180°C). Have 2 or 3 non-stick baking sheets on hand.

2 Put the butter, sugar, and flour in a large bowl, or into the bowl of a food processor.

3 Rub together, or pulse-blend, the ingredients until they look like fine bread crumbs.

4 Add the egg yolk and vanilla extract, and bring the mixture together into a dough.

5 Turn the dough out onto a lightly floured work surface and knead it briefly until smooth.

6 Flour the dough and work surface well, and roll it out to a thickness of about ¼in (5mm).

7 Use a palette knife to move the sheet of dough around, to prevent sticking.

8 If the dough is too sticky to roll well, chill for 15 minutes, then try again.

9 With the pastry cutter, cut out round cookies and transfer them to the baking sheets.

10 Re-roll the scraps to ¼in (5mm) thick, and cut out cookies until all the dough is used.

11 Bake in the preheated oven for 12–15 minutes, until golden brown at the edges.

12 Leave the cookies to cool until firm enough to handle, then transfer to a wire rack.

13 Leave the butter cookies to cool completely on the wire rack, before serving. **STORE** The cookies will keep well in an airtight container for 5 days.

Butter Cookie variations

Crystallized Ginger Cookies

Here crystallized ginger adds warmth and depth of flavor.

MAKES 30 | 15 MINS | 12–15 MINS | UP TO 8 WEEKS

Special equipment
food processor with blade attachment (optional)
3in (7cm) round cookie cutter

Ingredients
11 tbsp unsalted butter, softened and diced
½ cup sugar
1½ cups all-purpose flour, sifted, extra for dusting
1 tsp ground ginger
2oz (50g) crystallized ginger, finely chopped
1 large egg yolk
1 tsp pure vanilla extract

Method
1 Preheat the oven to 350°F (180°C). Combine the butter, sugar, and flour in a bowl, or in the bowl of a food processor fitted with a blade, and rub or process together until the mixture forms fine crumbs. Stir in the ground and crystallized gingers.

2 Add the egg yolk and vanilla extract, and bring the mixture together into a dough. Turn out onto a lightly floured work surface and knead it together briefly to form a smooth dough. Flour the dough and work surface lightly, and roll it out to ¼in (5mm) thick. Cut out cookies with the cookie cutter and transfer them to several non-stick baking sheets.

3 Bake in the oven for 12–15 minutes until they are golden brown at the edges. Leave on the baking sheets for a few minutes, then transfer to a wire rack to cool completely.

STORE The cookies will keep in an airtight container for 5 days.

Almond Butter Cookies

The addition of almond extract makes these delicious cookies quite grown up and not overly sweet.

MAKES 30 | 15 MINS | 12–15 MINS | UP TO 8 WEEKS

Special equipment
3in (7cm) round cookie cutter
food processor with blade attachment (optional)

Ingredients
11 tbsp unsalted butter, softened and diced
½ cup sugar
1½ cups all-purpose flour, sifted, more for dusting
⅓ cup sliced almonds, lightly toasted if preferred
1 tsp almond extract
1 large egg yolk

Method
1 Preheat the oven to 350°F (180°C). Combine the butter, sugar, and flour in a bowl, or in the bowl of a food processor with a blade attachment. Rub or process together until it forms fine crumbs. Mix in the almonds.

2 Add the egg yolk and almond extract, and bring the mixture together into a dough. Knead briefly to form a smooth dough. Roll out to ¼in (5mm) thick.

3 Cut out cookies with the cookie cutter and transfer to several non-stick baking sheets. Bake in the oven for 12–15 minutes until golden brown at the edges. Leave for a few minutes, then transfer to a wire rack to cool.

STORE The cookies will keep in an airtight container for 5 days.

BAKER'S TIP
Always look for almond extract, as bottles labeled "essence" are made from synthetic flavorings. For excellent after-dinner cookies to have with coffee, roll the cookies out as thin as you dare and bake for 5–8 minutes only.

Spritzgebäck Cookies

These delicate, buttery cookies are based on a traditional German cookie popular at Christmas. ▶

MAKES 45 | 45 MINS | 15 MINS

Special equipment
cookie press, or piping bag and star nozzle

Ingredients
28 tbsp unsalted butter, softened
1 cup sugar
few drops of pure vanilla extract
pinch of salt
3¼ cups all-purpose flour, sifted
1¼ cups (5oz) ground almonds
4oz (100g) dark or milk chocolate

Method
1 Preheat the oven to 350°F (180°C). Line 2–3 large baking sheets with parchment paper. Place the butter in a bowl and beat until smooth. Stir in the sugar, vanilla extract, and salt until the mixture is thick and the sugar is absorbed. Add two-thirds of the flour, stirring in a little at a time.

2 Add the rest of the flour and ground almonds and knead the mixture to make a smooth dough. Shape the dough into rolls and use the cookie press or piping bag to squeeze 3in (7.5cm) lengths of the dough onto the prepared baking sheets.

3 Bake for 12 minutes, or until lightly golden, and transfer to a wire rack to cool. Melt the chocolate gently in a microwave or in a bowl over a pan of simmering water. Dip one end of the cooled cookies into the chocolate, and return to the rack to set.

STORE The cookies will keep in an airtight container for 2–3 days.

Gingerbread Men

All children love to make gingerbread men. This recipe is quick and the dough is easy for little bakers to handle.

MAKES 16 · 20 MINS · 10–12 MINS · 8 WEEKS, UNBAKED

Special equipment
4½in (11cm) gingerbread man cutter
piping bag with thin nozzle (optional)

Ingredients
4 tbsp corn syrup
2⅓ cup all-purpose flour,
    plus extra for dusting
1 tsp baking soda
1½ tsp ground ginger
1½ tsp pumpkin pie spice
7 tbsp unsalted butter, softened
    and diced
¾ cup dark brown sugar

1 large egg
raisins, to decorate
confectioner's sugar, sifted (optional)

1 Preheat the oven to 375°F (190°C). Heat the corn syrup until it liquefies, then cool.

2 Sift the flour, baking soda, and spices into a large bowl. Add the butter.

3 Rub together with your fingertips until the mixture looks like fine breadcrumbs.

4 Add the sugar to the breadcrumbs mixture and mix well.

5 Beat the egg into the cooled syrup until well blended.

6 Make a well in the flour mixture. Pour in the syrup mix. Bring together to a rough dough.

7 On a lightly floured work surface, knead the dough briefly until smooth.

8 Flour the dough and the work surface well, and roll the dough out to ¼in (5mm) thick.

9 Using the cutter, cut out as many shapes as possible. Transfer to non-stick baking sheets.

10 Mix the scraps of dough, re-roll, and cut out more shapes, until all the dough is used.

11 Decorate the men with raisins, giving them eyes, a nose, and buttons down the front.

12 Bake for 10–12 minutes until golden. Transfer to a wire rack to cool completely.

13 If using, mix some confectioner's sugar in a bowl with enough water to form a thin icing.

14 Transfer the icing into the piping bag; placing the bag into a glass first will help.

15 Decorate the men with the piped icing to resemble clothes, hair, or whatever you prefer.

16 Leave the icing to set completely before serving or storing. **STORE** These gingerbread men will keep in an airtight container for 3 days.

Gingerbread variations

Swedish Spice Cookies

A version of the traditional Swedish Christmas cookies. Roll them as thin as you dare (and bake for less time) for a truly authentic result.

MAKES 60 | 20 MINS | 10 MINS | 8 WEEKS, UNBAKED

Chilling time
1 hr

Special equipment
3in (7cm) heart or star cookie cutters

Ingredients
9 tbsp unsalted butter, softened
⅔ cup sugar
1 large egg
1 tbsp corn syrup
1 tbsp light molasses
1⅓ cups all-purpose flour, plus extra for dusting
pinch of salt
1 tsp ground cinnamon
1 tsp ground ginger
1 tsp pumpkin pie spice

Method

1 With an electric hand mixer, cream the butter and sugar. Beat in the egg, corn syrup, and molasses. Sift together the flour, salt, and spices in a separate bowl. Add the flour mixture to the cookie batter and bring it all together to form a rough dough.

2 Briefly knead until smooth, place in a plastic bag and chill for 1 hour.

3 Preheat the oven to 350°F (180°C). Roll the cookie dough out on a lightly floured surface to a thickness of ⅛in (3mm) and cut out heart or star shapes with the pastry cutters.

4 Transfer the cookies to several non-stick baking sheets and bake in the top third of the oven for 10 minutes until edges darken slightly. Leave on sheets for a few minutes, then transfer on to a wire rack to cool.

STORE The cookies will keep in an airtight container for 5 days.

BAKER'S TIP
These are based on a Swedish Christmas cookie called *Pepparkakor*. To decorate a Christmas tree in traditional Swedish style, cut the cookies into heart shapes and use a straw to cut a hole out of the top before cooking. Once baked, you can tie the cookies on to the tree using red ribbon.

Gingernut Cookies

The addition of chopped nuts makes these cookies extra special.

MAKES 45 | 30 MINS | 8–10 MINS | 8 WEEKS, UNBAKED

Special equipment
3in (7cm) cookie cutters (any shape)

Ingredients
1⅓ cups all-purpose flour, plus extra for dusting
2 tsp baking powder
¾ cup sugar
a few drops of pure vanilla extract
½ tsp pumpkin pie spice
2 tsp ground ginger
⅓ cup honey
1 large egg, separated
4 tsp milk
9 tbsp butter, softened and diced
1¼ cups ground almonds
chopped hazelnuts or almonds, to decorate

Method

1 Preheat the oven to 350°F (180°C). Line 2 baking sheets with parchment paper.

2 Sift the flour and baking powder into a bowl. Add all the other ingredients except the chopped nuts. With a wooden spoon, bring the mixture together to form a soft dough. Use your hands to shape the dough into a ball.

3 Roll the dough out on a lightly floured surface to ¼in (5mm) thickness. Cut out the cookies with the shaped cutters, and place on the baking sheets, spaced apart to allow them to spread. Beat the egg white and brush over the cookies, then sprinkle over the nuts. Bake for 8–10 minutes, or until lightly golden brown.

4 Remove from the oven and allow to cool on the sheet for a few minutes, then transfer to a wire rack to cool completely.

STORE These gingernut cookies will keep in an airtight container for 3 days.

Cinnamon Stars

These classic German cookies make a great last-minute Christmas gift.

| MAKES 30 | 20 MINS | 12–15 MINS | 4 WEEKS, UNBAKED |

Chilling time
1 hr, or overnight (optional)

Special equipment
3in (7cm) star-shaped cookie cutter

Ingredients
2 large egg whites
1¾ cups confectioner's sugar, extra for dusting
½ tsp lemon juice
1 tsp ground cinnamon
2⅔ cups ground almonds
vegetable oil, for greasing
a little milk, if needed

Method

1 Whisk the egg whites until they are stiff. Sift in the confectioner's sugar, add the lemon juice, and continue to whisk for 5 more minutes, until thick and glossy. Take out 2 tablespoons of the mixture, cover, and set aside for topping the cookies later.

2 Gently fold the ground almonds and cinnamon into the egg white and sugar mixture. Cover and refrigerate for 1 hour or overnight. At this stage it will be a thick paste, rather than a dough.

3 Preheat oven to 325°F (160°C). Dust a work surface with sugar and turn the paste out onto it. Combine paste with some sugar to form a soft dough. Dust a rolling pin with sugar and roll out to ¼in (5mm) thick.

4 Oil the cutter and non-stick baking sheets. Cut star shapes out of the dough. Lay the cookies on the sheets. Brush a little of the meringue mix over each cookie, mixing it with a little milk, if too thick.

5 Bake in the top third of the oven for 12–15 minutes until the topping has set. Leave to cool for at least 10 minutes on the baking sheets, then transfer to a wire rack.

STORE The cookies will keep in an airtight container for 5 days.

Canestrelli

These delightful Italian cookies are as light as air and are traditionally made with a flower-shaped cutter, a fitting shape for such a delicate cookie.

MAKES 20–30 | **20 MINS** | **15–20 MINS** | **UP TO 4 WEEKS**

Chilling time
30 mins

Special equipment
flower-shaped, or 2 different-sized, round cookie cutters

Ingredients
3 large egg yolks, unbroken
11 tbsp unsalted butter, softened
1¼ cup confectioner's sugar, sifted
finely grated zest of ½ lemon
¾ cup potato flour
¾ cup all-purpose flour (or potato flour if you are wheat intolerant), plus extra for dusting
2 tsp baking powder
1 tsp salt

Method

1 Gently slide the egg yolks into a pan of simmering water over low heat. Poach for 5 minutes, until completely hard, then take them out of the water and set aside to cool. When they are cool, push the egg yolks through a fine metal sieve with the back of a spoon. Scrape into a small bowl.

2 Cream together the butter and confectioners' sugar with an electric hand mixer until light and fluffy. Add the egg yolks and lemon zest, and beat well to combine.

3 Sift the flours, baking powder, and salt together and add to the cookie batter, beating well to form a smooth, soft dough. Place the dough in a plastic bag and refrigerate for 30 minutes to firm up. Preheat the oven to 325°F (160°C).

4 Roll out the chilled dough on a lightly floured work surface to ½in (1cm) thick. Cut out traditional flower-shaped cookies, or other shapes. If you have no flower-shaped cutter, you can use a larger and a smaller cutter to make ring shapes instead.

5 Place the cookies on several non-stick baking sheets and bake in the top third of the oven for 15–17 minutes, until just turning golden. The canestrelli are very delicate when warm, so leave them to cool for at least 10 minutes on their baking sheets before removing to a wire rack to cool completely.

STORE The canestrelli will keep in an airtight container for 5 days.

BAKER'S TIP
These delicate cookies originate from the Liguria region of Italy. Their light texture comes from the traditional use of potato flour in the recipe. If you cannot find potato flour, an 00 grade flour (from larger supermarkets and Italian delicatessens), or even all-purpose flour, will make a good substitute.

Macaroons

These almond meringue cookies (not to be confused with French macarons) are crisp outside and chewy inside.

MAKES 24 | **10 MINS** | **12–15 MINS**

Special equipment
sheets of edible wafer paper

Ingredients
2 large egg whites
1 cup sugar
1¼ cups ground almonds
2 tbsp rice flour
a few drops of almond extract
24 blanched almonds

1 Preheat the oven to 350°F (180°C). Whisk the egg whites until stiff with an electric mixer.

2 Gradually whisk in the sugar, 1 tablespoon at a time, to give a thick, glossy meringue.

3 Fold in the ground almonds, rice flour, and almond extract until well combined.

4 Divide the sheets of edible wafer paper between 2 baking sheets.

5 Place 2 teaspoons in a cup of boiling water. Dry them, then use to scoop up the mixture.

6 Place 4 teaspoons of mixture, spaced apart, on each piece of edible wafer paper.

7 Keep the mixture in rounds. Put a blanched almond in the center of each cookie.

8 Bake the macaroons in the center of the oven for 12–15 minutes, or until lightly golden.

9 Transfer to a wire rack to cool completely, before peeling each cookie from the paper.

COOKIES AND SLICES

Macaroons are prone to sticking, but by using edible wafer paper, it doesn't matter if it tears off with the cookie. **STORE** Although macaroons will keep for 2–3 days in an airtight container, they tend to dry out and are always best eaten on the day.

Macaroon variations

Coconut Macaroons

Coconut macaroons are simple to make and completely wheat-free. I've omitted chocolate from my version so that they remain a light treat.

MAKES 18-20 | 20 MINS | 15–20 MINS

Chilling time
2 hrs

Special equipment
sheets of edible wafer paper (optional)

Ingredients
1 large egg white
½ cup sugar
pinch of salt
½ tsp pure vanilla extract
4oz (100g) sweetened, shredded coconut

Method

1 Preheat the oven to 325°F (160°C). In a large bowl with an electric hand mixer, whisk the egg whites until stiff. Add the sugar a little at a time, whisking between each addition, until the sugar is combined and the mixture is thick and glossy.

2 Add the salt and vanilla extract, and briefly whisk again to blend.

3 Gently fold in the coconut. Cover and refrigerate for 2 hours to firm up. This will also allow the shredded coconut to hydrate and soften.

4 Line a baking sheet with parchment or wafer paper. Place heaping teaspoons of the mixture onto the baking sheet; try to keep the mixture in a small heap.

5 Bake in the middle of the oven for 15–20 minutes, until golden brown in places. Leave the macaroons to cool on the sheets for at least 10 minutes to firm up, then transfer to a wire rack to cool completely.

STORE These macaroons will keep in an airtight container for 5 days.

Chocolate Macaroons

Add cocoa powder for a chocolate version of the basic macaroon.

MAKES 24 | 20 MINS | 15 MINS | UP TO 4 WEEKS

Chilling time
30 mins

Special equipment
sheets of edible wafer paper (optional)

Ingredients
2 large egg whites
1 cup sugar
1 cup ground almonds
2 tbsp rice flour
¼ cup cocoa powder
24 whole blanched almonds

Method

1 Preheat the oven to 350°F (180°C). In a large bowl with an electric hand mixer, whisk the egg whites until stiff. Add the sugar a little at a time, whisking between each addition, until all the sugar is combined and the mixture is thick and glossy.

2 Fold in the almonds, rice flour, and then the cocoa powder. Cover and refrigerate for 30 minutes to firm up. Line 2 baking sheets with parchment or wafer paper.

3 Place heaping teaspoons of the mixture onto the prepared baking sheets, spacing them at least 1½in (4cm) apart as they will spread. Try to keep each portion of the mixture in a small heap. Place a blanched almond in the center of each heap.

4 Bake the macaroons at the top of the oven for 12–15 minutes, until the exterior is crisp and the edges firm to the touch. Leave the macaroons to cool on the sheets for at least 5 minutes, then transfer to a wire rack to cool completely.

STORE Best eaten on the day they are made, these will keep in an airtight container for 2–3 days.

Coffee and Hazelnut Macaroons

These gorgeous little cookies are easy to prepare, infused with flavor, and look very pretty served after dinner with coffee, especially if you make them on the smaller side.

MAKES 20 | **30 MINS** | **20 MINS** | **UP TO 4 WEEKS**

Chilling time
30 mins

Special equipment
food processor with blade attachment
sheets of edible wafer paper (optional)

Ingredients
2 large egg whites
1 cup sugar
6oz (150g) whole hazelnuts, shelled, plus 20 extra
2 tbsp rice flour
1 tsp strong instant espresso powder, dissolved in 1 tsp boiling water and cooled, or equivalent cooled espresso

Method

1 Preheat the oven to 350°F (180°C). Place the hazelnuts on a baking sheet and toast for 5 minutes. Put them in a kitchen towel and rub to remove skin. Set aside to cool.

2 Whisk the egg whites until stiff. Add the sugar a little at a time, whisking, until all the sugar is combined and the mixture is thick.

3 In a food processor, pulse the hazelnuts to a powder. Fold them into the meringue mixture with the rice flour, and gently fold in 1 teaspoon of the coffee mixture. Cover and refrigerate for 30 minutes to firm up.

4 Place teaspoons of the mixture onto baking sheets lined with parchment or wafer paper, spacing them at least 1½in (4cm) apart. Keep each portion in a small heap and place a whole hazelnut in the center.

5 Bake the macaroons at the top of the oven for 12–15 minutes, until crisp and coloring slightly; check after 10 minutes if making them small. Leave on the sheets for 5 minutes and transfer to a wire rack to cool.

STORE Best eaten on the day, these will keep in an airtight container for 2–3 days.

BAKER'S TIP
Old-fashioned macaroons have been rather overshadowed of late by their prettier French cousins, macarons (see pages 246–251). However, macaroons are also wheat-free, easier to make, and just as pretty, in an understated kind of way.

Vanillekipferl

These crescent-shaped German cookies are often served at the same time as Cinnamon Stars (see page 199), making a truly festive platter.

MAKES 30 | 35 MINS | 15–17 MINS | UP TO 4 WEEKS

Chilling time
30 mins

Ingredients

1½ cup flour, plus extra for dusting
11 tbsp unsalted butter, softened and diced
⅔ cup confectioner's sugar
¾ cup ground almonds
1 tsp pure vanilla extract
1 large egg, beaten

Method

1 Sift the flour into a large bowl. Rub in the softened butter until the mixture resembles fine crumbs. Sift in the confectioner's sugar, and add the ground almonds.

2 Add the vanilla extract to the egg, then pour it into the flour mixture. Bring the mixture together to form a soft dough, adding a little more flour if the mixture is very sticky. Place the dough into a plastic bag and chill it for at least 30 minutes, to firm up.

3 Preheat the oven to 325°F (160°C). Divide the dough into 2 parts, and on a lightly floured work surface, roll each part into a sausage shape, approximately 1½in (3cm) in diameter. Use a sharp knife to cut ½in (1cm) pieces from the dough.

4 To form the cookies, take a piece of the dough and roll it between your palms to make a sausage shape of around 3½–¾in (8 x 2cm), tapering it slightly

at each end. Fold each end of the roll in slightly to form a crescent shape. Line 2 baking sheets with parchment paper, and place the formed cookies on them, leaving a little space between each.

5 Bake the vanillekipferl at the top of the oven for 15 minutes, until they are very lightly colored. They should not brown at all.

6 Leave the cookies to cool on their trays for 5 minutes, then transfer them to a wire rack. Scatter them liberally with confectioner's sugar, and leave them to cool completely.

STORE These will keep in an airtight container for 5 days.

BAKER'S TIP

A German Christmas tradition, these crescent-shaped biscuits rely on the use of ground almonds for their delicate, crumbly texture. Many recipes recommend tossing the finished cookies in vanilla sugar, but if that proves difficult to find, the vanilla extract in the cookie dough will do just as well.

Florentines

These crisp Italian cookies are packed full of fruit and nuts, and coated with luxurious dark chocolate. Wonderful for a quick afternoon treat.

MAKES 16–20   20 MINS   15–20 MINS

Ingredients
4 tbsp butter
¼ cup sugar
1 tbsp honey

½ cup all-purpose flour, sifted
¼ cup chopped mixed peel
¼ cup glacé cherries, finely chopped
¼ cup blanched almonds, finely chopped
1 tsp lemon juice
1 tbsp heavy cream
6oz (175g) good-quality dark chocolate, broken into pieces

Method

1 Preheat the oven to 350°F (180°C) and line 2 baking sheets with parchment paper.

2 Put the butter, sugar, and honey into a small saucepan and melt gently over low heat. Then allow to cool until it is just warm. Stir in all the other ingredients except the chocolate.

3 Using a teaspoon, drop spoonfuls of the mixture onto the baking sheets, leaving space between them for the cookies to spread.

4 Bake for 10 minutes, or until golden. Do not let them get too dark. Leave them on the baking sheets for a few minutes before transferring them to a wire rack to cool completely.

5 Melt the chocolate pieces in a heatproof bowl set over a pan of gently simmering water. Make sure the bowl is not touching the water.

6 Once the chocolate has melted, use a palette knife to spread a thin layer of chocolate on the bottom of each cookie. Place the cookies chocolate-side up on a wire rack to set. Spread a second layer of chocolate over the cookies. Then just before they set, make a wavy line in the chocolate with a fork.

STORE These will keep in an airtight container for 5 days.

BAKER'S TIP
You can make a beautiful display of three different colors of Florentines by topping a third with milk chocolate, another third with white chocolate, and the remainder with dark chocolate. Or use different tones of chocolate both to top and to drizzle over in a zigzag fashion, for a stunning effect.

Biscotti

These crisp Italian biscuits make great presents, as they can be prettily packaged and will keep for days.

MAKES 25–30 **15 MINS** **40–45 MINS** **UP TO 8 WEEKS**

Ingredients

1 cup whole almonds, skinned
1½ cups all-purpose flour
½ cup sugar
1 tsp baking powder
½ tsp salt
2 large eggs, at room temperature
1 tsp pure vanilla extract
4 tbsp unsalted butter, melted

1 Melt the butter in a small saucepan over low heat and then set aside to cool.

2 Preheat the oven to 350°F (180°C). Line a baking sheet with parchment paper.

3 Spread the almonds out on a non-stick baking sheet. Place in the center of the oven.

4 Bake the almonds for 5–10 minutes until slightly colored, tossing halfway.

5 Allow the almonds to cool until they are comfortable to handle. Roughly chop them.

6 Sift the flour through a fine sieve held over a large bowl.

7 Add the sugar and chopped almonds to the bowl and stir until well combined.

8 In a separate bowl, whisk together the eggs, vanilla extract, and the melted butter.

9 Gradually pour the egg mixture into the flour, while stirring with a fork.

10 Using your hands, bring the ingredients together to form a dough.

11 If the mixture seems too wet to shape easily, work in a little flour until it is pliable.

12 Turn the dough out onto a lightly floured work surface.

13 With your hands, form the dough into 2 log shapes, each about 8in (20cm) long.

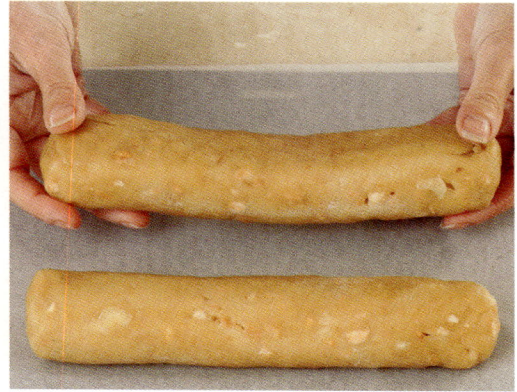

14 Place on the lined baking sheet and bake for 20 minutes in the middle of the oven.

15 Remove the logs from the oven. Cool slightly, then transfer to a chopping board.

16 With a serrated knife, cut the logs on a slant into 1½–2in (3–5cm) thick slices.

17 Put the biscotti on a baking sheet and return to the oven for 10 minutes to dry even more.

18 Turn the biscotti with a palette knife, and return to the oven for another 5 minutes.

19 Cool the biscotti on a wire rack to harden them and allow any moisture to escape.

TO FREEZE Place the cooled biscotti on baking sheets and freeze until solid.

Transfer to freezer bags. **STORE** Keep unfrozen in an airtight container for over 1 week.

BISCOTTI

Biscotti variations

Hazelnut and Chocolate Biscotti

Add chocolate chips to the biscotti dough for a child-friendly alternative.

SERVES 6–8 | 15 MINS | 40–45 MINS | UP TO 8 WEEKS

Ingredients

1 cup whole hazelnuts, shelled
1½ cup all-purpose flour, sifted, extra for dusting
1 tsp baking powder
½ tsp salt
½ cup sugar
¼ cup dark chocolate chips
2 large eggs
1 tsp pure vanilla extract
4 tbsp unsalted butter, melted and cooled

Method

1 Preheat the oven to 350°F (180°C). Spread the nuts on a baking sheet. Bake for 5–10 minutes, tossing halfway through, until slightly colored. Cool, rub in a kitchen towel to remove excess skin, then roughly chop.

2 In a bowl, mix together the flour, baking powder, salt, sugar, nuts, and chocolate chips. In a separate bowl, whisk the eggs, vanilla, and butter. Combine the wet and dry ingredients, mixing to form a dough. If the mixture is too wet, knead in a little extra flour to shape easily.

3 Put the dough onto a floured surface and form into 2 logs, each 8in (20cm) long by 3in (7cm). Place on a baking sheet lined with parchment paper and bake for 20 minutes in the middle of the oven. Take the logs out of the oven, allow them to cool slightly. Cut them diagonally into 1¼–2in (3–5cm) thick slices with a serrated knife.

4 Return the biscotti to the oven for another 15 minutes, turning after 10 minutes. They are ready when golden at the edges and hard to the touch. Cool the biscotti on a wire rack.

STORE These will keep in an airtight container for more than 1 week.

Chocolate and Brazil Nut Biscotti

These biscotti, darkened with cocoa powder, are ideal to serve after dinner with strong, black coffee.

SERVES 6–8 | 15 MINS | 40–45 MINS | UP TO 8 WEEKS

Ingredients

1 cup whole Brazil nuts, shelled
1⅓ cups all-purpose flour, sifted, extra for dusting
½ cup cocoa powder
½ cup sugar
1 tsp baking powder
½ tsp salt
2 large eggs
1 tsp pure vanilla extract
4 tbsp unsalted butter, melted and cooled

Method

1 Preheat the oven to 350°F (180°C). Spread the nuts on a baking sheet. Bake for 5–10 minutes. Cool slightly, rub in a kitchen towel to remove excess skin, then roughly chop.

2 Mix the flour, cocoa powder, sugar, baking powder, salt, and nuts. In a separate bowl, whisk together the eggs, vanilla extract, and butter. Combine the wet and dry ingredients to form a dough.

3 Turn the dough out onto a floured surface and form 2 logs, each 8in (20cm) long by 3in (7cm). Place on a baking sheet lined with parchment paper and bake for 20 minutes. Cool slightly, then cut diagonally into 1¼–2in (3–5cm) thick slices with a serrated knife.

4 Return to the oven for 15 minutes, turning after 10, until golden and hard to the touch.

STORE These will keep in an airtight container for more than 1 week.

BAKER'S TIP

The hard, crunchy texture and toasted taste of biscotti is obtained by double-baking. This technique also allows them to keep well for a relatively long time.

Pistachio and Orange Biscotti

These fragrant biscotti are delicious served either with coffee or dipped in a glass of sweet dessert wine. ▶

SERVES 6–8 | 15 MINS | 40–45 MINS | UP TO 8 WEEKS

Ingredients

1 cup whole pistachio nuts, shelled
1½ cups all-purpose flour, plus extra for dusting
½ cup sugar
finely grated zest of 1 orange
½ tsp baking powder
½ tsp salt
2 large eggs
1 tsp pure vanilla extract
4 tbsp unsalted butter, melted and cooled

Method

1 Preheat the oven to 350°F (180°C). Spread the nuts on a baking sheet. Bake for 5–10 minutes. Cool, rub in a kitchen towel to remove excess skin, then roughly chop.

2 In a bowl, mix the flour, sugar, zest, baking powder, salt, and nuts. In a separate bowl, whisk together the eggs, vanilla extract, and butter. Mix the wet and dry ingredients to form a dough.

3 Turn the dough out onto a floured surface and form into 2 logs, each 8in (20cm) long by 3in (7cm). Place them on a baking sheet lined with parchment paper and bake for 20 minutes in the middle of the oven. Cool slightly, then cut diagonally into ½in (1cm) thick slices with a serrated knife.

4 Bake for another 15 minutes, turning after 10, until golden and hard to the touch.

STORE These will keep in an airtight container for more than 1 week.

Tuiles

Basic tuile batter is very simple to master. Shaping the tuiles is where the skill comes in, and here are several ideas.

MAKES 15 · **15 MINS** · **5–7 MINS**

Ingredients
4 tbsp unsalted butter, softened
⅓ cup confectioner's sugar, sifted
1 large egg (room temperature)
  beaten
⅓ cup all-purpose flour
vegetable oil, for greasing

1 Preheat the oven to 400°F (200°C). Cream the butter and sugar with an electric hand mixer.

2 Add the egg and whisk to combine. Sift in the flour and fold in with a large metal spoon.

3 Baking up to 4 at a time, place tablespoons of batter well apart on non-stick baking sheets.

4 Using the back of a wet spoon, smooth them out to a thickness of 3¼in (8cm) in diameter.

For alternative shapes, cut stencils out of silicone paper. Try stars or scalloped circles.

Place the stencils on a baking sheet and smooth a spoonful of batter evenly over each.

5 Bake at the top of the oven for 5–7 minutes, until the edges start to color to a pale gold.

6 Use a palette knife to lift them; you have only a few minutes to shape them or they harden.

7 Drape over a greased rolling pin for a classic shape. If needed, re-bake for 1 minute to soften.

COOKIES AND SLICES

For a basket, press a tuile over the base of a small, greased, upturned circular bowl.

Use your hands, or another bowl, to hold it in place for a minute until it starts to harden.

For a spiral, twist an oblong tuile around the lightly greased handle of a wooden spoon.

8 Leave the tuiles to cool for 2–3 minutes before gently sliding them off the rolling pin. Place on a wire rack to cool and dry completely. Tuiles are best eaten the day they are made.

Tuile variations

Brandy Snaps

So easy to make, brandy snaps deserve to be back in fashion. A basket will transform a simple chocolate mousse into an elegant dessert.

MAKES 16–20 | 15 MINS | 6–8 MINS

Special equipment
piping bag and medium nozzle (optional)

Ingredients
7 tbsp unsalted butter, diced
½ cup sugar
¼ cup corn syrup
¾ cup all-purpose flour, sifted
1 tsp ground ginger
finely grated zest of ½ lemon
1 tbsp brandy (optional)
vegetable oil, for greasing

For the filling (optional)
1 cup heavy cream, whipped
1 tbsp confectioner's sugar
1 tsp brandy

Method

1 Preheat the oven to 350°F (180°C). Melt the butter and sugar in a pan over medium heat. Mix in the corn syrup well. Remove from the heat and beat in the flour, ginger, and zest. Stir in the brandy, if using.

2 Place heaped teaspoons of the mixture on 3 or 4 non-stick baking sheets, ensuring they are spaced well apart as they will spread to about 3¼in (8cm) in diameter. Bake at the top of the oven for 6–8 minutes, until golden brown and the edges are darkening slightly. If they become difficult to work with, bake for 1–2 minutes to soften.

3 Leave them to cool on their sheets for 3 minutes, until you are able to move them with a spatula, but they are still soft enough to shape. If they become difficult to work with, return them to the oven for 1–2 minutes to soften.

4 To make a classic shape, roll the cookies around the greased handle of a wooden spoon and wait until they harden before sliding them off onto a wire rack. See page 217, steps 10–11 for how to shape a basket.

5 To serve as a dessert, fold the filling ingredients together and pipe the mixture into the cooled, rolled brandy snaps. These are best eaten on the day they are made.

Parmesan Crisps

The simplest recipe imaginable—use these crisps as a garnish or canapé.

MAKES 24 | 5 MINS | 5–7 MINS

Special equipment
2¾in (7cm) pastry cutter

Ingredients

For the crisps
4oz (100g) Parmesan cheese, finely grated

For the additional ingredients (optional)
1 tbsp poppy seeds, or 1 tbsp sesame seeds, or 1 tbsp chopped herbs, such as rosemary, thyme, or sage

Method

1 Preheat the oven to 400°F (200°C). Mix the cheese in a bowl with any one of the additional ingredients (if using).

2 Place the pastry cutter on a non-stick baking sheet. Sprinkle 1 tablespoon of the grated cheese mixture inside the cutter, making sure to spread it out evenly. Gently remove the cutter. Repeat the process with the remaining cheese.

3 Bake them at the top of the oven for 5–7 minutes, or until the cheese has melted and started to brown slightly at the edges.

4 Leave the crisps to harden on their sheets for a couple of minutes, but transfer them to a wire rack before they cool completely, or they can be difficult to move. They are best eaten on the day they are made.

Almond Tuiles

These almond tuiles are so simple, yet they would enhance most desserts. Use them as a garnish for delicate fruit or vanilla-flavored desserts.

MAKES 15   **15 MINS**   **5–7 MINS**

Ingredients

4 tbsp unsalted butter, softened
⅓ cup confectioner's sugar, sifted
1 large egg
⅓ cup all-purpose flour, sifted
¼ cup sliced almonds
vegetable oil, for greasing

Method

1 Preheat the oven to 400°F (200°C). In a large bowl, or a food processor, cream together the butter and sugar until pale and fluffy. Add the egg and mix well to combine. Gently fold in the flour.

2 Place heaped tablespoons of the batter on a non-stick baking sheet. Wet the back of the spoon and smooth them out in a circular motion to even circles, about 3¼in (8cm) in diameter. You can use stencils to shape the tuiles (see page 216), but ensure they are always of an even thickness.

3 Scatter the surface with a few sliced almonds and bake them at the top of the oven for 5–7 minutes, depending on thickness. They are ready when the edges start to color and they are pale gold in the middle.

4 Remove the tuiles from the oven; you have only a couple of minutes to shape them before they harden. If they start to become difficult to work with, return them to the oven for 1–2 minutes until they soften.

5 To make a classic tuile, drape the cookies over a lightly greased rolling pin and leave them to cool for a couple of minutes before gently sliding them off (or shape differently, see page 216). Once the tuiles are set, put them on a wire rack to dry completely before storing in an airtight container. They are best eaten the day they are made.

BAKER'S TIP

Tuiles are deceptively simple to make, especially once you know that gently reheating them gives you more time to shape them. However, do not be tempted to shape these almond tuiles too tightly, as the almonds on the surface will not allow the cookie to be bent too much without cracking.

Shortbread

A Scottish classic, shortbread should only color very lightly in the oven, so remember to cover with foil if browning.

MAKES 8 WEDGES | **15 MINS** | **30–40 MINS**

Chilling time
1hr

Special equipment
8in (20cm) round cake pan
electric mixer with paddle
 attachment (optional)

Ingredients
11 tbsp unsalted butter, softened,
 plus extra for greasing
⅓ cup sugar, plus extra for sprinkling

1⅓ cups all-purpose flour, plus extra
 for dusting
½ cup cornstarch

1 Preheat the oven to 325°F (160°C). Grease the pan and line with parchment paper.

2 Place the softened butter and sugar in a large bowl.

3 Cream together the butter and sugar with an electric hand mixer until light and fluffy.

4 Stir in the flour and cornstarch very gently, stopping as soon as the flours are mixed in.

5 Bring together with your hands to form a rough, crumbly dough. Transfer to the pan.

6 Firmly push the dough down with your hands to form a compact, even layer.

7 Score the circle of shortbread lightly, with a sharp knife, into 8 wedges.

8 Prick the shortbread all over with a fork to make a decorative pattern.

9 Cover the shortbread with plastic wrap and chill in the refrigerator for 1 hour.

COOKIES AND SLICES

220

10 Bake in the center of the oven for 30–40 minutes. Cover with foil if it browns quickly.

11 Take the shortbread out of the oven, and re-score the wedges with a sharp knife.

12 While it is still warm, scatter a thin layer of sugar evenly over the top.

13 When cool, turn the shortbread gently out of its pan and break or cut it into wedges along the scored lines. **STORE** The shortbread will keep in an airtight container for 5 days.

Shortbread variations

Pecan Sandies

These addictive shortbread cookies are so-called because they are said to have the texture (though not the taste!) of fine sand.

MAKES 18–20 | **15 MINS** | **15 MINS**

Chilling time
30 mins (if needed)

Ingredients
7 tbsp unsalted butter, softened
¼ cup light brown sugar
¼ cup sugar
½ tsp pure vanilla extract
1 large egg yolk
1 cup all-purpose flour, sifted, plus extra for dusting
½ cup pecans, chopped

Method
1 Preheat the oven to 350°F (180°C). In a large bowl, cream together the butter and sugars with an electric hand mixer, until light and fluffy. Add the vanilla extract and the egg yolk, and mix well to combine. Mix in the flour, then the pecans, and bring the ingredients together to form a rough dough.

2 Turn the dough out onto a lightly floured work surface and knead it to form a smooth dough. Roll into a log about 8in (20cm) long. If the dough seems too soft to cut, refrigerate it for 30 minutes to allow it to firm up.

3 Slice ½in (1cm) disks from the log, and place a little apart on 2 baking sheets lined with parchment paper. Bake in the top third of the oven for 15 minutes, until golden brown at the edges. Leave on the sheets for a few minutes, then transfer them to a wire rack to cool completely.

STORE The sandies will keep in an airtight container for 5 days.

Chocolate Chip Shortbread Cookies

Chocolate chips make these shortbread cookies child-friendly.

MAKES 14–16 | **15 MINS** | **15–20 MINS**

Ingredients
7 tbsp unsalted butter, softened
⅓ cup sugar
¾ cup all-purpose flour, sifted, plus extra for dusting
¼ cup cornstarch, sifted
¼ cup dark chocolate chips

Method
1 Preheat the oven to 340°F (170°C). In a large bowl with an electric hand mixer, cream together the butter and sugar until light and fluffy. Stir in the flour, cornstarch, and chocolate chips, and bring together to form a rough dough.

2 Turn the dough out onto a lightly floured work surface and gently knead it together until it becomes smooth. Roll into a 2½in (6cm) diameter log, and slice at ¼in (5mm) intervals into cookies. Place spaced apart on 2 non-stick baking sheets.

3 Bake in the center of the oven for about 15–20 minutes until lightly golden. They should not color too much. Leave on the sheets for a few minutes before transferring to a wire rack to cool completely.

STORE These will keep in an airtight container for 5 days.

Marbled Millionaire's Shortbread

A modern classic—extremely sweet and rich, just as it should be.

| MAKES 16 SQUARES | 45 MINS | 35–40 MINS |

Special equipment
8in (20cm) square cake pan

Ingredients
1½ cups all-purpose flour, plus more for dusting
12 tbsp unsalted butter, softened,
  plus extra for greasing
½ cup sugar

For the caramel filling
4 tbsp unsalted butter
¼ cup light brown sugar
14oz (400g) can condensed milk

For the chocolate topping
7oz (200g) milk chocolate
2 tbsp unsalted butter
2oz (50g) dark chocolate

Method
1 Preheat the oven to 325°F (160°C). Put the flour, butter, and sugar in a bowl and rub together to make crumbs. Grease the pan and dust with flour. Put the mixture into the pan and press it down with your hands until it is compact and even. Bake in the center of the oven for 35–40 minutes, until light golden brown. Leave to cool in the pan.

2 For the caramel, melt the butter and sugar in a heavy-based saucepan over medium heat. Add the milk and bring to a boil, stirring constantly. Reduce the heat and cook on a steady simmer, still stirring constantly, for 5 minutes, until it thickens and darkens to a light caramel color. Pour the caramel over the cooled shortbread and leave to cool.

3 For the chocolate topping, put the milk chocolate and butter in a heatproof bowl over a pan of simmering water, without touching the water, until just melted. Stir well. Melt the dark chocolate without butter in a separate bowl in a similar way.

4 Pour the milk chocolate over the set caramel and smooth out. Pour the dark chocolate over the surface in a zigzag pattern and drag a fine skewer through the 2 chocolates to create a marbled effect. Leave to cool and harden before cutting into squares.

STORE These will keep in an airtight container for 5 days.

BAKER'S TIP
The secret to a good millionaire's shortbread is to make a caramel that sets enough so that it does not squish out of the sides on cutting, and a chocolate topping that is soft enough to cut easily. Add a little butter to the chocolate to soften it slightly, and gently cook the caramel until thickened to achieve a perfect result.

Flapjacks

These chewy bars are great energy boosters and very simple to make, using only a few pantry ingredients.

MAKES 16–20 **15 MINS** **40 MINS**

Special equipment
10in (25cm) square
cake pan

Ingredients
2 sticks butter, plus extra
 for greasing
1¼ cups light brown sugar
2 tbsp corn syrup
3¾ cups rolled oats

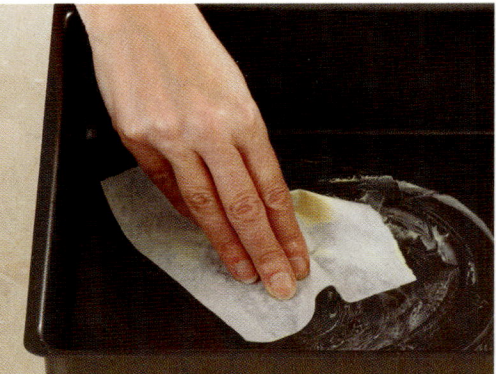

1 Preheat the oven to 300°F (150°C). Lightly grease the base and sides of the cake pan.

2 Put the butter, sugar, and syrup in a large saucepan and place over medium-low heat.

3 Stir constantly with a wooden spoon to prevent scorching. Remove from the heat.

4 Stir in the oats, making sure they are well coated, but do not over-work the mix.

5 Spoon the oat mixture from the saucepan into the prepared pan.

6 Press down firmly with the wooden spoon to make a roughly even layer.

7 To neaten the surface, dip a tablespoon in hot water and use the back to smooth the top.

8 Bake for 40 minutes or until evenly golden; you may need to turn the pan in the oven.

9 Leave to cool for 10 minutes, then cut into 16 squares, or 20 rectangles, with a sharp knife.

10 Leave in the pan to cool completely, then lever the flapjacks out of the pan; a spatula is a useful tool for this.
STORE The flapjacks will keep in an airtight container for 1 week.

Flapjack variations

Hazelnut and Raisin Flapjacks

Hazelnuts and raisins make these a chewy and wholesome treat.

MAKES 16-20 | **15 MINS** | **30 MINS** | **UP TO 4 WEEKS**

Special equipment
8 x 10in (20 x 25cm) brownie pan, or similar

Ingredients
4 tbsp unsalted butter,
  plus extra for greasing
1¼ cups light brown sugar
2 tbsp corn syrup
3¾ cups rolled oats
⅔ cup chopped hazelnuts
¼ cup raisins

Method
1 Preheat the oven to 325°F (160°C). Grease the pan and line the base and sides with parchment paper. Melt the butter, sugar, and syrup in a heavy saucepan over low heat until the butter has melted. Remove the pan from the heat and stir in the oats, hazelnuts, and raisins.

2 Transfer the mixture to the prepared pan and press it down firmly, until it is compact and even. Bake in the center of the oven for 30 minutes until golden brown and darkening slightly at the edges.

3 Leave in the pan for 5 minutes, then cut the flapjacks into squares with a sharp knife. Leave in the pan until cold before turning out with a metal spatula.

STORE The flapjacks will keep in an airtight container for 1 week.

BAKER'S TIP
Nuts and raisins make these flapjacks healthier and, as in the recipes for Oat Cookies (see page 188), you could also add a handful of pumpkin or sunflower seeds. Despite the health quotient of those ingredients, the butter content of flapjacks does make them a high-fat treat.

Cherry Flapjacks

These cherry flapjacks have the perfect texture, and a delicious, toasty flavor. ▶

MAKES 18 | **15 MINS** | **25 MINS**

Chilling time
10 mins

Special equipment
8in (20cm) square cake pan

Ingredients
11 tbsp unsalted butter, plus extra for greasing
⅓ cup light brown sugar
2 tbsp corn syrup
3¾ cups rolled oats
1 cup glacé cherries, quartered, or ½ cup dried
  cherries, coarsely chopped
⅓ cup raisins
4oz (100g) white or milk chocolate,
  broken into small pieces, for drizzling

Method
1 Preheat the oven to 350°F (180°C). Lightly grease the cake pan. Place the butter, sugar, and syrup in a medium saucepan over low heat, and stir until melted. Remove from the heat, add the oats, cherries, and raisins, and stir until well mixed.

2 Transfer to the prepared pan and press down. Bake in the top of the oven for 25 minutes. Remove, cool slightly in the pan, then mark into 18 pieces with a knife.

3 When the flapjacks are cold, place the chocolate in a small heatproof bowl set over a saucepan of simmering water. Make sure the bowl does not touch the water. Drizzle the melted chocolate over the flapjacks using a teaspoon, then chill for about 10 minutes, or until the chocolate has set. Remove the block of flapjacks from the pan and cut into pieces as marked.

STORE The flapjacks will keep in an airtight container for 1 week.

Sticky Date Flapjacks

The quantity of dates in this recipe gives these flapjacks a toffee-like flavor and wonderfully moist consistency.

MAKES 16 | **25 MINS** | **40 MINS**

Special equipment
8in (20cm) square cake pan
blender

Ingredients
1½ cups pitted dates (Medjool are best), chopped
½ tsp baking soda
14 tbsp unsalted butter
1¼ cups light brown sugar
2 tbsp corn syrup
3⅓ cups rolled oats

Method
1 Preheat the oven to 325°F (160°C). Line the pan with parchment paper. Place the dates and baking soda in a pan with enough water to cover, simmer for 5 minutes, then drain, reserving the liquid. Purée in a blender with 3 tablespoons of cooking liquid. Set aside.

2 Melt the butter, sugar, and syrup together in a large pan, stirring to mix. Stir in the oats, then press half the mixture into the pan.

3 Spread the date purée over the top of the oats, then spoon the remaining oat mixture over the top. Bake for 40 minutes, or until golden brown. Leave to cool in the pan for 10 minutes, then cut into 16 squares with a knife. Leave to cool completely in the pan before serving.

STORE The flapjacks will keep in an airtight container for 1 week.

Chocolate and Hazelnut Brownies

The classic recipe, these brownies are moist and soft in the center and crisp on top.

MAKES 24   **25 MINS**   **12–15 MINS**

Special equipment
9 x 13in (23 x 32cm) pan

Ingredients
1 cup hazelnuts
12 tbsp unsalted butter, diced
10oz (300g) dark chocolate (at least 50 percent cocoa solids, or higher for more bitter brownies), chopped
1⅓ cups sugar
4 large eggs, beaten
1½ cups all-purpose flour
½ cup cocoa powder, extra to dust

1 Preheat the oven to 400°F (200°C). Scatter the hazelnuts evenly over a baking sheet.

2 Toast the nuts in the oven for 5 minutes until browned, being careful not to scorch them.

3 Remove from the oven and rub the nuts in a kitchen towel to remove most of the skins.

4 Chop the hazelnuts roughly—some big chunks and some small. Set aside.

5 Line the base and sides of the pan with parchment paper, allowing some overhang.

6 Put chocolate and butter in a bowl over pan of simmering water, without touching water.

7 Melt the chocolate and butter, stirring until smooth. Remove and leave to cool.

8 Once the mixture has cooled, mix in the sugar until very well blended.

9 Now add the eggs, 1 at a time, making sure each is well mixed before you add the next.

COOKIES AND SLICES

10 Sift in the flour and cocoa powder, lifting the sieve up high above the bowl to aerate.

11 Mix in the flour and cocoa until the batter is smooth and no patches of flour are seen.

12 Stir in the chopped nuts to evenly distribute them in the batter; the mixture should be thick.

13 Pour into the prepared pan and spread so the mixture fills the corners. Smooth the top.

14 Bake for 12–15 minutes, or until just firm to the touch on top and still soft underneath.

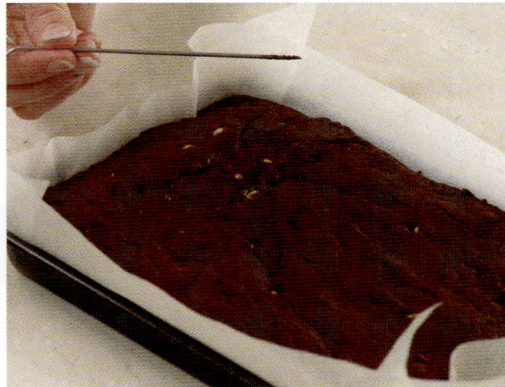

15 A skewer inserted should come out coated with a little batter. Remove from the oven.

16 Leave the brownie to cool completely in the pan to maintain the soft center.

17 Lift the brownie from the pan using the edges of the paper to get a good grip.

18 Using a long, sharp, or serrated knife, score the surface of the brownie into 24 even pieces.

19 Boil some water in a saucepan, and pour it into a shallow dish. Keep dish close at hand.

20 Cut the brownie into 24, wiping the knife between cuts and dipping it in the hot water.

21 Sift cocoa powder over brownies.
STORE Keep in an airtight container for 3 days.

CHOCOLATE AND HAZELNUT BROWNIES

Brownie variations

Sour Cherry and Chocolate Brownies

The sharp flavor and chewy texture of the dried sour cherries contrast wonderfully here with the rich, dark chocolate.

MAKES 16 · **15 MINS** · **20–25 MINS**

Special equipment
8in (20cm) square cake pan

Ingredients
11 tbsp unsalted butter, diced, extra for greasing
6oz (150g) good-quality dark chocolate
1¼ cups light brown sugar
1¼ cups all-purpose flour, extra for dusting
1¼ tsp baking powder
½ tsp salt
3 large eggs
1 tsp pure vanilla extract
½ cup dried sour cherries
4oz (100g) dark chocolate chunks

Method
1 Preheat the oven to 350°F (180°C). Grease the pan and dust with flour. Break up chocolate and place with butter in a heatproof bowl over simmering water, without touching water, until just melted. Remove from the heat, add the sugar, and stir to combine well. Cool slightly.

2 Sift the flour, baking powder, and salt into a separate bowl. Mix the eggs and vanilla extract into the chocolate mixture. Pour it into the flour and mix together. Be careful not to over-mix. Fold in the cherries and chocolate chunks.

3 Pour the mixture into the pan and bake in the center of the oven for 20–25 minutes. The brownies are ready when the edges are firm, but the middle is soft to the touch.

4 Cool in the pan for 5 minutes. Turn out and cut into squares. Cool further on a wire rack.

STORE The brownies will keep in an airtight container for 3 days.

BAKER'S TIP
The texture of a brownie is very much a matter of personal taste. Some people like them so squishy that they fall apart, others prefer a firmer cake. If you prefer soft brownies, reduce the cooking time slightly.

Walnut and White Chocolate Brownies

Slightly soft in the center, these make a tempting afternoon treat.

MAKES 16 · **10 MINS** · **1 HOUR 15 MINS**

Special equipment
8in (20cm) deep square pan

Ingredients
2 tbsp unsalted butter, diced, extra for greasing
2oz (50g) good-quality dark chocolate
3 large eggs
1 tbsp honey
1¼ cup light brown sugar
½ cup all-purpose flour
½ tsp baking powder
pinch salt
6oz (175g) walnut pieces
scant 1oz (25g) white chocolate, chopped

Method
1 Preheat the oven to 325°F (160°C). Lightly grease the pan, or line the base and sides with parchment paper.

2 Break the dark chocolate in pieces, and put it with the butter into a heatproof bowl over a saucepan of simmering water until melted, stirring occasionally. Don't let the bowl touch the water. Remove the bowl from the pan and set aside to cool slightly.

3 Beat the eggs, honey, and sugar together, then gradually beat in the melted chocolate mixture. Sift the flour, baking powder, and salt over, add the walnuts and white chocolate, and fold in the ingredients. Pour the mixture into the prepared pan.

4 Put the pan in the oven and bake for 30 minutes. Cover loosely with foil and bake for another 45 minutes. The center should be a little soft. Leave to cool completely in the pan on a wire rack. When cold, turn out onto a board and cut into squares.

STORE The brownies will keep in an airtight container for 5 days.

White Chocolate Macadamia Blondies

A white chocolate version of the ever-popular brownie.

MAKES 24   **15 MINS**   **20 MINS**

Special equipment
8 x 10in (20 x 25cm) baking dish, or similar

Ingredients
10oz (300g) white chocolate, chopped
12 tbsp unsalted butter, diced, more for greasing
1⅓ cup sugar
4 large eggs
1⅔ cups all-purpose flour, plus more to dust
1 cup macadamia nuts, roughly chopped

Method
1 Preheat the oven to 400°F (200°C). Grease the pan and dust with flour. In a bowl set over a pan of simmering water, melt the chocolate and butter together, stirring now and again until smooth. Do not allow the bowl to touch the water. Remove and leave to cool for about 20 minutes.

2 Once the chocolate has melted, mix in the sugar (the mixture may well become thick and grainy, but the eggs will loosen the mixture). Using a balloon whisk, stir in the eggs 1 at a time, making sure each is well mixed in before you add the next. Sift in the flour, mix it in, then stir in the nuts.

3 Pour the mixture into the pan and gently spread it out into the corners. Bake for 20 minutes, or until just firm to the touch on top, but still soft underneath. Leave to cool completely in the pan, then cut into 24 squares, or fewer rectangles for bigger blondies.

STORE The blondies will keep in an airtight container for 5 days.

Stilton and Walnut Biscuits

These savory biscuits are an ideal way to use up the leftover cheese and nuts you usually have after Christmas.

MAKES 24 · **10 MINS** · **20 MINS** · **12 WEEKS, UNBAKED**

Chilling time
1 hr

Special equipment
2in (5cm) round pastry cutter

Ingredients
5oz (120g) Stilton cheese, or other blue cheese
4 tbsp unsalted butter, softened
¾ cup all-purpose flour, sifted, plus extra for dusting
⅓ cup walnuts, chopped
freshly ground black pepper
1 large egg yolk, room temperature

1 Mix together the cheese and butter with an electric hand mixer until soft and creamy.

2 Add the flour to the cheese mixture and rub in with your fingertips to form breadcrumbs.

3 Add the walnuts and black pepper, and stir to mix through.

4 Finally add the egg yolk and bring the mixture together to form a stiff dough.

5 Knead the dough briefly on a lightly floured work surface to help blend in the walnuts.

6 Wrap the dough in plastic wrap. Chill for 1 hour. Preheat the oven to 350°F (180°C).

7 Turn the dough out onto a floured work surface and knead briefly to soften slightly.

8 Roll it out to a thickness of ¼in (5mm) and cut out the biscuits with the pastry cutter.

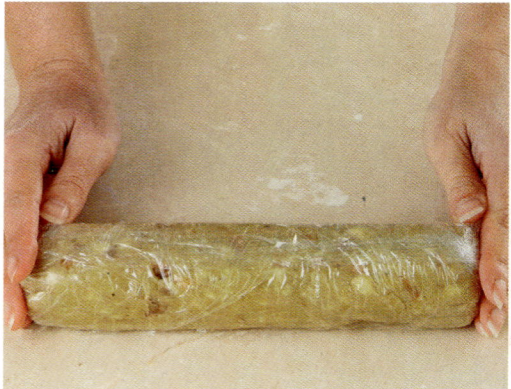

9 Alternatively, the dough can be chilled as an even 2in (5cm) diameter log.

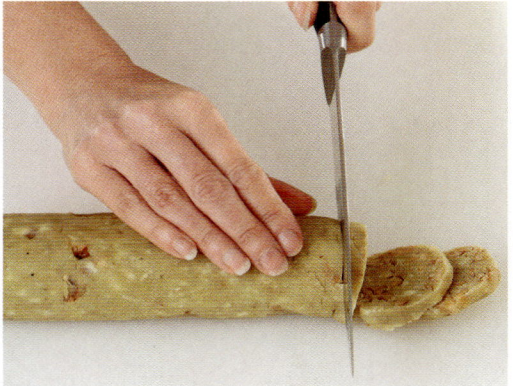  

10 Slice the dough log carefully into ¼in (5mm) rounds with a sharp knife.

11 Put the rounds on non-stick baking sheets and bake at the top of the oven for 15 minutes.

12 Turn them over and bake for another 5 minutes until golden brown on both sides.

13 Remove from the oven, allow to cool a little on their sheets, then transfer to a wire rack to cool completely.

STORE The biscuits will keep in an airtight container for 5 days.

Cheese Biscuit variations

Parmesan and Rosemary Thins

These savory crackers are light and elegant, and are equally good served as an appetizer before a meal or after dinner with cheese.

MAKES 15–20 | **10 MINS** | **15 MINS** | **12 WEEKS, UNBAKED**

Chilling time
1 hr

Special equipment
2½in (6cm) round cookie cutter
food processor with blade attachment (optional)

Ingredients
4 tbsp unsalted butter, softened and diced
½ cup all-purpose flour, plus extra for dusting
2oz (60g) Parmesan cheese, finely grated
freshly grated black pepper
1 tbsp chopped rosemary, or thyme, or basil

Method
1 Place the butter and flour in a bowl, or in the bowl of a food processor. Rub together with your fingertips—or pulse-blend — until the mixture resembles crumbs. Add the Parmesan, black pepper, and chopped herbs and mix in thoroughly. Bring the mixture together to form a dough.

2 Turn the dough out on to a lightly floured work surface and knead briefly to help it amalgamate, then wrap it in plastic wrap and chill for 1 hour.

3 Preheat the oven to 350°F (180°C). Turn the dough out on to a lightly floured work surface and knead briefly to soften slightly.

4 Roll the dough out to ½in (2mm) thick and cut out the thins with the cookie cutter. Place on 2 non-stick baking sheets and bake at the top of the oven for 10 minutes, then turn them over and continue to bake for 5 minutes, until lightly browned.

5 Remove from the oven and allow to cool on the sheets for 5 minutes, before transferring to a wire rack to cool.

STORE The thins will keep in an airtight container for 3 days.

Cheese Thins

These spicy crackerss can be made in bulk for an easy party snack.

MAKES 30 | **10 MINS** | **15 MINS** | **8 WEEKS, UNBAKED**

Chilling time
1 hr

Special equipment
2½in (6cm) round pastry cutter
food processor with blade attachment (optional)

Ingredients
4 tbsp unsalted butter, softened and diced
¾ cup all-purpose flour, plus extra for dusting
6oz (150g) strong Cheddar cheese, finely grated
½ tsp smoked paprika or cayenne pepper
1 large egg yolk, at room temperature

Method
1 Place the butter and flour in a bowl, or in the bowl of a food processor with a blade attachment. Rub together—or pulse-blend —until the mixture resembles crumbs. Add the Cheddar and the smoked paprika, and mix thoroughly. Add the egg yolk and bring the mixture together to form a dough.

2 Turn the dough out on to a lightly floured work surface and knead it briefly to help it amalgamate, then wrap it in plastic wrap and chill for 1 hour. When ready to bake, preheat the oven to 350°F (180°C). Turn the dough out and knead briefly to soften.

3 Roll the dough out to a thickness of ½in (2mm) and cut out the thins with the cookie cutter. Place them onto several non-stick baking sheets and bake at the top of the oven for 10 minutes, then turn them over, pressing down gently with a spatula to flatten any air bubbles that appear. Continue to bake for a further 5 minutes, until golden brown on both sides.

4 Remove from the oven and leave them on the sheets for 5 minutes, before transferring to a wire rack to cool completely.

STORE The thins will keep in an airtight container for 3 days.

Cheese Straws

A great way to use up any leftover pieces of hard cheese.

MAKES 15–20	10 MINS	15 MINS	12 WEEKS, UNBAKED

Chilling time
1 hr

Special equipment
food processor with blade attachment (optional)

Ingredients
½ cup flour, sifted, plus extra for dusting
pinch of salt
4 tbsp unsalted butter, softened and diced
1oz (30g) strong Cheddar cheese, finely grated
1 large egg yolk, plus 1 egg extra,
   beaten, for glazing
1 tsp Dijon mustard

Method

1 Place the flour, salt, and butter in a bowl, or the bowl of a food processor. Rub together with your fingertips, or pulse-blend, until the mixture resembles crumbs. Add the Cheddar and mix in. Whisk the egg yolk with 1 tablespoon cold water and the mustard until combined. Add to the crumbs and bring it together to form a dough.

2 Turn the dough out onto a lightly floured work surface and knead briefly. Wrap it in plastic wrap and chill for 1 hour. Preheat the oven to 400°F (200°C). When ready to cook, briefly knead the dough again.

3 Roll the dough out to a 12 x 6in (30 x 15cm) rectangle; it should be ¼in (5mm) thick. With a sharp knife, cut ½in (1cm) wide lengths along the shorter side. Brush the strips of pastry with a little beaten egg. Holding the top of each strip, twist the bottom of the strip gently a few times to form spirals.

4 Place the straws on non-stick baking sheets, pressing down the ends if the spirals appear to be unwinding. Bake at the top of the oven for 15 minutes. Cool on the sheets for 5 minutes, then transfer to a wire rack.

STORE The straws will keep in an airtight container for 3 days.

Oatcakes

These Scottish oatcakes are perfect with cheese and chutney. Made with just oats (see Baker's Tip), they become a good wheat-free option.

MAKES 16   **20 MINS**   **15 MINS**   **UP TO 4 WEEKS**

Special equipment
2½in (6cm) round cookie cutter

Ingredients
1¼ cups rolled oats, plus extra for dusting
¾ cup whole wheat flour, plus extra for dusting
¾ tsp salt
freshly ground black pepper
½ tsp baking soda
2 tbsp olive oil

Method

1 Preheat the oven to 350°F (180°C). Mix the dry ingredients together in a bowl. Whisk together the oil with 4 tablespoons freshly boiled water. Make a well in the center of the flour mixture and pour in the liquid, mixing it together with a spoon to form a thick paste.

2 Lightly flour a work surface with a mixture of flour and oats and turn the paste out onto it. Knead together briefly until it forms a dough. Gently roll the dough out, being aware that the more oats you use, the more delicate it will be and cracking is likely.

3 It is difficult to bring the pastry together again after the first rolling, cut as many oatcakes as possible with the first rolling. Roll the dough to a thickness of ¼in (5mm) and cut out the oatcakes. If the dough has difficulty coming together after the first cutting, put it back in the bowl and add a drop or two of water to help it amalgamate again, then re-roll and cut more oatcakes.

4 Place the oatcakes on several non-stick baking sheets and bake at the top of the oven for 10 minutes, then turn them over and continue to bake for a further 5 minutes, until golden brown on both sides. Remove the oatcakes from the oven and leave on the trays for 5 minutes, before transferring to a wire rack to cool completely.

STORE The oatcakes will keep in an airtight container for 3 days.

BAKER'S TIP

These traditional Scottish oatcakes can be made using just oats, or with a mixture of both oats and whole wheat flour. Made using only oats they are ideal for those who want to avoid wheat, but this does produce a more delicate, crumbly cake, and will need gentle handling when cutting out.

meringues & soufflés

Raspberry Cream Swiss Meringues

These mini meringues are filled with fresh raspberries and whipped cream, perfect for a summer buffet.

MAKES 6–8   **10 MINS**   **1 HOUR**

Special equipment
metal mixing bowl (optional)
piping bag with plain nozzle (optional)

Ingredients
4 egg whites (each medium egg white will weigh about 1oz/30g)
about 1 cup sugar, see step 3

For the filling
4oz (100g) raspberries
1 cup heavy cream
1 tbsp confectioner's sugar, sifted

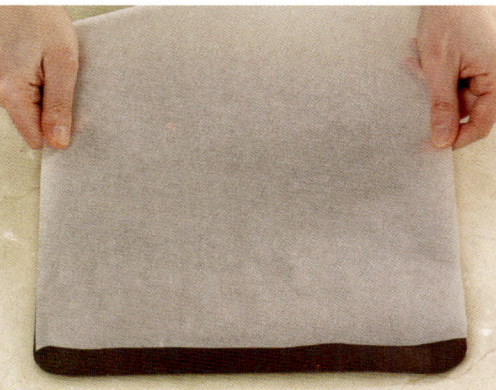

1 Preheat the oven to around 250°F (120°C). Line a baking sheet with parchment paper.

2 Make sure the metal bowl is clean and dry. Use a lemon to remove traces of grease.

3 Weigh the egg whites. You will need exactly double the weight of sugar to egg whites.

4 Whisk the egg whites in the metal bowl until they are stiff and form strong peaks.

5 Gradually add half the sugar, a couple of tablespoons at a time, whisking in between.

6 Gently fold the remaining sugar into the egg whites, trying to lose as little air as possible.

7 Put tablespoons of the mixture onto the baking sheet leaving 2in (5cm) gaps between.

8 Alternatively, pipe with a plain nozzle. Bake in the center of the oven for 1 hour.

9 They are ready when they lift easily from the parchment and sound hollow when tapped.

10 Turn off the oven and leave the meringues to cool inside. Remove to a wire rack until cold.

11 Put the raspberries in a bowl and crush them with the back of a fork, so they break up.

12 In a separate bowl whisk up the cream until firm but not stiff.

13 Gently fold together the cream and crushed raspberries. Mix with the confectioner's sugar.

14 Spread a little of the raspberry mixture onto half the meringues.

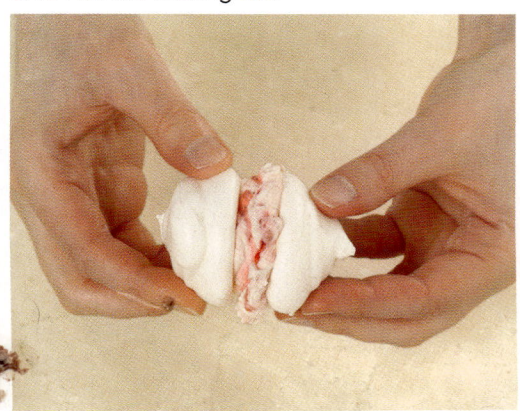

15 Top with the remaining meringue halves and gently press together to form sandwiches.

For sweet canapés, pipe smaller meringues and reduce the cooking time to 45 minutes; makes about 20 sandwiches. **PREPARE AHEAD** Keep unfilled in an airtight container for 5 days.

Meringue variations

Giant Pistachio Meringues

Too large to sandwich with cream, these beautiful creations are eaten like oversized cookies.

MAKES 8 | 15 MINS | 1½ HOURS

Special equipment
food processor with blade attachment
large metal mixing bowl

Ingredients
4 egg whites, at room temperature
about 1 cup sugar, see page 242, step 3
4oz (100g) unsalted, shelled pistachios

Method
1 Preheat the oven to the lowest setting, around 250°F (120°C). Spread the pistachios on a baking sheet and bake for 5 minutes then transfer them to a kitchen towel and rub to remove excess skin. Cool. Finely grind just less than half the nuts in a food processor, and coarsely chop the rest.

2 Put the egg whites into the metal bowl and whisk with an electric hand mixer until stiff peaks form. Add the sugar 2 tablespoons at a time, whisking between additions, until you have added at least half. Fold in the remaining sugar and the ground pistachios. Try to lose as little air as possible.

3 Line a baking sheet with parchment paper. Put large heaping tablespoons of the meringue mixture on to the sheet, leaving at least 2in (5cm) gaps between them. Scatter the tops with the chopped pistachios.

4 Bake in the center of the oven for 1½ hours. Turn off the oven and leave the meringues to cool inside, to prevent them from cracking. Transfer the meringues from the oven to a wire rack to cool completely.

5 Serve the meringues piled on top of each other, for maximum impact.

STORE These will keep in an airtight container for 3 days.

Lemon and Praline Meringues

Similar to Monts Blancs (see right), these have added crunch.

SERVES 6 | 35 MINS | 1½ HOURS

Special equipment
piping bag with star nozzle

Ingredients
3 egg whites, at room temperature
pinch of salt
about ¾ cup sugar, see page 242, step 3, plus an extra ¼ cup
vegetable oil, for greasing
2oz (60g) whole blanched almonds
pinch of cream of tartar
3oz (85g) dark chocolate, chopped
⅔ cup heavy cream
3 tbsp lemon curd

Method
1 Preheat the oven to 250°F (120°C) and line a baking sheet with parchment paper. Whisk the egg whites with the salt until stiff. Add 2 tablespoons sugar, and whisk until smooth and shiny. Add sugar, 1 tablespoon at a time, whisking well after each addition. Spoon into the piping bag, and pipe 6 x 4in (10cm) circles onto the baking sheet. Bake for 1½ hours, or until crisp.

2 Meanwhile, make the praline. Grease a baking sheet and put the ¼ cup sugar, almonds, and cream of tartar into a small, heavy saucepan. Set the pan over low heat and stir until the sugar dissolves. Boil until the syrup turns golden, then pour out onto the greased baking sheet. Leave until completely cold, then coarsely chop.

3 Melt the chocolate in a bowl set over simmering water. Whip the cream until just holding a trail, and fold in the lemon curd. Spread each meringue with chocolate. Allow to set, then pile the lemon curd cream on top, sprinkle with praline, and serve.

PREPARE AHEAD The meringue bases will keep in an airtight container for 5 days.

MERINGUES AND SOUFFLÉS

Monts Blancs

If using sweetened chestnut purée, omit the sugar in the filling.

MAKES 8   **20 MINS**   **45–60 MINS**

Special equipment
large metal mixing bowl
4in (10cm) pastry cutter

Ingredients
4 egg whites, at room temperature
about 1 cup sugar, see page 242, step 3
sunflower oil, for greasing

For the filling
14oz (435g) can unsweetened chestnut puree,
  or sweetened
½ cup sugar
1 tsp pure vanilla extract
2 cups heavy cream
confectioner's sugar, to dust

Method

1 Preheat the oven to the lowest setting, around 250°F (120°C).

2 Put the egg whites into a large, clean metal bowl and whisk them until they are stiff, and leave peaks when the whisk is removed from the egg whites. Gradually add the sugar 2 tablespoons at a time, whisking well between each addition, until you have added at least half. Gently fold the remaining sugar into the egg whites, trying to lose as little air as possible.

3 Lightly grease the pastry cutter. Line 2 baking sheets with parchment paper. Place the pastry cutter on the sheets, and spoon the meringue mixture into the ring, to a depth of 1¼in (3cm). Smooth over the top and gently remove the ring. Repeat until there are 4 meringue bases on each baking sheet.

4 Bake the meringues in the center of the oven for 45 minutes if you like them chewy, otherwise bake for 1 hour. Turn off the oven and leave the meringues to cool inside, to prevent them from cracking. Remove to a wire rack to cool completely.

5 Put the chestnut purée in a bowl with the sugar (if using), vanilla, and 4 tablespoons of heavy cream, and beat together until smooth. Push through a fine sieve to make a really light, fluffy filling. In a separate bowl whisk the remaining heavy cream until firm.

6 Gently smooth 1 tablespoon chestnut filling over the top of the meringues, using a palette knife to smooth the surface. Top each meringue with a spoonful of whipped cream, smoothed round with a palette knife to give the appearance of soft peaks. Dust with confectioner's sugar and serve.

PREPARE AHEAD The meringue bases can be prepared 5 days ahead and stored in an airtight container.

BAKER'S TIP
Make sure that the bowl you are using to whisk the egg whites in is completely clean and dry. For absolute accuracy, it is best to weigh the egg whites. You will need precisely double the weight of sugar to egg whites. An electronic scale is best.

Strawberries and Cream Macarons

The art of macaron making can seem complex, but here I have tried to devise a recipe that will suit the home cook.

MAKES 20	30 MINS	18–20 MINS

Special equipment
food processor with
   blade attachment
piping bag with small,
   plain nozzle

Ingredients
¾ cup confectioner's sugar
¾ cup ground almonds
2 large egg whites,
   at room temperature
⅓ cup sugar

For the filling
¾ cup heavy cream
5-10 very large strawberries,
   preferably the same diameter as
   the macarons

1 Preheat the oven to 300°F (150°C). Line 2 baking sheets with wax paper.

2 Trace 20 x 1¼in (3cm) circles, leaving 1¼in (3cm) between circles. Invert the paper.

3 In a food processor, pulse the almonds and confectioner's sugar to a very fine meal.

4 In a large bowl, whisk the egg whites to stiff peaks using an electric hand mixer.

5 Whisking, add the sugar a little at a time, whisking well between additions.

6 The meringue mixture should be very stiff at this point, more than for a Swiss meringue.

7 Gently fold in the almond mixture a spoonful at a time, until just incorporated.

8 Transfer the macaron mix to the piping bag, placing the bag into a bowl to help.

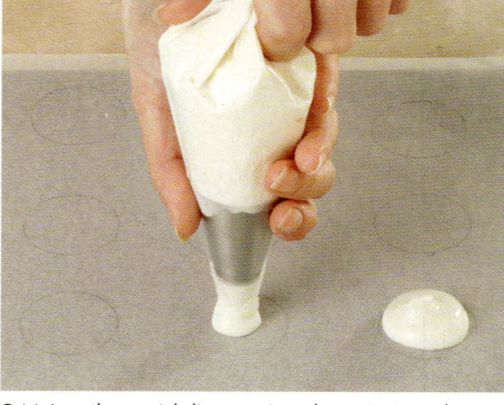

9 Using the guidelines, pipe the mix into the center of each circle, holding the bag vertically.

10 Try to keep the disks even in size and volume; the mix will spread very slightly.

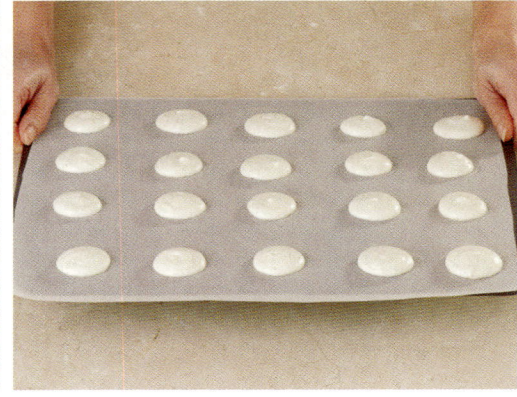

11 Bang the baking sheets down a few times if there are any peaks left in the center.

12 Bake in the middle of the oven for 18–20 minutes until the surface is set firm.

13 Test one shell: a firm prod with a finger should crack the top of the macaron.

14 Leave for 15–20 minutes, then transfer to a wire rack to cool completely.

15 Whisk the cream until thickened but not stiff; it should remain succulent.

16 Transfer the cream into the (cleaned) piping bag used earlier, with the same nozzle.

17 Pipe a blob of the whipped cream onto the flat side of half the macarons.

18 Slice the strawberries across into thin slices, the same diameter as the macarons.

19 Put a slice of strawberry on top of the cream filling of each macaron.

20 Add the remaining macaron shells and sandwich gently. The fillings should peek out.

21 Serve immediately. **PREPARE AHEAD** Unfilled macaron shells can be stored for 3 days.

MERINGUES AND SOUFFLÉS

Macaron variations

Tangerine Macarons

Sharp, zesty tangerines are used here, rather than the more usual oranges, to counterbalance the sweetness of the meringues.

MAKES 20 **30 MINS** **18–20 MINS**

Special equipment
food processor with blade attachment

Ingredients
¾ cup confectioner's sugar
¾ cup ground almonds
1 scant tsp finely grated tangerine zest
2 large egg whites, at room temperature
⅓ cup sugar
3–4 drops orange food coloring

For the filling
¾ cup confectioner's sugar
4 tbsp unsalted butter, softened
1 tbsp tangerine juice
1 scant tsp finely grated tangerine zest

Method
1 Preheat the oven to 300°F (150°C). Line 2 baking sheets with wax paper. Draw on 1¼in (3cm) circles with a pencil, leaving a 1¼in (3cm) gap between each one. Pulse the confectioner's sugar and almonds in a food processor, until finely mixed. Add the tangerine zest and pulse briefly.

2 In a bowl, whisk the egg whites to form stiff peaks with a hand mixer. Add the sugar a little at a time, whisking well with each addition. Whisk in the food coloring.

3 Fold in the almond mixture, a spoonful at a time. Transfer to the piping bag. Holding the bag vertically, pipe meringue into the center of each circle.

4 Bake in the middle of the oven for 18–20 minutes until the surface is set firm. Leave the macarons to cool on the baking sheets for 15–20 minutes and then transfer to a wire rack to cool completely.

5 For the filling, cream together the confectioner's sugar, butter, tangerine zest, and juice until smooth. Transfer into the (cleaned) piping bag, using the same nozzle. Pipe a blob of frosting onto the flat side of half the macarons, and sandwich with the rest. Serve the same day.

PREPARE AHEAD The unfilled shells can be stored for 3 days in an airtight container.

Chocolate Macarons

These delicious macarons are filled with a rich, dark chocolate buttercream.

MAKES 20 **30 MINS** **18–20 MINS**

Special equipment
food processor with blade attachment

Ingredients
½ cup ground almonds
¼ cup cocoa powder
¾ cup confectioner's sugar
2 large egg whites, at room temperature
⅓ cup sugar

For the filling
⅓ cup cocoa powder
1¼ cups confectioner's sugar
3 tbsp unsalted butter, melted
3 tbsp milk, plus a little extra if needed

Method
1 Preheat the oven to 300°F (150°C). Line 2 baking sheets with wax paper. In a food processor, pulse together the ground almonds, cocoa powder, and confectioner's sugar until very finely mixed, with no lumps.

2 Whisk the egg whites until stiff. Add the granulated sugar, whisking. The mixture should be stiff. Fold in the almond mixture a spoonful at a time. Transfer to the piping bag. Holding the bag vertically, pipe meringue into the center of each circle.

3 Bake in the middle of the oven for 18–20 minutes. Leave to cool on the sheets 15–20 minutes, before transferring to a wire rack.

4 For the filling, sift the cocoa and confectioner's sugar into a bowl. Add the butter and milk, and whisk. Add a little milk if too thick. Transfer to the piping bag and pipe frosting onto the flat side of half the macarons and sandwich together. Serve the same day, or the macarons will go soft.

PREPARE AHEAD The unfilled shells can be stored for 3 days in an airtight container.

Raspberry Macarons

Pretty as a picture, these macarons look almost too good to eat.

MAKES 20 · **30 MINS** · **18–20 MINS**

Special equipment
food processor with blade attachment

Ingredients
¾ cup confectioner's sugar
¾ cup ground almonds
2 large egg whites, at room temperature
⅓ cup sugar
3-4 drops of pink food coloring

For the filling
6oz (150g) mascarpone
2 tbsp good-quality seedless raspberry conserve

Method

1 Preheat the oven to 300°F (150°C). Line 2 baking sheets with wax paper. Draw 1¼in (3cm) circles with a pencil, leaving a 1¼in (3cm) gap between each. In a food processor, pulse the confectioner's sugar and almonds until finely mixed and smooth.

2 In a bowl, whisk the egg whites until they form stiff peaks. Add the sugar, a little at a time, whisking well between each addition. Whisk in the food coloring.

3 Fold in the almond mixture a spoonful at a time, until just mixed. Transfer the mix to the piping bag. Holding the bag vertically, pipe meringue into the center of each circle.

4 Bake in the middle of the oven for 18–20 minutes until the surface is firm. Leave to cool on the sheets for 15–20 minutes, before transferring to a wire rack to cool.

5 For the filling, beat the mascarpone and raspberry conserve until smooth and transfer to the (cleaned) piping bag used earlier, with the same nozzle. Pipe a blob of the filling onto the flat side of half the macarons, and sandwich together with the rest of the halves. Serve the same day, or the macarons will go soft.

PREPARE AHEAD The unfilled shells can be stored for 3 days in an airtight container.

BAKER'S TIP
The skill in making macarons comes in the technique, not in the proportions of the ingredients. Gentle folding, a heavy, flat baking sheet, and piping completely vertically downward should all help you to produce the perfect macaron.

Strawberry Pavlova

This well-loved dessert is named after Russian ballerina Anna Pavlova.

SERVES 8   15 MINS   1¼ HOURS

Ingredients

6 egg whites, at room temperature
pinch of salt
about 1½ cups sugar,
  see page 242, step 3
2 tsp cornstarch
1 tsp vinegar
1¼ cups heavy cream
strawberries, to decorate and serve

1 Preheat the oven to 350°F (180°C). Line a baking sheet with parchment paper.

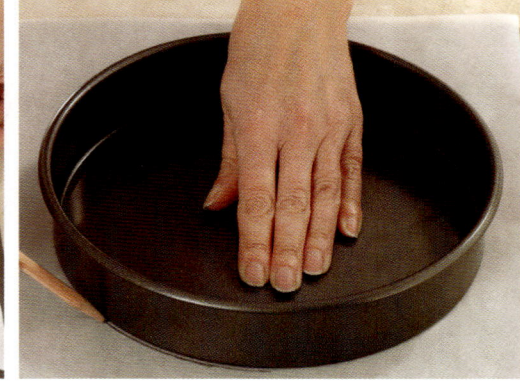

2 Draw a 8in (20cm) diameter circle on the parchment paper using a pencil.

3 Reverse the parchment, so the pencil mark is below and won't transfer to the meringue.

4 Put the egg whites in a large, clean, grease-free bowl with the salt.

5 Using an electric hand mixer, beat the egg whites until stiff peaks form.

6 Start whisking in the sugar 1 tablespoon at a time, whisking well after each addition.

7 Keep whisking until the whites are stiff and glossy. Whisk in the cornstarch and vinegar.

8 Spoon it into a mound inside the circle on the parchment. Spread it to the edges of the circle.

9 Form neat swirls, using a palette knife, as you spread out the meringue.

MERINGUES AND SOUFFLÉS

10 Bake for 5 minutes, then reduce the heat to 250°F (120°C) and cook for 75 minutes.

11 Leave to cool completely in the oven. Whip the cream until it holds its shape.

12 Spoon the cream onto the meringue base and decorate with the strawberries.

13 Serve in wedges, with extra berries, or a fruit coulis. **PREPARE AHEAD** The meringue will keep in a dry, airtight container for 1 week. Add the cream and berries just before serving.

Pavlova variations

Rhubarb Ginger Meringue Cake

A classic combination makes a tasty filling for this unusual cake.

SERVES 6–8 | **30 MINS** | **1 HOUR 5 MINS**

Ingredients

For the meringues
4 egg whites, at room temperature
pinch of salt
about 1 cup sugar, see page 242, step 3

For the filling
1lb 5oz (600g) rhubarb, chopped
⅓ cup sugar
4 pieces ginger, chopped
½ tsp ground ginger
1 cup heavy cream
confectioner's sugar, to dust

Method

1 Preheat the oven to 350°F (180°C). Line 2 baking sheets with parchment paper. Whisk the egg whites, salt, and ½ cup of the sugar in a large, clean bowl until stiff, glossy peaks form. Fold in the rest of the sugar a spoonful at a time.

2 Divide the meringue between the baking sheets and spread into 7in (18cm) circles. Bake for 5 minutes, then reduce the oven temperature to 250°F (120°C) and bake for 1 hour. Open the oven door and leave the meringue to cool completely.

3 Meanwhile, put the rhubarb, sugar, ginger, ground ginger, and a splash of water in a saucepan and cook, covered over low heat for 20 minutes, or until soft. Allow to cool. If too wet, drain to get rid of some of the liquid, and chill until required.

4 Whip the cream and fold in the rhubarb. Place 1 meringue on a serving plate, spread it with rhubarb and ginger filling, and top with the remaining meringue. Dust with confectioner's sugar and serve.

PREPARE AHEAD The meringue bases will keep in a dry, airtight container for 1 week.

Mini Pavlovas

A fantastic way to feed a crowd, the bases here can be prepared in advance and filled at the last moment with the best of the season's fruit.

MAKES 8 | **15 MINS** | **45–60 MINS**

Ingredients

6 egg whites, at room temperature
pinch of salt
about 1½ cups sugar, see page 242, step 3
2 tsp cornstarch
1 tsp vinegar
1¼ cups heavy cream
14oz (400g) mixed summer berries

Method

1 Preheat the oven to 250°F (120°C). Line 2 baking sheets with parchment paper. Using an electric hand mixer, beat the egg whites and salt until stiff peaks form. Whisk in the sugar 1 tablespoon at a time, then whisk in the cornstarch and vinegar.

2 Spoon tablespoons evenly onto the sheets, and smooth with the back of a spoon to 4in (10cm) wide and 1¼in (3cm) high.

3 Bake for 45 minutes–1 hour, until crisp. Cool and move to a serving plate. Whip the cream until it holds its shape. Top each pavlova with 1 tablespoon of cream and the berries.

PREPARE AHEAD The meringue bases will keep in a dry, airtight container for 1 week. Fill just before serving.

Mocha Coffee Pavlova

With its coffee-infused meringue and drizzled chocolate, this is an impressive and sophisticated pavlova to serve at a dinner party.

MAKES 8 | **15 MINS** | **1 HOUR 20 MINS**

Ingredients

6 egg whites, at room temperature
pinch of salt
about 1½ cups sugar, see page 242, step 3
2 tsp cornstarch
1 tsp vinegar
3 tbsp strong coffee powder mixed with 3 tbsp boiling water, cooled, or 3 tbsp cooled espresso
1¼ cups heavy cream
2oz (60g) good-quality dark chocolate, broken into pieces, plus extra to decorate
white chocolate, to decorate

Method

1 Preheat the oven to 350°F (180°C). Line a baking sheet with parchment. Put the egg whites in a grease-free bowl with the salt. Using an electric mixer, beat until stiff peaks form. Whisk in the sugar 1 tablespoon at a time, whisking well until stiff and glossy, then whisk in the cornstarch and vinegar.

2 Draw an 8in (20cm) diameter circle on the parchment paper with a pencil and reverse the paper. Spoon tablespoons of the meringue inside the circle and smooth out.

3 Bake for 5 minutes, then reduce to 250°F (120°C) and cook for 1 hour 15 minutes, or until crisp. Turn off the oven and leave the meringue inside to cool.

4 Melt the dark chocolate pieces in a heatproof bowl set over a pan of simmering water, and cool. Make white and dark chocolate shavings using a vegetable peeler. Before serving, whip the cream until it holds its shape. Top the pavlova with the cream. Drizzle with the melted chocolate and sprinkle with chocolate shavings.

PREPARE AHEAD The meringue base will keep in a dry, airtight container for 1 week. Fill just before serving.

MERINGUES AND SOUFFLÉS

Tropical Fruit Pavlova

The contrast between tangy passion fruit, cool whipped cream, and sweet meringue in this pavlova is really hard to beat. A refreshing dessert for a summer's day.

MAKES 8 **15 MINS** **65–80 MINS**

Ingredients

1 quantity meringue mix,
  see page 252, steps 4–7
1¼ cups heavy cream
14oz (400g) mango, and papaya,
  peeled and chopped
2 passion fruits

Method

1 Preheat the oven to 350°F (180°C). Line a baking sheet with parchment paper.

2 Take a 8in (20cm) round cake pan, and draw around it with a pencil on to the parchment paper. Invert so the pencil is on the underside. Spoon large tablespoons of the meringue evenly inside the circle, and smooth out with a palette knife.

3 Bake for 5 minutes, then reduce the temperature to 275°F (140°C) and cook for 1 hour 15 minutes, or until crisp and easy to remove from the parchment paper. Turn off the oven and leave the meringue inside to cool before transferring to a serving plate.

4 Just before serving, whip the cream until it holds its shape. Top the pavlova with the cream, then the chopped tropical fruits. Halve the passion fruits, squeeze out the juice and seeds, and pour over the pavlova just before serving.

PREPARE AHEAD The meringue base will keep in a dry, airtight container for 1 week. Fill just before serving.

BAKER'S TIP

Pavlovas do not keep very well, as the meringue base tends to go soggy after a few hours. However, to revitalize a leftover pavlova, try breaking it up into bite-sized chunks and folding with freshly whipped heavy cream and extra fruit.

Lemon Meringue Pie

With the sharpness of lemon combined with a smooth vanilla meringue topping, it is no wonder this pie is an American family favorite.

SERVES 8 | 30 MINS | 40–50 MINS

6 eggs, separated, at room temperature
3 tbsp cornstarch
1¾ cups sugar
juice of 3 lemons
1 tbsp finely grated lemon zest
½ tsp cream of tartar
½ tsp pure vanilla extract

Special equipment
9in (23cm) loose-bottomed tart pan
baking beans

Ingredients
3 tbsp butter, diced, plus extra for greasing
14oz (400g) store-bought pie dough
3 tbsp all-purpose flour, plus extra for dusting

Method

1 Preheat the oven to 400°F (200°C). Lightly grease the tart pan. Roll out the pie dough on a lightly floured surface and use it to line the pan.

2 Line the pie dough with parchment paper, then fill with baking beans. Place on a baking sheet and bake for 10–15 minutes, or until the pastry looks pale golden. Lift off the paper and beans, return to the oven, and bake for 3–5 minutes, or until the pastry is golden and dry. Transfer to a wire rack and leave to cool completely. Reduce the oven temperature to 350°F (180°C).

3 Place the egg yolks in a bowl and lightly beat. Combine the cornstarch, flour, and ½ cup of the sugar in a saucepan. Slowly add 1½ cups water and heat gently, stirring, until the sugar dissolves and there are no lumps. Increase the heat slightly and cook, stirring, for 3–5 minutes, or until the mixture starts to thicken.

4 Beat several spoonfuls of the hot mixture into the egg yolks. Pour this mixture into the pan and slowly bring to a boil, stirring constantly. Boil for 3 minutes, then stir in the lemon juice, zest, and butter. Continue boiling for a further 2 minutes, or until the mixture is thick and glossy, stirring constantly and scraping down the side of the pan as necessary. Remove the pan from the heat; cover to keep warm.

5 Whisk the egg whites in a large clean bowl until foamy. Sprinkle over the cream of tartar and whisk. Continue whisking, adding the remaining sugar, 1 tablespoon at a time. Add the vanilla with the last tablespoon of the sugar, whisking until the meringue is thick and glossy.

6 Pour the lemon filling into the pie crust, then top with the meringue, spreading it so it completely covers the filling right up to the pastry edge. Take care not to spill it over the pastry or the tart will be difficult to remove from the pan after baking.

7 Place the pie on a baking sheet, place in the oven, and bake for 12–15 minutes, or until the meringue is lightly golden. Place the pie on a wire rack and leave to cool completely before serving.

PREPARE AHEAD The unfilled pastry crust can be made 3 days in advance and stored in an airtight container.

BAKER'S TIP
The meringue topping of this pie has a tendency to slide around on top of the lemon filling, if you are not careful. Make sure that the meringue is touching the sides of the pastry crust around the entire pie before baking, as this will help to prevent it from dislodging.

Baked Alaska

The secret to this recipe is the cake base, which insulates the ice cream from the oven's heat when assembled and sealed properly.

SERVES 8–10 · **45–50 MINS** · **30–40 MINS**

Special equipment
8in (20cm) square cake pan
sugar thermometer (optional)
food processor with blade attachment

Ingredients
4 tbsp unsalted butter, plus extra for greasing
¾ cup all-purpose flour, plus extra for dusting

pinch of salt
4 eggs, at room temperature
⅔ cup sugar
1 tsp pure vanilla extract

For the filling
10oz (300g) strawberries
2–3 tbsp confectioner's sugar, to taste
3 pints (1.5 litres) vanilla ice cream

For the meringue
2 cups sugar, plus more for sprinkling
9 egg whites, at room temperature

Method
1 Preheat the oven to 350°F (180°C). Grease the pan, and sprinkle in 2 tablespoons flour. Turn the pan to coat the bottom and sides, then turn the pan upside down and tap to remove excess flour.

2 Sift the flour with the salt. Melt the butter in a small saucepan, and let cool. Beat the eggs with an electric mixer for a few seconds. Add the sugar, and beat at high speed for 5 minutes, or until the mixture is pale and thick. Beat in the vanilla extract.

3 Gently fold in the flour in stages, sifted over the egg mixture. Fold in the cooled, melted butter. Pour the cake mix into the pan. Bake in the oven for 30–40 minutes. Run a knife around the edge, and turn it out onto a wire rack. Peel off the paper and let cool.

4 Purée the strawberries in a food processor, then pour into a bowl. Stir in the confectioner's sugar. For the meringue, heat the sugar with 9fl oz (250ml) water in a pan, until dissolved. Boil until it reaches the hard ball stage. To test, remove the pan from the heat, take a teaspoon of syrup and let it cool for a few seconds, then take the syrup

between finger and thumb: it should form a ball. Alternatively, check if it registers 248°F (120°C) on a sugar thermometer.

5 Beat the egg whites until stiff peaks form. Pour in the hot syrup, beating constantly for 5 minutes, until the meringue is cool and stiff.

6 Butter a heatproof serving plate. Remove the ice cream from the freezer, and leave until soft enough to scoop. When the cake is cooled, use a serrated knife to cut the cake horizontally in 2 layers. Use one layer for the base and the other layer to make cake crumbs by pulsing it in a food processor.

7 Transfer the crumbs to a bowl and add 9fl oz (250ml) of the coulis. Blend to mix. Spread the remaining coulis over the cake.

8 Scoop the ice cream into balls, and place them in a layer on the cake. Scoop and arrange a second layer of ice-cream balls. Smooth the ice cream layers. Cover the top of the ice cream layer with the prepared strawberry cake crumbs. Using a metal spoon, spoon the meringue on top. Work quickly, as the ice cream must stay as firm as possible at this point before baking.

9 Spread the meringue over the top and sides to cover completely, and seal it to the serving plate to insulate the ice cream. Keep in the freezer for up to 2 hours. When ready to bake, preheat the oven to 425°F (220°C). Take the dessert from the freezer, sprinkle with sugar, and let stand for 1 minute. Bake for just 3–5 minutes, until lightly browned. Serve at once.

> ### BAKER'S TIP
> Baking a dessert filled with ice cream may seem like a foolish idea, but there are a few things you can do to ensure success. Make sure your cake base is thick enough, and that the ice cream is completely sealed in by the meringue, as these things will help to insulate the ice cream from the oven's heat.

Lemon Meringue Roulade

The traditional Lemon Meringue Pie filling is given a new twist in this impressive dinner party dessert.

SERVES 8 · **30 MINS** · **15 MINS** · **UP TO 8 WEEKS**

Special equipment
10 x 14in (25 x 35 cm) shallow baking pan or jelly roll pan

Ingredients
5 egg whites
1 cup sugar
½ tsp white wine vinegar
1 tsp cornstarch
½ tsp pure vanilla extract
1 cup heavy cream
4 tbsp good-quality lemon curd
confectioner's sugar, for dusting

1 Preheat the oven to 350°F (180°C) and line the baking pan with parchment paper.

2 Whisk the egg whites with an electric hand mixer until stiff peaks form.

3 Continue whisking at a slower speed and gradually add the sugar, a little at a time.

4 Gently fold in the vinegar, cornstarch, and vanilla, trying to keep all the air in the mixture.

5 Spread the mixture into the pan and bake in the center of the oven for 15 minutes.

6 Remove the meringue from the oven and allow to cool to room temperature.

7 Meanwhile, whisk the cream until thick but not stiff; it should remain unctuous.

8 Fold in the lemon curd until just well blended; a few ripples will enhance the roulade.

9 Sprinkle a fresh sheet of parchment paper with confectioner's sugar.

MERINGUES AND SOUFFLÉS

10 Carefully turn the cooled roulade out of the pan on to the sugared parchment.

11 Spread the lemon cream over the unbaked side of the roulade with a palette knife.

12 Roll the meringue up around the filling, being firm but not squeezing out the filling.

13 Place seam side down on a serving plate, cover, and chill. Sift over confectioner's sugar to serve. **PREPARE AHEAD** The meringue can be made up to 3 days in advance and stored, unfilled, in a dry, airtight container.

Meringue Roulade variations

Apricot Meringue Roulade

An impressive dessert that uses ingredients from the pantry.

SERVES 8 | **30 MINS** | **15–20 MINS** | **UP TO 8 WEEKS**

Special equipment
10 x 14in (25 x 35cm) jelly roll pan

Ingredients
4 large egg whites, at room temperature
pinch of salt
1 cup sugar
¼ cup sliced almonds
confectioner's sugar, for dusting
1¼ cups heavy cream
14oz (400g) can apricot halves
seeds and pulp from 2 passion fruits

Method
1 Preheat the oven to 375°F (190°C). Line the jelly roll pan with parchment paper. Place the egg whites in a bowl with the salt and whisk with an electric hand mixer until soft peaks form. Whisk in the sugar one tablespoon at a time until the mixture is stiff and shiny.

2 Spoon into the jelly roll pan and smooth into the corners. Scatter the sliced almonds over the top, then bake for 15–20 minutes, or until just firm to the touch and golden. Turn the meringue out onto a sheet of parchment paper dusted with confectioner's sugar, and leave to cool.

3 Meanwhile, place the cream in a bowl and whisk with an electric hand mixer until soft peaks form. Spread the cream over the meringue, then scatter over the apricots and passion fruit seeds. Roll the meringue up, starting from one short end and using the parchment paper to help you. When ready to serve, dust the roulade with more confectioner's sugar.

PREPARE AHEAD Make the meringue 3 days ahead and store, unfilled, in an airtight container.

Summer Fruit Meringue Roulade

Stuffed with seasonal fruits, this delicious roulade makes an ideal dessert for a summer buffet.

SERVES 8 | **25 MINS** | **15 MINS** | **UP TO 8 WEEKS**

Special equipment
10 x 14in (25 x 35cm) jelly roll pan

Ingredients
1 quantity meringue for roulade, see page 260, steps 1–6
1 cup heavy cream
9oz (250g) mixed summer fruits (strawberries, raspberries, cherries, blueberries), pitted, if necessary, and roughly chopped (see Baker's Tip)
confectioner's sugar, for dusting

Method
1 Whisk the cream until thick but not stiff. Place the cooled roulade on a piece of parchment dusted with confectioner's sugar.

2 Spread the cream over the unbaked side of the roulade with a palette knife. Sprinkle over the summer fruits. Roll the meringue up around the cream filling. Place seam side down on a serving plate, cover, and chill. Sift over confectioner's sugar to serve.

PREPARE AHEAD Make 3 days ahead and store, unfilled, in an airtight container.

BAKER'S TIP
Any soft fruits can be used to fill this summery dessert. The important thing is to cut them all to a uniform size, no more than ½-¾in (1.5cm). This will stop the roulade from appearing lumpy when it is rolled up, with large chunks of fruit bulging through the meringue base.

Chocolate and Pear Meringue Roulade

If you don't want to try fruit cake, make this rich, chocolatey roulade as an alternative Christmas dessert. ▶

SERVES 8 | **25 MINS** | **15 MINS** | **UP TO 8 WEEKS**

Special equipment
10 x 14in (25 x 35cm) jelly roll pan

Ingredients
5 large egg whites, at room temperature
1 cup sugar
½ tsp white wine vinegar
1 tsp cornstarch
½ tsp pure vanilla extract
¼ cup cocoa powder, sifted
1 cup heavy cream
14oz (410g) can pears in juice, drained and diced
confectioner's sugar, for dusting

Method
1 Preheat the oven to 350°F (180°C) and line the baking pan with parchment paper. Whisk the egg whites with an electric hand mixer until stiff peaks form. Continue whisking at a slower speed and gradually add the sugar, a little at a time. Gently fold in the vinegar, cornstarch, vanilla extract, and cocoa powder. Spread the mixture into the pan, smooth the surface, and bake in the center of the oven for 15 minutes.

2 Remove the meringue from the oven and allow to cool to room temperature. Meanwhile, whisk the cream until thick but not stiff. Turn the cooled roulade out of the pan on to another piece of parchment paper dusted with confectioner's sugar.

3 Spread the cream over the unbaked side of the roulade with a palette knife. Sprinkle over the pears. Roll the meringue up around the cream filling. Place seam side down on a serving plate, cover, and chill. Sift over confectioner's sugar to serve.

PREPARE AHEAD Make 3 days ahead and store, unfilled, in an airtight container.

MERINGUES AND SOUFFLÉS

Orange Soufflés

Soufflés are not difficult to make, but they do need a little care. This one is flavored with orange zest.

SERVES 4

20 MINS

12–15 MINS

4 WEEKS, UNBAKED

Special equipment
4 small ramekins

Ingredients
4 tbsp unsalted butter, melted
¼ cup sugar, plus extra for dusting
¼ cup all-purpose flour
1¼ cups milk
finely grated zest of 2 oranges
2 tbsp orange juice
3 eggs, separated, plus 1 egg white, at room temperature
confectioner's sugar

1 Place a baking sheet in the oven. Preheat to 400°F (200°C). Grease the ramekins.

2 Dust the insides of the buttered ramekins with sugar, making sure there are no gaps.

3 Add the flour to the butter and cook over low heat for 1 minute. Remove from the heat.

4 Add the milk, whisking to achieve a smooth sauce. Heat and stir, slowly bringing to a boil.

5 Simmer for 1–2 minutes, then remove from the heat and add the orange zest and juice.

6 Stir in all but 1 teaspoon of the sugar, stirring until all the sugar has dissolved.

7 When the mixture has cooled slightly, add the egg yolks to the sauce, beating in well.

8 Whisk the egg whites to medium peaks and beat in the remaining teaspoon of sugar.

9 Thoroughly mix 1 tablespoon of the egg whites into the sauce mixture to loosen it.

10 Now fold in the rest of the egg whites very gently, until all the ingredients are well mixed.

11 Pour the mixture into the ramekins so that it sits just above the rim of each ramekin.

12 Run a finger around the edge of the mix, for a "top hat" effect to help them rise straight.

13 Place on the hot baking sheet and bake for 12–15 minutes, or until the soufflés are golden and risen, but still a little runny in the center. Dust with a little confectioner's sugar and serve immediately.

Soufflé variations

Coffee Soufflés

Perfect served with coffee at the end of a special meal, the cardamom cream adds a Moorish flavor to the dish.

SERVES 6 | 30–35 MINS | 10–12 MINS

Special equipment
6 ramekins

Ingredients
1½ cups half-and-half
2 cardamom pods, lightly crushed
¼ cup coarsely ground coffee
1½ cups milk
4 egg yolks, at room temperature
⅔ cup sugar
⅓ cup all-purpose flour
⅓ cup Tia Maria, or other coffee liqueur
unsalted butter, to grease
6 egg whites, at room temperature
cocoa powder, to serve

Method

1 Put the cream and cardamom in a saucepan, and bring to a boil. Remove from the heat and infuse for 10–15 minutes, then strain, cover, and chill. At the same time, add the coffee to the milk, cover, and set aside to infuse for 10–15 minutes.

2 Bring the milk to a boil. Whisk the egg yolks with three-quarters of the sugar for 2–3 minutes. Whisk in the flour, then strain in the hot milk through a sieve until the mixture is smooth. Pour it back into the pan and bring it to a boil over medium heat, whisking constantly. Reduce the heat to low and cook for 2 minutes, whisking. Remove from the heat, and stir in the Tia Maria.

3 Preheat the oven to 400°F (200°C) and place a baking sheet to heat up. Brush butter into the ramekins to grease. Whisk the egg whites until stiff. Sprinkle in the remaining sugar, and whisk for 20 seconds to form a glossy meringue. Gently fold the meringue and coffee base together.

4 Divide the mix between the ramekins and run a finger around the top edge of the mix. Place the ramekins on the hot baking sheet. Bake for 10–12 minutes, until risen.

5 Sift cocoa powder over the top of the soufflé, and serve at once, with the spiced cardamom cream.

Cheese Soufflé

Any hard cheese can be used for this dish; pick one with a strong flavor.

SERVES 4 | 20 MINS | 30–35 MINS

Special equipment
1 quart (1.2-litre) soufflé dish

Ingredients
3 tbsp unsalted butter
¼ cup all-purpose flour
1 cup milk
salt and freshly ground black pepper
5oz aged Cheddar cheese, grated
½ tsp French mustard
5 large eggs, separated
1 tbsp grated Parmesan cheese

Method

1 Melt the butter in a small pan, stir in the flour until smooth, and cook over medium heat for 1 minute. Whisk in the milk until blended, then bring it to a boil, stirring, until thickened. Remove from the heat, season to taste, and stir in the cheese and mustard. Gradually stir in 4 of the egg yolks (save the remaining egg yolk for another recipe).

2 Preheat the oven to 375°F (190°C), and place a baking sheet to heat up. Whisk all the egg whites, until stiff peaks form. Stir 1 tablespoon of the egg whites into the cheese mixture to loosen it. Gently fold in the rest.

3 Pour the mixture into the dish, run a finger around the top edge of the mix, and sprinkle the Parmesan over it. Place the dish on the baking sheet, and bake for 25–30 minutes, or until puffed and golden brown. Serve at once with a green salad and crusty bread.

> **BAKER'S TIP**
> For perfect soufflés, always ensure you butter and sprinkle the sides of the ramekins with a sweet or savory dusting, to give the mix "grip" as it rises. Run your finger around the top edge of the mix so that it rises straight and high, like a "top hat." Also, always bake on a preheated baking sheet.

Raspberry Soufflés

Use only the sweetest, juiciest raspberries for this spectacular dish.

SERVES 6 | **20–25 MINS** | **10–12 MINS**

Special equipment
food processor with blade attachment
6 ramekins

Ingredients
unsalted butter, for greasing
½ cup sugar, plus extra for the ramekins
1lb 2oz (500g) raspberries
5 egg whites, at room temperature
2–3 tbsp confectioner's sugar, for sprinkling

For the Kirsch custard
1½ cups milk
¼ cup sugar
5 egg yolks, at room temperature
1 tbsp cornstarch
2–3 tbsp Kirsch

Method

1 For the custard, pour the milk into a saucepan and bring just to a boil over medium heat. Set aside ¼ of the milk. Add the sugar to the milk and stir until dissolved.

2 Put the yolks with the cornstarch into a bowl and whisk until smooth. Add the sweetened milk, whisking until just smooth. Cook over medium heat, stirring constantly, until thick. Remove from the heat. Stir in the reserved milk, strain it into a cold bowl, and let it cool. If it forms a skin, whisk to dissolve it. Stir in the Kirsch. Cover and refrigerate.

3 Brush the ramekins with butter and sprinkle with sugar. Preheat the oven to 375°F (190°C). Purée the raspberries with half the sugar. Work through a sieve. Whisk the egg whites until stiff. Add the remaining sugar and whisk until glossy. Add ¼ of the meringue to the purée and stir to combine. Add to the remaining meringue and fold in gently.

4 Spoon the mixture into the ramekins and run a finger around the top edge of the mix. Bake for 10–12 minutes, until puffed and lightly browned on top. Sift over confectioner's sugar and serve with the custard.

cheesecakes

Blueberry Ripple Cheesecake

The marbled effect on this cheesecake is simple to achieve and always looks impressive.

SERVES 8 · **20 MINS** · **40 MINS**

Special equipment
8in (20cm) round springform pan
food processor with
  blade attachment

Ingredients
4 tbsp unsalted butter, plus extra
  for greasing
5oz (140g) vanilla wafers (about
  34 cookies)
6oz (150g) blueberries
⅔ cup sugar, plus 3 tbsp extra
14oz (400g) cream cheese,
  at room temperature
9oz (250g) mascarpone,
  at room temperature
2 large eggs, plus 1 large egg yolk,
  at room temperature
½ tsp pure vanilla extract
2 tbsp all-purpose flour, sifted

For the compote
4oz (100g) blueberries
1 tbsp sugar
squeeze of lemon juice

1 Preheat the oven to 350°F (180°C). Grease the cake pan very well on its base and side.

2 Put the vanilla wafers in a large plastic bag and crush into fine crumbs with a rolling pin.

3 Melt the butter in a saucepan set over low heat; it should not begin to turn brown.

4 Add the crumbs to the saucepan, stir until coated in butter, and remove from the heat.

5 Press the crumbs into the base of the pan, pushing them down with the back of a spoon.

6 Put the blueberries and the 3 tbsp sugar in a food processor and purée until smooth.

7 Push the mixture through a nylon sieve (metal will taint it) into a small saucepan.

8 Bring to a boil, simmer for 3–5 minutes, or until thickened. Set aside.

9 Place the remaining sugar and the next 5 ingredients in the food processor.

10 Pulse the cream cheese mixture together until smooth and very well combined.

11 Pour the mixture on to the cookie base and smooth the top with a palette knife.

12 Drizzle over the berry jam and make swirls by drawing a metal skewer through the mix.

13 Boil a kettle of water. Put the cake in a deep roasting pan and wrap the sides with tin foil.

14 Pour hot water into the pan, to come halfway up the sides, to stop the cake from cracking.

15 Bake for 40 minutes, till set but a bit wobbly. Turn off the oven and wedge open the door.

16 After 1 hour, remove the cake and place on a wire rack. Remove the sides of the pan.

17 Slide 1 or 2 spatulas between the cookie base and the base of the pan.

18 Transfer the cheesecake to a serving plate or cake stand, and leave to cool completely.

19 Meanwhile, put all the ingredients for the compote in a small pan.

20 Heat the compote gently, stirring occasionally, until all the sugar dissolves.

21 Transfer to a pitcher to serve. **PREPARE AHEAD** Can be made 3 days in advance and chilled.

Baked Cheesecake variations

Chocolate Marble Cheesecake

This all-American favorite is dense, rich, and spectacular, making it an ideal dessert for entertaining.

SERVES 8–10 **35–40 MINS** **50–60 MINS**

Chilling time
4½–5 hrs

Special equipment
8in (20cm) springform pan

Ingredients
5 tbsp unsalted butter, plus extra for greasing
6oz (150g) vanilla wafers crushed or processed to crumbs (about 41 cookies)
6oz (150g) good-quality dark chocolate, chopped
1lb 2oz (500g) cream cheese, softened
⅔ cup sugar
1 tsp pure vanilla extract
2 large eggs, at room temperature

Method
1 Grease the pan with butter and chill. Add the butter to the cookie crumbs. Stir well and press the mixture onto the bottom and sides of the pan. Chill for 30–60 minutes, until firm.

2 Preheat the oven to 350°F (180°C). Place the chocolate in a heatproof bowl and set over a saucepan of simmering water. Allow to cool. Beat the cream cheese, until smooth. Add the sugar and vanilla, and beat just until smooth. Add the eggs, one at a time, beating well after each addition. Pour half the filling into the cookie base.

3 Mix the chocolate into the remaining filling. Spoon a ring of the chocolate filling over the plain filling. Using a knife or a metal skewer, swirl the fillings to make a marbled pattern. Bake for 50–60 minutes; the center should remain soft. Turn off the oven and leave the cheesecake inside until cool. Refrigerate for at least 4 hours. Run a knife around the side of the cheesecake to loosen it, remove the pan, and transfer to a serving plate.

PREPARE AHEAD The cheesecake can be made 3 days ahead and kept refrigerated; the flavor will mellow.

Vanilla Cheesecake

This rich yet light cheesecake is guaranteed to be a crowd pleaser.

SERVES 10–12 **20 MINS** **55 MINS**

Chilling time
6 hrs

Special equipment
9in (23cm) springform pan

Ingredients
4 tbsp unsalted butter, plus extra for greasing
8oz (225g), vanilla wafers finely crushed
1 tbsp brown sugar
1½lb (675g) cream cheese, at room temperature
4 large eggs (room temperature), separated
¾ cup sugar
1 tsp pure vanilla extract
16oz (1¾ cups) sour cream
kiwi fruit slices, to garnish

Method
1 Preheat the oven to 350°F (180°C). Grease the base of the pan and line with parchment paper. Melt the butter in a small saucepan over medium heat. Add the cookie crumbs and brown sugar and stir until blended. Press the crumbs over the base of the pan.

2 Combine the cream cheese, egg yolks, ⅔ cup of the sugar, and the vanilla in a bowl and beat until blended. In a separate bowl, beat the egg whites until stiff. Fold the egg whites into the cream cheese mixture. Pour the mixture into the pan and smooth the top.

3 Bake for 45 minutes, until just set in the middle. Remove from the oven and leave to stand for 10 minutes, or until it sinks back into the pan. Beat the sour cream and remaining sugar until the sugar has dissolved. Pour on top of the cake and smooth the surface.

4 Increase the oven temperature to 475°F (240°C), return to the oven, and continue baking for a further 5 minutes. Let cool on a wire rack, then cover and chill for at least 6 hours. To serve, garnish with slices of kiwi fruit.

PREPARE AHEAD Can be made 3 days ahead and kept chilled.

Ginger Cheesecake

Chopped ginger adds warmth to the zesty, smooth filling.

SERVES 8–10

40–45 MINS

50–60 MINS

Chilling time
4 hrs

Special equipment
8in (20cm) springform pan

Ingredients
5 tbsp unsalted butter, plus extra for greasing
6oz (150g) vanilla wafers (about 41 cookies)
1lb 2oz (500g) cream cheese
5oz (125g) pieces of preserved ginger in syrup,
 chopped, plus 3 tbsp syrup
finely grated zest of 1 lemon, plus 2 tsp juice
8fl oz (250ml) sour cream
⅔ cup sugar
1 tsp pure vanilla extract
4 large eggs, at room temperature
⅔ cup heavy cream (optional)

Method

1 Preheat the oven to 350°F (180°C). Beat the cream cheese in a bowl. Add all but 2 tablespoons of the ginger, ginger syrup, lemon zest and juice, sour cream, sugar, and vanilla. Beat until smooth. Add the eggs, one at a time, beating after each addition.

2 Pour the filling onto the base, and shake to level the surface. Place the pan on a baking sheet. Bake for 50–60 minutes. Turn off the oven but leave the cheesecake in there for 1½ hours. Then, chill for 4 hours.

3 Whip the cream, if using, to soft peaks. Run a knife around the cheesecake, then remove the pan. Swirl the cream on top. Scatter the reserved ginger on top before serving.

PREPARE AHEAD Can be made 3 days ahead and kept chilled.

BAKER'S TIP
When baking cheesecakes, there is always a danger that the surface will crack. To avoid this, allow the cheesecake to cool completely in the oven, so it deflates slowly, creating less chance of cracking.

German Cheesecake

The use of quark here is typical of German cooking. If you cannot find any, substitute it with low-fat cottage cheese puréed until smooth.

SERVES 8–12 | 30 MINS | 85–95 MINS

Chilling time
30 mins

Special equipment
9in (22cm) springform cake pan, ideally 1½in (4cm) deep
Food processor with blade attachment
Baking beans (optional)

Ingredients
1¾ cups all-purpose flour
¼ cup sugar
1 stick, plus 3 tbsp unsalted butter, diced
1 large egg yolk, at room temperature

For the filling
1lb 10oz (750g) quark, or fat-free cottage cheese processed until smooth
½ cup sugar
4 large eggs (room temperature), separated
finely grated zest and juice of 1 lemon
2 tsp pure vanilla extract

Method

1 Preheat the oven to 350°F (180°C). Line the bottom of the pan with parchment paper. To make the pastry, combine the flour, sugar, and butter in a food processor until they form fine breadcrumbs. Add the egg yolk and 2 tablespoons of water and bring together to form a dough. If it is dry add water, 1 tbsp at a time. Roll into a smooth ball, wrap in plastic wrap, and refrigerate for 30 minutes to allow the pastry to relax.

2 Once the dough has rested, roll it out to about ¼in (5mm) thick and line the cake pan with it. The pastry should be large enough to hang over the edge. Place another disk of parchment paper inside the pastry and weigh it down with baking beans, or raw rice. Chill for 30 minutes, to allow the pastry to rest. Bake for 20 minutes, then remove the beans and paper and bake for a further 5 minutes.

3 Meanwhile, blend the quark or processed cottage cheese, sugar, egg yolks, lemon zest and juice, and vanilla together until smooth. In a separate bowl, whisk the egg whites to soft peaks. Fold the egg whites gently into the cream cheese mixture until thoroughly blended. Pour the filling into the baked pastry crust.

4 Bake for a further 60–70 minutes. The cake is ready when golden brown and puffed up, often with a slight cracking of the surface. Turn the oven off and, leaving the door open, let the cheesecake cool in the oven for at least 30 minutes before allowing it to cool fully at room temperature for 1 hour. It will sink a little. Use a sharp knife to trim any excess pastry for an even finish. Serve slightly chilled or at room temperature, plain or with cream.

PREPARE AHEAD The pastry shell can be blind baked the day before and stored in an airtight container. The cheesecake can be stored in the refrigerator for 2 days, although the pastry will soften.

BAKER'S TIP
The whisked egg whites in this cheesecake make the filling puff up during baking. It always collapses down slightly as it cools, which can sometimes lead to a cracking of the surface of the cheesecake. Leaving it to cool in the oven helps prevent this.

Lemon Cheesecake

This no-cook cheesecake doesn't need baking, and thus produces a lighter, more delicate result.

SERVES 8   **30 MINS**

Chilling time
4 hrs, or overnight

Special equipment
9in (22cm) springform pan

Ingredients
9oz (250g) vanilla wafers
7 tbsp unsalted butter, diced
1 tbsp powdered, unflavored gelatin
finely grated zest and juice of 2
 small lemons
12oz (350g) cream cheese
¾ cup sugar
1¼ cups heavy cream

1 Line the pan with parchment paper. Put the cookies into a bag and crush with a rolling pin.

2 Melt the butter and combine it with the crushed cookies, mixing together well.

3 Press the cookie base firmly into the base of the pan, until a flat surface is achieved. Chill.

4 In a small heatproof bowl, soak the gelatin in the lemon juice for 5 minutes to soften.

5 Place the bowl over a pan of hot water and stir until the gelatin melts. Set aside to cool.

6 Beat the cream cheese, sugar, and lemon zest together until smooth.

7 In a separate bowl, whisk the cream to soft peaks. Make sure it is not stiff.

8 Beat the gelatin mixture into the cream cheese mixture and mix well to combine.

9 Gently fold the whipped cream into the cheese mixture. Be careful not to lose volume.

10 Pour the cheesecake filling on top of the cookie base, scraping it with a spatula.

11 Smooth the top well with a damp palette knife, or the back of a damp spoon.

12 Chill for at least 4 hours, or overnight. Run a sharp, thin knife around the inside of the pan.

13 Turn the cheesecake out gently onto a plate, making sure to remove the paper before cutting.
PREPARE AHEAD The cheesecake can be made 2 days ahead and stored in the refrigerator.

No-cook Cheesecake variations

Strawberry Cheesecake

This no-cook cheesecake takes very little time to make and is given a delicious twist with the use of mascarpone cheese.

SERVES 8–10 | 15 MINS | 5 MINS

Chilling time
at least 1 hr

Special equipment
8in (20cm) tart pan with removable bottom

Ingredients
4 tbsp unsalted butter
4oz (100g) good-quality dark chocolate,
  broken into pieces
6oz (150g) vanilla wafers, crushed
  (about 41 cookies)
14oz (400g) mascarpone,
  at room temperature
finely grated zest and juice of 2 limes
2–3 tbsp confectioner's sugar,
  plus extra for dusting
8oz (225g) strawberries, hulled and halved

Method

1 Melt the butter and chocolate in a small saucepan over very gentle heat, and stir in the cookie crumbs. Transfer the mixture to the pan and press it down firmly and evenly. Beat the mascarpone in a bowl with the lime zest and juice. Stir in the confectioner's sugar, to taste. Spread the cheese mixture over the cookie base and refrigerate for at least 1 hour.

2 To serve, arrange the strawberries over the cheesecake. Dust with confectioner's sugar and cut into slices.

PREPARE AHEAD The cheesecake can be made 1 day in advance, covered, and chilled until required.

BAKER'S TIP
Try using different cookie bases to complement your choice of filling. I used ginger biscuits for the Marmalade and Ginger Cheesecake (see right), but Oreos or other chocolate cookies work well with a chocolate filling, and crushed shortbread cookies would complement the strawberries well here.

Marmalade and Ginger Cheesecake

Spicy preserved ginger and zesty marmalade revive this old classic.

SERVES 8–10 | 30 MINS | 5 MINS

Chilling time
at least 4 hrs, or overnight

Special equipment
9in (22cm) springform pan

Ingredients
7 tbsp unsalted butter, diced
9oz (250g) gingersnaps, crushed
1 tbsp unflavored powdered gelatin
finely grated zest and juice of 2 small oranges
12oz (350g) cream cheese, at room temperature
¾ cup sugar
2 heaped tbsp orange marmalade
1 piece of preserved ginger in syrup, drained,
  and finely chopped
1¼ cups heavy cream

Method

1 Line the pan with parchment paper. Melt the butter and combine it with the crushed cookies, mixing well. Press the cookie base firmly into the cake pan. Cover, and chill.

2 Meanwhile, in a saucepan, combine the gelatin and orange juice. Heat gently, and stir until the gelatin is dissolved. Let cool.

3 In a large mixing bowl, beat the cream cheese, sugar, orange zest, marmalade, and ginger together until smooth. Whisk the cream to soft peaks. Beat the cooled gelatin mixture into the cream cheese mixture and mix well. Fold in the cream.

4 Pour the cheesecake filling on top of the cookie base and smooth the top with a palette knife. Chill the cheesecake for at least 4 hours. To serve run a sharp, thin knife around the inside of the pan to loosen the sides of the cheesecake. Turn out gently on to a plate. Remove the paper before cutting.

PREPARE AHEAD Cover the cheesecake and chill for 2 days.

Cherry Cheesecake

Light and luscious, this is a great dessert for any time of year.

SERVES 6 · **30 MINS** · **5 MINS**

Chilling time
at least 2 hrs

Special equipment
8in (20cm) round springform cake pan

Ingredients
5 tbsp unsalted butter, plus extra for greasing
7oz (200g) vanilla wafers, crushed
2 x 8oz (250g) tubs ricotta cheese
¼ cup sugar
finely grated zest and juice of 4 lemons
½ cup heavy cream
1 tbsp powdered gelatin
14oz (400g) can black cherries or morello
   cherries in juice

Method

1 Grease and line the cake pan with parchment paper. Melt the butter in a saucepan, add the cookie crumbs, and stir well. Transfer the mixture to the pan, pressing down firmly with the back of a spoon.

2 Mix together the ricotta, sugar, and zest. In a separate bowl, whisk the cream to soft peaks. Add to the ricotta mixture and beat with a wooden spoon until well combined.

3 Mix the lemon juice and gelatin in a small bowl, then sit the bowl over a pan of simmering water and stir until the gelatin dissolves. Add to the ricotta mixture and stir well. Pour the mixture on top of the cookie crumbs, spreading evenly. Place in the refrigerator for 2 hours, or until set and firm.

4 In a pan, bring the cherry juice to a boil, then simmer until reduced by about three-quarters. Leave to cool, then arrange the cherries on top of the cheesecake, spoon over the sauce, and serve.

PREPARE AHEAD Cover the cheesecake and chill for 2 days.

Crostata di ricotta

Ricotta is mixed with candied peel and almonds, and baked in a sweet lemon pastry crust in this Italian classic. The fresher the cheese, the better.

SERVES 8–10

35–40 MINS

1–1¼ HOURS

Chilling time
45–60 mins

Special equipment
9-10in (23-25cm) springform pan

Ingredients
1 stick, plus 4 tbsp unsalted butter
1¾ cups all-purpose flour, plus extra for dusting
finely grated zest of 1 lemon
¼ cup sugar
4 large egg yolks, at room temperature
pinch of salt
1 large egg, for glazing

For the filling
2¾lb (1.25kg) ricotta cheese
½ cup sugar
1 tbsp all-purpose flour
1 tsp salt
finely grated zest of 1 orange
2 tbsp chopped candied orange peel
1 tsp pure vanilla extract
⅓ cup golden raisins
¼ cup sliced almonds
4 large egg yolks, at room temperature

Method

1 Pound the butter between 2 sheets of parchment paper with a rolling pin, to soften. Sift the flour on to a work surface and make a large well in the center. Put the lemon zest, sugar, butter, egg yolks, and salt into the well. Using your fingertips, work together the ingredients until well mixed. Gradually draw in the flour, and press the dough into a ball.

2 Lightly flour the work surface, then knead the dough for 1-2 minutes until very smooth. Shape into a ball, wrap in plastic wrap, and chill for 30 minutes. Grease the pan. Lightly flour the work surface and roll out ¾ of the dough to make a 14-15in (35–37cm) round. Roll up the dough around the rolling pin, then drape it over the pan. Press it well into the bottom of the pan, and gently up the side. Trim the excess dough. Chill the shell, together with the remaining dough and trimmings, for 15 minutes.

3 Place the ricotta in a large bowl and beat in the sugar, flour, and half the salt. Add the orange zest, candied peel, vanilla, golden raisins, almonds, and egg yolks. Beat the mixture together thoroughly to combine. Spoon the filling into the chilled pastry shell. Tap the pan on the work surface to eliminate any air pockets. Smooth the top of the filling, using the back of a wooden spoon.

4 Press any dough trimmings into the remaining dough and roll it into a 10in (25cm) round on a floured surface. Cut it into strips ½in (1cm) wide and use to lattice the top of the pie. Trim off the overhanging ends of dough, so that the pastry strips are even with the edge of the shell.

5 Lightly beat the whole egg with the remaining salt. Glaze the ends of the strips, then seal to the edge. Brush the lattice with the glaze and chill until firm, 15–30 minutes. Preheat the oven to 350°F (180°C) and put a baking sheet near the bottom of the oven.

6 Bake on the heated baking sheet until the top is firm and golden brown, 1–1¼ hours. Let cool in its pan until just warm, then remove the side of the pan and let cool completely. Transfer to a large serving plate, cut into wedges, and serve.

PREPARE AHEAD The cheesecake can be made up to 1 day ahead and kept refrigerated, though the texture will not be as light.

BAKER'S TIP

This traditional Italian version of the cheesecake uses ricotta for a very light texture and taste. The ricotta must be fresh and of the very best quality for perfect results, so buy it from an Italian delicatessen.

sweet
tarts
& pies

Normandy Pear Tart

This almond cream-filled fruit tart is a signature dish of Normandy, France, where they grow wonderful pears.

SERVES 6–8 | **40–45 MINS** | **37–45 MINS**

Chilling time
45 mins

Special equipment
9–10in (23–25cm) tart pan
food processor with
  blade attachment

Ingredients
1⅓ cups all-purpose flour, plus extra
  for dusting
3 large egg yolks, room temperature
¼ cup sugar

pinch of salt
5 tbsp unsalted butter, plus extra
  for greasing
½ tsp pure vanilla extract

For the almond cream
1 cup whole blanched almonds
1 stick, plus 1 tbsp unsalted butter
½ cup sugar
1 egg, plus 1 egg yolk

1 tbsp Kirsch
2 tbsp all-purpose flour, sifted

For the pears
3–4 ripe pears
juice of 1 lemon

For the glaze
⅓ cup apricot jam
2–3 tbsp Kirsch or water

1 To make the pastry, sift the flour on to a work surface. Make a well in the center.

2 Add the egg yolks, sugar, and salt to the well. Using a rolling pin, pound the butter.

3 Add the butter and vanilla. Using your fingertips, work the ingredients until mixed.

 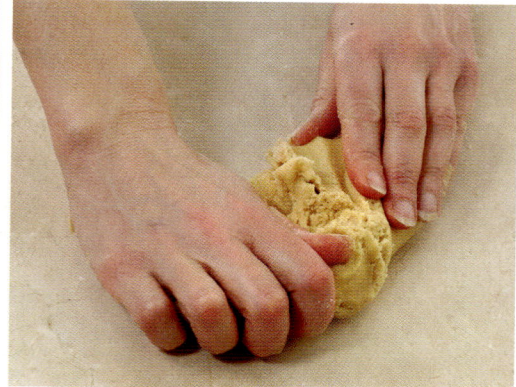 

4 Work the flour into the other ingredients until crumbs form. If dry, add a little water.

5 Flour a work surface, then knead the dough for 1–2 minutes. Wrap, and chill for 30 minutes.

6 Grease the pan. On a floured surface, roll the dough to a round, 2in (5cm) larger than the pan.

7 Roll the dough around the rolling pin, then unroll it over the pan and use to line the case.

8 Prick the bottom with a fork. Chill for at least 15 minutes, until firm.

9 Preheat the oven to 400°F (200°C). Grind the almonds to a "flour" in the food processor.

10 With an electric hand mixer, beat the butter and sugar for 2–3 minutes, until fluffy.

11 Gradually add the eggs, beating well after each addition.

12 Add the Kirsch, then gently stir in the almonds and flour until well blended.

13 Peel and core the pears, cut into neat wedges, and toss with the lemon juice.

14 Spoon the almond cream into the pastry shell, and spread evenly with a palette knife.

15 Place the pears in a spiral pattern. Set the pan on a baking sheet. Bake for 12–15 minutes.

16 Reduce the heat to 350°F (180°C), and bake for 25–30 minutes, until the almond cream sets.

17 Make a glaze by melting the jam with the Kirsch, and working it through a sieve.

18 Cool and unmold the tart, then brush with the glaze. Serve at room temperature.
STORE Best eaten the same day but can be kept up to 2 days in an airtight container.

Almond Cream Tart variations

Normandy Peach Tart

When pears are not in season, use the very ripest of the summer's peaches in this version for a wonderfully indulgent dessert.

SERVES 6–8 **40–45 MINS** **37–45 MINS**

Chilling time
45 mins

Special equipment
9–10in (23–25cm) tart pan
food processor with blade attachment

Ingredients
1 sweet pastry shell, see page 286, steps 1–8
1 cup whole blanched almonds
9 tbsp unsalted butter
½ cup sugar
1 large egg, plus 1 large egg yolk
1 tbsp Kirsch
2 tbsp all-purpose flour, sifted
2¼lb (1kg) ripe peaches
⅓ cup apricot jam
2–3 tbsp Kirsch or water

Method

1 Make the pastry shell. Preheat the oven to 400°F (200°C). Heat a baking sheet in the bottom of the oven. For the almond cream, grind the almonds to a "flour" in the food processor. Beat the butter and sugar until fluffy. Add the eggs and egg yolk, beating well. Add the Kirsch, then stir in the almonds and flour. Spoon into the pastry shell.

2 Immerse the peaches in a pan of boiling water, leave for 10 seconds, then transfer to a bowl of cold water. Cut each peach in half, remove the pit, and peel off the skin. Cut each half into thin slices and arrange on the almond cream.

3 Set the pan on the baking sheet, and bake for 12–15 minutes. Reduce the oven heat to 350°F (180°C), and bake for another 25–30 minutes, until the almond cream is puffed up and set. Leave to cool in the pan.

4 Make a glaze by melting the jam with the Kirsch, and work through a sieve. Unmold the tart, then brush with the glaze.

STORE Best eaten the same day but can be kept for 2 days in an airtight container.

BAKER'S TIP

Almond cream makes a delicious filling, and its flavor pairs well with certain fruits. Stone fruits such as peaches, nectarines, cherries, and plums make the best flavor pairings with almonds, but play around by adding apples, raspberries, or gooseberries.

Prune and Almond Tart

Prunes and brandy are a classic combination in French cuisine and work especially well with the almond flavor of this filling.

MAKES 8 SLICES **20 MINS** **45 MINS**

Chilling time
30 mins

Special equipment
food processor with blade attachment
9in (23cm) tart pan with removable bottom
baking beans

Ingredients
1⅓ cups all-purpose flour, plus extra for dusting
1 tbsp sugar
6 tbsp unsalted butter, chilled
1 small egg

For the filling
7oz (200g) pitted prunes
2 tbsp brandy
1 cup sliced almonds, toasted
⅓ cup sugar
2 large eggs, plus 1 large egg yolk
1 tbsp finely grated orange zest
few drops of almond extract
2 tbsp unsalted butter, softened
½ cup heavy cream

Method

1 Place the flour, sugar, and butter into a food processor and pulse until it forms crumbs. Add the egg, and process until the pastry forms a ball. Roll out on a floured surface and use to line the tart pan. Chill for at least 30 minutes.

2 Preheat the oven to 375°F (190°C). Line the tart dough with parchment paper and baking beans. Bake for 10 minutes, then remove the paper and beans, and bake for a further 5 minutes. Cool on a wire rack.

3 Reduce the oven temperature to 350°F (180°C). Place the prunes in a saucepan, cover with water, and add the brandy. Simmer for 5 minutes, then turn off the heat and set aside. Place half the sliced almonds with the sugar in a food processor, and pulse until finely ground. Add the eggs, egg yolk, orange zest, almond extract, butter, and cream, and process until smooth.

4 Drain the prunes, and cut any large ones in half. Pour the almond cream into the tart, and arrange the prunes on top. Scatter the remaining sliced almonds on top, and bake for 30 minutes, or until just set. Serve with cream or ice cream.

STORE Best eaten the same day, but can be kept for 2 days in an airtight container.

Almond and Peach Tart

This easy tart is even quicker with store-bought pastry.

| SERVES 8 | 20 MINS | 30 MINS | UP TO 8 WEEKS |

Special equipment
5 x 14½in (12 x 36cm) rectangular tart pan

Ingredients
¼ cup all-purpose flour, sifted, plus extra for dusting
9oz (250g) store-bought pie dough, or see page 290, step 1
7 tbsp unsalted butter, at room temperature
½ cup sugar
2 large eggs, at room temperature
1 cup ground almonds
4 peaches, halved and pitted
confectioner's sugar, for dusting

Method

1 Preheat the oven to 400°F (200°C). Put a baking sheet in the oven to heat up. On a surface lightly dusted with flour, roll out the dough to a thickness of about ¼in (5mm), then use to line the pan. Trim off the excess dough and set aside.

2 Place the butter and sugar in a bowl and beat with an electric hand mixer until creamy, then beat in the eggs. Mix in the ground almonds and flour until well combined, then smooth into the pie dough. Press the peach halves cut-side down into the almond mixture. Sit the pan on the hot baking sheet, then bake for 30 minutes or until the almond mixture is golden brown and cooked through.

3 Serve warm, or leave to cool completely, dusted with confectioner's sugar.

STORE Best eaten the same day, but can be kept for 2 days in an airtight container.

Bakewell Tart

With its almond cream topping and buttery pastry crust, this version of an English teatime classic can be served warm with cream as a dessert.

SERVES 6–8 | **30 MINS** | **60–65 MINS** | **12 WEEKS, PIE SHELL**

Chilling time
1 hr

Special equipment
9in (22cm) tart pan
food processor with blade attachment (optional)
baking beans

Ingredients
1¼ cups all-purpose flour, sifted, plus extra for dusting
7 tbsp unsalted butter, chilled and diced

¼ cup sugar
1 large egg yolk
finely grated zest of ½ lemon

For the filling
1 stick, plus 1 tbsp unsalted butter, softened
½ cup sugar
3 large eggs, at room temperature
½ tsp almond extract
1¼ cups ground almonds
⅓ cup good-quality raspberry jam
¼ cup sliced almonds
confectioner's sugar, to serve

Method

1 To make the pastry, rub the flour and butter together until they form fine crumbs, or pulse-blend in a food processor. Stir in the sugar. Beat the egg yolk with the lemon zest and add to the crumbs, bringing the mixture together to form a soft dough. Wrap in plastic wrap and chill for 1 hour.

2 Preheat the oven to 350°F (180°C). Roll out the pastry on a well floured surface to a thickness of no more than ⅛in (3mm). Should it begin to crumble, bring it together with your hands. Use it to line the pan, leaving an overlapping edge of at least ¾in (2cm). Prick the base all over with a fork. Line the pastry shell with parchment paper and weigh it down with baking beans.

3 Place the pan on a baking sheet and blind bake it for 20 minutes. Remove the beans and the paper and return it to the oven for a further 5 minutes if the center still looks a little uncooked.

4 To make the filling, cream together the butter and sugar until pale and fluffy. Beat in the eggs and almond extract until well combined. Fold in the ground almonds to form a thick paste.

5 Spread the jam over the base of the cooked crust. Pour the almond cream over the jam layer and use a palette knife to spread evenly. Scatter with the almonds.

6 Bake in the center of the oven for 40 minutes, until golden brown. Remove from the oven and allow to cool for 5 minutes. Then take a small, sharp knife and use it to trim the excess pastry from the edges of the tart, being careful to cut down and away from the tart so that no crumbs go on to the surface of the tart. Allow to cool before dusting with confectioner's sugar to serve.

STORE The baked tart will keep in an airtight container for 2 days.

PREPARE AHEAD The unfilled pastry shell can be prepared ahead, and stored in an airtight container for up to 3 days or frozen for 12 weeks.

BAKER'S TIP

Leaving an overlapping edge to the pastry allows you to trim after baking for a neat, professional finish. When trimming, be careful to cut down and away from the tart, so that no crumbs fall on the surface.

Strawberry Tart

Master the basics of this fresh fruit tart and you can adapt it by replacing the strawberries with other soft fruit.

SERVES 6–8 | **40 MINS** | **20–25 MINS** | **12 WEEKS, TART CASE**

Chilling time
1 hr

Special equipment
9in (22cm) tart pan
baking beans

Ingredients
1¼ cups all-purpose flour, plus extra
  for dusting
7 tbsp unsalted butter, chilled
  and diced
¼ cup sugar
2 large egg yolks
½ tsp pure vanilla extract
6 tbsp red currant jelly, for glazing

For the crème pâtissière
½ cup sugar
½ cup cornstarch
2 large eggs, at room temperature
1 tsp pure vanilla extract
1¾ cups whole milk
10oz (300g) strawberries, washed
  and thickly sliced

1 In a bowl, rub the flour and butter together until they form fine crumbs. Stir in the sugar.

2 Beat the egg yolks with the vanilla extract and add them to the flour mixture.

3 Bring together to form a soft dough, wrap in plastic wrap, and chill for 1 hour.

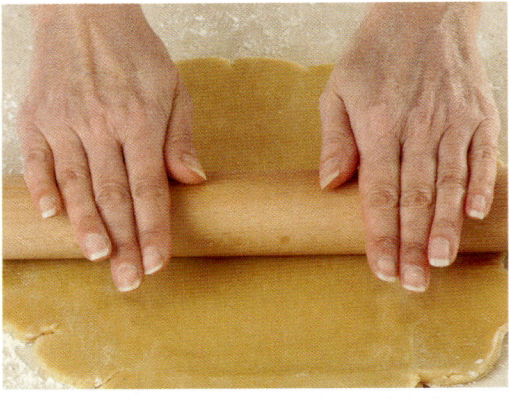

4 Preheat the oven to 350°F (180°C). Roll out the pastry to ⅛in (3mm) thick.

5 Being fragile, it may crumble. If so, bring it together with your hands and gently knead.

6 Use the rolled out pastry to line the pan, leaving an overlapping edge of ¾in (2cm).

7 Use a pair of scissors to trim any excess pastry that hangs down further than this.

8 Prick the pastry base all over with a fork, to prevent air bubbles forming during baking.

9 Carefully line the pastry shell with parchment paper.

SWEET TARTS AND PIES

10 Scatter baking beans over the paper. Place on a baking sheet and bake for 20 minutes.

11 Remove the beans and paper, and bake for 5 minutes more. Trim any excess pastry.

12 Melt the jelly with 1 scant tablespoon water, and brush over the pastry shell. Leave to cool.

13 For the crème pâtissière, beat the sugar, cornstarch, eggs, and vanilla in a bowl.

14 In a heavy saucepan, bring the milk to a boil and take it off the heat just as it bubbles.

15 Pour the hot milk on to the egg mixture, whisking all the time.

16 Return the custard to a pan and bring to a boil over medium heat, whisking constantly.

17 When the custard thickens, reduce heat to low and continue to cook for 2–3 minutes.

18 Turn into a bowl, cover the surface with plastic wrap, and leave it to cool.

19 Beat the crème pâtissière and spread it over the pastry shell. Top with the strawberries.

20 Heat the jelly glaze again and brush over the strawberries, then leave to set.

21 Remove from the pan to serve. **STORE** Best eaten on the day but will keep chilled overnight.

Crème Pâtissière Tart variations

Raspberry Tart with Chocolate Cream

A fruit tart with a twist, here chocolate is baked into and brushed over the pastry shell, and the crème pâtissière is enriched with melted dark chocolate—a perfect partner for fresh raspberries.

| SERVES 6–8 | 40 MINS | 20–25 MINS | 12 WEEKS, PASTRY |

Chilling time
1 hr

Special equipment
9in (22cm) tart pan
baking beans

Ingredients
1 cup all-purpose flour, plus extra for dusting
¼ cup cocoa powder
7 tbsp unsalted butter, chilled and diced
¼ cup sugar
2 large egg yolks
½ tsp pure vanilla extract
½ cup sugar
½ cup cornstarch, sifted
2 large eggs, at room temperature
1 tsp pure vanilla extract
1¾ cups whole milk
6oz (175g) dark chocolate, chopped
14oz (400g) raspberries
confectioner's sugar, to dust

Method

1 Rub the flour, cocoa powder, and butter together until they resemble fine crumbs. Stir in the sugar. Beat the egg yolk with the vanilla extract and add it to the flour mixture, bringing it together to form a soft dough. Add a little cold water if the mixture seems too stiff. Wrap in plastic wrap. Chill for 1 hour.

2 Preheat the oven to 350°F (180°C). Roll the pastry out to a thickness of ⅛in (3mm). Use it to line the pan, leaving an overlapping edge of ¾in (2cm); trim excess with scissors. Prick the base all over with a fork.

3 Line the pastry with parchment paper and add baking beans. Place on a baking sheet and bake for 20 minutes. Remove the beans and paper and return it to the oven for another 5 minutes. Trim excess pastry.

4 For the crème pâtissière, beat together the sugar, cornstarch, eggs, and 1 teaspoon vanilla extract. In a pan, bring the milk and 4oz (100g) of the chocolate to a boil, whisking all the time. Take it off the heat just as it starts to bubble up. Pour the milk onto the egg mixture, whisking all the time.

5 Return to the cleaned-out pan and bring to a boil over medium heat, whisking. When it thickens, reduce the heat to its lowest and cook for 2–3 minutes, whisking. Turn into a bowl, cover the surface with plastic wrap to prevent a skin forming, and leave to cool.

6 Melt the remaining chocolate in a bowl set over a pan of simmering water and brush around the inside of the crust. Leave to set. Beat the cold crème pâtissière with a wooden spoon and transfer into the crust. Arrange the raspberries over, remove from the pan, and dust with confectioner's sugar.

STORE Best eaten the same day it is made, this will store in the refrigerator overnight.

Fruit Tartlets

Any mix of fruits will look attractive; choose whatever is in season.

SERVES 8   40–45 MINS   11–13 MINS   12 WEEKS, PASTRY

Chilling time
1 hr

Special equipment
8 x 4in (10cm) tartlet pans

Ingredients
1⅓ cups all-purpose flour, plus extra for dusting
4 large egg yolks
⅓ cup sugar
½ tsp salt
½ tsp pure vanilla extract
6 tbsp unsalted butter, diced,
  plus extra for greasing

For the filling
1½ cups milk
1 vanilla pod or 2 tsp pure vanilla extract
5 large egg yolks, at room temperature
¼ cup sugar
¼ cup all-purpose flour
1lb 2oz (500g) mixed fresh fruit, such as kiwi fruit,
  raspberries, grapes, peaches
⅓ cup apricot jam or red currant jelly, for glazing

Method

1 Sift the flour on to a work surface and make a well in the center. Add the egg yolks, sugar, salt, vanilla, and butter. Work the ingredients in the well until thoroughly mixed, then draw in the flour until coarse crumbs form. Press the dough into a ball, and knead for 2 minutes, until smooth. Wrap in plastic wrap, and chill for 30 minutes.

2 Bring the milk to a boil in a medium saucepan with the split-open vanilla pod, if using. Remove the pan from the heat, cover, and let stand for 10–15 minutes. In a bowl, whisk together the egg yolks, sugar, and flour. Whisk in the hot milk. Return the mixture to the cleaned-out pan and cook over low heat, whisking constantly, until the flour has cooked and the cream is thick. Simmer over low heat for 2 minutes.

3 Transfer the pastry cream to another bowl and remove the vanilla pod if using, or stir in the vanilla extract. Press plastic wrap over the surface to prevent a skin from forming. Let cool.

4 Grease the tartlet pans. Lightly flour a work surface. Roll out the dough to ⅛in (3mm) thick. Group the pans together, with their edges nearly touching. Roll the dough loosely around the rolling pin and drape it over the pans so all are covered. Roll the rolling pin over the tops of the pans to remove excess dough. Press up the dough edges to form a deep shell. Set the tartlet pans on a baking sheet and prick the dough with the fork. Chill for 30 minutes.

5 Preheat the oven to 400°F (200°C). Line each tartlet shell with a piece of foil, pressing it down well. Bake for 6–8 minutes, then remove the foil and bake for 5 minutes longer. Transfer to a wire rack to cool. When cold, remove each shell from its pan.

6 Peel and slice the kiwi. Peel and slice the peaches. Melt the jam or jelly with 2–3 tablespoons water in a saucepan. Work it through a sieve. Brush the inside of each tartlet shell with the glaze. Half fill each shell with the cooled pastry cream, smoothing the top with the back of a spoon. Arrange the fruit on top and brush with the jam glaze.

STORE These will keep in an airtight container in the refrigerator for 2 days.

BAKER'S TIP
Crème pâtissière is one of the most useful sweet recipes to master. Once you get the hang of it, it is very impressive to serve. For a lighter finish to the pastry cream, fold about 3½fl oz (100ml) whipped heavy cream into the cooled crème pâtissière.

Tarte aux pommes

This French classic uses two types of apples: those that cook down to a purée, and those that keep their shape.

MAKES 8 SLICES — **20 MINS** — **45–55 MINS** — **12 WEEKS, PIE SHELL**

Chilling time
30 mins

Special equipment
9in (23cm) fluted tart pan
baking beans

Ingredients

1 x 9-inch (23cm) store-bought pie dough
all-purpose flour, for dusting
4 tbsp unsalted butter
1lb 10oz (750g) cooking apples, peeled, cored,
    and chopped (such as Braeburn, Granny Smith,
    or Honeycrisp)
½ cup sugar
finely grated zest and juice of ½ lemon
2 tbsp Calvados or brandy
2 dessert apples (such as Fuji, Gala, or McIntosh)
2 tbsp apricot jam, sieved

Method

1 Roll the pastry out on a lightly floured surface and line the pan. Trim around the top of the pan and prick the pastry base with a fork. Chill the pastry crust for at least 30 minutes.

2 Preheat the oven to 400°F (200°C). Line the pastry crust with parchment paper and fill with baking beans. Bake for 15 minutes. Remove the paper and beans, then return to the oven for another 5 minutes, or until the pastry is a light golden color.

3 Melt the butter in a saucepan and add the cooking apples. Cover and cook over low heat, stirring occasionally, for 15 minutes, or until soft and mushy.

4 Push the cooked apple through a sieve to produce a smooth purée, then return it to the saucepan. Reserve 1 tablespoon sugar and add the rest to the apple purée, then stir in the lemon zest and Calvados. Return the pan to the heat and simmer, stirring continuously until it thickens.

5 Spoon the purée into the pastry crust. Peel, core, and thinly slice the dessert apples and arrange on top of the purée. Brush with the lemon juice and sprinkle with the reserved sugar.

6 Bake for 30–35 minutes, or until the apple slices have softened and are starting to turn pale golden. Use a small, sharp knife to trim the excess pastry for a neat edge (see Baker's Tip, page 290).

7 Warm the apricot jam and brush it over the top. Cut into slices and serve.

STORE The baked tart will keep in an airtight container for 2 days.

PREPARE AHEAD The unfilled pastry shell can be prepared ahead and stored in an airtight container for up to 3 days, or frozen for 12 weeks.

BAKER'S TIP

A glaze will help make any homemade tart look as appetizing as those in the top pâtisseries. For a red fruit tart, use warmed red currant jelly brushed over the fruits. Otherwise, as here, apricot jam is most suitable. Press the jam through a sieve first, to remove any lumps of fruit.

SWEET TARTS AND PIES

Pumpkin Pie

This version of the classic dessert produces a delicate result, gently set and fragrant with warm tones of cinnamon and mixed spice.

SERVES 6–8 | **30 MINS** | **1 HOUR 5 MINS** | **12 WEEKS, PIE SHELL**

Chilling time
1 hr

Special equipment
9in (22cm) tart pan
food processor with blade attachment (optional)
baking beans

Ingredients
1 cup all-purpose flour, plus extra for dusting
7 tbsp unsalted butter, chilled and diced

¼ cup sugar
1 large egg yolk
½ tsp pure vanilla extract

For the filling
3 medium eggs, at room temperature
½ cup light brown sugar
1 tsp cinnamon
1 tsp pumpkin pie spice
¾ cup heavy cream
14oz (425g) canned pumpkin, or 14oz (400g) roasted and puréed pumpkin

Method

1 To make the pastry, rub the flour and butter together until they form fine crumbs. Stir in the sugar. Beat the egg yolk with the vanilla extract and add to the dry ingredients, bringing the mixture together to form a soft dough. Wrap in plastic wrap and chill in the refrigerator for 1 hour.

2 Preheat the oven to 350°F (180°C). Roll out the pastry on a well floured surface to ⅛in (3mm) thick. It will be quite fragile, so should it begin to crumble, just bring it together again with your hands and give it a gentle knead to get rid of any joins. Use it to line the pan, leaving an overlapping edge of ¾in (2cm). Use a pair of scissors to trim any excess pastry that hangs down further than this. Prick it all over with a fork. Line the pastry shell with parchment paper and weigh it down with baking beans.

3 Place the shell on a baking sheet and blind bake it for 20 minutes. Remove the beans and the parchment paper and return it to the oven for a further 5 minutes if the center still looks a little uncooked.

4 In a large bowl, whisk together the eggs, sugar, spices, and cream. When they are well blended, beat in the canned or puréed pumpkin to make a smooth filling. Partially pull out an oven rack from the center of the oven, place the pastry crust on it, then pour in the filling. Bake until the filling is quite set, but before it begins to bubble up at the edges. Leave the pie to cool in the pan for at least 20 minutes. Serve warm with thick cream or vanilla ice cream.

STORE The pie can be kept in an airtight container in the refrigerator for 2 days.

PREPARE AHEAD The unfilled pastry shell can be prepared ahead and stored in an airtight container for 3 days, or frozen for 12 weeks.

BAKER'S TIP

Cans of ready prepared pumpkin are a short cut to producing this delicate pie, full of fall flavors. However, fresh pumpkin or even butternut squash can be roasted until tender and puréed for a homemade version. It will be denser than the canned pumpkin, so a little less is needed to set the filling.

Almond and Raspberry Lattice Tart

This is the Viennese specialty "Linzertorte" made with almond lattice pastry.

SERVES 6–8 **30–35 MINS** **40–45 MINS**

Chilling time
1¼–2¼ hrs

Special equipment
9in (23cm) tart pan
food processor with
  blade attachment
fluted pastry wheel (optional)

Ingredients
¾ cup all-purpose flour,
  plus extra for dusting
½ tsp ground cinnamon
pinch of ground cloves
1½ cups ground almonds
9 tbsp unsalted butter, softened and
  diced, plus extra for greasing
1 large egg yolk
½ cup sugar
¼ tsp salt
finely grated zest of 1 lemon
  and juice of ½

For the filling
½ cup sugar
13oz (375g) raspberries
1–2 tbsp confectioner's sugar,
  for dusting

1 Sift the flour into a bowl. Mix in the cloves, cinnamon, and almonds, and make a well.

2 Using your fingers, mix the butter, yolk, sugar, salt, juice, and zest. Place in the well.

3 Draw in the flour and work it until coarse crumbs form. Mix the dough into a ball.

4 Knead dough for 1–2 minutes until smooth. Wrap in plastic wrap. Chill for 1–2 hours.

5 Cook the sugar and raspberries in a saucepan for 10–12 minutes, until thick. Cool.

6 With the back of a wooden spoon, press half of the fruit pulp through a sieve.

7 Stir in the remaining pulp. Grease the pan and preheat the oven to 375°F (190°C).

8 Flour the work surface. Roll out two-thirds of the dough into a 11in (28cm) round.

9 Use the dough to line the pan, and cut off any excess overhanging the sides.

10 Spread the filling in the shell. Roll the rest of the dough to a 6 x 12in (15 x 30cm) rectangle.

11 Using a fluted wheel for a decorative edge, cut the dough into 12 x ½in- (1cm) strips.

12 Arrange half the strips from left to right over the tart, ¼in (2cm) apart. Turn the tart 45°.

13 Place the other strips diagonally. Trim, roll out the trimmings, and cut 4 strips.

14 Brush the edge with water and fix the edge strips. Chill for 15 minutes.

15 Bake for 15 minutes. Reduce to 350°F (180°C) and bake for 25–30 minutes more.

16 Leave to cool then remove from the pan and, about 30 minutes before serving, lightly dust with confectioner's sugar.
STORE The tart can be stored in an airtight container for up to 2 days; the flavor will mellow.

Lattice Tart and Pie variations

Cherry Pie

One of the most famous of all American pies. The juice from the fruit is thickened with flour to help bring the filling together.

SERVES 8 | 40–45 MINS | 40–45 MINS

Chilling time
45 mins

Special equipment
9in (23cm) pie pan

Ingredients
1¾ cups all-purpose flour, plus extra for dusting
½ tsp salt
½ cup vegetable shortening, chilled and diced
5 tbsp unsalted butter, chilled and diced

For the filling and glaze
1lb 2oz (500g) cherries, pitted
¾ cup sugar
¼ cup all-purpose flour
¼ tsp almond extract (optional)
1 large egg
½ tsp salt

Method
1 Sift the flour and salt into a large bowl. Add the shortening and butter, and rub with your fingers until the mixture forms coarse crumbs. Sprinkle with 3 tablespoons water, and blend until the dough forms a ball.

Wrap in plastic wrap, and chill for 30 minutes. Preheat the oven to 400°F (200°C), and put in a baking sheet. Roll out two-thirds of the dough on a floured work surface, about 2in (5cm) larger than the pan. Press the dough well into the pan. Chill for 15 minutes.

2 Put the cherries in a bowl and add the sugar, flour, and almond extract (if using). Stir well, then spoon into the pan.

3 Roll out the remaining dough on a floured work surface into a rectangle. Cut out 8 strips ½in (1cm) wide. Weave them into a lattice on top of the pie. Lightly beat together the egg and salt, and use this to glaze the lattice. Bake for 40–45 minutes, until the pastry is golden brown. Serve at room temperature, or chilled, with cream.

STORE Will keep in an airtight container for 2 days, but best eaten on the day of baking.

Crostata di marmellata

This Italian tart is quickly made with a few pantry essentials.

SERVES 6–8 | 30 MINS | 50 MINS | 12 WEEKS, PASTRY

Chilling time
1 hr

Special equipment
9in (22cm) tart pan
baking beans

Ingredients
1⅓ cups all-purpose flour, plus extra for dusting
7 tbsp unsalted butter, chilled and diced
¼ cup sugar
1 egg yolk, plus 1 egg, beaten, for glazing
2 tbsp milk, plus extra if needed
½ tsp pure vanilla extract
14oz (450g) jar good-quality raspberry, cherry, or apricot jam

Method
1 Rub the flour and butter together in a bowl until they form fine crumbs. Stir in the sugar. Beat the egg yolk with the milk and vanilla and add it to the dry ingredients, bringing the mixture together to form a soft dough. Use an extra tablespoon of milk if the mixture seems a little dry. Wrap in plastic wrap and chill for 1 hour.

2 Preheat the oven to 350°F (180°C). Roll out the pastry on a well floured surface to ⅛in (3mm) thick. It will be quite fragile, so should it begin to crumble, just bring it together again with your hands and give it a gentle knead to get rid of any joins. Use it to line the pan, leaving an overlapping edge of ¾in (2cm). Use a pair of scissors to trim any excess pastry that hangs down further than this. Prick the base all over with a fork. Roll up the excess pastry and chill for later use.

3 Line the pastry crust with a piece of parchment paper and weigh it down with baking beans. Place the crust on a baking sheet and blind bake for 20 minutes. Remove the beans and paper and return it to the oven for a further 5 minutes if the center still looks a little uncooked.

4 Increase the oven temperature to 400°F (200°C). Spread the jam in a ½-¾in (1-2cm) layer over the pastry crust. Roll out the remaining pastry into a square just larger than the tart and ⅛in (3mm) thick. Cut the pastry into at least 12 strips, ½in (1cm) wide, and use these to top the tart in a criss-cross fashion, making a lattice effect.

5 Use a little beaten egg to secure the strips to the side of the tart and to gently brush the lattice. Return the tart to the oven for 20–25 minutes until the pastry lattice is cooked through and golden brown on top. Cool for at least 20 minutes before eating while still warm with thick cream, or cold.

STORE The tart will keep in an airtight container for 2 days.

Peach Pie

Less famous than its cherry cousin but no less tasty, this classic is a splendid summer dessert. Choose perfectly ripe peaches full of juice. ▲

SERVES 8   **40–45 MINS**   **40–45 MINS**

Chilling time
45 mins

Special equipment
9in (23cm) pie pan

Ingredients
4–5 ripe peaches
¼ cup all-purpose flour
⅔ cup sugar, plus extra if needed
pinch of salt
1–2 tbsp lemon juice (optional)

For the glaze
1 large egg
½ tsp salt

Method
1 Immerse the peaches in boiling water for 10 seconds, then transfer to a bowl of cold water. Halve the peaches, remove the pits, and peel off the skins. Cut into ½in (1cm) slices and put in a large bowl.

2 Sprinkle the peaches with the flour, sugar, salt, and lemon juice, to taste. Carefully stir the peaches, then transfer them to the pastry crust, in the pie pan, with their juices.

3 Lightly beat together the egg and salt, and use this to glaze the pie.

4 Bake for 40–45 minutes, until the pastry is golden brown, and the peaches are soft and bubbling. Serve warm, with vanilla ice cream.

STORE The pie can be kept in an airtight container for 2 days, but is really best eaten on the day it is baked.

Pecan Pie

This sweet, crunchy pie originated in the southern United States, where pecan nuts are widely grown.

SERVES 6–8	15 MINS	1½ HOURS	12 WEEKS, PIE SHELL

Chilling time
30 mins

Special equipment
9in (22cm) tart pan with removable bottom
food processor with blade attachment (optional)
baking beans

Ingredients
1 cup all-purpose plain flour, plus extra
  for dusting
7 tbsp unsalted butter, chilled and diced
¼ cup sugar
1 egg yolk
½ tsp pure vanilla extract
crème fraîche or whipped cream,
  to serve (optional)

For the filling
⅔ cup maple syrup
4 tbsp butter
1 cup light brown sugar
few drops of pure vanilla extract
pinch of salt
3 large eggs
7oz (200g) pecan nuts

Method

1 Using your fingertips, rub the flour and butter together, or pulse-blend in a food processor, until they form fine crumbs. Stir in the sugar. Beat the egg yolk with the vanilla and add to the dry ingredients, bringing the mixture together to form a soft dough. Wrap in plastic wrap and chill for 1 hour. Preheat the oven to 350°F (180°C).

2 Roll out the pastry on a well floured surface to ⅛in (3mm) thick. It will be fragile, so should it begin to crumble, just bring it together again with your hands and give it a gentle knead to get rid of any joins. Use it to line the pan, leaving an overlapping edge of at least ¾in (2cm). Prick the base all over with a fork.

3 Line the pastry crust with parchment and weigh it down with baking beans. Place the crust on a baking sheet and blind bake it for 20 minutes. Remove the beans and paper and bake for a further 5 minutes if the center still looks a little uncooked.

4 Pour the maple syrup into a pan, and add the butter, sugar, vanilla extract, and salt. Place the pan over low heat, and stir constantly until the butter has melted and the sugar dissolved. Remove the pan from the heat and leave the mixture to cool until it feels just tepid, then beat in the eggs, 1 at a time. Stir in the pecan nuts, then pour the mixture into the pastry crust.

5 Bake for 40–50 minutes, or until just set. Cover with a sheet of foil if it is browning too quickly. Remove the pie from the oven, transfer it to a wire rack, and leave to cool for 15–20 minutes. Remove from the pan and either serve it warm or leave it on the wire rack to cool completely. Serve with crème fraîche or whipped cream.

STORE The tart will keep in an airtight container for 2 days.

PREPARE AHEAD The unfilled pastry crust can be prepared ahead and stored in an airtight container for up to 3 days, or frozen for 12 weeks.

BAKER'S TIP
Try to buy nuts fresh, each time you want to bake with them. Remember to buy them in small batches, and never store them for very long. Nuts turn rancid very quickly, due to the large amount of oil they contain, and just one rancid nut can taint and ruin this tart.

Treacle Tart

A classic English tart that remains a favorite with young and old alike. Try making this more sophisticated version, rich with cream and eggs.

SERVES 6–8	30 MINS	50–55 MINS	12 WEEKS, PIE SHELL

Chilling time
1 hr

Special equipment
9in (22cm) tart pan
food processor with blade attachment (optional)
baking beans
handheld blender (optional)

Ingredients
1¼ cups all-purpose flour, plus extra for dusting
7 tbsp unsalted butter, chilled and diced
¼ cup sugar
2 large egg yolks
½ tsp pure vanilla extract

For the filling
¾ cup corn syrup
¾ cup heavy cream
2 large eggs
finely grated zest of 1 orange
1½ cups (3½oz) brioche or croissant crumbs

Method

1 To make the pastry, rub the flour and butter together until they form fine crumbs. Stir in the sugar. Beat the egg yolks with the vanilla extract and add them to the dry ingredients, bringing the mixture together to form a soft dough. Wrap in plastic wrap and chill for 1 hour. Preheat the oven to 350°F (180°C).

2 Roll out the pastry on a well floured surface to ⅛in (3mm) thick. It will be quite fragile, so should it begin to crumble, just bring it together again with your hands and give it a gentle knead to get rid of any joins. Use it to line the pan, leaving an overlapping edge of ¾in (2cm). Use a pair of scissors to trim any excess pastry that hangs down further than this. Prick the base all over with a fork. Roll up the excess pastry and chill for later use.

3 Line the pastry crust with parchment paper and weigh it down with baking beans. Place the crust on a baking sheet and blind bake it for 20 minutes. Remove the baking beans and parchment paper and return the crust to the oven for a further 5 minutes if the center still looks a little uncooked when first removed.

4 Measure out the corn syrup into a large measuring cup. Measure the cream on top of it (the density of the syrup will keep the 2 separate, making measuring easy.) Add the eggs and orange zest and blend together with a handheld blender until well combined. Gently fold in the brioche crumbs.

5 Place the pastry crust on to a baking sheet, pull out an oven rack from the center of the oven and put the baking sheet on top. Pour the filling into the crust and carefully slide the rack into the oven.

6 Bake the tart for 30 minutes until just set, but before the filling starts to bubble up. Remove the tart from the oven and cool for at least 20 minutes before eating warm with thick cream or ice cream.

STORE The tart will keep in an airtight container for 2 days.

PREPARE AHEAD The unfilled pastry crust can be prepared ahead and stored in an airtight container for up to 3 days, or frozen for 12 weeks.

BAKER'S TIP
Traditional treacle tarts are made from little more than pastry, syrup, and breadcrumbs. For a delicious, more luxurious tart, try using cream and eggs to lighten the filling. They lend a smoothness and incorporate air, to give a more mousse-like result than the sometimes stolid original recipe.

Tarte Tatin

Named after two French sisters who earned a living by baking their father's favorite apple tart.

SERVES 8 | 45–50 MINS | 35–50 MINS

Chilling time
30 mins

Special equipment
9–10in (23–25cm) ovenproof pan or Tatin dish

Ingredients
5 tbsp unsalted butter, softened
1⅓ cups all-purpose flour, plus extra for dusting
2 large egg yolks

1½ tbsp sugar
pinch of salt

For the filling
14–16 apples, total weight about 5lb 6oz (2.4kg)
1 lemon
1 stick, plus 1 tbsp unsalted butter
¾ cup sugar
crème fraîche, to serve

1 For the pastry, sift the flour into a bowl and make a well in the center.

2 Put the egg yolks, sugar, and salt in the well, then add the butter and 1 tablespoon water.

3 Using your fingertips, work the ingredients in the well until thoroughly mixed.

4 Work the flour into the mixture until coarse crumbs form. Press the dough into a ball.

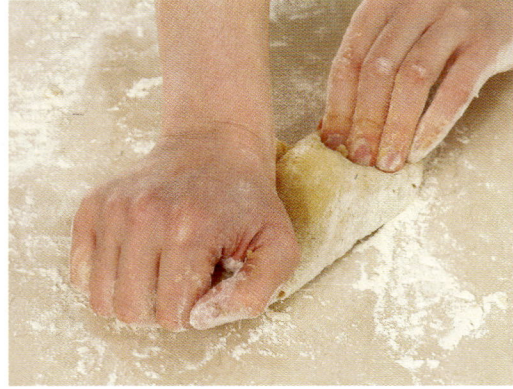

5 Lightly flour the work surface, then knead the dough for 1–2 minutes, until very smooth.

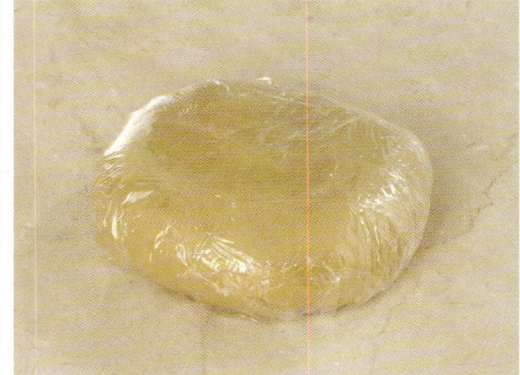

6 Shape into a ball, wrap in plastic, and chill for about 30 minutes, until firm.

7 With a vegetable peeler, carefully peel the apples, then halve and core them.

8 Cut the lemon in half, and rub the apples all over with it, to prevent discoloration.

9 Melt the butter in the frying pan. Add the sugar and stir it together.

10 Cook over medium heat, stirring now and then, until caramelized to a deep golden brown.

11 Remove from the heat, and let cool to tepid. Put the apple in concentric circles to fill the pan.

12 Cook the apples over high heat for 15–25 minutes, until caramelized. Turn once.

13 Remove from the heat. Cool for 10–15 minutes. Preheat the oven to 375°F (190°C).

14 Roll out the pastry to a round 1in (2.5cm) larger than the pan. Drape it over the pan.

15 Tuck the edges of the pastry around the apples. Bake for 20–25 minutes until golden.

16 Cool to tepid, then set a plate on top, hold firmly together, and invert. Spoon some caramel over the apples. Serve with crème fraîche.

Tarte Tatin variations

Pear Tarte Tatin

Pears are an easy substitute for apples, but will take longer to cook. Use pears that are ripe but still holding their shape—Comice pears are a good choice.

SERVES 8 **30 MINS** **40–55 MINS**

Chilling time
40–45 mins

Special equipment
9–10in (23–25cm) ovenproof pan or Tatin dish

Ingredients

For the pastry
1 cup all-purpose flour,
  plus extra for dusting
2 large egg yolks
1½ tbsp sugar
pinch of salt
5 tbsp unsalted butter, softened

For the filling
9 tbsp unsalted butter
¾ cup sugar
12–14 pears, total weight 5½lb (2.4kg), peeled,
  halved, cored, and rubbed with lemon halves
crème fraîche, to serve (optional)

Method

1 For the pastry, sift the flour into a large bowl and make a well in the center. Put the egg yolks, sugar, and salt in the well. Add the butter and 1 tablespoon of water. Using your fingertips, work the ingredients in the well until thoroughly mixed. Work the flour into the mixture until coarse crumbs form.

2 Press the dough into a ball. Flour the work surface and knead the dough for 2 minutes, until smooth. Wrap in plastic wrap and chill for about 30 minutes, until firm.

3 Melt the butter in the frying pan. Add the sugar and stir it together. Cook over medium heat, stirring, until caramelized to a deep golden brown; about 3–5 minutes. Remove from the heat, and let cool.

4 Arrange the pear halves on their sides in the pan with the tapered ends toward the center of the pan. Cook the pears over high heat for 20–30 minutes, until caramelized. Turn once to caramelize on both sides. The pears should be tender but still retain their shape, and very little juice should remain.

5 Take the pan from the heat and cool for 10–15 minutes. Preheat the oven to 375°F (190°C). Roll out the pastry to a round 1in (2.5cm) larger than the pan. Drape it over the pan and tuck the edges around the pears. Bake for 20–25 minutes.

6 Cool to tepid, then set a plate on top, hold together, and invert. Spoon some caramel over the apples. Serve with crème fraîche.

PREPARE AHEAD The tart can be baked 6–8 hours ahead and warmed briefly on the stove before unmolding.

BAKER'S TIP
Pears may produce more liquid than apples and so take longer cook in the caramel until the liquid has evaporated. Make sure very little liquid remains or the Tatin may be soggy.

Caramel Banana Tart

Not one for purists, but this tropical take on a tarte Tatin is so delicious and easy to prepare, no one will mind—and the flavors are particularly appealing to kids.

SERVES 6 **15 MINS** **30–35 MINS**

Special equipment
8in (20cm) tart dish (not loose-bottomed)

Ingredients
5 tbsp butter
⅔ cup corn syrup
4 medium bananas, peeled and sliced
  ½in (1cm) thick
7oz (200g) puff pastry, store-bought or see
  Palmiers, page 178
all-purpose flour, to dust
vanilla ice cream or crème fraîche,
  to serve (optional)

Method

1 Preheat the oven to 400°F (200°C). Heat the butter and syrup in a small pan until the butter has melted and the mixture is smooth, then allow to boil for 1 minute. Pour into the tart dish. Arrange the banana slices on top of the syrup mixture; this will be the top of the dessert when it's turned out. Place the dish on a baking sheet and bake for 10 minutes.

2 Meanwhile, on a lightly floured surface, roll the pastry out into a round about 9in (23cm) in diameter. It should be about ¼in (5mm) thick. Trim off any excess, if necessary. Carefully remove the tart dish from the oven and place the pastry circle on top of the caramelized banana mix. Use the handle of a small knife to tuck the edge of the pastry down into the dish, being very careful of the hot caramel.

3 Return the tart to the oven and bake for a further 20–25 minutes, or until the pastry is golden brown. Leave to stand for 5–10 minutes, then place a serving plate on top and turn the tart upside-down. Serve with vanilla ice cream.

Peach Tarte Tatin

This more unusual tarte Tatin is a good choice for a late summer dessert. Choose firm peaches to ensure the fruit holds its shape as it cooks. Mango slices would also work well here.

SERVES 6 **40–45 MINS** **20–25 MINS**

Chilling time
45 mins

Special equipment
10in (25cm) round baking dish

Ingredients
6 tbsp unsalted butter, diced
3 large egg yolks
½ tsp pure vanilla extract
1⅔ cups all-purpose flour, plus extra for dusting
¼ cup sugar
¼ tsp salt

For the filling
¾ cup sugar
2¼lb (1kg) peaches

Method

1 In a small bowl, mix the egg yolks with the vanilla. Mix together the flour, sugar, and salt in a large bowl. Add the butter and, with your fingertips, mix to form crumbs. Stir in the egg yolks, and transfer to a floured work surface. Knead until smooth. Chill for 30 minutes, until firm.

2 Place the sugar for the filling in a saucepan, and heat gently until dissolved, stirring occasionally. Boil, without stirring, until the mixture starts to turn golden around the edge. Do not stir, or it may crystallize. Lower the heat and continue cooking, swirling the saucepan once or twice so the syrup colors evenly, until the caramel is golden. Cook the caramel only until medium gold; if it gets too dark, it will become bitter in the oven.

3 Remove the saucepan from the heat, and immediately plunge the base of the saucepan into a bowl of cold water, until cooking stops. Stand back in case of splashes. Pour the caramel into the bottom of the baking dish. Working quickly, tilt the dish so the bottom is thoroughly coated with a thin, even layer. Let cool.

4 Immerse the peaches in a saucepan of boiling water for 10 seconds, then transfer to a bowl of cold water. Cut them in half, remove the pit, and peel off the skin. Cut the peach halves lengthways into two. Tightly pack the peach wedges on top of the caramel, rounded-side down, in concentric circles.

5 On a lightly floured work surface, roll out the dough into a 11in (28cm) round. Wrap it around the rolling pin and drape over the dish. Tuck the edge of the dough down around the peaches. Chill for 15 minutes. Preheat the oven to 400°F (200°C).

6 Bake for 30–35 minutes. Let the tart cool to tepid. To unmold, set a platter on top of the baking dish. Hold dish and platter firmly together and invert them, then remove the baking dish. Serve at once, cut into wedges.

Custard Tart

A filling of gently set egg custard, delicately spiced with nutmeg, makes a simple yet elegant tart.

SERVES 8	20 MINS	45–50 MINS	12 WEEKS, CRUST

Chilling time
1 hr

Special equipment
9in (22cm) tart pan
baking beans

Ingredients
1¼ cups all-purpose flour, plus extra
  for dusting
7 tbsp unsalted butter, chilled
  and diced
¼ cup sugar
2 large egg yolks
½ tsp pure vanilla extract

For the filling
¾ cup milk
⅔ cup heavy cream
2 large eggs
¼ cup sugar
½ tsp pure vanilla extract
¼ tsp freshly grated nutmeg

1 In a bowl, mix the flour and butter together until they form fine crumbs. Stir in the sugar.

2 Beat the egg yolks with the vanilla extract and add them to the dry ingredients.

3 Bring the mixture together to form a soft dough. Wrap in plastic wrap and chill for 1 hour.

4 Preheat the oven to 350°F (180°C). Roll out the pastry to ⅛in (3mm) thick.

5 It will be fragile, so should it crumble, bring it together with your hands and knead gently.

6 Use it to line the pan, leaving an overlapping edge of ¾in (2cm).

7 Prick the pastry all over with a fork, to prevent air bubbles forming during baking.

8 Line with parchment and weigh it down with beans. Bake for 20 minutes on a baking sheet.

9 Remove the beans and paper and bake for 5 minutes more. Trim the overhanging pastry.

SWEET TARTS AND PIES

314

10 Reduce the temperature to 340°F (170°C). Heat the milk and the cream in a pan.

11 Meanwhile, whisk together the eggs, sugar, vanilla extract, and nutmeg.

12 Once the milk and cream have come to a boil, pour them over the egg mixture, whisking.

13 Place the pastry crust on a baking sheet; this will make it easier to transfer to the oven.

14 Pour the filling into the crust and place the baking sheet in the top third of the oven.

15 Bake for 20–25 minutes, or until just set but still with a slight wobble in the center.

16 Remove the tart from the oven and leave to cool, then remove from the pan.
STORE The tart will keep in an airtight container in the refrigerator for 1 day.

Custard Tart variations

Gooseberry Tart

The sharp gooseberries quiver in smooth, just-set custard, all held together in a light, sweet pastry crust for a sublime seasonal treat.

SERVES 6–8 | 30 MINS | 1 HOUR | 12 WEEKS, PIE CASE

Chilling time
30 mins

Special equipment
10in (24cm) tart pan with removable bottom
baking beans

Ingredients
1¼ cups all-purpose flour
¼ cup sugar
5 tbsp butter
1 large egg yolk

For the filling
14oz (400g) gooseberries
1 cup heavy cream
2 large eggs
¼ cup sugar

Method

1 For the pastry, combine the flour, sugar, and butter, and mix in a food processor to form fine breadcrumbs. Add the egg yolk and process until the mixture forms a ball, adding a little cold water, 1 tablespoon at a time, if necessary. Wrap in plastic wrap and chill for 30 minutes.

2 Preheat the oven to 350°F (180°C). Meanwhile, pull the tops and tails off the gooseberries and set aside. To make the custard, whisk together the cream, eggs, and sugar. Put in the refrigerator.

3 Roll out the pastry into a circle a little larger than the pan. Line the tart pan with the pastry. Line the pastry crust with parchment paper and baking beans, and bake blind for 15 minutes. Remove the beans and paper, and bake for another 10 minutes until cooked through but still pale.

4 Remove the pan from the oven and put a single layer of gooseberries in the pastry crust. Pour the custard over and return it to the oven for a further 35 minutes until the custard is set and golden at the edges. Leave to cool slightly before removing from the pan and serving with thick cream.

Flan nature

A classic French dessert, this custard tart is best served chilled.

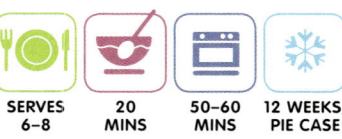

SERVES 6–8 | 20 MINS | 50–60 MINS | 12 WEEKS, PIE CASE

Chilling time
1 hr

Special equipment
8in (20cm) springform cake pan
baking beans

Ingredients
1 sweet pastry crust, see page 314, steps 1–9
¾ cup all-purpose flour
½ cup sugar
3 large eggs
3 tbsp unsalted butter, melted and cooled
½ tsp pure vanilla extract
2 cups milk

Method

1 Make the pastry crust. Preheat the oven to 300°F (150°C). In a bowl, whisk the flour, sugar, eggs, butter, and vanilla extract to a thick, smooth paste. Whisk in the milk and transfer the mixture to a large measuring cup.

2 Rest the baking sheet that holds the pastry crust on the edge of the middle oven shelf, and, holding it with one hand, pour the filling carefully into the tart crust with the other. When it is as full as you can make it without spilling, gently push the tart on to the oven shelf and close the door.

3 Bake for 50 minutes to 1 hour until just set, but not at all puffed up. The surface should be golden brown. Trim the excess pastry from the sides of the pan with a sharp knife. Let cool completely in the pan.

STORE This will keep in an airtight container in the refrigerator for 2 days.

Tarta di nata

These bite-sized custard pastries are a Portuguese favorite.

MAKES 16   30 MINS   20–25 MINS

Special equipment
muffin pan

Ingredients
all-purpose flour, for dusting
1lb 2oz (500g) store-bought all-butter puff pastry, or see page 178, steps 1–9
2 cups milk
1 cinnamon stick
1 large piece lemon zest
4 large egg yolks
½ cup sugar
¼ cup all-purpose flour
1 tbsp cornstarch

Method

1 Preheat the oven to 425°F (220°C). On a well floured work surface roll out the puff pastry to a 16 x 12in (40 x 30cm) rectangle. Roll up the pastry to make a log. Trim the ends, and cut into 16 equal-sized slices.

2 Take a piece of rolled pastry and tuck the loose end underneath it. Lay it down and roll into a thin circle, about 4in (10cm) in diameter, turning it over only once to ensure a natural curve. You should be left with a shallow, bowl-type piece of pastry. Use your thumbs to press it into a muffin pan, ensuring it is well shaped to the pan. Prick the bottom of the pastry with a fork. Repeat the process with all the pastry. Rest it in the refrigerator while you make the filling.

3 Heat the milk, cinnamon stick, and lemon zest in a heavy-based saucepan. When the milk starts to boil, take it from the heat.

4 In a bowl, whisk together the egg yolks, sugar, flour, and cornstarch until you have a thick paste. Remove the cinnamon stick and the lemon peel from the hot milk and pour it gradually over the egg yolk mixture, whisking constantly. Return the custard to the cleaned-out pan and place over medium heat, whisking constantly, until it thickens. Take it immediately from the heat.

5 Fill each pastry crust two-thirds full of the custard and bake at the top of the oven for 20-25 minutes, until the custards are puffed and blackened in places on their surface. Remove from the oven and allow to cool. The custards should deflate slightly, but this is quite normal. Leave for at least 10–15 minutes before eating warm or cold.

STORE The finished tarts will keep in an airtight container for 1 day.

PREPARE AHEAD Both the custard and the pastry crusts can be prepared ahead and stored separately in the refrigerator overnight before finishing.

Tarte au citron

Variations of this ever-popular tart often appear on restaurant menus the world over, and it is a vital baking recipe to have in your repertoire.

| 8 SLICES | 35 MINS | 45 MINS | 12 WEEKS, TART CASE |

Chilling time
1½ hrs

Special equipment
food processor with blade attachment
9in (23cm) tart pan with removable bottom
baking beans

Ingredients
1⅓ cups all-purpose flour, plus extra for dusting
6 tbsp butter, chilled
¼ cup sugar
1 large egg

For the filling
5 large eggs
¾ cup sugar
finely grated zest and juice of 4 lemons
1 cup heavy cream
confectioner's sugar, to serve
lemon zest, to serve

Method

1 To make the pastry, place the flour, butter, and sugar into a food processor and pulse until it resembles crumbs. Add the egg and process until the pastry draws together into a ball. Roll out the pastry on a floured surface into a large circle, and use it to line the tart pan. Chill for at least 30 minutes.

2 Beat the eggs and sugar together until combined. Beat in the lemon zest and juice, then whisk in the cream. Chill in the refrigerator for 1 hour.

3 Preheat the oven to 375°F (190°C). Line the pastry crust with parchment paper, fill with baking beans, and bake blind for 10 minutes. Remove the paper and beans, and bake the pastry for another 5 minutes, or until the base is crisp.

4 Reduce the oven temperature to 275°F (140°C). Place the tart pan on a baking sheet. Pour in the lemon filling, being careful not to allow the filling to spill over the edges. Bake for 30 minutes, or until just set.

5 Remove from the oven and cool. Serve, dusted with confectioner's sugar and sprinkled with lemon zest.

STORE The tart will keep in an airtight container in the refrigerator for 2 days.

BAKER'S TIP

When baking with lemons, try to choose unwaxed fruits, especially if a recipe calls for lemon zest. If unwaxed lemons are unavailable, scrub the fruits to remove the wax. Pick lemons that are heavy for their size, indicating that they have lots of juice.

Key Lime Pie

This pie takes its name from the small limes that grow in the Florida Keys, where the recipe originated.

8 SLICES **20–25 MINS** **15–20 MINS**

Special equipment
9in (23cm) tart pan with removable bottom
zester (optional)

Ingredients
7 tbsp unsalted butter
8oz (225g) vanilla wafers, crushed
5 limes, plus 1 extra, cut into thin slices,
 to decorate
3 large egg yolks
14oz (400g) can sweetened condensed milk

Method

1 Preheat the oven to 350°F (180°C). Melt the butter in a saucepan over low heat. Add the vanilla wafer crumbs and stir until well combined. Remove from the heat and place the mixture into the tart pan, then use the base of a metal spoon to press it evenly and firmly all over the base and sides of the pan. Place on a baking sheet and bake for 5–10 minutes.

2 Meanwhile, grate the zest of 3 of the limes into a bowl. Juice all 5 of the limes, and set aside.

3 Place the egg yolks into the bowl with the lime zest, and whisk until the egg has thickened. Pour in the condensed milk and continue whisking for 5 minutes if using an electric hand mixer, or for 6–7 minutes if

whisking by hand. Add the lime juice, and whisk again until it is incorporated. Pour the mixture into the pan and bake for 15–20 minutes, or until it is set.

4 Remove the pie from the oven and leave it to cool completely. Serve the pie decorated with the lime slices, with whipped cream.

STORE The pie will keep in an airtight container in the refrigerator for 2 days.

BAKER'S TIP
A common baking mistake with sweet tarts with a deep filling is to overcook them. Remove them from the oven when they still are slightly wobbly at the center. They will cool and set to an unctuous, creamy texture. Overcooking will result in a tart with an unpleasantly "rubbery" texture.

Chocolate Tart

This rich, dark chocolate tart is best served just set, while still warm, and with plenty of thick, cold cream.

SERVES 8–10 | 30 MINS | 40 MINS | 12 WEEKS, PIE CASE

Chilling time
1 hr

Special equipment
9in (22cm) tart pan
baking beans

Ingredients
1¼ cups all-purpose flour
7 tbsp unsalted butter, chilled
   and diced

For the filling
1 stick, plus 3 tbsp unsalted butter,
   cut into pieces
7oz (200g) good-quality dark
   chocolate, broken into pieces

¼ cup sugar
2 large egg yolks
½ tsp pure vanilla extract

3 large eggs
¼ cup sugar
½ cup heavy cream

1 In a bowl, rub the flour and butter together until they form fine crumbs.

2 Add the sugar to the crumb mixture and stir to combine.

3 Beat the egg yolks with the vanilla extract and add them to the dry ingredients.

4 Bring the mixture together to form a soft dough. Wrap in plastic wrap. Chill for 1 hour.

5 Preheat the oven to 350°F (180°C). Roll out the pastry to ⅛in (3mm) thick.

6 It will be fragile, so should it crumble, bring it together with your hands and knead gently.

7 Use it to line the pan, leaving an overlapping edge of ¾in (2cm).

8 Use a pair of scissors to trim any excess pastry that hangs down further than this.

9 Prick the pastry base all over with a fork, to prevent air bubbles forming during baking.

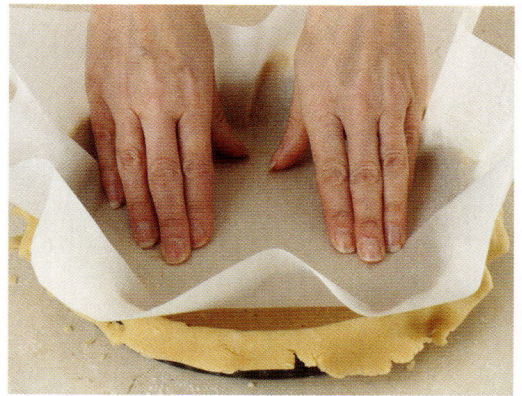

10 Carefully line the pastry crust with a piece of parchment paper.

11 Scatter baking beans over the paper, place on a baking sheet, and bake for 20 minutes.

12 Remove the beans and paper and bake for 5 minutes more. Trim any excess pastry.

13 Melt the butter and chocolate in a bowl over a pan of simmering water, stirring.

14 When just melted, remove from the heat and set aside to cool.

15 Whisk together the eggs and sugar until well blended.

16 Pour in the cooled chocolate mixture and whisk gently but thoroughly to combine.

17 Finally, mix in the cream then transfer the chocolate mixture to a large measuring cup.

18 Place the pastry crust on a baking sheet so that it is easy to carry to the oven.

19 Pour the filling into the pastry crust and transfer to the top of the preheated oven.

20 Bake for 10–15 minutes until just set. Leave to cool for 5 minutes; it will continue to harden.

21 Transfer to a serving plate. **STORE** Keep refrigerated in an airtight container for 2 days.

CHOCOLATE TART

323

Chocolate Tart variations

Double Chocolate Raspberry Tart

This impressive dessert is even quicker with a store-bought crust.

SERVES 6–8 | 40 MINS | 20–25 MINS | 12 WEEKS PASTRY

Chilling time
1 hr

Special equipment
9in (22cm) tart pan
baking beans

Ingredients
1 chocolate crust, store-bought, or see pages 322–323, steps 1–12, reducing the quantity of all-purpose flour to 1 cup and adding ¼ cup cocoa instead

For the filling
½ cup sugar
½ cup cornstarch, sifted
2 large eggs, at room temperature
1 tsp pure vanilla extract
1¾ cups whole milk
6oz (175g) good-quality dark chocolate, chopped
14oz (400g) raspberries
confectioner's sugar, for dusting

Method
1 Melt the white chocolate in a heatproof bowl set over a pan of barely simmering water. Leave to cool.

2 Melt the dark chocolate in the same way, and use a pastry brush to paint the inside of the pastry crust with a layer of chocolate. This will stop the pastry from going soggy once it is filled with the filling. Leave to set.

3 Whip the cream stiffly. Fold the cooled white chocolate into the whipped cream. Crush half the raspberries and fold them through the cream mixture. Pile the filling into the crust evenly. Decorate with the remaining raspberries, dust with confectioner's sugar, and serve.

STORE The tart will keep in an airtight container in the refrigerator for 2 days.

Chocolate Walnut Truffle Tart

The Italian sweet pastry *pasta frolla* acts as a container for a rich filling. Cocoa powder sifted over the tart echoes the coating for chocolate truffles.

SERVES 6–8 | 45–50 MINS | 35–40 MINS

Chilling time
45 mins

Special equipment
9in (23cm) springform pan
food processor with blade attachment

Ingredients
1¼ cups all-purpose flour, plus extra for dusting
5 tbsp unsalted butter, plus extra for greasing
¼ cup sugar
¼ tsp salt
1 large egg

For the filling
1½ cups walnuts
½ cup sugar
2oz (60g) good-quality dark chocolate, chopped
11 tbsp unsalted butter
2 tsp all-purpose flour
2 large egg yolks, plus 1 large whole egg
1 tsp pure vanilla extract

For the chocolate glaze
16oz (175g) good-quality dark chocolate, chopped
5 tbsp unsalted butter
2 tsp Grand Marnier
cocoa powder, for dusting

Method
1 Sift the flour on to a work surface and make a well in the center. Pound the butter with a rolling pin to soften. Put the butter, sugar, salt, and egg into the well. With your fingertips, work the ingredients in until well mixed. Work the flour until coarse crumbs form. Press the dough into a ball. Knead for 1–2 minutes, until smooth. Wrap in plastic wrap and chill for 30 minutes.

2 Grease the pan. Roll the dough into a 11in (28cm) round. Wrap it around the rolling pin and gently press into the pan, sealing any cracks. Prick the bottom of the shell with a fork. Chill for 15 minutes, until firm.

3 Preheat the oven to 350°F (180°C). Spread out the nuts on a baking sheet, and toast in the heated oven until they are lightly browned, 5–10 minutes. Stir occasionally, so they color evenly. Let cool. Return the baking sheet to the oven. Reserve 8 walnut halves. Grind the remaining nuts with the sugar in a food processor, then empty into a bowl. Chop the chocolate in a food processor. Beat the butter until creamy. Add the flour and the hazelnut mixture and continue beating for 2–3 minutes, until light and fluffy. Add the yolks and egg, one at a time, beating after each addition. Mix in the chocolate and vanilla extract. Spread the filling over the pastry shell and smooth the top. Bake 35–40 minutes, until a metal skewer inserted in the center comes out clean. Let cool on a wire rack.

4 While the tart cools, put the chocolate for the glaze in a bowl set over a saucepan of simmering water, stirring occasionally, just until melted. Dip the reserved walnuts in the chocolate to coat, then set aside.

5 Cut the butter into small pieces and gently stir it into the warm melted chocolate in 2–3 batches. Add the Grand Marnier. Let cool to tepid. Set the tart pan on a bowl to loosen and remove the side. Spread the glaze over to the tart. Let cool. Just before serving, sift cocoa powder over and arrange the walnuts on top. Serve at room temperature.

STORE The tart can be baked and stored for up to 2 days in an airtight container, and the flavors will mellow. Add the glaze not more than 4 hours before serving.

PREPARE AHEAD This can be made up to 2 days ahead and kept, tightly wrapped, in the refrigerator.

BAKER'S TIP
Toasting nuts intensifies their flavor and adds crunch to their texture. You can tell that they are toasted when the skins start to pop and the nuts smell fragrant. Though the walnut skins are not removed in this recipe, toasting also makes it easier to remove thin skins from nuts.

Banoffee Pie

This version of the modern classic is incredibly rich and sweet, just as it should be. Great for a party, as a little goes a long way.

SERVES 6–8 | 20 MINS | 8 WEEKS

Chilling time
1 hr

Special equipment
9in (22cm) springform pan

Ingredients
9oz (250g) vanilla wafers
7 tbsp unsalted butter, melted and cooled

For the caramel
4 tbsp unsalted butter
1/3 cup light brown sugar
14oz (397g) can condensed milk

For the topping
2 large, ripe bananas
1 cup heavy cream, whipped
a little dark chocolate, for grating

Method

1 Line the pan with parchment paper. Put the cookies in a sturdy plastic bag and use a rolling pin to crush them as finely as possible. Mix the cookies with the melted butter, and place them into the prepared pan. Press down firmly to create an even finish. Cover, and refrigerate.

2 To make the caramel, melt the butter and sugar in a small saucepan over medium heat. Add the condensed milk and bring to a boil. Reduce the heat and cook the caramel, stirring constantly, on a steady simmer for 2-3 minutes. It will thicken and darken to a light caramel color. Pour over the cookie base and leave to set.

3 Once cool, slice the bananas thinly into 1/4in (5mm) disks, cut slightly on a diagonal, and use them to cover the surface of the caramel. Whip the cream and smooth it over the bananas using a spatula. Finally grate over a little dark chocolate using a fine grater, or decorate with chocolate curls.

STORE The pie will keep in an airtight container in the refrigerator for 2 days.

BAKER'S TIP
This no-cook dessert is a favorite with children and adults alike. The base and caramel layers need to be chilled to firm up, but take the pie out of the refrigerator for 30 minutes before topping it with bananas and cream to serve. This will allow the cookie and caramel base to be cut more easily.

Apple Pie

Perhaps the ultimate in home-baked comfort food, this fall pie is best served warm with vanilla ice cream.

SERVES 6–8 **30–35 MINS** **50–55 MINS**

Chilling time
45 mins

Special equipment
9in (23cm) pie dish

Ingredients
2½ cups all-purpose flour, plus extra
  for dusting
½ tsp salt
¾ cup vegetable shortening,
  plus extra for greasing
2 tbsp sugar, plus extra for glazing
1 tbsp milk, to glaze

For the filling
2¼lb (1kg) tart apples
juice of 1 lemon
½ cup sugar, or to taste
2 tbsp all-purpose flour
½ tsp cinnamon, or to taste
¼ tsp nutmeg, or to taste

1 Sift the flour and salt into a bowl. Add the shortening, cutting it in with 2 butter knives.

2 With your fingertips, rub the fat into the flour until crumbs form. Lift the mixture to aerate it.

3 Add the sugar. Sprinkle over 6–7 tablespoons cold water, mixing lightly with a fork.

4 Press the crumbs into a ball, wrap, and chill for 30 minutes. Meanwhile, grease the dish.

5 Flour a surface. Roll out ⅔ of the dough into a round 2in (5cm) larger than the dish.

6 Using the rolling pin, drape the pastry over the dish, then gently push it in to the contours.

7 Trim any excess pastry, then chill for 15 minutes, until firm.

8 Peel the apples, then cut off the ends. Halve the apples and scoop out the cores.

9 Set each apple, cut-side down, on a chopping board and cut into medium slices.

SWEET TARTS AND PIES

10 Put the apple slices in a bowl, and sprinkle with the lemon juice. Toss to coat.

11 Sprinkle the flour, cinnamon, nutmeg, and sugar over the apples. Toss to coat.

12 Put the apples in the pie dish and arrange so that it is slightly mounded in the center.

13 Brush the edge of the shell with water. Roll out the remaining dough into a 11in (28cm) round.

14 Wrap it around the rolling pin and drape it over the filling. Trim the top crust.

15 Press the edges together to seal, crimping with the back of a knife as you go.

16 Cut an "x" in the top crust. Gently pull back the point of each triangle to reveal the filling.

17 Roll out the trimmings, cut into strips, and moisten. Lay on the pie in a criss-cross pattern.

18 Using a pastry brush, glaze the pie with the milk so that it bakes to a golden color.

19 Sprinkle with sugar. Chill until firm; about 30 minutes. Preheat the oven to 425°F (220°C).

20 Bake for 20 minutes. Reduce to 350°F (180°C) and bake for 30–35 minutes longer.

21 Insert a skewer through the steam vent to check the apples are tender. Serve warm.

Fruit Pie variations

Rhubarb and Strawberry Pie

Make this pie in late spring, when both rhubarb and strawberries are at their very best.

SERVES 6–8 | **30–35 MINS** | **50–55 MINS**

Chilling time
45 mins

Special equipment
9in (23cm) pie dish

Ingredients
1 uncooked pie crust and pastry for lid, see pages 330, steps 1–7

For the filling
2¼lb (1kg) rhubarb, sliced
finely grated zest of 1 orange
1 cup sugar, plus 1 tbsp to glaze
¼ tsp salt
¼ cup flour
13oz (375g) strawberries, hulled, and halved or quartered
1 tbsp unsalted butter
1 tbsp milk, to glaze

Method

1 In a bowl, combine the rhubarb, orange zest, sugar, salt, and flour, and stir to mix. Add the strawberries and toss. Spoon the fruit mixture into the pie dish already lined with pastry, doming the mixture slightly. Cut the butter into small pieces and dot the pieces all over the filling.

2 Brush the edge of the pastry shell with cold water. Roll out the remaining dough into an 11in (28cm) round. Drape the pastry over the filling, trim it even with the bottom crust, and press the edges to seal.

3 Cut a steam vent in the center of the pie. Brush with milk and sprinkle with the sugar. Chill for 15 minutes. Preheat the oven to 425°F (220°C). Put a baking sheet in the center of the oven to heat up.

4 Bake on the baking sheet for 20 minutes. Reduce the temperature to 350°F (180°C) and bake for another 30–35 minutes, until the crust is browned. Test the fruit with a skewer and if it needs longer but the top could burn, loosely cover with foil. Transfer to a wire rack and let cool. Serve in generous slices with ice cream.

PREPARE AHEAD The dough can be made 2 days ahead and kept in the refrigerator.

Cherry Pie

An iconic American pie, perfect for summer gatherings.

SERVES 4–6 | **30 MINS** | **45 MINS**

Chilling time
1 hr

Special equipment
8in (20cm) metal pie dish with a lip

Ingredients
1½ cups all-purpose flour, plus extra for dusting
9 tbsp unsalted butter, chilled and diced
¼ cup sugar
2 tbsp milk

For the filling
¼ cup sugar
1lb 2oz (500g) cherries, pitted
juice of 1 small lemon
1 tbsp cornstarch
1 large egg, beaten

Method

1 For the pastry, sift the flour into a large bowl. Add the butter and rub with your fingertips until the mixture forms fine crumbs. Stir in the sugar. Add the milk, bringing the mixture together to form a soft dough. Wrap in plastic wrap and chill for 30 minutes. Preheat the oven to 350°F (180°C).

2 For the filling, melt the sugar and 3½ tablespoons of water in a saucepan. Once the sugar has dissolved, add the cherries and lemon juice. Bring to a boil, cover, and simmer for 5 minutes. Mix the cornstarch with 1 tablespoon water to make a paste, then add it to the cherries. Continue to cook over low heat until the mixture thickens.

3 On a floured surface, roll out the pastry to ⅛-¼in (3-5cm) thick. Lift it over the pie dish and line the bottom and the sides of the dish with the pastry. Use scissors to trim off the excess pastry, leaving an overhang of ¾in (2cm). Brush the edge of the pastry with a little beaten egg.

4 Make a ball from the excess pastry and roll it out again, making a circle just bigger than the dish. Fill the crust with the cherries

and put the remaining pastry on top, pressing down firmly. Trim overhanging pastry with a sharp knife and brush top with beaten egg. Cut two slits in the top to allow steam to escape.

5 Bake for 40-45 minutes, until the pastry is golden brown. Serve at room temperature, or chilled, with ice cream or whipped cream.

PREPARE AHEAD The pie can be kept in an airtight container for 2 days, but is best eaten on the day. The filling can be made 3 days ahead and refrigerated. The pastry can be made 1 day ahead and refrigerated.

Blackberry and Apple Pie

This pie is best eaten on the day it is baked, which will not be difficult! ▶

SERVES 4–6   **35–40 MINS**   **50–60 MINS**

Chilling time
45 mins

Special equipment
9½in pie dish
pie funnel

Ingredients
1⅔ cups all-purpose flour, plus extra for dusting
1½ tbsp sugar
¼ tsp salt
3 tbsp vegetable shortening, chilled and diced
4 tbsp unsalted butter, chilled and diced

For the filling
1lb 15oz (875g) apples, peeled, cored, cut in half lengthwise, and sliced into 6 chunks
juice of 1 lemon
⅔ cup sugar, or to taste
1lb 2oz (500g) blackberries

Method
1 Sift the flour, sugar, and salt into a bowl. Add the vegetable shortening and butter, and rub together with your fingertips until crumbs form. Sprinkle water over the mix, 1 tablespoon at a time, stopping as soon as clumps form; too much water toughens the

pastry. Press the dough into a ball, wrap in plastic wrap, and chill for 30 minutes.

2 Put the apples in a bowl, add the lemon juice and all but 2 tablespoons of sugar and toss. Add the blackberries and toss again.

3 Roll out the dough to a shape 3in (7.5cm) larger than the top of the dish. Invert the dish onto the pastry. Cut a ¾in (2cm) strip the dough, leaving a shape 1½in (4cm) larger than the dish. Place a pie funnel in the center. Spoon the fruit around.

4 Moisten the edge of the dish with water and transfer the strip of pastry, pressing firmly. Brush the strip with cold water and transfer the pastry top, pressing down to seal. Cut a hole over the pie funnel and trim the edges. Chill for 15 minutes. Preheat the oven to 375°F (190°C). Bake for 50–60 minutes, until lightly browned and crisp. Sprinkle with sugar and serve hot or warm.

PREPARE AHEAD The dough can be made 2 days ahead and kept in the refrigerator, wrapped in plastic wrap.

Mince Pies

The mincemeat in this classic English recipe is quick to prepare and needs no time to mature, making these a very easy, festive treat to bake.

MAKES 18　**20 MINS**　**10–12 MINS**　**UP TO 8 WEEKS**

Chilling time
10 mins

Special equipment
3in (7.5cm) and 2½in (6cm) biscuit cutters

Ingredients
1 small apple
2 tbsp butter, melted
½ cup golden raisins
½ cup raisins
¼ cup currants
¼ cup mixed peel, chopped
⅓ cup chopped almonds or hazelnuts
finely grated zest of 1 lemon
1 tsp pumpkin pie spice
1 tbsp brandy or whisky
2 tbsp dark brown sugar
1 small banana
1 9-inch (23 cm) store-bought pie dough
all-purpose flour, for dusting
confectioner's sugar, for dusting

Method

1 Preheat the oven to 375°F (190°C). Grate the apple (including the skin), and place in a large bowl. Add the melted butter, golden raisins, raisins, currants, mixed peel, nuts, lemon zest, pumpkin pie spice, brandy, and sugar, and mix. Chop the banana into small dice, and add to the bowl. Mix well.

2 Roll out the pastry on a lightly floured surface to a thickness of ⅛in (2mm) and cut out 18 circles using the larger biscuit cutters. Re-roll the pastry, and cut a further 18 smaller circles or shapes, such as stars.

3 Line a muffin pan with the larger pastry circles, and place a heaped teaspoon of mincemeat in each small pastry shell. Top with the smaller circles or shapes. Chill for 10 minutes, and then bake for 10–12 minutes, or until the pastry is golden. Carefully remove from the pans, and cool on a wire rack. Dust with confectioner's sugar to serve.

STORE The pies will keep for 3 days in an airtight container.

PREPARE AHEAD The dough can be made 2 days ahead and kept in the refrigerator, wrapped in plastic wrap.

BAKER'S TIP

Home-made mincemeat will always taste far superior to any store-bought version. The diced banana used in this mincemeat recipe might not be an orthodox ingredient, but it does lend a rich, velvety texture to the mincemeat.

Galette des rois

Traditionally, rum or brandy is used to flavor the filling in this classic French pie, but milk can easily be substituted for a child-friendly version.

SERVES 6–8 | **25 MINS** | **30 MINS** | **UP TO 8 WEEKS**

Ingredients
½ cup sugar
7 tbsp unsalted butter, softened
1 large egg, plus 1 more, beaten, for glazing
1 cup ground almonds
1 tsp almond extract
1 tbsp brandy, rum or milk
all-purpose flour, for dusting
1lb 2oz (500g) store-bought all-butter puff pastry, or see page 178, steps 1–9

Method

1 Preheat the oven to 400°F (200°C). In a bowl with an electric hand mixer, or in an electric mixer with paddle attachment, cream together the sugar and butter. Beat in the egg.

2 Mix in the ground almonds, almond extract, and rum, brandy, or milk, to make a thick paste.

3 On a well-floured work surface, roll out the pastry to a 20 x 10in (50 x 25cm) rectangle. The measurements do not have to be exact, but the pastry should be ⅛–¼in (3–5mm) thick.

4 Fold the pastry in half and use a 10in (25cm) dinner plate or similar to cut out 2 disks. Lay 1 disk out on a non-stick baking sheet. Use a little beaten egg to brush around the edge of the disk. Spread the almond filling on to the pastry disk, spreading it out smoothly to within ½in (1cm) of the edge.

5 Put the other pastry disk on top of the filling, and use your fingers or the back of a fork to press down and seal the two disks together. Use a small, sharp knife to score a series of thin slivers in the top of the pastry, in a spiral design, being careful not to allow them to meet in the center or the pastry will pull apart when cooking. If you are feeling very artistic, you could also try cutting the edges of the pastry into a scalloped edge before cooking.

6 Brush the top of the pastry with beaten egg and bake at the top of the oven for 30 minutes, until golden brown and puffed up. Allow the galette to cool for 5 minutes on its baking sheet before removing to a wire rack to cool completely. Serve warm or cold.

STORE The galette will keep in an airtight container for 3 days.

PREPARE AHEAD The almond cream can be prepared 3 days ahead of time and stored in the refrigerator.

BAKER'S TIP
In France, this almond cream puff pastry is eaten on January 6, to celebrate Epiphany. However, it is so simple and delicious that it should definitely be eaten more than once a year. It makes a great picnic dish.

Cherry Strudel

Don't be intimidated by the making of this ultra-thin pastry; the trick is to knead it well so the dough is elastic.

SERVES 6–8 | **45–50 MINS** | **30–40 MINS** | **UP TO 4 WEEKS**

Ingredients

1¾ cups all-purpose flour, plus extra for dusting
1 large egg
½ tsp lemon juice
pinch of salt
9 tbsp unsalted butter, plus extra for greasing

For the filling

1lb 2oz (500g) cherries
1 lemon
⅔ cup walnuts
½ cup light brown sugar
1 tsp ground cinnamon
confectioner's sugar, for sprinkling

1 Sift the flour onto a work surface and make a well in the center.

2 In a bowl, beat the egg with ½ cup water, the lemon juice, and salt. Pour into the well.

3 Work the ingredients in the well, drawing in a little of the flour with your fingertips.

4 Gradually knead in just enough flour so the dough forms a ball; it should be quite soft.

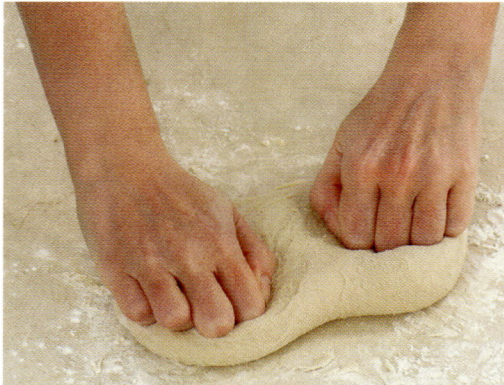

5 On a floured work surface, knead for 10 minutes until shiny and smooth.

6 Shape into a ball, cover with a bowl, and let rest for 30 minutes.

7 Pit the cherries. Grate the zest from the lemon onto a plate to retain the essential oils.

8 Coarsely chop the walnuts until even in size but with some larger chunks. Set aside.

9 Cover a work table with an old, clean bed sheet. Lightly and evenly flour it.

10 Roll out the dough to a very large square. Cover with damp kitchen towels for 15 minutes.

11 Preheat the oven to 375°F (190°C). Grease a baking sheet. Melt the butter in a saucepan.

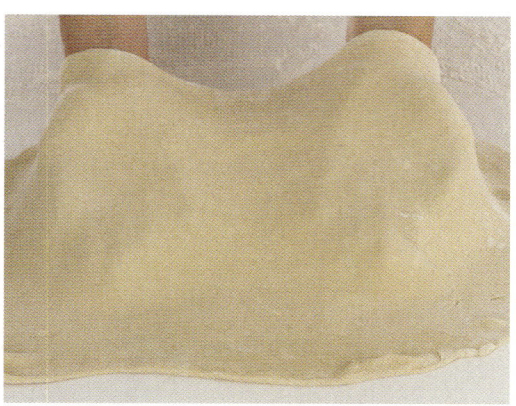

12 Flour your hands and stretch the dough, starting at the center and working outward.

13 Continue to work outward until the dough is as thin as possible; it should be translucent.

14 Immediately brush the dough evenly with about three-quarters of the melted butter.

15 Sprinkle the buttered dough with the cherries, walnuts, sugar, zest, and cinnamon.

16 Trim off the thicker edges, pulling them out and pinching them off with your fingers.

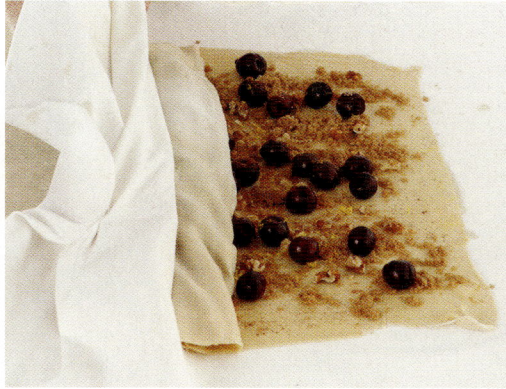

17 Roll up the strudel using the sheet, working gently but firmly and ensuring even pressure.

18 Transfer the roll to the baking sheet and shape it into a crescent, or a loose circle.

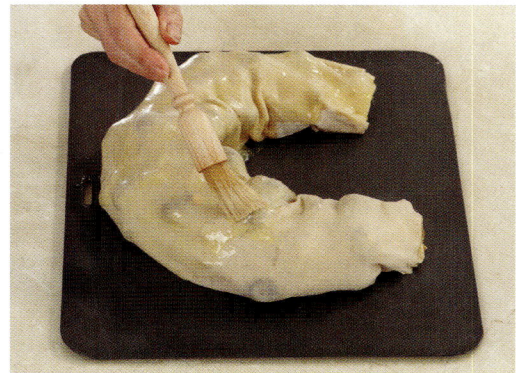

19 Brush with the remaining melted butter and bake for 30–40 minutes, until crisp.

20 Leave for a few minutes before moving to a wire rack, using a metal spatula.

21 Sprinkle with confectioner's sugar and serve warm, with crème fraîche.

Strudel variations

Dried Fruit Strudel

Ideal for the colder months, when many fresh fruits are out of season, this strudel would make an impressive alternative Christmas dessert.

SERVES 6–8 | 45–50 MINS | 30–40 MINS | UP TO 4 WEEKS

Ingredients

1lb 2oz (500g) mixed dried fruit (apricots, prunes, dates, raisins, figs)
½ cup dark rum
5 tbsp unsalted butter, melted, plus extra for greasing
4 10 x 18in (25 x 45cm) sheets filo pastry, thawed if frozen
⅔ cup walnuts, coarsely chopped
½ cup light brown sugar
1 tsp ground cinnamon
confectioner's sugar, for sprinkling

Method

1 Put the dried fruit into a saucepan with the rum and ½ cup water. Place over low heat and stir occasionally for 5 minutes. Remove from the heat and leave to cool. The fruit will plump up. Grease a baking sheet. Preheat the oven to 375°F (190°C).

2 Place a sheet of filo on a clean work surface and brush with melted butter. Lay another sheet on top and brush with butter. Repeat with the remaining pastry sheets.

3 Drain the dried fruit, and sprinkle on to the filo pastry, leaving a ¾in (2cm) border all the way around the edge. Sprinkle on the walnuts, brown sugar, and cinnamon.

4 Roll the pastry, starting from one of the longer sides, and press the ends together tightly. Transfer the strudel on to the baking sheet and brush with a little melted butter.

5 Bake for 30–40 minutes, until golden. Leave on the baking sheet for a few minutes then transfer to a wire rack. Sprinkle with confectioner's sugar and serve warm.

PREPARE AHEAD The uncooked strudel can be stored in the refrigerator a few hours before baking. The cooked strudel can be warmed in the oven 1 day later.

Squash and Goat Cheese Strudel

This makes a good vegetarian alternative at a festive gathering.

MAKES 4 | 15 MINS | 20–25 MINS | UP TO 4 WEEKS

Ingredients

2 tbsp olive oil
3 red onions, finely sliced
2 tbsp balsamic vinegar
pinch of sugar
sea salt
freshly ground black pepper
all-purpose flour, for dusting
1 pack (12 sheets) ready-made filo, about 10 x 10in (25 x 25cm)
4 tbsp unsalted butter, melted
1lb 2oz (500g) peeled and seeded butternut squash, coarsely grated (about 5 cups)
2 tbsp sage, finely chopped
9oz (250g) soft goat cheese, crumbled

Method

1 Preheat the oven to 400°F (200°C). Heat the olive oil in a frying pan over medium heat. Add the onions and cook for around 5 minutes, until soft. Add the balsamic vinegar, sugar, and a generous amount of salt and pepper, and cook over a low heat for a further 5 minutes.

2 On a well floured work surface lay out 4 sheets of filo pastry, overlapping slightly. Brush each one with melted butter, and cover with a second layer. Brush with butter again and cover with a third layer. Brush the top layer with any remaining butter, being careful to brush around the edges first (this will help to seal the strudels later).

3 Now scatter the butternut squash evenly over the surface of the 4 pastry bases, leaving a clean border of at least ¾in (2cm) around all the edges except those nearest to you. Scatter the onions on top, then the sage. Finally, add the goat cheese and season with black pepper and a little salt.

4 Fold in the 2 sides of the strudel that are free of filling, then roll each up, starting with the side nearest you. Tuck the sides in as you roll, and finish with the join tucked underneath. Carefully transfer to a baking sheet and brush with any remaining butter.

5 Bake the strudels at the top of a hot oven for 20–25 minutes until golden brown and crispy. Leave to cool for at least 10 minutes before serving, although the strudels can be served either hot or cold.

PREPARE AHEAD The uncooked strudels can be stored in the refrigerator, covered, a few hours before baking. The cooked strudels can be warmed in the oven 1 day later.

BAKER'S TIP
This vegetarian strudel takes only minutes to make with the help of store-bought filo pastry. Grating the squash adds a nice texture and if you have a food processor with a grater attachment, the preparation is even quicker.

Apple Strudel
A Viennese speciality, this is delicious served warm or cold. ▶

| SERVES 10–12 | 50 MINS | 40 MINS | UP TO 4 WEEKS |

Ingredients
4 tbsp unsalted butter, melted,
  plus extra for greasing
2¼lb (1kg) crisp apples, such as Gala or Braeburn
finely grated zest of ½ lemon
3 tbsp rum
¼ cup raisins
½ cup sugar
few drops of pure vanilla extract
⅓ cup blanched almonds, chopped
4 10 x 18in (25 x 45cm) sheets filo pastry,
  thawed if frozen
½-⅔ cup fresh breadcrumbs
confectioner's sugar, for dusting

Method
1 Preheat the oven to 350°F (180°C). Grease a baking sheet. To make the filling, peel, core, and cut the apples into pieces. Place in a bowl and mix with the lemon zest, rum, raisins, sugar, vanilla extract, and almonds.

2 Place a sheet of filo on a clean work surface and brush with melted butter. Lay another sheet on top and brush with butter. Repeat with the remaining pastry sheets.

3 Sprinkle the breadcrumbs over the pastry, leaving a ¾in (2cm) border. Spoon the filling over the breadcrumbs and fold the edges of the short sides over the filling. Roll the pastry, starting from one of the longer sides, and press the ends together tightly. Transfer the strudel to the baking sheet and brush with a little melted butter.

4 Bake in the oven for 30–40 minutes, brushing the strudel with the remaining melted butter after the first 20 minutes.

5 Remove the strudel from the oven and allow to cool on the baking sheet. Sprinkle with confectioner's sugar and serve warm or cold.

PREPARE AHEAD The uncooked strudel can be stored in the refrigerator a few hours before baking. The cooked strudel can be warmed in the oven 1 day later.

Baklava

This crispy Middle Eastern confection, filled with chopped nuts and spices and drenched with honey syrup, has long been a favorite.

MAKES 36	50-55 MINS	1¼-1½ HOURS

Special equipment

12 x 16in (30 x 40cm) baking dish with deep sides
sugar thermometer (optional)

Ingredients

9oz (250g) shelled unsalted pistachio nuts, coarsely chopped
9oz (250g) walnut pieces, coarsely chopped
1 cup sugar
2 tsp ground cinnamon
large pinch of ground cloves
1lb 2oz (500g) package of filo pastry
18 tbsp unsalted butter
1 cup honey
juice of 1 lemon
3 tbsp orange flower water

Method

1 Set aside 3–4 tablespoons of the chopped pistachios for decoration. Put the remainder in a bowl with the walnuts, ¼ cup of the sugar, cinnamon, and cloves. Stir to mix.

2 Preheat the oven to 350°F (180°C). Lay a damp kitchen towel on a work surface, unroll the filo sheets on it, and cover with a second damp towel. Melt the butter in a small saucepan. Brush the baking dish with a little butter. Take 1 sheet of filo and line the dish with it, folding over one end to fit.

3 Brush the filo with butter, and gently press it into the corners and sides of the dish. Lay another sheet on top, brush it with butter, and press it into the dish as before. Continue layering the filo, buttering each sheet, until one-third has been used. Scatter half the nut filling over the top sheet.

4 Layer another third of the filo sheets as before, then sprinkle the remaining nut filling over it. Layer the remaining sheets in the same way. Trim off excess with a knife. Brush with butter, and pour any remaining butter on top. With a small knife, cut diagonal lines, ½in (1cm) deep, in the filo to mark out 1½in (4cm) diamond shapes. Do not press down when cutting.

5 Bake on a low shelf for 1¼–1½ hours, until golden. A skewer inserted in the center for 30 seconds should come out clean.

6 For the syrup, put the remaining sugar and 1 cup of water in a pan and heat until dissolved, stirring occasionally. Pour in the honey and stir to mix. Boil for about 25 minutes without stirring, until the syrup reaches the soft ball stage, 239°F (115°C) on a sugar thermometer. To test the syrup without a thermometer, take the pan from the heat and dip a teaspoon in the hot syrup. Let the syrup cool a few seconds, then take a little between your finger and thumb; it should form a soft ball.

7 Remove the syrup from the heat and let it cool to lukewarm. Add the lemon juice and orange flower water. Remove the dish from the oven and immediately pour the syrup over the pastries. With a sharp knife, cut along the marked lines, almost to the bottom (see Baker's Tip), then let the pastries cool.

8 Cut through the marked lines completely. Carefully lift out the pastries with a palette knife and arrange them on each dessert plate. Sprinkle the top of each pastry with the reserved chopped pistachio nuts.

PREPARE AHEAD The pastries can be made 5 days before serving. Store in an airtight container; the flavor will mellow.

BAKER'S TIP

Filo pastry is very delicate, and can crumble slightly when cut. The syrup used in this recipe will help minimize this, but not stop it completely. Make sure you use a very sharp, slim blade to cut the baklava, and be sure to score it first, as instructed in the recipe, for the neatest looking baklava.

Blueberry Cobbler

A classic summer-fruit pudding, easy to make and great for a hungry family.

SERVES 6–8 | **15 MINS** | **30 MINS**

Special equipment
shallow ovenproof dish

Ingredients

For the filling
1lb (3½ cups) blueberries
2 large peaches or 2 apples, cored, peeled, and diced
finely grated zest of ½ lemon
2 tbsp sugar

For the cobbler
1½ cups all-purpose flour
1 tsp baking powder
⅓ cup sugar, plus 1 tbsp for sprinkling
pinch of salt
5 tbsp unsalted butter, chilled and diced
½ cup buttermilk
1 large egg
handful of sliced almonds

1 Preheat the oven to 375°F (190°C). Put the fruit in the dish and add sugar and zest.

2 For the cobbler topping, sift the flour, baking powder, sugar, and salt into a bowl.

3 Add the butter and mix with your fingers until the mixture resembles breadcrumbs.

4 Beat together the buttermilk and egg, add to the dry ingredients, and mix to form a dough.

5 Place walnut-sized spoonfuls over the fruit, leaving space for the mix to spread.

6 Press the balls of mixture down lightly, to help them combine with the fruit.

7 Evenly sprinkle over the flaked almonds and the remaining 1 tablespoon sugar.

8 Bake for 30 minutes, until golden and bubbling. If it browns quickly, cover with foil.

9 Insert a skewer into the middle of the center "cobble." It should emerge clean.

SWEET TARTS AND PIES

10 If the skewer has uncooked mixture on it, return the cobbler to the oven for another 5 minutes, then take out and test again. Leave the cobbler to cool briefly before serving straight from the dish, with plenty of custard or cream. Best eaten the same day.

Cobbler variations

Peach Cobbler

Gently poaching the peaches for a few minutes first helps them to break down to a delicious, sticky mass after baking. Really ripe peaches will need no poaching.

SERVES 6–8   **20 MINS**   **30–35 MINS**

Special equipment
shallow ovenproof dish

Ingredients

For the filling
¼ cup sugar
8 ripe peaches, peeled, stoned, and quartered
1 tsp cornstarch
juice of ½ lemon

For the cobbler
1½ cups all-purpose flour
1 tsp baking powder
pinch of salt
½–¾ tsp ground cinnamon, to taste
5 tbsp unsalted butter
⅓ cup sugar
1 large egg
½ cup buttermilk
1 tbsp light brown sugar

Method

1 Preheat the oven to 375°F (190°C). Heat the sugar and 3–4 tablespoons water together in a large, heavy-based saucepan. Once the sugar has dissolved, add the peaches and cook over medium heat, covered, for 2–3 minutes. Mix the cornstarch with the lemon juice to make a paste, then add it to the peaches. Continue to cook, uncovered, over low heat until the liquid thickens around the peaches. Put the peaches in the dish.

2 Sift the flour, baking powder, salt, and cinnamon into a bowl. Rub in the butter until the mixture resembles fine breadcrumbs. Stir in the sugar. Whisk together the egg and the buttermilk. Add the liquid to the dry ingredients and bring it together to form a soft, sticky dough.

3 Drop heaped tablespoonfuls of the dough over the surface of the fruit, leaving a little space between them. Sprinkle with the brown sugar. Bake at the top of the oven for 25–30 minutes, or until golden and bubbling. The cobbler is ready when a skewer inserted into the center of the topping comes out clean. Leave to cool for at least 5 minutes before serving with ice cream, custard, or cream.

BAKER'S TIP

Once you have mastered the art of making a cobbler topping, you can use it as a quick finishing touch to any fresh fruit you have on hand. Harder fruits may need to be poached first, but most can be tossed in sugar and a few spices before topping with the cobbler mix.

Apple and Blackberry Cobbler

The classic autumnal fruit pairing of blackberry and apple is given a twist here with a cobbler topping, rather than the more usual pie crust or crumble top.

SERVES 6–8   **20 MINS**   **30 MINS**

Special equipment
shallow ovenproof dish

Ingredients

For the filling
2¼lb (1kg) apples, peeled, cored and roughly chopped
9oz (250g) blackberries
juice of ½ lemon
2 tbsp sugar
2 tbsp light brown sugar
2 tbsp unsalted butter, chilled and diced

For the cobbler
1½ cups all-purpose flour
1 tsp baking powder
pinch of salt
½–¾ tsp ground cinnamon, to taste
5 tbsp unsalted butter
⅓ cup sugar
1 large egg
½ cup buttermilk
1 tbsp light brown sugar

Method

1 Preheat the oven to 375°F (190°C). Toss the apples and blackberries in the lemon juice, then mix them together with the two types of sugar. Put them in the ovenproof dish and dot with the butter.

2 Sift the flour, baking powder, salt, and cinnamon into a bowl. Rub in the butter until the mixture resembles fine breadcrumbs. Stir in the sugar. Whisk together the egg and the buttermilk. Add the liquid to the dry ingredients and bring it together to form a soft, sticky dough.

3 Drop heaped tablespoonfuls of the dough over the surface of the fruit, leaving a little space between them. Sprinkle with the light brown sugar. Bake in the center of the oven for 30 minutes, or until golden and bubbling. The cobbler is ready when a skewer inserted into the center of the topping comes out clean. Leave to cool for at least 5 minutes before serving with ice cream, custard, or cream.

Cinnamon and Plum Cobbler

Use brown sugar and cinnamon to add a sweet, dark, spicy flavor to really ripe plums. Cobblers are quick to make, but to speed things up even more, use a food processor to make the crumbs for the cobbler dough.

SERVES 6–8   **20 MINS**   **30 MINS**

Special equipment
shallow ovenproof dish

Ingredients

For the filling
2¼lb (1kg) plums, pitted and halved
¼ cup light brown sugar
1 tsp cinnamon
2 tbsp unsalted butter, chilled and diced

For the cobbler
1½ cups all-purpose flour
1 tsp baking powder
pinch of salt
½–¾ tsp ground cinnamon, to taste
5 tbsp unsalted butter
⅓ cup sugar
1 large egg
½ cup buttermilk
1 tbsp light brown sugar

Method

1 Preheat the oven to 375°F (190°C). Toss the plums with the sugar and cinnamon. Put them in the ovenproof dish and dot with the butter.

2 Sift the flour, baking powder, salt, and cinnamon into a bowl. Rub in the butter until the mixture resembles fine breadcrumbs. Stir in the sugar. Whisk together the egg and the buttermilk. Add the liquid to the dry ingredients and bring it together to form a soft, sticky dough.

3 Drop heaped tablespoonfuls of the dough over the surface of the fruit, leaving a little space between them. Sprinkle with the soft light brown sugar.

4 Bake in the center of the preheated oven for 30 minutes, or until golden and bubbling. The cobbler is ready when a skewer inserted into the center of the topping comes out clean. Leave to cool for at least 5 minutes before serving with ice cream, custard, or cream.

Plum Crumble

This popular dessert is quick and easy to make, and suitable for any occasion.

| SERVES 4 | 10 MINS | 30–40 MINS | 4 WEEKS, TOPPING |

Ingredients

For the crumble topping
1¼ cups all-purpose flour
7 tbsp unsalted butter, chilled and cubed
½ cup light brown sugar
¾ cup rolled oats

For the filling
1lb 5oz (600g) plums, pitted and halved
maple syrup or honey, to drizzle

Method

1 Preheat the oven to 400°F (200°C). To make the crumble topping, place the flour in a large mixing bowl. Rub in the butter with your fingertips until the mixture resembles breadcrumbs. Do not make it too fine or your crumble will have a soggy top. Stir in the sugar and the oats.

2 Place the plums in a medium ovenproof dish, drizzle the maple syrup over, and top with the crumble.

3 Bake for 30–40 minutes, or until the top is golden brown and the plum juices are beginning to bubble.

PREPARE AHEAD The crumble mix can be made 1 month in advance and kept frozen until ready to use.

BAKER'S TIP
Though a homey dessert, there are few more welcome sights on the dinner table than a crumble. Use a recipe when making a crumble topping: it may seem like child's play, but it is easy to include too much fat, creating a topping that "melts" when baked, or too little, resulting in a dry crumble.

Apple Brown Betty

A "betty" is a baked fruit dessert topped with buttered bread crumbs. This dessert was made popular during the Colonial era.

SERVES 4   30 MINS   35–45 MINS

Special equipment
1 quart (1.2 liter) baking dish

Ingredients

6 tbsp unsalted butter
1¾ cups (6oz) fresh bread crumbs
2lb (900g) apples, such as Bramley, Granny Smith, or Golden Delicious (about 4 apples)
¾ cup brown sugar
1 tsp ground cinnamon
½ tsp pumpkin pie spice
finely grated zest of 1 lemon
2 tbsp lemon juice
1 tsp pure vanilla extract

Method

1 Preheat the oven to 350°F (180°C). Melt the butter in a saucepan, add the bread crumbs, and mix well.

2 Peel, quarter, and core the apples. Cut each quarter into slices and place in a bowl. Add the sugar, cinnamon, pumpkin pie spice, lemon zest and juice, and vanilla extract, and mix well.

3 Put half the apple mixture into the baking dish. Cover with half the bread crumbs, then put in the rest of the apples and top with the remaining bread crumbs.

4 Bake for 35–45 minutes, checking after 35 minutes. If it is getting too brown, reduce the oven temperature to 325°F (160°C) and cover with parchment paper. It is cooked when the crumbs are golden brown and the apples are soft. Serve warm.

BAKER'S TIP

A betty is simplicity itself to make. The recipe lends itself very well to all sorts of different fruits, though orchard fruits suit it best. And try changing the spices to suit your palate. Be creative: try lemon thyme with pears, or star anise or cardamom with plums.

SWEET TARTS AND PIES

savory
tarts
& pies

Swiss Chard and Gruyère Tart

If chard proves difficult to find, you can substitute spinach in step 14, cooking it for slightly less time.

SERVES 6–8 | **20 MINS** | **55–70 MINS** | **8 WEEKS, PIE CASE**

Chilling time
1 hr

Special equipment
9in (23cm) fluted tart pan with removable bottom
baking beans

Ingredients

For the pastry
⅔ cup all-purpose flour, plus extra for dusting

5 tbsp unsalted butter, chilled and diced
1 egg yolk

For the filling
1 tbsp extra virgin olive oil
1 onion, finely chopped
sea salt
2 garlic cloves, finely chopped

few sprigs of fresh rosemary, leaves picked and finely chopped
9oz (250g) Swiss chard, stalks trimmed
5oz (125g) Gruyère cheese, grated
5oz (125g) feta cheese, cubed
freshly ground black pepper
¾ cup whipping cream
2 large eggs

1 For the pastry, rub the flour and butter together until the mixture forms fine crumbs.

2 Lightly beat the egg yolk with 1 tablespoon of cold water.

3 Add to the crumbs and bring together to form a soft dough. Add extra water if too dry.

4 Wrap in plastic wrap and chill for 1 hour. Preheat the oven to 350°F (180°C).

5 On a floured work surface, roll the pastry out to a large circle around ⅛in (3mm) thick.

6 Lift the pastry carefully, using the rolling pin to help you, and place it into the tart pan.

7 Push it in with your fingers. The pastry should overlap the sides by at least ¾oz (2cm).

8 Prick the bottom all over with a fork, and line with parchment paper.

9 Weigh the parchment down with baking beans. Place the pastry shell on a baking sheet.

SAVORY TARTS AND PIES

10 Bake in the center of the oven for 20–25 minutes. Remove the beans and paper.

11 Bake for 5 more minutes to crisp the bottom. Leave to cool and trim the edges with a knife.

PREPARE AHEAD The pastry can be made 2 days ahead, wrapped in plastic, and chilled.

12 Meanwhile, heat the oil in a pan over low heat. Add the onion and a pinch of salt.

13 Sweat the onion until soft. Add the garlic and rosemary, and cook for a few seconds.

14 Roughly chop the Swiss chard and add to the pan. Stir for about 5 minutes until it wilts.

15 Set the pastry shell on a baking sheet and spoon in the onion and chard mixture.

16 Sprinkle over the Gruyère cheese, and scatter with the feta. Season well.

17 With a fork, mix together the cream and the 2 eggs until well combined.

18 Carefully pour the cream and egg mix over the tart filling.

19 Bake for 30–40 minutes until golden. Leave to cool before releasing from the pan.

20 Serve warm or at room temperature. Best eaten the same day. Can be chilled overnight.

Savory Tart variations

Onion Tart

A deep-filled onion tart is one of my favorite dishes—it is amazing how a simple filling of onions, cream, and eggs can produce such delicious results.

| SERVES 6–8 | 25 MINS | 80–85 MINS | UP TO 8 WEEKS |

Chilling time
1 hr

Special equipment
9in (22cm) tart pan
baking beans

Ingredients
1 pastry shell, see pages 358–359, steps 1–11

For the filling
2 tbsp olive oil
2 tbsp butter
1lb 2oz (500g) finely sliced onions
sea salt
freshly ground black pepper
¾ cup heavy cream
1 large egg, plus 1 egg yolk

Method

1 Heat the olive oil and butter in a pan and add the onions. Season well and, when sizzling, reduce the heat and cook over low heat, covered, for 20 minutes, stirring occasionally. The onions should soften, but not brown. Take the lid off, increase the heat, and cook the onions for 5–10 minutes to allow any water to dry.

2 Place the onions in the pastry shell and spread them out. Whisk together the heavy cream, egg, egg yolk, and seasoning. Place the tart back on a baking sheet and pour the cream mixture over the onions. Use a fork to help distribute the cream evenly, by pushing the onions from side to side a little.

3 Bake in the center of the oven for 30 minutes, until the mixture has just set, and is lightly golden and slightly puffy. Remove the tart from the oven, trim the edges of the pastry, and allow it to cool for at least 20 minutes before eating warm or cold.

STORE This is best eaten the day it is made, but the tart can be chilled overnight.

PREPARE AHEAD The pastry shell can be prepared 2 days in advance, and wrapped in plastic wrap until needed.

Smoked Trout Tartlets

These tartlets are perfect for taking on a picnic lunch or as part of a buffet spread, and work equally well as a first course or for a light supper.

| MAKES 6 | 30 MINS | 25–30 MINS | UP TO 4 WEEKS |

Chilling time
30 mins

Special equipment
food processor with blade attachment
6 x 4in (10cm) tartlet pans
baking beans

Ingredients
1 cup all-purpose flour, plus extra for dusting
3 tbsp unsalted butter, chilled and diced
pinch of salt
1 small egg

For the filling
4oz (115ml) crème fraîche
1 tsp creamed horseradish
½ tsp lemon juice
finely grated zest of ½ lemon
1 tsp capers, rinsed and chopped
sea salt
freshly ground black pepper
4 large egg yolks, beaten
7oz (200g) smoked trout
bunch of dill, chopped

Method

1 To make the pastry, place the flour, butter, and salt in a food processor, and process until the mixture forms crumbs. Add the egg and mix until incorporated.

2 Roll out the dough on a well floured surface, and line the tartlet pans. Line the tart crusts with parchment paper, fill with baking beans, and chill for 30 minutes.

3 Preheat the oven to 400°F (200°C). Blind bake the pastry crusts for 10 minutes, then remove the beans and parchment, and bake for a further 5 minutes.

4 Mix the crème fraîche, horseradish, lemon juice and zest, and capers in a bowl, and season to taste with salt and pepper. Stir in the egg yolks, fish, and herbs.

5 Divide the mixture among the tart crusts and return to the oven for 10–15 minutes, or until set. Allow to cool for 5 minutes before removing from the pans and serving with a mixed leaf salad.

STORE These are best eaten the day they are made, but can be chilled overnight.

PREPARE AHEAD The pastry shells can be prepared 2 days in advance, and wrapped in plastic wrap until needed.

BAKER'S TIP

A good quiche or savory tart is a simple combination of short, buttery pastry, cream, and eggs, plus filling, of course. I always blind bake the crusts for these types of tarts before filling them, as this helps the pastry to remain crisp at the base even after contact with the creamy filling.

Quiche Lorraine

A French classic, this egg and bacon flan is the original quiche.

SERVES 4–6 | 35 MINS | 47–52 MINS

Chilling time
30 mins

Special equipment
9in (23cm) x 1½in (4cm) deep tart pan
baking beans

Ingredients
1⅓ cups all-purpose flour, plus extra for dusting
1 stick unsalted butter, cubed
1 large egg yolk

For the filling
7oz (200g) thick-cut bacon, cut into ½ in thick slices
1 onion, finely chopped
3oz (75g) Gruyère cheese, grated
4 large eggs, lightly beaten
⅔ cup heavy cream
⅔ cup milk
freshly ground black pepper

Method

1 To make the pastry, place the flour and butter in a large bowl and rub with your fingertips until the mixture resembles fine crumbs. Add the egg yolk, and 3–4 tablespoons chilled water, and mix to make a smooth dough. Turn out on a floured surface and knead briefly. Wrap in plastic wrap and chill for 30 minutes. Preheat the oven to 375°F (190°C).

2 On a lightly floured surface, roll out the pastry and line the dish, pressing the dough to the sides. Prick the base of the pastry with a fork and line with parchment paper and baking beans. Bake blind for 12 minutes, then remove the paper and beans, and bake for a further 10 minutes, or until lightly golden.

3 Meanwhile, heat a large frying pan and dry–fry the bacon for 3–4 minutes. Add the onion, fry for a further 2–3 minutes, then spread the onions and bacon over the pastry crust. Add the cheese. Whisk together the eggs, cream, milk, and black pepper, and pour into the pastry crust. Place the dish on a baking sheet and bake for 25–30 minutes, until golden and just set. Allow to set, then slice and serve the quiche while still piping hot.

PREPARE AHEAD Cook up to 48 hours in advance, let cool, then refrigerate. Reheat at 325°F (160°C) for 15–20 minutes.

SAVORY TART VARIATIONS

Savory Tart variations

Crab and Shrimp Tart with Saffron

A tart to impress, the delicate flavors of crab and shrimp balance wonderfully with the assertive pungency and musky taste of saffron, in turn balanced by the fresh zest of the herbs.

| SERVES 2–4 | 20 MINS | 50–65 MINS | UP TO 8 WEEKS |

Chilling time
1 hr

Special equipment
6in (15cm) tart pan
baking beans

Ingredients
1 cup all-purpose flour, plus extra for dusting
4 tbsp unsalted butter, chilled and diced
1 large egg yolk

For the filling
pinch of saffron
5oz (125g) white crab meat
4oz (100g) small cold water shrimp
¾ cup heavy cream
1 large egg
1 tbsp finely chopped tarragon or chervil
sea salt
freshly ground black pepper

Method

1 Rub the flour and butter together until the mixture forms fine crumbs. Add the egg yolk and 1 tablespoon cold water and bring the mixture together to form a soft dough. Add a little extra water if the mixture is too dry to form a dough easily. Wrap in plastic wrap and chill for 1 hour.

2 Preheat the oven to 350°F (180°C). On a well floured work surface, roll the pastry out to a large circle, around ⅛in (3mm) thick. Lift the pastry carefully, using the rolling pin to help you, and place it into the tart pan, making sure it overlaps the sides. Take a pair of scissors and trim off all but ¾in (2cm) of the overhanging pastry. Use your fingers to push the pastry down into the pan. Prick the bottom all over with a fork, line with parchment paper, weigh it down with baking beans, and place it on a baking sheet.

3 Blind bake the tart crust in the center of the oven for 20–25 minutes, until lightly cooked. Remove the beans and paper and return the pastry crust to the oven for 5 minutes to crisp up the bottom, if necessary. Allow to cool.

4 Bring a small saucepan of water to a boil and splash 1 tablespoon hot water over the saffron in a small bowl to allow the color to develop. Put the crab meat and shrimp into a sieve and press down well over a sink to remove any excess water, as this will make the tart soggy. Use your fingers to mix the crab and shrimp together, then scatter them over the surface of the tart.

5 Whisk the cream and the egg together in a measuring cup or pitcher. Add the herbs, the saffron and its soaking water, and seasoning, and mix well. Place the pastry crust back on a baking sheet and, with the oven door open, rest it half on, half off the middle oven shelf. Hold the tart with one hand and with the other carefully pour as much of the cream and egg mixture as possible into the tart, then carefully slide it in to the oven.

6 Bake for 30–35 minutes until lightly golden and slightly puffed up. Remove from the oven and let cool for at least 10-15 minutes. Trim the overhanging pastry, and remove from the pan. Serve warm or cold.

PREPARE AHEAD The pastry crust can be prepared 2 days in advance, wrapped in plastic wrap, and chilled until needed.

BAKER'S TIP
Tarts containing crab are very rich, and you may find that a little goes a long way. For a more pronounced crab flavor, replace the total weight of white crab meat and shrimp with a mixture of white and brown crab meat, which will also usually be more economical.

SAVORY TARTS AND PIES

Spinach and Goat Cheese Tart

Fast becoming a modern classic, vegetarians can omit the pancetta.

| SERVES 6–8 | 20 MINS | 55–65 MINS | UP TO 8 WEEKS |

Chilling time
1 hr

Special equipment
9in (22cm) tart pan with removable bottom
baking beans

Ingredients
1 pastry shell, see pages 358–359, steps 1–11

For the filling
6oz (150g) pancetta, diced
1 tbsp olive oil
6oz (150g) baby spinach, washed
4oz (100g) goat cheese
sea salt
freshly ground black pepper
1¼ cups heavy cream
2 large eggs

Method

1 In a frying pan, cook the pancetta in the olive oil for 5 minutes, until golden brown. Add the spinach and cook it for a few minutes until it wilts. If there is water, drain it off before using the filling. Leave to cool.

2 Spread the spinach and pancetta mixture over the base of the pastry crust. Cube or crumble the goat cheese and spread it over the spinach. Season with a little salt (the pancetta is salty) and lots of black pepper.

3 Whisk the cream and eggs in a large measuring cup or pitcher. Place the pastry crust onto a baking sheet and, with the oven door open, rest it half on, half off the middle oven shelf. Hold the sheet with one hand and with the other pour the mixture into the tart, then slide it in to the oven.

4 Bake for 30–35 minutes until lightly golden in places and slightly puffed up. Remove from the oven and leave to cool for at least 10–15 minutes before trimming off the overhanging pastry and removing the tart from the pan. Serve warm or cold.

STORE The tart can be chilled overnight and gently reheated in an oven set to medium heat.

PREPARE AHEAD The pastry crust can be prepared 2 days in advance, wrapped in plastic wrap, and chilled until needed

Flamiche

This classic leek pie originates from the Picardy region of northern France. Although not traditional, the inclusion of blue cheese adds piquancy.

SERVES 4–6 · **20 MINS** · **40–45 MINS**

Special equipment
7in (18cm) springform pan

Ingredients
4 tbsp unsalted butter
2 tbsp olive oil, plus extra for greasing
1lb 2oz (500g) leeks, washed, trimmed, and finely shredded
sea salt and freshly ground black pepper
nutmeg
2 tbsp all-purpose flour, plus extra for dusting
1 cup milk
4oz (100g) blue cheese, such as Stilton (optional)
1lb 2oz (500g) store-bought puff pastry, or 1 quantity puff pastry, see page 178, steps 1–9
1 large egg, beaten

Method

1 Preheat the oven to 400°F (200°C). In a large saucepan, melt the butter and olive oil. Add the leeks and cook over low heat for 10 minutes, stirring occasionally, until well softened but not browned. Season well with salt, pepper, and a little grated nutmeg. Scatter the flour over the surface of the leeks and stir it in well.

2 Pour the milk onto the leeks, a little at a time, stirring constantly. The mixture will thicken to begin with, then gradually loosen as all the milk is added. Bring to a boil, reduce the heat, and cook for 3–5 minutes, until well thickened. Remove from the heat and stir in the cheese (if using).

3 Roll out the puff pastry on a well floured work surface into a 8 x 16in (20 x 40cm) rectangle. It should be ⅛–¼in (3–5mm) thick. Place the pan onto one short edge of the pastry and cut a circle around it to make the lid; the remaining pastry should be large enough to line the bottom of the pan.

4 Oil the pan, trim the remaining pastry and use it to line the pan, allowing the sides to overhang slightly. Brush the interior with a little beaten egg and set aside for 5 minutes; this may seem unusual, but the dried egg wash creates a kind of lacquer that prevents the pastry from going soggy.

5 Fill the pastry crust with the leek mixture and brush a little beaten egg around the edges of the pastry. Top with the disk of pastry and press around the edges to seal together. Brush the top of the flamiche with beaten egg, then cut 2 small slits in the top to allow the steam to escape.

6 Bake in the top third of the oven for 25–30 minutes, until puffed up and golden brown. Remove the flamiche from the oven, trim the excess pastry, and cool for at least 10 minutes before serving warm or cold.

PREPARE AHEAD The flamiche will keep overnight, covered, and chilled in the refrigerator. Gently reheat, or bring back to room temperature, before eating.

> **BAKER'S TIP**
> A flamiche is traditionally decorated by scoring a crisscross pattern of lines over the top of the uncooked pastry. In my experience, however, such overlapping lines can cause the pastry to split. I simply use a very sharp knife to draw lines coming out of the center, like the spokes of a wheel.

Zweibelkuchen

The combination of sour cream and caraway seeds contrast well with the sweet, melting onions used to top this traditional German tart.

SERVES 8   30 MINS   60–65 MINS

Rising and proofing time
1½–2½ hrs

Special equipment
10 x 13in (26 x 32cm) rimmed baking sheet

Ingredients
4 tsp quick-rise dried yeast
3 tbsp olive oil, plus extra for greasing
3¼ cup bread flour, plus extra for dusting
1 tsp salt

For the filling
4 tbsp unsalted butter
2 tbsp olive oil
1lb 5oz (600g) onions, finely sliced
½ tsp caraway seeds
sea salt
freshly ground black pepper
½ cup sour cream
½ cup crème fraîche
3 large eggs
1 tbsp all-purpose flour
3oz (75g) bacon, cooked and crumbled

Method

1 To make the crust, dissolve the yeast in 1 cup warm water. Add the olive oil and set aside. Sift the flour and salt into a large bowl. Make a well in the middle of the flour mixture and pour in the liquid ingredients, stirring all the time. Use your hands to bring the mixture together to form a soft dough. Turn it out onto a well-floured work surface and knead for 10 minutes, until soft, smooth, and elastic.

2 Place the dough in a large, lightly oiled bowl, cover with plastic wrap and leave to rise in a warm place for 1–2 hours, until doubled in size.

3 To make the filling, heat the butter and olive oil in a large, heavy saucepan. Put in the onions and caraway seeds, and season well with salt and pepper. Cook gently for about 20 minutes, covered, until they are soft but not brown. Remove the lid and cook for another 5 minutes until any excess water evaporates.

4 In a separate bowl, whisk together the sour cream, crème fraîche, eggs, and flour, and season well. Mix in the cooked onions and set aside to cool.

5 When the dough has risen well, turn it out onto a floured work surface and push it down gently with your knuckles to "knock it back." Lightly oil the baking sheet. Roll the dough out to roughly the size of the sheet and line the sheet with it, making sure the pie has an upturned edge. Use your fingers to ease the dough into position, if necessary. Cover with lightly oiled plastic wrap and leave to rise in a warm place for another 30 minutes until puffy in places.

6 Preheat the oven to 400°F (200°C). Gently push down the dough if it has risen too much around the edges of the sheet. Spread the filling out over the pie base, and sprinkle the top with bacon.

7 Place the baking sheet in the top shelf of the oven, and bake for 35–40 minutes until golden brown. Remove from the oven and leave to cool for at least 5 minutes before serving. Serve warm or cold.

PREPARE AHEAD Cover and chill overnight.

BAKER'S TIP
This delicious onion and sour cream tart looks like a cross between a pizza and a tart, and is indeed made with a traditional pizza dough base. It is not much known outside its native country, but is well worth making. It was traditionally served during grape harvesting time in parts of Germany.

SAVORY TARTS AND PIES

Steak and Wild Mushroom Pie

A quick puff pastry recipe is incredibly useful in your repertoire, but use store-bought pastry if you're short on time.

SERVES 4–6 **50–55 MINS** **2½–3 HOURS**

Chilling time
1 hr

Special equipment
2 quart pie dish

Ingredients
1lb 2oz (500g) mixed wild mushrooms, sliced, or 3oz (75g) dried wild mushrooms
¼ cup all-purpose flour
2¼lb (1kg) sirloin steak, cut into 1in (2.5cm) cubes
3 cups beef stock or water, plus extra if needed

4 shallots, finely chopped
leaves from 6 parsley sprigs, finely chopped

For the quick puff pastry
1⅓ cups all-purpose flour, plus extra for dusting
salt and pepper

1 stick, plus 4 tbsp cold unsalted butter
1 egg, beaten, to glaze

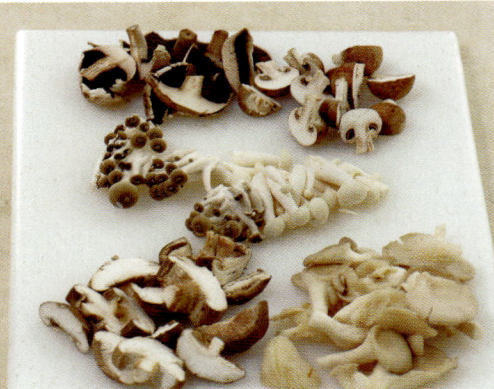

1 Preheat the oven to 350°F (180°C) and slice the mushrooms.

2 Season the flour with salt and pepper. Toss the steak in the flour to coat.

3 Put the meat, mushrooms, and shallots in a casserole. Add the stock and heat, stirring well.

4 Bring to a boil, stirring constantly. Cover and cook in the oven for 2–2¼ hours, until tender.

5 To make the pastry, sift the flour and ½ tsp salt into a bowl. Rub in a third of the butter.

6 Mix to a dough with ½ cup water. Chill in the refrigerator for 15 minutes.

7 Roll out the dough on a lightly floured surface to a 6 x 15in (15 x 38cm) rectangle.

8 Dot the rest of the butter over two-thirds. Fold the unbuttered side over half the buttered side.

9 Fold the dough again so the butter is completely enclosed in layers of dough.

10 Turn it over and roll over the edges to seal. Wrap in plastic wrap and chill for 15 minutes.

11 Roll to 6 x 18in (15 x 45cm), fold in thirds, make a quarter turn. Seal. Chill for 15 minutes.

12 Repeat step 11 three more times, chilling the dough for 15 minutes between each turn.

13 Add the parsley to the meat and season to taste. Spoon it into the dish.

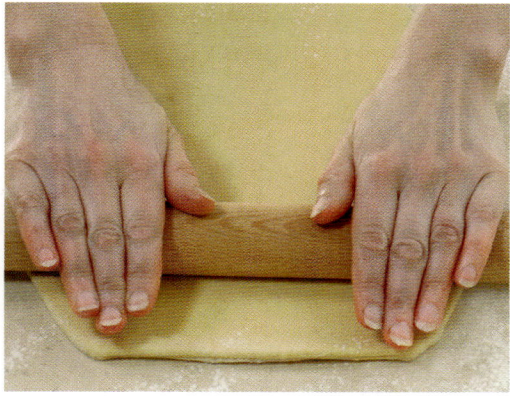

14 Increase the heat to 425°F (220°C). Flour a work surface and roll out the dough.

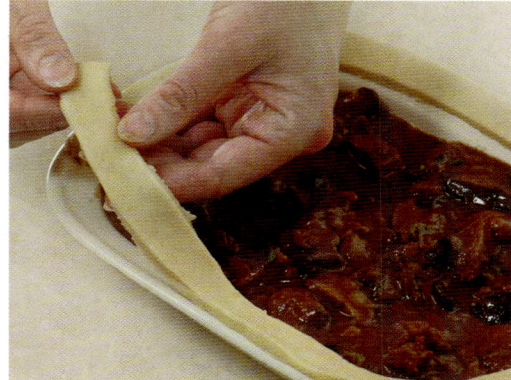

15 Cut a strip from the edge. Moisten the rim of the pie dish, and press the strip onto it.

16 Place the rolled-out dough over the pie. Press firmly to seal it to the rim of the dish.

17 Brush with the beaten egg. Make a hole in the center of the lid to allow steam to escape.

18 Chill the pie for 15 minutes, then bake for 25–35 minutes, until golden brown. If browning too quickly, cover with foil. **PREPARE AHEAD** The pie filling can be made 2–3 days ahead.

STEAK AND WILD MUSHROOM PIE

Savory Pie variations

Fish Pie

Try to use small, cold-water shrimp in this dish, which are not only tastier, but also less likely to have been farmed, making them more sustainable.

SERVES 4   20 MINS   20–25 MINS

Special equipment
7in (18cm) metal pie dish or cake pan

Ingredients
10oz (300g) salmon fillet
7oz (200g) undyed smoked haddock
4 tbsp unsalted butter
5 tbsp all-purpose flour, plus extra for dusting
1½ cups milk
sea salt and freshly ground black pepper
pinch of freshly grated nutmeg
7oz (200g) shrimp
4oz (100g) baby spinach, washed
9oz (250g) ready-made all-butter puff pastry, or see pages 370–371, steps 5–12, reducing by one-third
1 egg, beaten, for glazing

Method
1 Preheat the oven to 400°F (200°C). Gently poach the salmon and haddock in lightly simmering water for 5 minutes, until just cooked. Drain and cool. Melt the butter in a pan. Remove from the heat and whisk in the flour until a thick paste is formed. Add the milk a little at a time, whisking to avoid any lumps. Season and add nutmeg. Bring the sauce to a boil, stirring. Reduce the heat and cook for 5 minutes, stirring.

2 Remove skin and bones and flake the fish into a bowl. Add the shrimp. Spread the uncooked spinach over the top and pour the hot sauce over it. Season to taste. When the spinach is wilted, mix the filling and transfer to the pie dish.

3 On a floured surface, roll out the pastry to a circle bigger than the pie dish, ⅛–¼in (3–5mm) thick. Cut a circle to fit the pie. Roll some of the trimmings out into long strips. Brush the rim of the dish with egg and press the pastry strips around the rim.

4 Brush the edging with egg and top with the pastry lid. Press down to seal the lid and trim off any overhang. Brush the top with egg and cut 2 slits in it. Bake in the top of the oven for 20–25 minutes, until golden, and allow to rest for 5 minutes before serving.

PREPARE AHEAD Chill overnight and reheat.

Chicken Pie

Store-bought pastry makes this an easy option for a weekday supper.

SERVES 4   20 MINS   20–25 MINS

Special equipment
7in (18cm) metal pie dish or cake pan

Ingredients
1 onion, finely chopped
3 tbsp olive oil
2oz (50g) diced pancetta
2 leeks, about 7oz (200g), cut in ½in (1cm) slices
6oz (150g) button mushrooms, washed, halved, or quartered if necessary
2 large chicken breasts, about 14oz (400g), cut in 1in (2.5cm) chunks
1 heaping tbsp chopped thyme
1 heaping tbsp chopped parsley
1 tbsp all-purpose flour, plus extra for dusting
1¼ cups half-and-half
1 tbsp Dijon mustard
sea salt and freshly ground black pepper
9oz (250g) ready-made all-butter puff pastry, or see pages 370–371, steps 5–12, reducing quantities by one-third
1 egg, beaten, for glazing

Method
1 Preheat the oven to 400°F (200°C). In a pan, cook the onion in 2 tablespoons of the olive oil for 5 minutes, until softened, but not brown. Add the pancetta and cook for 2 minutes. Add the leeks and button mushrooms and cook for another 3–5 minutes until the pancetta is crispy.

2 Add the remaining olive oil to the pan and add the chicken and herbs. Cook over high heat for 3–4 minutes until colored on all sides. Sprinkle the flour over the pie filling and stir it in well. Pour in the half-and-half, add the mustard and salt and pepper and bring to a boil, stirring. The mixture should thicken as it heats. Continue to cook for 5 minutes over low heat until the liquid has reduced. Turn the filling out into the pie dish.

3 Roll out the pastry, cover the pie, and bake as directed for Fish Pie, see left, steps 3–4.

Steak and Kidney Double Crust Pie

A classic savory pie with a light, crumbly finish to the crust.

SERVES 4 | 30 MINS | 2¾–3¼ HOURS | 8 WEEKS, UNBAKED

Special equipment
7in (18cm) metal pie dish or cake pan

Ingredients

For the filling
¼ cup olive oil, plus extra for greasing
2 onions, roughly chopped
4oz (100g) button mushrooms, wiped, halved or quartered, if necessary
1lb 5oz (600g) chuck roast, in 1¼in (3cm) chunks
sea salt and freshly ground black pepper
¼ cup all-purpose flour
2 cups beef stock
large sprig of thyme
2 tbsp unsalted butter, softened
4 fresh lamb's kidneys, about 7oz (200g)

For the crust pastry
1½ cups all-purpose flour
1 tsp baking powder
¾ cup cold vegetable shortening, diced
½ tsp salt
1 egg, beaten, for glazing

Method

1 In a pan, heat 2 tablespoons of oil and fry the onion for 5 minutes, until softened but not browned. Add the mushrooms and fry for 3–4 minutes until they begin to color in places. Remove the vegetables from the pan with a slotted spoon and set aside.

2 Toss the diced steak in 2 tablespoons of seasoned flour. Heat the remaining oil in the pan, on high heat, and fry off the meat, until browned. Take care not to overcrowd the pan or the meat will begin to steam rather than brown. Remove the meat as it cooks and add it to the vegetables.

3 Once the meat is seared, return it and the vegetables to the pan. Cover with the beef stock. Season, add the thyme, and bring to a boil. When boiled, reduce the heat to low, cover, and cook for 2–2½ hours, until tender.

4 Rub together the flour, baking powder, salt, and shortening until it looks like crumbs. Add enough cold water to bring the mixture together to a soft dough. Wrap in plastic wrap. Rest the dough for at least 1 hour.

5 Make a paste out of 2 tablespoons of flour mashed into the butter. Uncover the stew and increase the heat. When it begins to boil, add the flour mixture a little at a time, stirring. Reduce the heat and cook over low heat for 30 minutes, until the sauce thickens.

6 Preheat the oven to 350°F (180°C). Trim the kidneys of any skin, cut out the central core, and cut into chunks. Add them to the stew. Roll out the pastry on a floured surface into a 8 x 16in (20cm x 40cm) rectangle. It should be ⅛-¼in (3–5mm) thick. Place the pie dish onto a short edge of the pastry and cut a circle around it for the lid.

7 Oil the pan, trim the remaining pastry and use it to line the pie dish, allowing the sides to overhang. Fill the case with the pie filling and brush egg around the edges of the pastry. Top with the disk of pastry and press down around the edges to seal.

8 Brush the pie with egg, then cut 2 small slits in the top to allow the steam to escape. Bake in the middle of a preheated oven for 40–45 minutes, until golden brown. Remove the pie from the oven and allow it to cool for at least 5 minutes before serving.

PREPARE AHEAD The filling can be made 2 days ahead, and chilled until needed. Do not add the uncooked kidneys until you are ready to bake the pie. This pie is best eaten the day it is made, but can be chilled overnight. Reheat well before eating.

Beef and Ale Cobbler

Great for feeding a crowd, the filling can be prepared days ahead and the whole dish needs no additional attention once it has gone into the oven.

| SERVES 4 | 40 MINS | 2½–3¼ HOURS | 8 WEEKS, STEW |

Special equipment
2in (5cm) pastry cutter

Ingredients

For the filling
¼ cup olive oil
2 onions, finely chopped
1 celery stick, finely diced
1 leek, trimmed and finely sliced
6oz (150g) button mushrooms, wiped, halved or quartered, if needed
1lb 5oz (600g) chuck roast, in 1¼in (3cm) chunks
2 tbsp all-purpose flour

sea salt
freshly ground black pepper
16fl oz (500ml) dark beer or ale, or beef stock
1 beef bouillon cube
1 bouquet garni
1 tbsp sugar
2 large carrots, in ¾in (2cm) chunks

For the cobbler
1¾ cups all-purpose flour, plus extra for dusting
2 tsp baking powder
1 tsp salt
9 tbsp unsalted butter, chilled and diced
1 tbsp finely chopped parsley
3 tbsp horseradish sauce, or horseradish cream
2–4 tbsp milk
1 egg, beaten, for glazing

Method

1 In a large ovenproof Dutch oven, heat 2 tablespoons olive oil and fry the onion, celery, and leek for about 5 minutes, until soft but not brown. Add the mushrooms and fry for 3–4 minutes until they begin to color in places. Remove the vegetables with a slotted spoon and set aside.

2 Toss the steak in 2 tablespoons seasoned flour. Heat the remaining oil in the Dutch oven and fry the meat, a few pieces at a time, until well browned on all sides. Take care not to overcrowd it, or the meat will begin to steam rather than brown. Remove the meat as it cooks, and add it to the vegetables.

3 Return the meat and vegetables to the Dutch oven, and cover with the beer. Add the beef bouillon cube, 1¼ cups boiling water, bouquet garni, sugar, and carrots. Check for seasoning, and bring to a boil. Reduce heat

to its lowest setting, cover, and cook for 2–2½ hours, until the meat is tender. Check it from time to time, and add some water if dry.

4 Preheat the oven to 400°F (200°C). Sift together the flour, baking powder, and salt. Rub in the butter until the mixture resembles fine crumbs. Mix in the parsley. Whisk together the horseradish sauce and milk, and use the liquid to bind the dry ingredients to form a soft dough.

5 On a floured surface, roll out the dough to a thickness of ¾in (2cm). Using the pastry cutter cut out circles. Re-roll the offcuts and re-cut until the dough is used up. When the stew is cooked, remove the bouquet garni and top it with the disks of cobbler topping. Overlap them slightly so that there are very few gaps where the filling can be seen.

6 Brush the tops with beaten egg, and bake the cobbler in the middle of the oven for 30–40 minutes, until it is puffed up and golden brown. Remove it from the oven and let it rest for 5 minutes before serving.

PREPARE AHEAD Prepare the filling 2 days ahead and chill, before topping with the cobbler and baking. The cooked cobbler can be chilled overnight; reheat before eating.

BAKER'S TIP

A cobbler topping is easier to make than dumplings or pastry, and can turn a simple stew into a hearty, one-pot meal. Any kind of meat or vegetable stew can be transformed with the addition of these savory scones; try adding mustard, horseradish, herbs, or spices to the mix to complement the filling.

Chicken Pot Pies with Herb Crust

A delicious and deeply comforting recipe with a tasty scone topping. Best of all, no accompaniments are needed.

SERVES 6 **25–35 MINS** **22–25 MINS**

Special equipment
3½in (8.5cm) pastry cutter
6 large ramekins

Ingredients
1 quart chicken stock
3 carrots, sliced
1lb 10oz (750g) large potatoes, diced
3 celery sticks, thinly sliced
6oz (175g) peas
1lb 2oz (500g) cooked skinless, boneless chicken
4 tbsp unsalted butter
1 onion, chopped
¼ cup all-purpose flour
¾ cup heavy cream
pinch of ground nutmeg
sea salt and freshly ground black pepper
leaves from 1 small bunch of parsley, chopped
1 egg

For the topping
1⅓ cups all-purpose flour, plus extra for dusting
1 tbsp baking powder
1 tsp salt
4 tbsp unsalted butter, diced
leaves from 1 small bunch of parsley, chopped
⅔ cup milk, more if needed

Method

1 Boil the stock in a large saucepan. Add the carrots, potatoes, and celery, and simmer for 3 minutes. Add the peas and simmer for about 5 minutes, until all the vegetables are tender. Drain, reserving the stock. Cut the chicken into slivers and put in a bowl. Add the vegetables.

2 Melt the butter in a small saucepan over moderate heat. Add the onion and cook for 3–5 minutes, until softened but not browned. Sprinkle the flour over the onions and cook, stirring, for 1–2 minutes. Add 2 cups stock and heat, whisking, until the sauce comes to a boil and thickens. Simmer for 2 minutes, then add the cream and a pinch of nutmeg, and taste for seasoning. Pour the sauce over the chicken and vegetables, add the parsley and mix gently.

3 Sift the flour into a large bowl with the baking powder and salt. Make a well in the center and add the butter. Rub with your fingertips to form fine crumbs. Add the parsley, make a well again and pour in the milk, cutting in quickly with a knife to form coarse crumbs. Add more milk if it is dry. Bring the dough together with your fingers.

4 Knead the dough lightly on a well-floured surface until smooth. Pat the dough out to a thickness of ½in (1cm). Cut out rounds with the pastry cutter. Pat out the trimmings and cut additional rounds, for a total of 6.

5 Preheat the oven to 425°F (220°C). Divide the chicken filling evenly among the 6 dishes. Place a scone round on each pie (it's nice if the scone is positioned slightly off-center, so you can see some of the creamy filling). Lightly beat the egg with a pinch of salt and use to glaze the rounds.

6 Bake for 15 minutes. Reduce the heat to 350°F (180°C) and bake until the crust is golden brown and the filling is bubbling. It should take 7–10 minutes longer. If the scone topping threatens to scorch, cover the pies loosely with a sheet of foil.

PREPARE AHEAD The filling can be prepared 1 day ahead, covered, and chilled. Bring it to room temperature before baking.

BAKER'S TIP
Though this scone topping is very easy to make, you can also make this pie with a puff pastry (see pages 370–1, steps 5–12) or shortcrust (see page 358, steps 1–5) topping instead. Try experimenting with the filling too, adding different herbs; tarragon is a particularly good choice here.

Cold Chicken and Ham Pie

This is wonderful to take on a picnic, served with chutney and a crisp green salad.

SERVES 8–10 **50–60 MINS** **1½ HOURS**

Special equipment
8–9in (20–23cm) springform pan
meat grinder (optional)
food processor with blade
  attachment (optional)

Ingredients

For the pastry
4 cups all-purpose flour, plus extra
  for dusting
2 tsp salt
5 tbsp butter, chilled and diced
⅓ cup lard or vegetable shortening,
  chilled and diced

For the filling
4 skinless, boneless chicken breasts,
  total weight about 1lb 10oz (750g)
13oz (375g) lean boneless pork
finely grated zest of ½ lemon
1 tsp dried thyme
1 tsp dried sage
ground nutmeg
sea salt
freshly ground black pepper
9 large eggs
13oz (375g) cooked lean ham

1 Sift the flour and salt into a large bowl. Rub in the butter and lard until fine crumbs form.

2 Make a well in the center, add ⅔ cup water, and mix quickly with a knife to form crumbs.

3 Turn onto a floured surface and knead until smooth. Wrap and chill for 30 minutes.

4 In a pan, place 6 eggs in water, bring to boil, simmering for 7 minutes. Drain, cool, and peel.

5 Cut 2 of the chicken breasts and pork into chunks. Grind or process, but not too finely.

6 Put the ground meats in a bowl. Add lemon zest, thyme, sage, nutmeg, salt, and pepper.

7 Beat 2 eggs and add to the ground meats. Beat the filling until it pulls away from the sides.

8 Cut the reserved chicken breasts and ham into ¾in (2cm) cubes and stir into the filling.

9 Grease the pan. Shape about three-quarters of the dough into a ball; keep the rest covered.

10 On a floured surface, roll the dough out to the size of the pan, with a ½in (1cm) overhang.

11 Preheat the oven to 400°F (200°C). Spread half the filling and arrange the eggs on top.

12 Gently push in the eggs and cover with the remaining mix. Fold over the dough overhang.

13 Beat the remaining egg with a pinch of salt, and brush the edges with the egg glaze.

14 Roll out the remaining dough ¼in (5mm) thick. Lay on top, press to seal, and trim.

15 Poke a hole in the lid. Insert a roll of foil to form a chimney. Decorate with the trimmings.

16 Cut out strips, 1in (2.5cm) wide, and cut them into leaf shapes. Mark veins with a knife.

17 Arrange the leaves, glaze, and bake for 1 hour. Reduce the heat to 350°F (180°C).

18 Bake for another 30 minutes. Discard the foil chimney and chill before unmolding. Serve at room temperature. **STORE** The pie will keep in the refrigerator for 3 days.

Raised Pie variations

Game Pie

This traditional raised pie makes an impressive centerpiece for a summer buffet and keeps well for days in the fridge.

| SERVES 8 | 30 MINS | 1¾ HOUR |

Chilling time
overnight

Special equipment
2lb (900g) loaf pan
small funnel

Ingredients

For the hot water pastry
2¼ cups all-purpose flour, plus extra for dusting
½ tsp fine salt
11 tbsp lard or beef dripping, cubed
1 egg, beaten, for glazing

For the filling
6oz (150g) pork shoulder, cut in 1cm (½in) chunks
6oz (150g) pork belly, trimmed, cut in ½in (1cm) chunks
9oz (250g) venison, cut in ½in (1cm) chunks
2 pheasant breasts, cut in ½in (1cm) slices
sea salt and freshly ground black pepper

For the jelly
1 tbsp unflavored, powdered gelatine
1½ cups chicken stock

Method

1 Preheat the oven to 400°F (200°C). To make the hot water crust, place the flour and salt in a bowl and make a well. Boil a small pan of water then measure out ⅔ cup of boiling water into a heat-proof measuring cup. Add the lard or dripping to the water, and stir until the fat has melted. This reduces the temperature of the water and makes it easy to work with.

2 Pour the liquid into the center of the flour and mix together with a wooden spoon. At the end you will need to use your hands to bring it all together into a soft dough. Be careful, as it will be hot. Cut off one-quarter of the pastry, wrap it in a clean kitchen towel and put it somewhere warm for later.

3 Working quickly, as the pastry will harden as it cools, turn the dough out on to a well floured work surface and roll it out to a thickness of ¼in (5mm). Use the rolling pin to carefully lift the pastry into the loaf pan. Press it firmly all around the bottom and the sides of the pan. Trim off any excess pastry, allowing an overhang of ¾in (2cm).

4 Pack the pastry crust with layers of the pork, venison, and pheasant, seasoning liberally between each layer. Brush the edges of the pastry with a little beaten egg. Now roll out the set aside pastry and use it to top the pie. Press down all around the edges of the pan with your fingers to seal, and trim off any excess. Decorate the pie, if desired, with pastry leaves made from the offcuts, and brush the top with a little beaten egg. Use a chopstick or other implement to make a hole in the top of the pie, so you can fill with jelly after it has cooked.

5 Bake the pie in the center of the oven for 30 minutes, then reduce the heat to 325°F (160°C) and cook for a further 1¼ hours until golden brown. Remove the pie from the oven and leave it to cool in the pan.

6 Heat the chicken stock and add the gelatine, stirring until it dissolves. Leave it to cool. Once the liquid starts to thicken, but not solidify, pour it with a small funnel into the top of the pie, a little at a time. You may need to re-open the hole in the top of the pie if it has closed up when cooking. Refrigerate to set the jelly overnight before eating.

PREPARE AHEAD The pie will keep for 3 days in an airtight container in the refrigerator.

BAKER'S TIP

Hot water pastry has a reputation for being difficult to handle. It does need to be used quickly, before it starts to cool and harden, but is remarkably pliable and can be squashed and shaped to fit the pan far more easily than other types of pastry. It is also extremely resilient, and will remain crisp for days.

Individual Pork Pies

Try making these bite-sized pork pies for a special picnic treat.

| MAKES 12 | 40 MINS | 1 HOUR |

Chilling time
overnight

Special equipment
food processor with blade attachment (optional)
12-hole muffin pan
small funnel (optional)

Ingredients

For the filling
7oz (200g) pork belly, trimmed of fat and skin, and cubed
7oz (200g) pork shoulder, trimmed and cubed
2oz (50g) unsmoked back or streaky bacon, trimmed and diced
10 sage leaves, finely chopped
sea salt and freshly ground black pepper
¼ tsp nutmeg
¼ tsp allspice

For the hot water pastry
3¼ cups all-purpose flour, plus extra for dusting
½ tsp fine salt
¾ cup lard or beef dripping, cubed
1 egg, beaten, for glazing

For the jelly (optional)
1½ tsp unflavored powdered gelatin
1 cup chicken stock

Method

1 Preheat the oven to 400°F (200°C). Put the pork belly, pork shoulder, bacon, herbs, seasoning, and spices into a food processor and puree until the meat is chopped, but not mushy. If you do not have a processor, cut the meat into ¼in (5mm) dice, then mix in the other ingredients.

2 To make the hot water crust, put the flour and salt in a bowl and make a well. Bring a pan of water to a boil and measure out ⅔ cup boiling water into a measuring cup. Add the lard or dripping to the water, and stir until the fat has melted. This will also take the temperature of the water down and make it easier to work with.

3 Pour the liquid into the center of the flour and mix together with a wooden spoon. At the end you will need to use your hands to bring it all together into a soft dough. Be careful, as it will be hot. Cut off one-quarter of the pastry, wrap it in a clean kitchen towel and put it somewhere warm for later.

4 You will need to work quickly as the pastry will begin to harden as it cools. Turn the dough out onto a well floured work surface and roll it out to ¼in (5mm) thick. Cut circles big enough to line the muffin pan, allowing the pastry to overlap the edges slightly. Make 12 pastry crusts. Pack the pork filling into each of the lined muffin crusts, and brush a little beaten egg around the edges of each.

5 Roll out the set-aside pastry. Cut out 12 lids to fit the muffin crusts. Top the filling with the lids, and press down the sides to seal. Brush the tops with egg. Use a chopstick or other implement to make a hole in each pie if you wish to fill it with jelly later, or cut 2 slits to allow the steam to escape if you don't.

6 Bake the pies in the center of the oven for 30 minutes, then reduce the heat to 325°F (160°C) and cook for a further 30 minutes, until golden brown. Remove from the oven and leave to cool in the pan for 10 minutes before turning out. At this stage they can be eaten hot with gravy, allowed to cool, or cooled and filled with jelly.

7 To make the jelly (if using), heat the chicken stock and add the softened gelatine, stirring constantly until it dissolves. Cool. Once the liquid starts to thicken, but not solidify, use a small funnel to pour it into each cooled pie, a little at a time. You may need to re-open the holes in the tops of the pies if they have closed up a little when cooking. Each pie will need only 2–3 tablespoons of liquid. Refrigerate to set the jelly overnight before eating.

PREPARE AHEAD The pies will keep for 3 days in an airtight container in the refrigerator.

Beef Wellington

Also known as Boeuf en croûte, this is always an impressive dinner-party main course.

SERVES 6 **45 MINS** **42–60 MINS**

Ingredients

2¼lb (1kg) fillet of beef, cut from the thick end, trimmed of fat
sea salt
freshly ground black pepper
2 tbsp sunflower oil
3 tbsp unsalted butter
2 shallots, finely chopped
1 garlic clove, crushed

9oz (250g) mixed wild mushrooms, finely chopped
1 tbsp brandy or Madeira
18oz (500g) packet ready-made all-butter puff pastry, or see page 370–1, steps 5–12
beaten egg, to glaze

1 Preheat the oven to 425°F (220°C). Season the meat with salt and pepper.

2 Heat the oil in a large frying pan, and fry the beef until browned all over.

3 Place the beef in a roasting pan and roast for 10 minutes. Remove and leave it to cool.

4 Melt the butter in a pan. Fry the shallots and garlic for 2–3 minutes, stirring, until softened.

5 Add the mushrooms, and cook, stirring, for 4–5 minutes, until the juices evaporate.

6 Add the brandy. Let it bubble for 30 seconds. Remove from the heat and leave to cool.

7 Roll out one-third of the pastry to a rectangle, about 2in (5cm) larger than the beef.

8 Place on a baking sheet and prick with a fork. Bake for 12–15 minutes, until crisp. Cool.

9 Spread one-third of the mushroom mixture on the center of the cooked pastry.

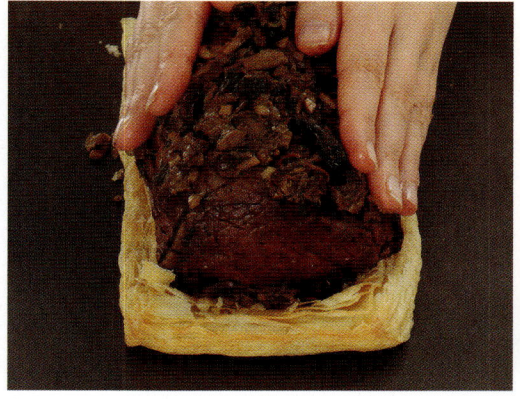

10 Place the beef on top and spread the remaining mushroom mixture over the meat.

11 Roll out the remaining pastry and place it over the beef, tucking in the edges.

12 Brush the beaten egg around the edges, and press down the raw pastry to seal.

13 Brush the egg all over the uncooked pastry case to glaze.

14 Slit the top for steam to escape. Bake 30 minutes for rare, and 45 minutes for well done.

15 If the pastry starts to become too brown, cover loosely with a sheet of foil.

16 Remove from the oven and let it stand for 10 minutes before serving. Slice the dish using a very sharp knife.

En Croûte variations

Sausage Rolls

Perfect finger food for picnics and parties, sausage rolls are so easy to make from scratch you will never go back to store-bought.

MAKES 24 | 30 MINS | 10–12 MINS | 12 WEEKS, UNCOOKED

Chilling time
30 mins

Ingredients
14oz (400g) ready-made puff pastry, or see pages 370–371, steps 5–12
1½lb (675g) sausage meat
1 small onion, finely chopped
1 tbsp thyme leaves
1 tbsp finely grated lemon zest
1 tsp Dijon mustard
1 large egg yolk
sea salt and freshly ground black pepper
all-purpose flour, for dusting
1 egg, beaten, for glazing

Method
1 Preheat the oven to 400°F (200°C). Line a baking sheet with parchment paper and chill. Cut the pastry in half lengthwise. Roll each piece out to form a 12 x 6in (30 x 15cm) rectangle. Cover with plastic wrap and chill for 30 minutes. Combine the sausage meat with the onion, thyme, lemon zest, mustard, and egg yolk. Season with salt and pepper.

2 Lay the pastry on a floured surface. Form the sausage mixture into 2 thinly rolled tubes and place in the center of each piece of pastry. Brush the inside of the pastry with the beaten egg, then roll the pastry over and press to seal. Cut each roll into 12 pieces.

3 Place the rolls on the chilled sheet, make 2 snips at the top of each with scissors, then brush with the beaten egg. Bake for 10–12 minutes, or until the pastry is golden and flaky. Serve warm, or transfer to a wire rack to cool completely.

PREPARE AHEAD These can be stored in an airtight container in the fridge for 2 days.

Venison Wellingtons

Perfect for a special occasion meal or dinner party.

SERVES 4 | 40 MINS | 20–25 MINS

Ingredients
¼oz (10g) dried wild mushrooms (optional)
2 tbsp olive oil
4 venison loin steaks, each 4–6oz (120–150g)
sea salt and freshly ground black pepper
2 tbsp unsalted butter
2 shallots, finely chopped
1 garlic clove, finely chopped
7oz (200g) mixed mushrooms, including wild mushrooms if possible
1 tbsp thyme leaves
1 tbsp brandy or Madeira
1lb 2oz (500g) ready-made all-butter puff pastry, or see page 178, steps 1–9
1 egg, beaten, for glazing

Method
1 Preheat the oven to 400°F (200°C). If no fresh wild mushrooms are available, put the dried wild mushrooms in a bowl and cover with boiling water. Leave for at least 15 minutes.

2 Heat the olive oil in a frying pan. Season the venison steaks on all sides with salt and pepper and fry them, 2 at a time, for 2 minutes each side, until they are browned all over. Take them out of the pan and set aside to cool completely.

3 Melt the butter in the same pan. Add the shallot and cook it for 5 minutes over medium heat until softened, but not brown. Add the garlic and cook for 1–2 minutes.

4 Roughly chop the fresh mushrooms and add them to the pan with the thyme. Season and cook for 5 minutes until they are well softened and any juices have evaporated. Add the brandy and cook over high heat for 1 minute until that has evaporated too. Remove from the heat and let cool. If using dried mushrooms, drain them, chop them roughly, and add to the mushroom mixture.

5 Divide the pastry into four equal pieces and roll out rectangles about ¼in (5mm) thick and large enough to wrap around each steak. Pat each steak dry with paper towel.

6 Place a quarter of the mushroom filling in a rectangle roughly the same shape as the venison steak to one side of the pastry, leaving a clean edge of at least ¾in (2cm). Flatten the mushrooms down and place a steak on top. Brush the edges of the pastry with beaten egg and fold the pastry over the meat. Press the edges down firmly to seal in the meat. Crimp them in to give an attractive finish. Repeat with the remaining steaks and pastry. Cut small slits in the top of the wellingtons to allow the steam to escape, and brush the tops with more beaten egg.

7 Place the pastries on a heavy baking sheet with a rim and bake in the top third of the oven for 20–25 minutes, or until puffed up and golden. The longer the wellington is cooked, the more well done the meat will be. Remove from the oven and allow to cool for 5 minutes before serving.

Salmon En Croûte

Baking salmon in puff pastry keeps it moist and succulent. ▶

SERVES 4   **25 MINS**   **30 MINS**

Ingredients
3oz (85g) watercress, coarse stems removed
½ cup cream cheese
sea salt and freshly ground black pepper
1lb 5oz (600g) skinless salmon fillet
14oz (400g) ready-made puff pastry,
  or see pages 370–371, steps 5–12
all-purpose flour, for dusting
unsalted butter, for greasing
beaten egg or milk, for glazing

Method
1 Preheat the oven to 400°F (200°C). Chop the watercress very finely, place in a bowl, add the cream cheese, season with salt and pepper, and mix well.

2 Cut the salmon fillet into 2 pieces. Roll out the pastry on a lightly floured surface to a thickness of ⅛in (3mm). It should be roughly 3in (7.5cm) longer than the salmon pieces and just over twice as wide. Trim the edges straight. Transfer to a lightly greased baking sheet.

3 Place 1 piece of salmon in the middle of the pastry. Spread the top with the watercress cream and place the other piece of salmon on top. Lightly brush the pastry edges with water, then fold both ends over the salmon. Fold in the sides so they overlap slightly and press together to seal. Re-roll the trimmings and use to decorate the top of the pastry, if liked. Brush with the beaten egg, and make 2 or 3 holes with a skewer to allow steam to escape.

4 Bake for 30 minutes, or until the pastry is well risen and golden brown. Test if the salmon is cooked by pushing a skewer halfway through the thickest part and leaving it for 4–5 seconds; when removed, it should feel hot.

5 Remove from the oven and allow to stand for a few minutes, then slice and serve.

PREPARE AHEAD The whole dish can be made up to 12 hours before baking. Cover with plastic wrap and chill until ready to cook.

Feta Filo Pie

Crisp pastry encases a delicious blend of spinach, feta, and pine nuts in this classic Middle Eastern dish.

SERVES 6 | **30 MINS** | **35–40 MINS**

Special equipment
8in (20cm) springform pan

Ingredients
2lb (900g) fresh spinach leaves
7 tbsp unsalted butter,
  plus extra for greasing
1 tsp ground cumin
1 tsp ground coriander
1 tsp ground cinnamon
2 red onions, finely chopped
¼ cup dried apricots, chopped

½ cup pine nuts, toasted
6 sheets filo pastry, 16 x 12in
  (40 x 30cm), thawed if frozen
sea salt
freshly ground black pepper
10oz (300g) feta cheese, crumbled

1 Rinse the spinach leaves, shake off excess water, and pack into a large saucepan.

2 Cover and cook over medium heat for 8–10 minutes, turning occasionally, until just wilted.

3 Drain through a colander, pressing against the sides to extract as much water as possible.

4 Leave to cool slightly. When cool enough, squeeze out more water with your hands.

5 Meanwhile, melt 2 tablespoons of the butter in a small frying pan, until it begins to bubble.

6 Gently fry the spices with the onions over low heat, stirring occasionally.

7 Fry for 7–8 minutes until the onions are softened but not browned.

8 Stir in the apricots and pine nuts, then set aside to cool slightly.

9 Preheat the oven to 400°F (200°C). Grease and line the springform pan with parchment.

10 To assemble the pie, melt the remaining butter. Brush the pan with melted butter.

11 Cover the base with a sheet of filo pastry, leaving the edges overhanging.

12 Brush melted butter over the pastry sheet, including the overhang.

13 Layer 5 more sheets, brushing each with butter and leaving the edges overhanging.

14 Blot the cooled spinach with paper towel to remove moisture completely. Chop it finely.

15 Stir the spinach into the cooked onion mixture, and season with salt and pepper.

16 Pile half the spinach mixture into the pastry case and spread evenly.

17 Sprinkle the feta cheese over the top, and cover with the remaining spinach mixture.

18 Fold the overhanging pastry over the spinach, piece by piece, brushing with butter.

19 Brush the top with any remaining butter, and place the pan on a baking sheet.

20 Bake for 35–40 minutes, until crisp and golden. Leave to cool for 10 minutes.

21 Release it from the pan and serve hot or warm, cut into wedges.

FETA FILO PIE

Filo Pie variations

Filo Pie with Spicy Kale and Sausage

In their native Greece, filo pies are made with a mixture of wild bitter greens, but any greens work well provided they have a pronounced, slightly bitter flavor. Try substituting the kale for spring greens or spinach.

| SERVES 6 | 35–40 MINS | 45–55 MINS | 8 WEEKS, UNBAKED |

Special equipment
11in (28cm) springform pan

Ingredients
14 tbsp unsalted butter
9oz (250g) sausage meat
3 onions, finely chopped
1lb 2oz (500g) package filo sheets
1lb 10oz (750g) kale, washed, trimmed, and shredded
½ tsp ground allspice
sea salt and freshly ground black pepper
2 large eggs, beaten

Method

1 Heat 2 tablespoons of the butter in a sauté pan, add the sausage meat, and cook, stirring, until it is crumbly and brown. Transfer to a bowl with a slotted spoon, leaving the fat behind. Add the onions to the pan and cook, stirring, until soft. Add the kale, cover, and cook very gently until the kale is wilted. Remove the lid and cook for 5 minutes, stirring constantly, until the moisture has evaporated.

2 Return the sausage meat to the pan with the allspice and stir into the kale mixture. Season to taste. Remove from the heat and let cool completely. Stir in the eggs.

3 Preheat the oven to 350°F (180°C). Melt the remaining butter in a saucepan; brush the pan with a little butter.

4 Lay a folded damp kitchen towel on the work surface. Unroll the filo sheets onto the towel. Using the pan as a guide, cut through the pastry sheets to leave a 3in (7.5cm) border around the pan where possible. Cover the sheets with a second folded damp towel.

5 Put 1 filo sheet on top of a third damp towel and brush with butter. Transfer to the pan, pressing it well into the side. Butter another filo sheet and put it in the pan at a right angle to the first. Continue buttering and layering until half the filo is used, arranging alternate layers at right angles.

6 Spoon the kale and sausage meat filling into the case. Butter another sheet of filo and cover the filling with it. Top with the remaining sheets of filo, brushing each, including the top one, with melted butter. Fold the overhanging dough over the top and drizzle with the remaining butter.

7 Bake the pie in the heated oven for 45-55 minutes, until golden brown. Let cool slightly, then cut into wedges and serve hot or at room temperature.

PREPARE AHEAD The pie can be prepared ahead up to the point of baking, wrapped in plastic wrap, and refrigerated for 2 days.

Potato and Blue Cheese Filo Pie

An excellent dish to prepare ahead for a mid-week meal.

SERVES 6 | 35–40 MINS | 45–55 MINS

Special equipment
11in (28cm) springform pan

Ingredients
2¼lb (1kg) potatoes, very thinly sliced
12 tbsp unsalted butter
1lb 2oz (500g) package filo pastry
5oz (125g) blue cheese, crumbled
4 shallots, finely chopped
4½oz (125g) bacon, cut into strips
4–5 sprigs each parsley, tarragon, and chervil, leaves finely chopped
sea salt and freshly ground black pepper
3–4 tbsp sour cream

Method

1 Preheat the oven to 350°F (180°C). Melt 1 tablespoon butter in a frying pan and cook the bacon until brown, about 5 minutes. Drain on paper towels. Melt the rest of the butter in a saucepan. Brush the pan with a little butter. Lay a damp kitchen towel on a work surface, and unroll the filo pastry sheets onto the towel.

2 Using the pan as a guide, cut through the pastry to leave a 3in (7.5cm) border around the pan. Reserve the trimmings. Cover with a second damp towel.

3 Put a filo sheet on a third damp towel and brush with butter, then press into the pan. Repeat with another sheet, putting it in the pan at a right angle to the first. Continue until half the filo is used.

4 Arrange half the potatoes in the pan. Sprinkle with half the cheese, shallots, herbs, salt, and pepper. Repeat, then pour over the sour cream. Cover the pie with the rest of the filo, buttering and layering. Cut a 3in (7.5cm) hole from the center, so the filling shows. Bake for 45–55 minutes, until golden brown. Serve in wedges, with a crisp green salad.

PREPARE AHEAD This can be prepared ahead up to the point of baking, wrapped in plastic wrap and refrigerated for 2 days.

Cornish Pasties

Although not traditional, I find a splash of Worcestershire sauce adds a depth of flavor to the pasty filling.

MAKES 4 LARGE | **20 MINS** | **40–45 MINS**

Chilling time
1 hr

Ingredients
7 tbsp lard, chilled and diced
4 tbsp unsalted butter, chilled and diced
1½ cups all-purpose flour, plus extra for dusting
½ tsp salt

For the filling
9oz (250g) skirt steak, trimmed, in ½in (1cm) cubes
3oz (80g) rutabaga, peeled, and cut into ¼in (5mm) cubes
4oz (100g) waxy potatoes, peeled, and cut into ¼in (5mm) cubes
1 large onion, finely chopped

splash of Worcestershire sauce
1 tsp all-purpose flour
sea salt
freshly ground black pepper
1 egg, beaten, for glazing

SAVORY TARTS AND PIES

1 Rub the lard and butter into the flour until the mixture resembles fine crumbs.

2 Add the salt and enough cold water to bring the mixture together into a soft dough.

3 Knead the dough briefly on a lightly floured surface. Wrap in plastic wrap. Chill for 1 hour.

4 Preheat the oven to 375°F (190°C). Mix all the filling ingredients and season well.

5 On a well floured work surface roll the pastry out to a thickness of ¼in (5mm).

6 Using a side plate or saucer, cut 4 circles from the dough. Re-roll the offcuts.

7 Fold the circles in half, then flatten them out again, leaving a slight mark down the center.

8 Pile a quarter of the filling into each circle, leaving a ¾in (2cm) border all around.

9 Brush the border of the pastry with a little beaten egg.

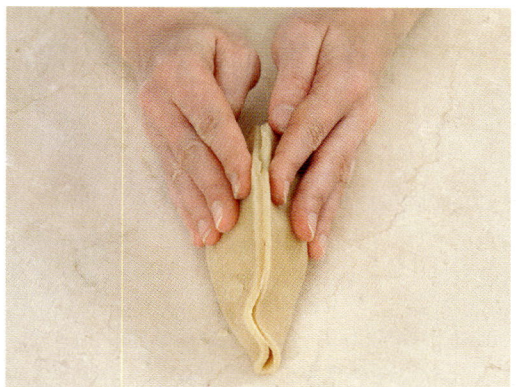

10 Pull both edges up over the filling and press together to seal.

11 Crimp the sealed edge with your fingers to form a decorative ridge along the top.

12 Brush all over the finished pasties with a little beaten egg.

13 Bake in the center of the oven for 40–45 minutes, until golden brown. Remove the pasties from the oven and allow to cool for at least 15 minutes before eating warm or cold. **STORE** These will keep in the refrigerator for 2 days.

Pasty variations

Chicken Pasties

A complete and filling lunch in a pastry packet, these chicken pasties, a lighter alternative to the traditional beef pasties, go down particularly well with children.

SERVES 4   30 MINS   35 MINS

Chilling time
20 mins

Ingredients
1 quantity pasty dough, see page 392, steps 1–3
1 large egg, beaten, for glazing

For the filling
½ cup cream cheese
6 scallions, sliced
2 tbsp chopped parsley
sea salt and freshly ground black pepper
2–3 chicken breasts, about 12oz (350g),
   cut into ¾in (2cm) chunks
1 potato, about 6oz (150g), in ½in (1cm) cubes
1 sweet potato, about 6oz (150g),
   in ½in (1cm) cubes

Method

1 Mix the cream cheese, onions, and parsley in a bowl, and season to taste with salt and pepper. Stir in the chicken, potato, and sweet potato.

2 Preheat the oven to 400°F (200°C). Divide the pastry into 4 pieces. Roll out each piece on a lightly floured surface and, using a small plate as a guide, cut into a 8in (20cm) round. Spoon a quarter of the filling into the center of each round. Brush the edges with water and bring together to seal, then crimp for a decorative finish.

3 Place the pasties on a baking sheet and brush with the reserved egg mixture. Make a slit in the tops and bake for 10 minutes, then reduce the heat to 350°F (180°C) and cook for 25–30 minutes, or until a thin knife comes out clean when inserted into the center. Remove from the oven and serve the pasties hot or cold.

STORE The pasties will keep in the refrigerator for 2 days.

Empanadas

These bite-sized savory pastries originated from Spain and Portugal, the name translating as "wrapped in bread." Perfect for a buffet or picnic, they make very versatile nibbles.

MAKES 24   45 MINS   40–50 MINS

Chilling time
30 mins

Special equipment
3½in (9cm) round pastry cutter

Ingredients
2½ cups all-purpose flour, plus extra for dusting
sea salt
6 tbsp unsalted butter, diced
2 large eggs, beaten, plus extra for glazing

For the filling
1 tbsp olive oil, plus extra for greasing
1 onion, finely chopped
½ cup drained canned tomatoes
2 tsp tomato paste
6oz can tuna, drained
2 tbsp finely chopped parsley
freshly ground black pepper

Method

1 To make the pastry, sift the flour into a large mixing bowl with ½ teaspoon salt. Add the butter and rub in with your fingertips until it resembles fine crumbs. Add the beaten eggs with 4–6 tablespoons water and combine to form a dough. Wrap in plastic wrap and chill for 30 minutes.

2 Meanwhile, heat the oil in a frying pan, add the onion, and fry over a medium heat, stirring often, for 5–8 minutes, or until translucent. Add the tomatoes, tomato paste, tuna, and parsley, and season to taste with salt and pepper. Reduce the heat and simmer for 10–12 minutes, stirring occasionally. Allow to cool completely.

3 Preheat the oven to 375°F (190°C). Roll out the pastry to a thickness of ⅛in (3mm). Cut out 24 rounds with the pastry cutter.

Put 1 teaspoon of the filling on each, then brush the edges with water, fold over, and pinch together.

4 Place the empanadas on an oiled baking sheet and brush with egg. Bake for 25–30 minutes, or until golden brown. Serve warm.

STORE The empanadas will keep in the refrigerator for 2 days.

SAVORY TARTS AND PIES

Forfar Bridie

These simple savory pastries are a classic Scottish dish.

MAKES 4 | **15 MINS** | **20–25 MINS**

Chilling time
1 hr

Ingredients
¾ cup lard, chilled and diced
1½ cups all-purpose flour, plus extra for dusting
2 tsp baking powder
1 tsp salt

For the filling
10oz (300g) finely chopped sirloin steak,
  or skirt steak
1 onion, finely chopped
splash of Worcestershire sauce
sea salt and freshly ground black pepper
1 egg, beaten, for glazing

Method

1 To make the pastry, rub the lard into the flour until the mixture resembles fine crumbs. Add the baking powder and salt and enough cold water to form a soft dough. Bring the dough together, wrap it in plastic wrap, and chill for 1 hour. Preheat the oven to 400°F (200°C). Mix the beef, onion, Worcestershire sauce, and seasoning together and set aside.

2 On a floured work surface, roll the pastry out to ¼in (5mm) thick. Using a side plate or saucer, cut 4 circles out of the pastry. You may need to re-roll the off cuts to get all 4. If the pastry cracks on rolling, gather it together and start again; the re-rolling will make it more robust. Fold the circles in half, trim the sides so that they are a bit rectangular, then flatten them out again.

3 Pile a quarter of the filling onto one half of each pastry circle. Leave a ¾in (2cm) border. Brush the border with a little beaten egg. Now fold the pastry over and crimp the edges together. Brush the finished bridies with a little beaten egg, and cut a slit in the top of each one to allow the steam to escape.

4 Bake in the center of the oven for 20-25 minutes, until golden brown. Remove the bridies from the oven and allow them to cool for at least 10 minutes before eating.

STORE The bridies will keep in the refrigerator for 2 days.

BAKER'S TIP

This traditional Scottish pastry is a close relation to the Cornish pasty, despite being from opposite ends of Britain. Here, a simple filling of chopped or ground steak and onions is cooked in a crumbly pastry. As there are very few ingredients, it is worth using the best meat possible; I prefer finely chopped skirt steak.

classic
& artisan
breads

Whole Wheat Cottage Loaf

Stone-ground whole wheat flour can vary in its absorbency, and you may need more or less water.

MAKES 2 LOAVES   **35–40 MINS**   **40–45 MINS**   **UP TO 8 WEEKS**

Rising and proofing time
1¾–2¼ hrs

Ingredients

4 tbsp unsalted butter, plus extra for greasing
3 tbsp honey
3 tsp dried yeast
1 tbsp salt
¾ cup all-purpose flour, plus extra for dusting
5 cups stone-ground whole wheat flour

1 Melt the butter. Mix 1 tablespoon of honey and ¼ cup lukewarm water in a small bowl.

2 Sprinkle the yeast over the honey mixture. Leave it for 5 minutes to dissolve, stirring once.

3 Mix the butter, remaining honey, 1½ cups lukewarm water, yeast, and salt in a bowl.

4 Stir in the white flour with half the whole wheat flour, and mix with your hands.

5 Add the remaining whole wheat flour, ¾ cup at a time, mixing well after each addition.

6 Stop adding wheat flour when the dough pulls away from the side of the bowl in a ball.

7 Turn the dough out onto a floured work surface, and sprinkle it with white flour.

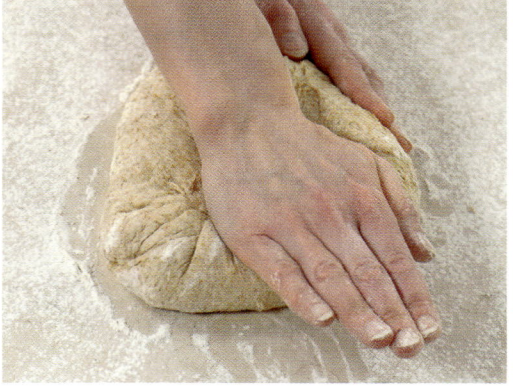

8 Knead for 10 minutes until it is very smooth, elastic, and forms a ball.

9 Grease a large bowl with butter. Put in the dough and flip it to butter the surface lightly.

10 Cover with a damp kitchen towel. Leave it in a warm place for 1–1½ hours until doubled.

11 Grease a baking sheet. Place the dough on a floured work surface and knock out the air.

12 Cover and let it rest for 5 minutes. Cut it into 3 equal pieces, then cut 1 piece in half.

13 Cover 1 large and 1 small piece of dough with a kitchen towel while shaping the others.

14 Shape 1 large piece into a loose ball. Fold in the sides, turn, and pinch to make a tight ball.

15 Flip the ball, seam side down, onto the prepared baking sheet.

16 Similarly, shape 1 small piece into a ball. Set it, seam-side down, on top of the first ball.

17 Using your forefinger, press through the center of the balls down to the baking sheet.

18 Repeat with the remaining 2 dough balls to shape a second loaf.

19 Cover both loaves with kitchen towels. Leave in a warm place for 45 minutes, or until doubled.

20 Preheat the oven to 375°F (190°C). Bake for 40–45 minutes, until well browned.

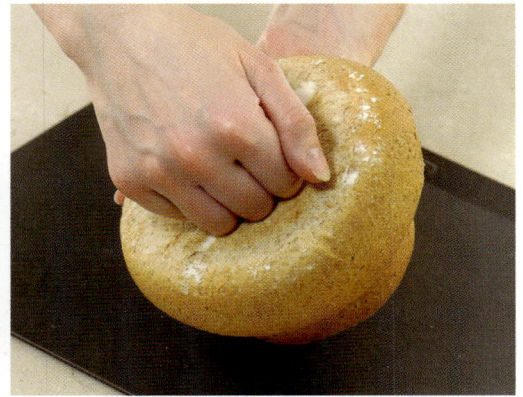

21 The loaves should sound hollow when tapped on the base. Cool on a wire rack.

Classic Loaf variations

White Loaf

Mastering a classic white loaf should be a rite of passage for all amateur bakers. Nothing beats the taste of fresh, crusty white bread, still warm from the oven.

MAKES 1 LOAF   **20 MINS**   **40–45 MINS**   **UP TO 4 WEEKS**

Rising and proofing time
2–3 hrs

Ingredients
4 cups bread flour, plus extra for dusting
1 tsp fine salt
2 tsp dried yeast
1 tbsp sunflower or vegetable oil, plus extra for greasing

Method

1 Put the flour and salt into a large bowl. In a small bowl, dissolve the dried yeast in 1¼ cups warm water. Once it has dissolved, add the oil. Make a well in the center of the flour. Pour in the liquid, stirring to form a rough dough. Use your hands to bring the dough together.

2 Turn the dough out onto a lightly floured work surface. Knead for 10 minutes until smooth, glossy, and elastic. Put the dough in a lightly oiled bowl, cover loosely with plastic wrap and leave to rise in a warm place for up to 2 hours, until twice its size.

3 When the dough has risen, put it onto a floured surface and knock it back to its original size. Knead it and shape it into the desired shape; I prefer a long, curved oval shape known as a bloomer. Place the dough on a baking sheet, cover it with plastic wrap and a kitchen towel, and leave it to proof in a warm place until risen and doubled. This could take 30 minutes–1 hour. The bread is ready when it is tight and well risen, and a finger poked into the dough leaves a dent, which springs back quickly.

4 Preheat the oven to 425°F (220°C). Place one oven shelf in the middle of the oven, and one below it, close to the bottom of the oven. Bring a small pan of water to a boil. Now slash the top of the loaf two or 3 times with a knife on the diagonal. This will allow the bread to continue to rise in the oven. Dust the top with flour, if wanted, and place it on the middle shelf. Place a roasting pan on the bottom shelf of the oven and then quickly pour the boiling water into it and shut the door. This will allow steam to be created in the oven and help the bread to rise.

5 Bake the bread for 10 minutes, then reduce to 375°F (190°C) and bake it for 30–35 minutes until the crust is golden brown and the bottom sounds hollow when tapped. Reduce to 350°F (180°C) if it is starting to brown too quickly. Remove the bread from the oven and leave to cool on a wire rack.

STORE Best eaten the day it is made, the loaf will store, well wrapped, in an airtight container overnight.

BAKER'S TIP
Tempting as it may be to taste the loaf as soon as it comes out of the oven, try to leave the bread to cool for at least 30 minutes before cutting. This will vastly improve the taste and texture of the finished loaf.

CLASSIC AND ARTISAN BREADS

Walnut and Rosemary Loaf

A perfect combination of flavors; the texture of the nuts is fabulous.

MAKES 2 LOAVES | **20 MINS** | **30–40 MINS** | **UP TO 12 WEEKS**

Proofing time
2 hrs

Ingredients
3 tsp dried yeast
1 tsp sugar
3 tbsp olive oil, plus 2 tsp extra for oiling and glazing
2½ cups bread flour, plus extra for dusting
1 tsp salt
6oz (175g) walnuts, roughly chopped
3 tbsp finely chopped fresh rosemary

Method

1 Mix the yeast and sugar in a small bowl, then stir in ½ cup lukewarm water. Leave for 10–15 minutes, or until the mixture becomes creamy. Lightly oil a large bowl.

2 Put the flour in bowl with salt and the olive oil, then add the yeast mixture and ¾ cup water. Mix until ingredients form a dough. Knead the dough on a floured surface for 15 minutes. Knead in the walnuts and rosemary, then put dough in the oiled bowl. Cover with a towel. Put in a warm place for 1½ hours until dough is twice its size.

3 Knock air from the dough and knead it for a few more minutes. Halve it, and shape each half into a 6in (15cm) round loaf. Cover with a towel and leave for 30 minutes to rise. Preheat oven to 450°F (230°C) and oil a large baking sheet.

4 When the dough has doubled, brush with oil and place on the baking sheet. Bake on the middle shelf for 30–40 minutes, until the loaves sound hollow when tapped on the base. Cool on a wire rack.

STORE Will keep for 1 day, wrapped in paper.

Pane di patate

Bread made with mashed potato has a soft crust and moist center. In this recipe, the dough is coated in butter and baked in a ring mold.

| MAKES 1 LOAF | 50–55 MINS | 40–45 MINS | UP TO 8 WEEKS |

Rising and proofing time
1½–2¼ hrs

Special equipment
3-pint (1.75-liter) ring mold, or 10in (25cm) round cake pan, with 8oz (250ml) ramekin (optional)

Ingredients
9oz (250g) potatoes, peeled and cut into 2–3 pieces
2½ tsp dried yeast
9 tbsp unsalted butter, plus extra for greasing
1 large bunch of chives, snipped
2 tbsp sugar
2 tsp salt
2¼ cups all-purpose flour, plus extra for dusting

Method

1 Place the potatoes in a saucepan with plenty of cold water. Bring to a boil and simmer until tender. Drain, reserving 1 cup of the cooking liquid. Mash with a potato masher. Let cool.

2 In a small bowl, sprinkle the yeast over ¼ cup lukewarm water. Leave for 5 minutes until dissolved, stirring once. Melt half the butter in a saucepan. Put the reserved liquid, mashed potato, dissolved yeast, and melted butter into a large bowl. Add the chives, sugar, and salt, and mix together with your hand.

3 Stir in half the flour and mix well with your hand. Add the remaining flour, ½ cup at a time, mixing well after each addition, until the dough pulls away from the sides of the bowl. It should be soft and slightly sticky. Turn the dough onto a floured work surface. Knead for 5–7 minutes, until very smooth and elastic.

4 Grease a large, clean bowl. Put the dough in the bowl, and flip it so the surface is lightly buttered. Cover with a damp kitchen towel and let the dough rise in a warm place for 1–1½ hours, until doubled in size.

5 Grease the ring mold or cake pan. If using a pan, grease the outside of the ramekin and place it upside down in the center. Melt the remaining butter. Turn the dough out onto a lightly floured work surface and knock back. Cover and let rest for 5 minutes. Flour your hands and pinch off walnut-sized pieces of dough, making about 30 pieces. Roll each piece of dough into a smooth ball.

6 Put a few balls into the dish of melted butter and turn them with a spoon until coated. Transfer the balls of dough to the prepared mold or pan. Repeat with the remaining dough. Cover with a dry kitchen towel, and let the loaf rise in a warm place for 40 minutes, until the mold or pan is full.

7 Preheat the oven to 375°F (190°C). Bake the bread for 40–45 minutes, until it is golden brown and starts to shrink away from the mold. Let it cool slightly on a wire rack, then carefully unmold. With your fingers, pull the bread apart while still warm.

STORE This bread is delicious still warm from the oven, but can be tightly wrapped with paper and kept for 2–3 days.

PREPARE AHEAD The dough can be made, kneaded, and left to rise in the refrigerator overnight. Shape the dough, let it come to room temperature, then bake as directed.

BAKER'S TIP
This is both a classic Italian and an American recipe, where it is known as "monkey bread." It is designed to be placed in the center of the dinner table and for diners to pull apart the sections with their fingers. It is best for a family, or more casual, gathering.

Dinner Rolls

You can shape the rolls however you like, though an assortment of different shapes looks very nice in a basket.

MAKES 16 | **45–55 MINS** | **15–18 MINS** | **8 WEEKS, UNBAKED**

Rising and proofing time
1½–2 hrs

Ingredients

1⅛ cup milk
4 tbsp unsalted butter, cubed, plus extra for greasing
2 tbsp sugar
2½ tsp dried yeast
2 large eggs, plus 1 yolk, for glazing
2 tsp salt

4⅓ cups all-purpose flour, plus extra for dusting
poppy seeds, for sprinkling (optional)

1 Bring the milk to a boil. Put ¼ cup into a small bowl and let cool to lukewarm.

2 Add the butter and sugar to the remaining milk in the pan until melted. Cool to lukewarm.

3 Sprinkle the yeast over the ¼ cup of milk. Leave for 5 minutes to dissolve. Stir once.

4 In a large bowl, lightly beat the eggs. Add the sweetened milk, salt, and dissolved yeast.

5 Gradually stir in the flour, until the dough forms a ball. It should be soft and slightly sticky.

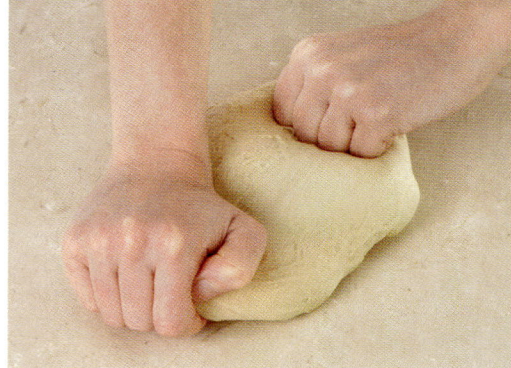

6 Knead the dough on a floured work surface for 5–7 minutes, until very smooth and elastic.

7 Put in an oiled bowl. Cover with plastic wrap. Put in a warm place for 1–1½ hours till doubled.

8 Grease two baking sheets. Put the dough on a floured work surface and knock it back.

9 Cut in half, and roll each piece into a cylinder. Cut each cylinder into 8 equal pieces.

10 To shape round rolls, roll the dough in a circular motion so it forms a smooth ball.

11 For a baker's knot, roll into a rope, shape into an 8, and tuck the ends through the holes.

12 For a snail, roll into a long rope and wind it around in a spiral, tucking the end underneath.

13 Put on baking sheets. Cover with a kitchen towel. Leave in a warm place for 30 minutes.

14 Preheat the oven to 425°F (220°C). Beat the egg yolk with 1 tablespoon of water.

15 Brush the rolls with the glaze and sprinkle evenly with poppy seeds, if you like.

16 Bake for 15–18 minutes until golden brown. Serve warm. **PREPARE AHEAD** These rolls can be frozen at the shaping stage, brought back to room temperature, then glazed and baked.

Bread Roll variations

Spiced Cranberry and Pecan Rolls

These sweetened, fragrant rolls were adapted from a basic white bread recipe. Try adapting your own dough with different combinations of dried fruit, nuts, seeds, and spices.

MAKES 8 ROLLS | 20 MINS | 20–25 MINS | UP TO 4 WEEKS

Rising and proofing time
2–3 hrs

Ingredients
4 cups bread flour, plus extra for dusting
1 tsp fine salt
1 tsp pumpkin pie spice
2 tbsp sugar
2 tsp dried yeast
2/3 cup whole milk
1/2 cup dried cranberries, coarsely chopped
1/3 cup pecans, coarsely chopped
1 tbsp sunflower oil, plus extra for greasing
1 egg, beaten, for glazing

Method
1 Put the flour, salt, pumpkin spice, and sugar into a large bowl. Dissolve the yeast in 2/3 cup warm water. Once it has dissolved, add the milk and oil. Pour the liquid into the flour mixture, stirring it together to form a rough dough. Use your hands to bring the dough together. Turn the dough out onto a floured surface. Knead the dough for 10 minutes, until it becomes smooth, glossy, and elastic.

2 Stretch the dough out thinly, scatter the cranberries and pecans over the surface, and knead for 1–2 minutes more until the added ingredients are well incorporated. Put the dough in an oiled bowl, cover with plastic wrap, and leave to rise in a warm place for up to 2 hours, until doubled.

3 Turn the dough out onto a floured work surface and gently knock it back. Knead it briefly and divide it into 8 equal-sized pieces. Shape each into a plump, round roll. Try and poke any bits of fruit or nut that are sticking out back into the rolls, as these may burn while baking.

4 Place the rolls onto a large baking sheet, cover loosely with plastic wrap and a clean kitchen towel, and leave them to rise in a warm place for 1 hour, until almost doubled in size. Preheat the oven to 400°F (200°C). Gently slash the top of the rolls in the shape of a cross with a sharp knife. This will allow the rolls to continue to rise in the oven. Lightly brush the tops with beaten egg and place them on the middle rack of the oven.

5 Bake for 20-25 minutes until golden brown and the bottoms sound hollow when tapped. Remove the rolls from the oven and leave to cool on a wire rack.

STORE These are best eaten the day they are made, but will store, well wrapped in paper, in an airtight container overnight.

BAKER'S TIP
These are a delightful alternative to traditional breakfast rolls. Try making a double quantity of the White Loaf dough (see page 402) and using half of it to make these rolls. They are especially welcome on Christmas morning, with the festive colors of the cranberries and warming fragrance of spices.

Sesame Seed Buns

These soft bread rolls are very easy to make and great for picnics or packed lunches, or for burgers at a summer barbecue.

MAKES 8 BUNS | 30 MINS | 20 MINS

Rising and proofing time
1 1/2 hrs

Ingredients
2 1/2 cups bread flour, plus extra for dusting
1 tsp salt
1 tsp dried yeast
1 tbsp vegetable oil, sunflower oil, or light olive oil, plus extra for greasing
1 egg, beaten
1/4 cup sesame seeds

Method
1 Stir the flour, salt, and yeast together in a large bowl, then make a well in the middle. Pour the oil into 1 1/2 cups tepid water, then pour this liquid into the well and quickly stir together. Leave to stand for 10 minutes.

2 Turn the dough out onto a floured surface. Knead for 5 minutes, or until smooth and elastic. Shape into a ball by bringing the edges into the middle, then turn into an oiled bowl, smooth side up. Cover with oiled plastic wrap and leave in a warm place for 1 hour, or until doubled.

3 Meanwhile, dust a baking sheet with flour. Scoop the dough onto a floured surface, dust with a little flour, then knead briefly. Pull the dough into 8 even-sized pieces, then shape into rounds. Place onto the floured baking sheet, well spaced apart, then leave for 30 minutes, or until larger and pillowy. Preheat the oven to 400°F (200°C).

4 Once risen, brush the buns with egg and sprinkle sesame seeds over each. Bake for 20 minutes, or until golden, risen, and round. Cool on a wire rack.

STORE These are best eaten the day they are made, but will store, well wrapped in paper, in an airtight container overnight.

Whole Wheat Fennel Seed Rolls

Fennel seeds and cracked black pepper make these savory rolls perfect for smoked ham sandwiches, or as buns for chorizo or pork burgers. Try experimenting with different whole spices, such as caraway or cumin.

MAKES 6 ROLLS | **20 MINS** | **25–35 MINS** | **UP TO 12 WEEKS**

Rising and proofing time
2 hrs

Ingredients
2 tsp dried yeast
1 tsp brown sugar
3¾ cups whole wheat flour, plus extra for dusting
1½ tsp fine salt
2 tsp fennel seeds
1 tsp black peppercorns, cracked
olive oil, for greasing
1 tsp sesame seeds (optional)

Method

1 Sprinkle the yeast into a small bowl, add the sugar, and mix in ⅔ cup lukewarm water. Leave for about 15 minutes for the mixture to become creamy and frothy.

2 Mix the flour with a pinch of salt in a bowl, then add the yeast mixture, and gradually add a further ⅔ cup of lukewarm water. Mix until it comes together (it may need a little more water if it is too dry). Transfer to a lightly floured board and knead for about 10–15 minutes until smooth and elastic, then knead in the fennel seeds and cracked black pepper.

3 Lightly grease a bowl with olive oil. Sit the dough in the prepared bowl, cover with a kitchen towel, and leave somewhere warm for 1½ hours until doubled in size.

4 Knock back the dough and knead for a few more minutes, then divide into six pieces and shape each into a roll. Place them on an oiled baking sheet, cover, and leave to rise again for about 30 minutes. Preheat the oven to 400°F (200°C).

5 Brush the rolls with a little water, then sprinkle with sesame seeds (if using) and bake for about 25–35 minutes until the rolls are golden and sound hollow when tapped on the base. Allow to cool on the baking sheet for a few minutes, then transfer to a wire rack to cool completely.

STORE These are best eaten the day they are made, but will store, well wrapped in paper, in an airtight container overnight.

Pão de queijo

These unusual miniature cheese rolls, crisp on the outside and chewy on the inside, are a popular Brazilian street food.

MAKES 16	10 MINS	30 MINS	8 WEEKS, UNBAKED

Special equipment
food processor with blade attachment

Ingredients
½ cup milk
3–4 tbsp sunflower or vegetable oil
1 tsp salt
1⅔ cups tapioca or cassava flour,
  plus extra for dusting
2 large eggs, beaten, plus extra for glazing
5oz (125g) Parmesan cheese, grated

Method

1 Put the milk, ½ cup water, sunflower oil, and salt in a small saucepan and bring to a boil. Put the flour into a large bowl and quickly mix in the hot liquid. The mixture will be very clumpy and stuck together. Put it aside to cool.

2 Preheat the oven to 375°F (190°C). Once the tapioca mixture has cooled, put it into a food processor. Add the eggs and process until all the lumps disappear, and it resembles a thick, smooth paste. Add the cheese and process together until it begins to form a sticky, elastic dough.

3 Turn the mixture out onto a well-floured work surface and knead for 2–3 minutes, until it is smooth and pliable. Divide the mixture into 16 equal pieces. Roll each piece into golf ball-sized balls and place, spaced apart, on a baking sheet lined with parchment paper.

4 Brush the balls with a little beaten egg and bake in the middle of the oven for 30 minutes, until well risen and golden brown. Remove them from the oven and cool for a few minutes before eating. These are best eaten the same day they are made, preferably still warm from the oven.

PREPARE AHEAD These can be open frozen on the baking sheet at the end of step 3 and transferred to freezer bags. Simply defrost for 30 minutes and bake as usual.

BAKER'S TIP

These classic Brazilian cheese rolls are made from manioc, tapioca or cassava flour, and are thus wheat-free. The flour clumps when mixed with the liquid at first, but the use of a food processor will help enormously here. You will find that it soon forms a smooth mass.

CLASSIC AND ARTISAN BREADS

Seeded Rye Bread

A crusty loaf accented by aromatic caraway seeds. Low-gluten rye is mixed with white flour to lighten it.

MAKES 1 LOAF | **35–40 MINS** | **50–55 MINS** | **UP TO 8 WEEKS**

Rising and proofing time
2¼–2¾ hrs

Ingredients
2½ tsp dried yeast
1 tbsp molasses
1 tbsp vegetable oil, plus extra
  for greasing
1 tbsp caraway seeds
2 tsp salt
8oz (250ml) lager
2½ cups rye flour
1¼ cups all-purpose flour,
  plus extra for dusting
polenta, for dusting
1 egg white, for glazing

1 Put the dissolved yeast, molasses, two-thirds of the caraway seeds, salt, and oil into a bowl.

2 Pour in the lager. Stir in the rye flour and mix together well with your hands.

3 Gradually add the all-purpose flour until it forms a soft, slightly sticky dough.

4 Knead for 8–10 minutes, until the dough is smooth and elastic. Put in an oiled bowl.

5 Cover with a damp kitchen towel. Leave in a warm place for 1½–2 hours, until doubled.

6 Sprinkle a baking sheet with polenta. Knock back the dough on a floured work surface.

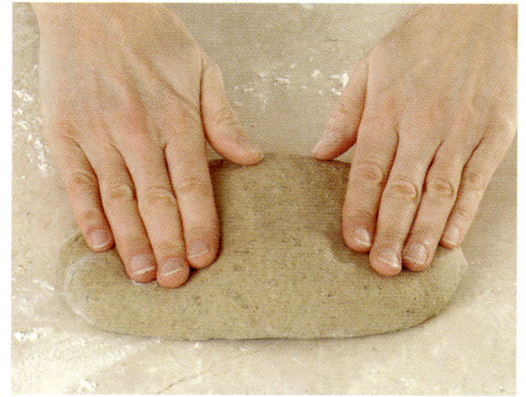

7 Cover and let it rest for 5 minutes. Pat the dough into an oval, about 10in (25cm) long.

8 Roll it back and forth on the work surface, exerting pressure on the ends to taper them.

9 Transfer to the baking sheet. Cover and leave in a warm place for 45 minutes until doubled.

CLASSIC AND ARTISAN BREADS

412

10 Preheat the oven to 375°F (190°C). Beat the egg white until frothy. Brush with the glaze.

11 Sprinkle with the remaining caraway seeds, and press them into the dough.

12 With a sharp knife, make 3 diagonal slashes, about ¼in (5mm) deep, on top.

13 Bake for 50–55 minutes, until well browned. The bread should sound hollow when tapped on the base. Transfer to a wire rack and cool completely. **STORE** This loaf will keep, tightly wrapped in paper, for 2 days.

Rye Bread variations

Apricot and Pumpkin Seed Rolls

Rye flour is very dense, so mix it with bread flour for a lighter texture.

MAKES 8 ROLLS | 20 MINS | 30 MINS | UP TO 4 WEEKS

Rising and proofing time
up to 4 hrs

Ingredients
2½ tsp dried yeast
1 tbsp molasses
1 tbsp sunflower or vegetable oil, plus extra for greasing
2½ cups rye flour
2 cups bread flour, plus extra for dusting
1 tsp fine salt
½ cup dried apricots, coarsely chopped
¼ cup pumpkin seeds, lightly toasted
1 egg, beaten, for glazing

Method

1 Dissolve the dried yeast in 1¼ cups warm water. Add the molasses and oil and whisk well to dissolve the molasses evenly. Put the two types of flour and the salt into a large bowl or the bowl of a electric mixer fitted with a dough hook.

2 Gradually pour the liquid into the flour mixture, stirring it to form a rough dough. Turn the dough out onto a floured work surface. Knead the dough for up to 10 minutes, or 5–7 minutes in an electric mixer on medium speed, until elastic.

3 Stretch the dough out thinly, scatter the apricots and pumpkin seeds over the surface, and knead for a minute or two more until well incorporated. Put into a lightly oiled bowl, cover loosely with plastic wrap, and leave to rise in a warm place for up to 2 hours, until well risen. This dough will not double in size, as rye flour is very low in gluten, and rises slowly.

4 Turn it out onto a lightly floured work surface and gently knock it back. Knead it briefly and divide it into 8 equal sized pieces. Shape each into a plump, round shape. Try and poke any bits of fruit or seed that are sticking out back into the rolls, as these may burn easily when baking.

5 Place the rolls onto a baking sheet, cover loosely with plastic wrap and a kitchen towel, and leave to rise in a warm place until well risen. This could take up to 2 hours. The rolls are ready to bake when they are tight and well risen, and a finger poked into the dough leaves a dent, which springs back quickly.

6 Preheat the oven to 375°F (190°C). Brush the rolls with beaten egg and bake in the middle of the oven for 30 minutes until golden brown and the bottoms sound hollow when tapped. Remove the rolls from the oven and leave to cool on a wire rack.

STORE These are best eaten the same day, but will store overnight, well wrapped.

ALSO TRY...

Walnut Rye Bread Toast 2½oz (75g) walnuts by dry frying in a pan for 3–4 minutes. Rub in a clean kitchen towel to remove excess skin and coarsely chop, then scatter the nuts over the thinly stretched dough instead of the apricots and pumpkins. Once risen, shape into a single ball-shaped loaf, tucking the sides under the center of the dough to get a tight, even shape, leaving the seam at the bottom; this is known as a boule. After it has risen a second time, bake for 45 minutes.

BAKER'S TIP
Here I have used apricot and pumpkin seeds, but dried cranberries, raisins, or blueberries would all work well, too. As an extra alternative, you could also try other seeds, such as sesame or poppy seeds.

CLASSIC AND ARTISAN BREADS

Pesto Garland Bread

A loaf lightly flavored with rye and spread with fragrant homemade pesto, this bread is perfect for serving at a buffet lunch or taking on a picnic, as the slices can be pulled off in individual portions. It also looks amazing!

MAKES 1 LOAF   **35–40 MINS**   **30–35 MINS**

Rising and proofing time
1¾–2¼ hrs

Special equipment
food processor with blade attachment

Ingredients
2½ tsp dried yeast
¾ cup rye flour
1½ cups all-purpose flour, plus extra for dusting
2 tsp salt
extra virgin olive oil for greasing and glazing
leaves from 1 large bunch of basil
3 garlic cloves, peeled
3 tbsp olive oil
⅓ cup pine nuts, coarsely chopped
2oz (60g) freshly grated Parmesan cheese
freshly ground black pepper

Method

1 In a small bowl, sprinkle the yeast over ¼ cup taken from 1¼ cups lukewarm water. Let stand for about 5 minutes, until dissolved, stirring once. Put the rye flour and half the all-purpose flour in the bowl of a food processor with the salt. Combine the yeast and remaining water and pour in, blending just until mixed. Add the remaining flour, ½ cup at a time. Mix after each addition, until the dough is soft and slightly sticky.

2 Continue working the dough for 60 seconds, until elastic. Turn onto a floured work surface and remove the blade. Shape into a ball. Place in an oiled bowl. Cover with a damp kitchen towel and let rise in a warm place for 1–1½ hours, until doubled in bulk.

3 Pulse the basil and garlic in the food processor. Work until coarsely chopped. With the blades turning, gradually add 3 tablespoons oil until smooth. Transfer the pesto to a bowl and stir in the pine nuts, Parmesan, and plenty of black pepper.

4 Brush a baking sheet with oil. Place the dough onto a floured surface and knead to knock out the air. Cover and let rest for about 5 minutes. Flatten the dough, then roll it into a 16 x 12in (40 x 30cm) rectangle with a rolling pin. Spread the pesto evenly over the dough, leaving a ½in (1cm) border. Starting with a long end, roll up the rectangle into an even cylinder. Running the length of the cylinder, pinch the seam firmly together. Do not seal the ends.

5 Transfer the cylinder, seam-side down, to the baking sheet. Curve it into a ring, sealing the ends. With a sharp knife, make a series of deep cuts around the ring, about 2in (5cm) apart. Pull the slices apart slightly and twist them over to lie flat. Cover with a dry kitchen towel and let rise in a warm place for about 45 minutes, until doubled in bulk.

6 Preheat the oven to 425°F (220°C). Brush the loaf with oil. Bake for 10 minutes. Reduce to 375°F (190°C), and bake for 20–25 minutes, until golden. Cool slightly on a wire rack. Serve the same day.

Multi-grain Breakfast Bread

This hearty bread combines rolled oats, wheat bran, polenta, whole wheat and all-purpose flours, with sunflower seeds for added crunch.

MAKES 2 LOAVES   **45–50 MINS**   **40–45 MINS**   **UP TO 8 WEEKS**

Rising and proofing time
2½–3 hrs

Ingredients
¾ cup sunflower seeds
1½ cups buttermilk
2½ tsp quick-rising dried yeast
½ cup rolled oats
⅓ cup wheat bran
½ cup polenta, plus extra for dusting
¼ cup brown sugar
1 tbsp salt
2 cups whole wheat flour
2 cups all-purpose flour,
  plus extra for dusting
unsalted butter, for greasing
1 egg white, beaten, for glazing

Method

1 Preheat the oven to 350°F (180°C). Spread the seeds on a baking sheet and toast in the oven until lightly browned. Let cool, then coarsely chop.

2 Pour the buttermilk into a saucepan and heat to just lukewarm. Sprinkle the yeast over ¼ cup lukewarm water. Set aside for 2 minutes, stir gently, then leave for 2–3 minutes, until completely dissolved.

3 Put the sunflower seeds, rolled oats, wheat bran, polenta, brown sugar, and salt in a large bowl. Add the dissolved yeast and buttermilk, and mix together. Stir in the whole wheat flour with half the all-purpose flour, and mix well with your hand.

4 Add the remaining all-purpose flour, ½ cup at a time, mixing well after each addition, until the dough pulls away from the sides of the bowl in a ball. It should be soft and slightly sticky. Turn the dough onto a floured work surface. Knead for 8–10 minutes, until it is very smooth, elastic, and forms into a ball.

5 Grease a large bowl with butter. Put the dough in the bowl, and flip it so the surface is lightly buttered. Cover with a damp kitchen towel and leave to rise in a warm place for 1½–2 hours, until doubled in size.

6 Sprinkle 2 baking sheets with polenta. Turn the dough out onto a lightly floured work surface and knock back. Cover, and let it rest for 5 minutes. With a sharp knife, cut the dough in half. Shape each half into a thin oval. Cover with a dry kitchen towel and leave to rise in a warm place for 1 hour, or until doubled in size again.

7 Preheat the oven to 375°F (190°C). Brush the loaves with egg white, and bake for 40–45 minutes, until the base of the loaves sound hollow when tapped. Transfer the loaves to a wire rack to cool completely.

STORE This bread is best on the day of baking, but can be tightly wrapped in paper and kept for 2–3 days.

BAKER'S TIP
Buttermilk is a great ingredient for bakers. Try adding it to any baking recipe that calls for milk. Its mild acidity brings a slight tang of sourness, while its active ingredients will lighten and soften the texture of most baked goods. You can find it in most supermarkets.

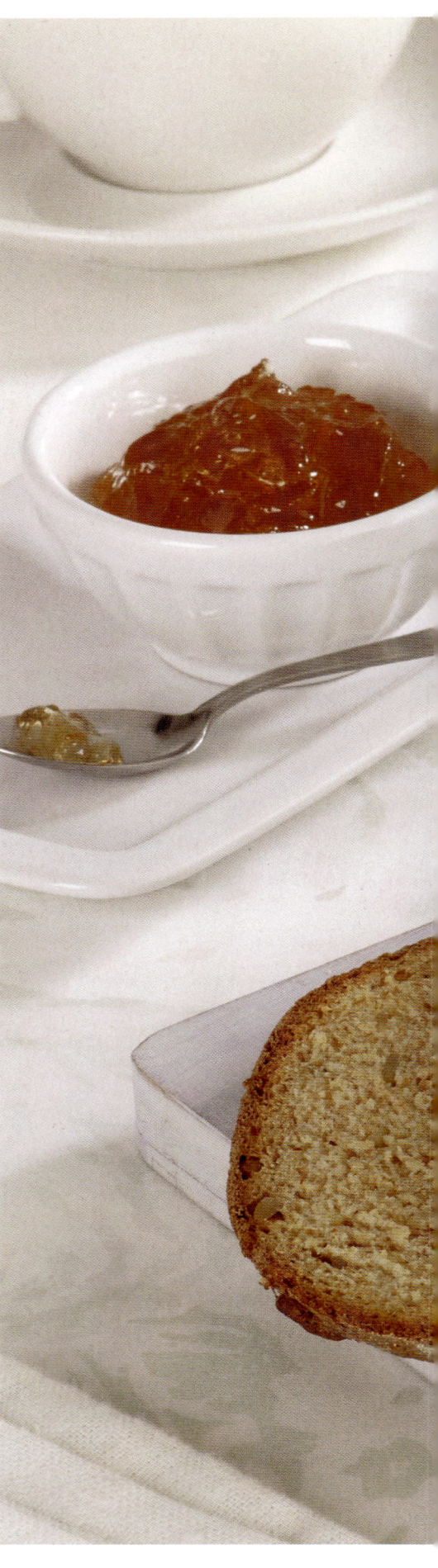

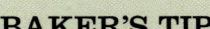

Anadama Cornbread

This dark, sweet cornbread originally hails from New England. It is curiously sweet and savory at the same time, and keeps very well.

MAKES 1 LOAF | **25 MINS** | **45–50 MINS** | **UP TO 8 WEEKS**

Rising and proofing time
4 hrs

Ingredients
½ cup milk
½ cup fine cornmeal
4 tbsp unsalted butter, softened
½ cup molasses
2 tsp dried yeast
2½ cups all-purpose flour, plus extra for dusting
1 tsp salt
vegetable oil, for greasing
1 egg, beaten, for glazing

Method

1 Heat ½ cup water and the milk in a small saucepan. Bring to a boil and add the cornmeal. Cook for a minute or two until it thickens, then remove from the heat. Add the butter and stir until it is well mixed. Beat in the molasses, then set aside to cool.

2 Dissolve the yeast in ⅓ cup warm water and stir well. Put the flour and salt into a bowl and make a well. Gradually stir in the cornmeal mixture, then add the yeast mixture to make a soft, sticky dough.

3 Turn the dough out onto a lightly floured work surface. Knead for about 10 minutes, until soft and elastic. It will remain fairly sticky, but should not stick to your hands. Knead in a little flour if it seems too wet. Put the dough in a lightly oiled bowl, cover loosely with plastic wrap, and leave to rise in a warm place for up to 2 hours. The dough will not double in size, but should be very soft and pliable when well risen.

4 Turn the dough out onto a lightly floured work surface and gently knock it back. Knead it briefly and shape it into a flattened oval, tucking the sides underneath the center of the dough to get a tight, even shape. Place on a large baking sheet, and cover loosely with plastic wrap and a clean kitchen towel. Leave it to rise in a warm place for about 2 hours. The dough is ready to bake when it is tight and well risen, and a finger gently poked into the dough leaves a dent, which springs back quickly.

5 Preheat the oven to 350°F (180°C). Place one oven shelf in the middle of the oven, and one below it, close to the bottom. Bring a small pan of water to a boil. Brush the loaf all over with a little beaten egg, and gently slash the top 2–3 times with a sharp knife on the diagonal. This will alllow the bread to continue to rise in the oven. Dust the top with a little flour, if desired, and place it on the middle shelf. Place a roasting pan on the bottom shelf, then quickly pour the boiling water into it and shut the door.

6 Bake for 45–50 minutes, until the crust is nicely darkened and the bottom sounds hollow when tapped. Remove from the oven and leave to cool on a wire rack.

STORE The bread will keep, well wrapped in paper, in an airtight container for 5 days.

BAKER'S TIP
This dark, sweet cornbread originally hails from New England. It is curiously sweet and savory at the same time, and keeps very well. Anadama tastes wonderful with cheeses such as Emmental or Gruyère, or simply buttered and topped with some good ham and a little mustard.

Rosemary Focaccia

A good-tempered dough that can be left in the refrigerator to rise overnight. Bring back to room temperature to bake.

SERVES 6–8 | **30–35 MINS** | **15–20 MINS**

Rising and proofing time
1½–2¼ hrs

Special equipment
15 x 9in (38 x 23cm) jelly roll pan

Ingredients
3 tsp dried yeast
2¼ cups all-purpose flour, plus extra
  for dusting
2 tsp salt
leaves from 5–7 rosemary sprigs
⅓ cup extra virgin olive oil, plus extra
  for greasing
¼ tsp freshly ground black pepper
Sea salt flakes

1 Sprinkle the yeast over 4 tablespoons of warm water. Leave for 5 minutes, stirring once.

2 In a large bowl, mix the flour with the salt and make a well in the center.

3 Add the chopped rosemary, 4 tablespoons oil, yeast, pepper, and 1 cup lukewarm water.

4 Gradually draw in the flour and work it into the other ingredients to form a smooth dough.

5 The dough should be soft and sticky. Do not be tempted to add more flour to dry it out.

6 Sprinkle the dough with flour and knead for 5–7 minutes on a floured work surface.

7 When ready, the dough will be very smooth and elastic. Place in an oiled bowl.

8 Cover with a damp kitchen towel. Leave to rise in a warm place for 1–1½ hours, until doubled.

9 Put the dough on a floured work surface and knock out the air.

10 Cover with a dry kitchen towel and let it rest for about 5 minutes. Brush the pan with oil.

11 Transfer the dough to the pan. With your hands, flatten the dough to fill the pan evenly.

12 Cover with a kitchen towel and leave to rise in a warm place for 35–45 minutes, until puffed.

13 Preheat the oven to 400°F (200°C). Scatter the reserved rosemary leaves on top.

14 With your fingertips, poke the dough all over to make deep dimples.

15 Pour spoonfuls of the remaining oil all over the dough and sprinkle with the salt flakes.

16 Bake on the top shelf for 15–20 minutes, until browned. Transfer to a wire rack. **ALSO TRY...**
Sage Focaccia Omit rosemary and black pepper at step 3. Add 3–5 sage sprigs, chopped.

ROSEMARY FOCACCIA

Focaccia variations

Blackberry Focaccia

A sweet twist on a classic bread, perfect for a late summer picnic.

SERVES 6–8 **30–35 MINS** **15–20 MINS**

Rising and proofing time
1½–2¼ hrs

Special equipment
15 x 9in (38 x 23cm) jelly roll pan

Ingredients
1 tbsp dried yeast
2¼ cups all-purpose flour, plus extra for dusting
1 tsp salt
2 tbsp sugar, plus 1 tbsp for sprinkling
⅓ cup extra virgin olive oil, plus extra for greasing
10oz (300g) blackberries

Method

1 In a small bowl, sprinkle the yeast over 4 tablespoons lukewarm water. Let stand for 5 minutes until dissolved, stirring once.

2 In a large bowl, mix the flour with the salt and 2 tablespoons of the sugar. Make a well in the center and add the dissolved yeast, 4 tablespoons of the oil, and 1 cup lukewarm water. Draw in the flour and mix to form a smooth dough. The dough should be soft and sticky; avoid adding more flour to dry it out.

3 Flour your hands and the dough, and turn it out onto a floured surface. Knead for 5–7 minutes, until smooth and elastic. Transfer to an oiled bowl and cover with a damp kitchen towel. Leave to rise in a warm place until doubled in bulk; about 1–1½ hours.

4 Generously brush the pan with olive oil. Turn out the dough and knock out the air. Cover with a dry kitchen towel and leave to rest for 5 minutes. Transfer to the pan, flattening with your hands to fill it. Scatter the blackberries over the surface of the dough, cover, and leave to rise in a warm place for 35–45 minutes, until puffed.

5 Preheat the oven to 400°F (200°C). Brush the dough with the remaining oil and sprinkle with the rest of the sugar. Bake in the top of the oven for 15–20 minutes, until lightly browned. Cool slightly on a wire rack, then serve warm.

PREPARE AHEAD After kneading, at the end of step 3, the dough can be loosely covered with plastic wrap and left to rise in the refrigerator overnight.

Fougasse

Fougasse is the French equivalent of the Italian focaccia, most associated with the region of Provence. The traditional leaf effect is surprisingly easy to achieve and looks lovely.

MAKES 3 LOAVES   **30–35 MINS**   **15 MINS**

Rising and proofing time
6 hrs

Ingredients
5 tbsp olive oil, plus extra for greasing
1 onion, finely chopped
2 strips bacon, finely chopped
3 cups bread flour, plus extra for dusting
¼ oz packet dried yeast
1 tsp salt
sea salt flakes, for sprinkling

Method

1 Heat 1 tbsp of the oil in a frying pan. Fry the onion and bacon until browned, remove from the pan, and set aside.

2 Mix 1½ cups of the flour with the yeast. Add about ⅔ cup water, then mix for 3–4 minutes. Cover and leave to rise and then fall again. This should take about 4 hours.

3 Add the remaining flour, the salt, ⅔ cup water, and the remaining ¼ cup olive oil, and mix well. Turn out onto a lightly floured work surface and knead to a smooth dough. Return to the bowl to rise for 1 hour, or until doubled in size.

4 Line 3 baking sheets with parchment paper. Punch down the dough, then add the onion and bacon. Knead well, then divide the dough into 3 balls. Flatten each ball to about 1in (2.5cm) high with a rolling pin, then shape each into a rough circle.

5 Put the dough circles onto baking sheets. To create the traditional leaf shapes, cut each circle with a sharp knife, twice down the center, then 3 times on either side on a slant. Cut all the way through the thickness of the dough, but not through the edges. Brush with olive oil, sprinkle with sea salt, and leave to rise for 1 hour, or until doubled in size. Preheat the oven to 450°F (230°C).

6 Bake the loaves for 15 minutes, until golden. Remove from the oven and allow to cool before serving.

Ciabatta

One of the simplest breads to master, a good ciabatta should be well risen and crusty, with large air pockets.

MAKES 2 LOAVES | **30 MINS** | **30 MINS** | **UP TO 8 WEEKS**

Rising and proofing time
3 hrs

Ingredients
2 tsp dried yeast
2 tbsp olive oil,
  plus extra for greasing
2½ cups bread flour, plus extra
  for dusting
1 tsp sea salt

1 Dissolve the yeast in 1½ cups warm water. Once it has dissolved, add the oil.

2 Put the flour and salt in a bowl. Make a well, pour in the yeast, and stir to form a soft dough.

3 Knead on a floured surface for 10 minutes, until smooth, soft, and somewhat slippery.

4 Put the dough in a lightly oiled bowl and cover loosely with plastic wrap.

5 Leave to rise in a warm place for 2 hours until doubled. Turn out onto a floured surface.

6 Gently knock back the dough with your fists, then divide it into 2 equal pieces.

7 Knead them briefly and shape into traditional slipper shapes, around 12 x 4in (30 x 10cm).

8 Place each loaf on a lined baking sheet, with enough space around to allow it to expand.

9 Cover loosely with plastic wrap and a towel. Leave for 1 hour until doubled in volume.

10 Preheat the oven to 450°F (230°C). Spray the loaves with a fine mist of water.

11 Bake on the middle shelf for 30 minutes, spraying them with water every 10 minutes.

12 It is cooked when the top is golden brown and the base sounds hollow when tapped.

13 When cooked, turn the loaves out onto a wire rack to cool for at least 30 minutes before cutting. **STORE** These are best eaten the same day, but can be stored overnight, wrapped in paper.

Ciabatta variations

Green Olive and Rosemary Ciabatta

Green olives and rosemary make a vibrant alternative to plain ciabatta.

MAKES 2 LOAVES | 40 MINS | 30 MINS | UP TO 8 WEEKS

Rising and proofing time
3 hrs

Ingredients
1 quantity ciabatta dough,
  see pages 424, steps 1–3
4oz (100g) good-quality pitted green olives,
  drained, roughly chopped
2 good sprigs of rosemary, leaves only,
  coarsely chopped

Method
1 Knead the dough for 10 minutes. Then stretch it out thinly on the work surface, scatter evenly with the olives and rosemary, and bring the sides together to cover the ingredients. Knead the dough until well incorporated. Put it in an oiled bowl, cover with plastic wrap, and leave to rise in a warm place for up to 2 hours, until doubled.

2 Turn the dough out onto a floured work surface and knock it back. Divide it into two equal pieces. Knead the pieces and shape them into two traditional slipper shapes, each 12 x 4in (30 x 10cm). Put each loaf on a lined baking sheet with enough space around it to allow it to expand as it rises. Cover with plastic wrap and a kitchen towel and leave for 1 hour until twice its volume.

3 Preheat the oven to 450°F (230°C). Spray the loaves with a fine mist of water and bake in the center of the oven for 30 minutes until golden brown; spray the loaves with water every 10 minutes. The bread is cooked when the underneath sounds hollow when tapped. Cool on a wire rack for 30 minutes before cutting.

STORE Best eaten on the same day. Can be stored overnight, wrapped in paper.

Ciabatta Crostini

Don't waste day-old ciabatta; slice it and bake the slices to make crostini, which will keep for days and can be used for snacks, canapés, or croutons. ▶

MAKES 25–30 | 15 MINS | 10 MINS

Ingredients
1 loaf day-old ciabatta bread, see pages 424–425
olive oil

For the toppings
½ cup arugula pesto, or 4oz (100g) roasted red peppers, sliced and mixed with chopped basil, or ½ cup black olive tapenade topped with 4oz (100g) goat cheese

Method
1 Preheat the oven to 425°F (220°C). Slice the ciabatta into ½in (1cm) slices. Brush the tops with olive oil.

2 Bake them on the top rack for 10 minutes, turning them after 5 minutes. Remove from the oven and cool on a wire rack.

3 Once cooled, top with any of the three suggested toppings, just before serving. If using the tapenade and goat cheese topping, briefly grill before serving.

PREPARE AHEAD The baked, unadorned crostini will keep in an airtight container for 3 days. Add the topping just before serving.

Black Olive and Peppadew Ciabatta

Try using black olives and Peppadew peppers for a delicious ciabatta loaf studded with red and black. **PICTURED OVERLEAF**

MAKES 2 LOAVES | 40 MINS | 30 MINS | UP TO 8 WEEKS

Rising and proofing time
3 hrs

Ingredients
1 quantity ciabatta dough,
  see pages 424, steps 1–3
2oz (50g) pitted black olives, drained, coarsely chopped
2oz (50g) Peppadew small red peppers, drained, coarsely chopped

Method
1 Once the dough has been kneaded for 10 minutes, stretch it out thinly on the work surface, scatter with the olives and peppers, and bring the sides together to cover the ingredients. Knead the dough briefly until they are incorporated. Put the dough in an oiled bowl, cover loosely with plastic wrap, and leave to rise in a warm place for up to 2 hours, until doubled in size.

2 Turn the dough out onto a floured work surface and knock it back. Divide it into two pieces. Knead the pieces and shape them into two slipper shapes, each 12 x 4in (30 x 10cm). Place each loaf on a lined baking sheet. Cover with plastic wrap and a kitchen towel and leave for an hour until doubled.

3 Preheat the oven to 450°F (230°C). Mist the bread with water and bake in the center of the oven for 30 minutes until golden brown. Mist every 10 minutes. The bread is cooked when the base sounds hollow when tapped. Cool for 30 minutes before cutting.

STORE Best eaten on the same day. Can be stored overnight, wrapped in paper.

BAKER'S TIP
Ciabatta dough should be wet and loose on kneading, as this will help to create the large air pockets traditionally found in the finished loaf. Wet doughs are easier to knead in a machine fitted with a dough hook, as they are a little sticky to manage well with your hands.

Sesame Grissini

Tradition has it that breadsticks should be pulled the length of the baker's arm—these are more manageable!

MAKES 32 **40–45 MINS** **15–18 MINS**

Rising time
1–1½ hrs

Ingredients
2½ tsp dried yeast
2¼ cups bread flour,
　plus extra for dusting
1 tbsp sugar
2 tsp salt
2 tbsp extra virgin olive oil, plus
　extra for glazing and greasing
½ cup sesame seeds

1 Sprinkle the yeast over ¼ cup lukewarm water. Leave for 5 minutes, stirring once.

2 Put the flour, sugar, and salt in a bowl. Add the yeast and 1 cup more lukewarm water.

3 Add the oil and draw the flour into the liquid, mixing to form a soft, slightly sticky dough.

4 Knead the dough on a floured surface for 5–7 minutes, until very smooth and elastic.

5 Cover the dough with a damp kitchen towel and let it rest for about 5 minutes.

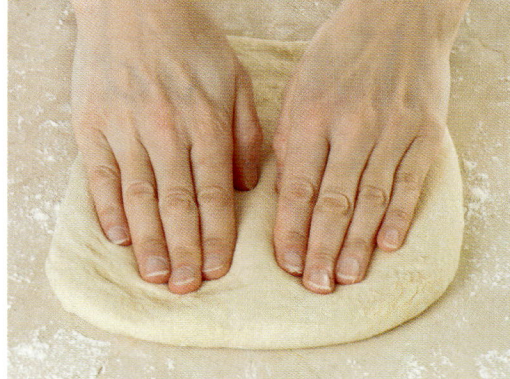

6 Flour your hands and pat the dough into a rectangle on a well-floured work surface.

7 Roll the dough out to a 16 x 6in (40 x 15cm) rectangle. Cover it with a damp kitchen towel.

8 Leave in a warm place for 1–1½ hours until doubled. Preheat oven to 425°F (220°C).

9 Dust 3 baking sheets with flour. Brush the dough with water. Sprinkle with sesame seeds.

10 With a sharp knife, cut the dough into 32 strips, each about ½in (1cm) wide.

11 Stretch 1 strip to the width of a baking sheet. Set it on 1 of the prepared baking sheets.

12 Repeat with the remaining strips, arranging them ¾in (2cm) apart.

13 Bake for 15–18 minutes, until golden and crisp. Transfer to a wire rack and let cool completely.
STORE These will keep in an airtight container for 2 days.

Grissini variations

Spanish Picos

These miniature Spanish breadsticks are made by tying strips of dough in loops and are a great addition to a tapas meal.

MAKES 16 · 40–45 MINS · 18–20 MINS

Rising time
1–1½ hrs

Ingredients
½ quantity grissini dough, see page 430, steps 1–6
1½ tbsp sea salt

Method

1 Roll out the dough to a 8 x 6in (20 x 15cm) rectangle. Cover with a damp kitchen towel and leave to rise in a warm place for 1–1½ hours until doubled in size.

2 Preheat the oven to 425°F (220°C). Dust 2 baking sheets with flour. Cut the dough into 16 strips, then cut each strip into half. Take a half strip, loop it, and twist the ends in a single knot, and transfer to a prepared baking sheet. Repeat to shape the remaining strips.

3 Lightly brush the loops with water and sprinkle with the sea salt. Bake the loops for 18–20 minutes, until golden and crisp. Let cool as directed.

STORE The picos can be kept for 2 days in an airtight container.

Parmesan Grissini

Smoked paprika adds a depth of flavor to these cheesy grissini.

MAKES 32 · 40–45 MINS · 10 MINS

Rising time
1–1½ hrs

Ingredients
2½ tsp dried yeast
2¼ cups all-purpose flour, plus extra for dusting
1 tbsp sugar
2 tsp salt
1½ tsp smoked paprika
2 tbsp olive oil, extra for glazing and greasing
2oz (50g) Parmesan cheese, grated

Method

1 Sprinkle the yeast over ¼ cup lukewarm water. Leave for 5 minutes until dissolved, stirring once. Put the flour, sugar, salt, and smoked paprika in a bowl. Pour in the oil, dissolved yeast, and 1 cup more lukewarm water.

2 Draw in the flour to form a dough; it should be soft and sticky. Flour the surface and knead for 5–7 minutes, until it is smooth and forms a ball. Cover with a damp kitchen towel and leave for 5 minutes. Flour your hands and pat the dough into a rectangle on a floured surface. Roll it out to a 16 x 6in (40 x 15cm) rectangle. Cover with the kitchen towel, and leave for 1–1½ hours, until doubled in size.

3 Preheat the oven to 425°F (220°C). Dust 3 baking sheets with flour and lightly brush the dough with water. Sprinkle with Parmesan, pressing it down gently. With a sharp knife, cut the dough into 32 strips, each ½in (1cm) wide. Stretch 1 strip to the width of a baking sheet, and set on 1 of the prepared sheets. Repeat with the remaining strips, placing them ¾in (2cm) apart. Bake for 10 minutes, until golden and crisp. Transfer to a wire rack to cool.

STORE Best eaten fresh, these will keep in an airtight container for 2 days.

Prosciutto-wrapped Canapés

Try dipping these quick homemade canapés in herb mayo or salsa verde.

MAKES 32 · 45 MINS · 15–18 MINS

Rising time
1–1½ hrs

Ingredients
1 quantity grissini dough,
  see page 430, steps 1–8
3 tbsp sea salt
12 slices prosciutto

Method

1 Preheat the oven to 425°F (220°C) and dust 3 baking sheets with flour. Brush the rolled out dough with water and sprinkle with sea salt crystals.

2 With a sharp knife, cut the dough into 32 strips, each ½in (1cm) wide. Stretch each one to the width of the baking sheet and position ¾in (2cm) apart. Bake for 15–18 minutes, until golden and crisp. Cool on a wire rack.

3 Cut each slice of prosciutto lengthwise into 3. Wrap each grissini at one end with one-third of a slice of ham just before serving as a canapé.

PREPARE AHEAD The grissini can be made 1 day ahead and stored unwrapped in an airtight container.

BAKER'S TIP

Homemade grissini are a lovely addition to a party menu. Experiment by adding flavor and texture, using things such as chopped olives, or smoked paprika, or your favorite cheeses; or leave them plain for a healthy and child-friendly snack. They will be at their best if eaten on the day they are baked.

Bagels

Making bagels is surprisingly simple. Try sprinkling with poppy or sesame seeds after brushing with egg.

MAKES 8–10 **40 MINS** **20–25 MINS** **8 WEEKS, UNBAKED**

Rising and proofing time
1½–3 hrs

Ingredients
3¼ cups bread flour, plus extra
  for dusting
2 tsp fine salt
2 tsp sugar
2 tsp dried yeast
1 tbsp sunflower or vegetable oil,
  plus extra for greasing
1 egg, beaten, for glazing

1 Put the flour, salt, and sugar in a bowl. Dissolve the yeast in 1¾ cups warm water.

2 Add the oil and pour the liquid into the flour mixture, stirring together to form a soft dough.

3 Knead for 10 minutes on a floured surface until smooth. Transfer to an oiled bowl.

4 Cover loosely with plastic wrap and let rise in a warm place for 1–2 hours, until doubled.

5 Transfer to a floured surface, push it down to its original size, and divide into 8–10 pieces.

6 Take each piece of dough and roll it under your palm to make a fat log shape.

7 Using your palms, continue to roll it toward each end, until it is about 10in (25cm) long.

8 Wrap the dough around your knuckles, so the ends are underneath your palm.

9 Squeeze gently, then roll briefly to seal the end. The hole should still be big at this stage.

10 Transfer to 2 baking sheets lined with parchment. Repeat to shape all the bagels.

11 Cover with plastic wrap and a towel. Leave in a warm place until doubled; up to 1 hour.

12 Preheat the oven to 425°F (220°C) and set a large saucepan of water to boil.

13 Poach the bagels in gently simmering water for 1 minute on either side.

14 Remove them from the water with a slotted spoon. Dry them briefly on a clean kitchen towel.

15 Return the bagels to the baking sheets and brush them with a little beaten egg.

16 Bake in the center of the oven for 20–25 minutes until golden. Cool for 5 minutes on a wire rack before serving. **STORE** Best the day they are made, but still good toasted the next day.

Bagel variations

Cinnamon and Raisin Bagels

These sweet and spicy bagels are delicious fresh from the oven. Any leftovers can be trimmed of the crusts and turned into an alternative Bread and Butter Pudding (see page 92).

MAKES 8–10 | **40 MINS** | **20–25 MINS** | **8 WEEKS, UNBAKED**

Rising and proofing time
1½–3 hrs

Ingredients
3¼ cups bread flour, plus extra for dusting
2 tsp fine salt
2 tsp sugar
2 tsp ground cinnamon
2 tsp dried yeast
1 tbsp sunflower or vegetable oil, plus extra for greasing
¼ cup raisins
1 egg, beaten, for glazing

Method
1 Put the flour, salt, sugar, and cinnamon into a large bowl. Dissolve the yeast in 1¾ cups warm water, whisking gently to help it dissolve, then add the oil. Gradually pour the liquid into the flour mixture, stirring to form a soft dough. Knead on a well floured work surface, until smooth, soft, and pliable.

2 Stretch the dough out thinly, scatter the raisins evenly over it, and knead briefly until well mixed. Put it in an oiled bowl, cover with plastic wrap and leave to rise in a warm place for 1–2 hours, until nearly doubled.

3 Place the dough on a floured surface and gently push it down until it is back to its original size. Divide it into 8–10 equal pieces. Take each piece and roll it under your palm to make a fat log shape. Using both your palms, continue to roll the dough outward toward each end, until it is about 10in (25cm) long.

4 Wrap the dough around your knuckles, so the join is underneath your palm. Squeeze gently, then roll the bagel briefly to seal the join. The hole should still be quite big at this stage. Transfer to 2 baking sheets lined with parchment paper and cover loosely with plastic wrap and a kitchen towel. Leave in a warm place for up to 1 hour, until well puffed up and doubled in size.

5 Preheat the oven to 425°F (220°C) and set a large pan of water to boil. Gently poach the bagels, in batches of 3 or 4, in the simmering water for 1 minute, then flip them over and poach for another minute. Remove with a slotted spoon, dry briefly on a kitchen towel, then return to the baking sheets. Brush with the beaten egg. Bake in the center of the oven for 20–25 minutes until golden brown. Remove from the oven and cool for at least 5 minutes on a wire rack before eating.

STORE Best served the day they are made, but good toasted the next day.

Mini Bagels

Great for parties, try serving halved and topped simply with cream cheese, a curl of smoked salmon, lemon juice, and a sprinkling of cracked black pepper. ▶

MAKES 16–20 | **45 MINS** | **15–20 MINS** | **8 WEEKS, UNBAKED**

Rising and proofing time
1½–3 hrs

Ingredients
1 quantity bagel dough, see page 434, steps 1–4

Method
1 When the dough has risen, place it on a floured work surface and knock it back. Divide it into 16–20 equal pieces, depending on the size you want. Take each piece and roll it under your palm to make a log shape. Use both your palms to roll the dough outward toward each end, until it is 6in (15cm) long.

2 Take the dough and wrap it around the three middle fingers of your hand, so the join is under your palm. Pinch gently, then roll briefly to seal the join. The hole should still be big at this stage. Put the bagels on 2 baking sheets lined with parchment paper, and cover with plastic wrap and a ktichen towel. Leave in a warm place for 30 minutes, until well puffed up.

3 Preheat the oven to 425°F (220°C) and set a large pan of water to boil. Gently poach the bagels in batches of 6–8, poaching each side for just 30 seconds. Briefly dry the bagels with a kitchen towel, brush with the beaten egg, and bake for 15–20 minutes until golden brown. Remove from the oven and cool for at least 5 minutes on a wire rack before eating.

STORE These mini bagels are best served fresh the day they are made, but are also good toasted the next day.

BAKER'S TIP
The secret to cooking an authentic bagel is to poach the proofed bagels briefly in simmering water before baking. It is this unusual step that helps to give them their classic chewy texture and soft inside crumb.

Soft Pretzels

These German breads are great fun to make; the two-stage glazing method gives an authentic result.

Ingredients
2 cups bread flour, plus extra
  for dusting
1 cup all-purpose flour
1 tsp salt
2 tbsp sugar
2 tsp dried yeast
1 tbsp sunflower or vegetable oil,
  plus extra for greasing

For the glaze
¼ tsp baking soda
coarse sea salt
1 egg, beaten

1 Put the two types of flour, salt, and sugar into a large bowl.

2 Sprinkle the yeast over 1¼ cups warm water. Stir, leave for 5 minutes, and add the oil.

3 Gradually pour the liquid into the flour mixture, stirring to form a soft dough.

4 Knead for 10 minutes until smooth, soft, and pliable. Transfer to an oiled bowl.

5 Cover loosely with plastic wrap and leave in a warm place for 1–2 hours, until nearly doubled.

6 Turn the dough out onto a lightly floured work surface, and gently knock it back.

7 Divide the dough into 16 equal sized pieces, using a sharp knife to cut it cleanly.

8 Take each piece of dough and roll it under your palm to make a log shape.

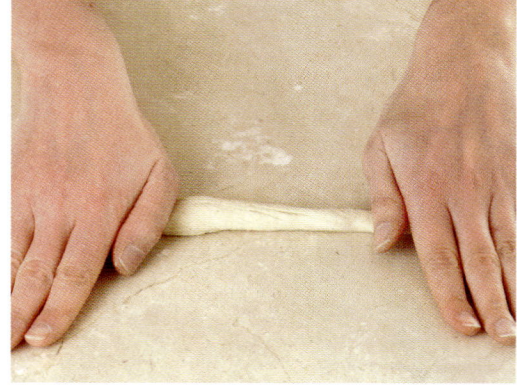

9 Using your palms, continue to roll the dough toward each end, until it is 18in (45cm) long.

10 If difficult to stretch, hold by either end and rotate in a looping action, like a skipping rope.

11 Take each end of the dough and cross them over each other, forming a heart shape.

12 Now twist the ends around each other, as though they had linked arms.

13 Secure the ends to the sides of the pretzel; it will appear quite loose at this stage.

14 Repeat to make 16 pretzels, placing them on baking sheets lined with parchment.

15 Cover with plastic wrap and a towel. Leave in a warm place for 30 minutes, until puffed up.

16 Preheat the oven to 400°F (200°C). Mix the soda in 2 tablespoons boiling water.

17 Brush the pretzels with the mixture. This gives them a dark color and chewy exterior.

18 Scatter flakes of sea salt or sesame seeds over the brushed pretzels. Bake for 15 minutes.

19 Remove from the oven and brush with a little beaten egg. Bake for another 5 minutes.

20 Remove from the oven. The pretzels should be dark golden brown with a shiny finish.

21 Transfer to a wire rack and leave to cool for at least 5 minutes before serving.

Soft Pretzel variations

Sugar and Cinnamon Pretzels

A delicious sweet alternative to plain pretzels, these are definitely best eaten straight from the oven. Try toasting any leftover pretzels or gently reheating in a medium oven.

MAKES 16 | **50 MINS** | **20 MINS** | **UP TO 8 WEEKS**

Rising and proofing time
1½–2½ hrs

Ingredients
1 quantity unbaked pretzels,
  see pages 440–441, steps 1–15

For the glaze
¼ tsp baking soda
1 egg, beaten
2 tbsp unsalted butter, melted
¼ cup sugar
2 tsp ground cinnamon

Method

1 Preheat the oven to 400°F (200°C). Dissolve the baking soda in 2 tablespoons boiling water and brush it all over the shaped and risen pretzels. Bake for 15 minutes. Remove from the oven, brush all over with egg, and return to the oven for 5 minutes until dark golden brown and shiny.

2 Remove the pretzels from the oven and brush each one with melted butter. Mix the sugar and cinnamon on a plate and dip the buttered side of the pretzels into the mix. Leave to cool on a wire rack for at least 5 minutes before serving.

STORE These can be stored in an airtight container overnight.

BAKER'S TIP
Pretzels get their traditional mahogany coloring and chewy texture from a quick dip in baking soda before cooking. The dough can be tricky to handle at home, so be sure to brush twice: first with the baking soda solution, and later with some beaten egg, for an easy way to perfect pretzels.

Hot Dog Pretzels

These pretzeldogs are guaranteed to be a big hit at a children's party and are simple to prepare. Warming and festive in appearance, they are also great for a winter celebration. ▶

MAKES 8 | **30 MINS** | **15 MINS** | **UP TO 8 WEEKS**

Rising and proofing time
1½–2½ hrs

Ingredients
1 tsp dried yeast
½ tbsp sunflower or vegetable oil,
  plus extra for greasing
1 cup bread flour, plus extra for dusting
¾ cup all-purpose flour
½ tsp salt
1 tbsp sugar
8 hot dogs
mustard (optional)

For the glaze
1 tbsp baking soda
coarse sea salt

Method

1 Put the two types of flour, salt, and sugar into a bowl. Sprinkle the yeast over 1¼ cups warm water. Stir once, then leave for 5 minutes, until dissolved. Once it has dissolved, add the oil.

2 Pour the liquid into the flour mixture, stirring it together to form a soft dough. Knead by hand for 10 minutes on a floured work surface until smooth, soft, and pliable. Put in a lightly oiled bowl, cover loosely with plastic wrap, and leave in a warm place for 1–2 hours, until nearly doubled in size.

3 Turn the dough out onto a floured work surface and knock it back. Divide it into 8 equal pieces. Take each piece of dough and roll it under your palm to make a log shape. Use both your palms to continue to roll the dough outward toward each end, until it is about 18in (45cm) long. If the dough is difficult to stretch, hold it by either end and gently rotate it in a looping action as you would a skipping rope.

4 Take each hot dog and, if you like mustard (and don't mind the mess) brush with a little mustard. Starting at the top, wrap the pretzel dough around it in a circular twisting motion, so that the hot dog is completely sealed in, with only the top and the bottom showing. Pinch the dough together at the top and bottom to make sure it doesn't unwrap.

5 Place on baking sheets lined with parchment paper, cover with oiled plastic wrap and a kitchen towel, and leave in a warm place for about 30 minutes, until well puffed up. Preheat the oven to 400°F (200°C).

6 Dissolve the baking soda in 1 quart boiling water in a large saucepan. Poach the hotdogs, in batches of 3, in the simmering water for 1 minute. Remove with a slotted spatula, dry briefly on a kitchen towel, and return to the baking sheets.

7 Scatter with sea salt and bake for 15 minutes until golden brown and shiny. Remove from the oven and cool on a wire rack for 5 minutes before serving.

STORE These are best eaten while still warm, but can be stored in an airtight container in the refrigerator overnight.

English Muffins

This soft, traditional English teatime bread crossed the Atlantic to become an American brunch favorite.

MAKES 10   25–30 MINS   13–16 MINS

Rising and proofing time
1½ hrs

Ingredients

2½ cups all-purpose flour,
  plus extra for dusting
1 tsp quick-rising dried yeast
1 tsp salt
2 tbsp unsalted butter, melted,
  plus extra for greasing
vegetable oil, for greasing
2 tbsp ground rice or semolina

Method

1 Pour 1¼ cups tepid water into a bowl, sprinkle over the yeast, and leave for 5 minutes to dissolve, stirring once. Mix the flour and salt in a large bowl. Make a well and pour in the yeast mixture and melted butter. Gradually draw in the flour to form a soft, pliable dough.

2 Knead the dough on a lightly floured surface for 5 minutes. Shape it into a ball and place in a large greased bowl. Cover with oiled plastic wrap and leave in a warm place for 1 hour, or until doubled in size.

3 Lay a kitchen towel on a sheet, and scatter with most of the ground rice. Turn the dough out onto a floured surface, knead briefly, and divide it into 10 balls.

Place the balls on the towel and press them into flattish rounds. Sprinkle with the rest of the ground rice, and cover with another kitchen towel. Leave to prove for 20–30 minutes, or until risen.

4 Heat a large, lidded frying pan and cook the muffins in batches. Cover with the lid and cook very gently for 10–12 minutes, or until they puff up and the undersides are golden and toasted. Turn over and cook for 3–4 minutes, or until golden underneath. Cool on a wire rack. Great split, toasted, and spread with butter and jam, or as the base for eggs Benedict.

BAKER'S TIP
Homemade muffins are far superior to anything you can buy, so it really is worth the extra effort of making them. Prepare the dough in the morning, and you can enjoy a freshly cooked batch for afternoon tea. Alternatively, leave to rise overnight, ready to bake for a leisurely breakfast.

Hefezopf

This traditional German bread is similar to brioche. Like all yeasted sweet breads, it is at its best the day of baking.

MAKES 1 LOAF · **20 MINS** · **25–35 MINS** · **UP TO 8 WEEKS**

Rising and proofing time
4–4½ hrs

Ingredients

1½ tsp dried yeast
1¼ cup warm milk
1 large egg
2½ cups all-purpose flour,
  plus extra for dusting
¼ cup sugar
¼ tsp fine salt

5 tbsp unsalted butter, melted
vegetable oil, for greasing
1 egg, beaten, for glazing

1 Dissolve the yeast in the warm milk. Let it cool, then add the egg and beat well.

2 Put the flour, sugar, and salt in a large bowl. Make a well and pour in the milk mixture.

3 Add the melted butter and gradually draw in the flour, stirring to form a soft dough.

4 Knead for 10 minutes on a floured surface, until smooth, soft, and pliable.

5 Put in an oiled bowl and cover with plastic wrap. Leave for 2–2½ hours until doubled.

6 Put the dough on a floured work surface and gently knock it back. Divide into 3 equal pieces.

7 Take each piece of dough and roll it under your palm to make a fat log shape.

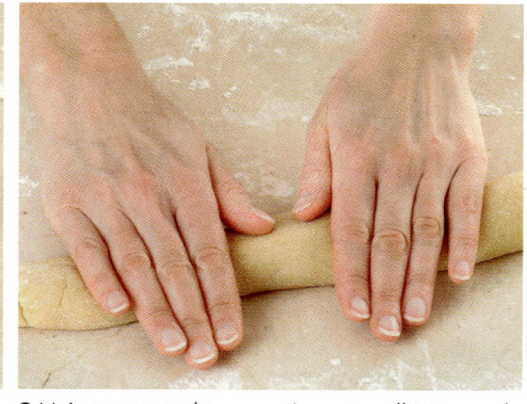

8 Using your palms, continue to roll it toward each end, until it is about 12in (30cm) long.

9 Pinch the tops of the 3 pieces together, and tuck the join underneath to start the braid.

10 Loosely braid the dough, leaving room for it to rise. Pinch and tuck the ends underneath.

11 Put on a baking sheet lined with parchment. Cover with oiled plastic wrap and a towel.

12 Leave in a warm place for 2 hours; it will not double now, but will rise on baking.

13 Preheat the oven to 375°F (190°C). Brush liberally with beaten egg.

14 Bake for 25–30 minutes, until golden. Check if undercooked where the braids meet.

15 If undercooked, cover with foil and bake for 5 minutes. Cool for 15 minutes before serving.

STORE Wrap in plastic wrap for 2 days. **ALSO TRY...** For variety, add 3oz (75g) golden raisins at step 2 and scatter 2 tablespoons sliced almonds after brushing with egg at step 13.

Hefezopf variations

Spiced Pecan and Raisin Hefezopf

The nuts and spices make this bread even tastier toasted.

MAKES 1 LOAF | **30 MINS** | **25–35 MINS** | **UP TO 8 WEEKS**

Rising and proofing time
4–4½ hrs

Ingredients

3 x "logs" hefezopf dough, approx. 12in (30cm) long, see page 446, steps 1–8
¼ cup raisins
¼ cup pecans, roughly chopped
2 tbsp light brown sugar
1 tsp pumpkin pie spice

Method

1 Roll each "log" of dough out crosswise, so that you have three pieces each 12 x 3¼in (30 x 8cm). The measurements do not have to be precise, but the pieces of dough should be roughly the same shape.

2 Mix together the raisins, pecans, sugar, and pumpkin pie spice. Scatter a third of the mixture over each piece of dough, and press down with your palms firmly. Roll up each piece along its longest side, tucking the dough in firmly as you go. You should be left with three 12in (30cm) "ropes" of dough stuffed with the raisin and nut mix.

3 Pinch the tops of the 3 pieces of dough together and tuck the join underneath. Now loosely braid the dough together, leaving room for it to rise, and pinch and tuck the ends underneath.

4 Transfer the loaf to a baking sheet lined with parchment paper, cover with lightly oiled plastic wrap and a kitchen towel, and leave in a warm place for a further 2 hours. This dough will rise, but not double in size. Preheat the oven to 375°F (190°C).

5 Brush the loaf with egg, making sure to get into the joins of the braid. Bake in the preheated oven for 25–30 minutes, until well risen and golden brown. If the bread is undercooked where the braids meet, but has browned well, cover loosely with foil and cook for a further 5 minutes. Remove from the oven and leave to cool on a wire rack for at least 15 minutes before serving.

STORE This loaf is best eaten the day it is baked, but will store, wrapped in plastic wrap, for 2 days.

BAKER'S TIP

Hefezopf is a sweet yeasted bread, traditionally braided and baked at Easter all over Germany. It is quite similar to a brioche dough recipe, and can be baked plain or stuffed with a variety of dried fruits and nuts. Try experimenting with this recipe to include your favorites.

Challah

This traditional Jewish bread is baked for holidays and the Sabbath.

MAKES 1 LOAF · 45–55 MINS · 35–40 MINS · UP TO 8 WEEKS

Proofing time
1¾–2¼ hrs

Ingredients
2½ tsp dried yeast
4 tbsp vegetable oil, plus extra for greasing
4 tbsp sugar
2 eggs, plus 1 yolk, for glazing
2 tsp salt
2¼ cups bread flour,
  plus extra for dusting
1 tsp poppy seeds, for sprinkling (optional)

Method

1 Put 1 cup of water into a pan, and bring just to a boil. Pour 4 tablespoons into a bowl, and let cool to lukewarm. Sprinkle over the yeast and let stand, stirring once, for 5 minutes, until dissolved. Add the oil and sugar to the remaining water in the pan and heat until melted. Let cool to lukewarm.

2 In a large bowl, beat the eggs just until mixed. Add the cooled sweetened water, salt, and dissolved yeast. Stir in half the flour and mix well. Add the remaining flour gradually, until the dough forms a ball. It should be soft and slightly sticky.

3 Turn onto a floured work surface. Knead for 5–7 minutes, until very smooth and elastic. Oil a large bowl. Put the dough in the bowl, and flip it. Cover with a damp kitchen towel and let rise in a warm place for 1–1½ hours, until doubled in bulk.

4 Lightly brush a baking sheet with oil. Turn the dough onto a lightly floured work surface and knock back. Cut the dough into 4 equal pieces. Flour the work surface. Roll each piece of dough with your hands to a 25in (63cm) strand.

5 Line the strands up next to each other. Starting from your left, lift the first strand to cross over the second. Lift the third strand to cross over the fourth. Now lift the fourth strand and lay it between the first and second strands. Finish braiding the strands, pinching the ends together and tucking them under the braided loaf.

6 Transfer the loaf to the prepared baking sheet. Cover with a dry kitchen towel and let rise in a warm place for about 45 minutes, until doubled in bulk. Preheat the oven to 375°F (190°C). Make the glaze by beating the egg yolk with 1 tablespoon water until it looks frothy. Brush the loaf with the glaze, and sprinkle with poppy seeds, if you like.

7 Bake in the oven for 35–40 minutes, until golden and the bread sounds hollow when the bottom is tapped.

STORE Challah is best eaten the day it is made, but will store, wrapped in plastic wrap, for up to 2 days.

CLASSIC AND ARTISAN BREADS

Pane al latte

This soft, slightly sweet Italian milk bread is perfect for small children —though adults will enjoy it for breakfast or lunch as well!

MAKES 1 LOAF   **30 MINS**   **20 MINS**

Rising and proofing time
2½–3 hrs

Ingredients

4 cups all-purpose flour, plus extra for dusting
1 tsp salt
2 tbsp sugar
2 tsp dried yeast
¾ cup warm milk
2 large eggs, plus 1 egg, beaten, for glazing
4 tbsp unsalted butter, melted
vegetable oil, for greasing

Method

1 Put the flour, salt, and sugar into a bowl and mix well. Dissolve the yeast in the milk, whisking to help it dissolve. Once the liquid has cooled, add the eggs and beat well.

2 Gradually pour the milk mixture, then the butter, into the flour mixture, stirring it to form a soft dough. Knead the dough for 10 minutes on a floured work surface, until smooth, glossy, and elastic.

3 Put the dough in a lightly oiled bowl, cover loosely with plastic wrap, and leave to rise in a warm place for up to 2 hours, until doubled in size. Turn the dough out onto a lightly floured work surface and gently knock it back. Divide it into 5 roughly equal pieces. Ideally, 2 should be slightly bigger than the rest.

4 Knead each piece briefly, and roll it out to a long, fat log shape. The 3 smaller pieces should be about 8in (20cm) long, and the 2 larger ones about 10in (25cm) long. Take the 3 shorter pieces and position them side-by-side on a baking sheet

lined with parchment paper. Place the 2 longer ones on each side and draw the tops and bottoms together, flaring out the centers to form a "circle." Pinch the top of the loaf together to ensure that the dough does not come apart.

5 Cover it loosely with lightly oiled plastic wrap and a clean kitchen towel, and leave it in a warm place to rise, until almost doubled in size. This could take 30 minutes to 1 hour. Preheat the oven to 375°F (190°C

6 Gently brush with a little beaten egg and bake for 20 minutes, until golden brown. Remove from the oven and leave to cool for at least 10 minutes before serving.

STORE Best eaten still warm from the oven, the bread can be wrapped in paper overnight and toasted the next day.

BAKER'S TIP

The use of eggs, milk, and sugar give this very soft Italian bread a sweet, gentle flavor and velvety texture. It toasts well, but is at its best served still warm with plenty of cold, unsalted butter and homemade strawberry jam. It is especially popular with children.

Sourdough Bread

A true sourdough starter uses naturally-occurring yeasts to ferment. Dried yeast is a bit of a cheat, but more reliable.

MAKES 2 LOAVES · **45–50 MINS** · **40–45 MINS** · **UP TO 8 WEEKS**

Fermenting time
4–6 days

Rising and proofing time
2–2½ hrs

Ingredients

For the sourdough starter
1 tbsp dried yeast
1⅓ cups bread flour

For the sponge
1⅓ cups bread flour, plus extra
  for sprinkling

For the bread
1½ tsp dried yeast
2¼ cups bread flour, plus extra
  for dusting
1 tbsp salt
vegetable oil, for greasing
polenta or fine yellow cornmeal,
  for dusting

1 Make the starter 3–5 days ahead. Dissolve the yeast in 2 cups lukewarm water.

2 Stir in the flour, and cover. Let it ferment in a warm place for 24 hours.

3 Look at the starter; it should have become frothy and have a distinct, sour odor.

4 Stir, cover, and ferment for 2–4 days longer, stirring it each day. Then use, or refrigerate.

5 To make the sponge, mix 1 cup starter with 1 cup lukewarm water in a large bowl.

6 Stir in the flour and mix vigorously. Sprinkle with 3 tablespoons flour.

7 Cover with a damp kitchen towel, and let ferment in a warm place overnight.

8 To make the bread, dissolve the yeast in ¼ cup lukewarm water. Mix into the sponge.

9 Stir in half the flour and the salt, and mix well to combine all the ingredients.

10 Gradually add the remaining flour. Mix well, until the dough forms a soft, slightly sticky ball.

11 Knead for 8–10 minutes, until very smooth and elastic. Put in an oiled bowl.

12 Cover with a damp kitchen towel and let rise in a warm place for 1–1½ hours, until doubled.

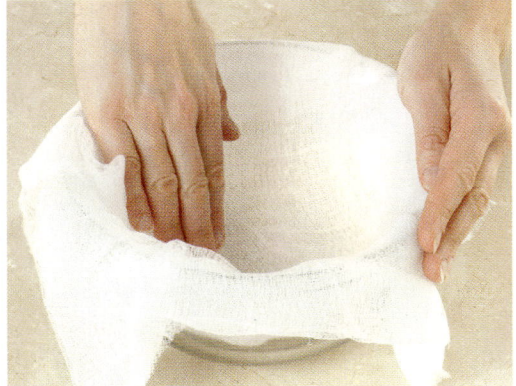

13 Line 2 x 8in (20cm) bowls with pieces of cloth, and sprinkle generously with flour.

14 Knock back the dough on a floured surface, cut in half, and shape each half into a ball.

15 Place in the bowls, covering with kitchen towels. Keep warm for 1 hour.

16 Put a pan on the oven floor and heat to 400°F (200°C). Sprinkle 2 baking sheets with polenta.

17 Turn the loaves, seam-side down, onto the baking sheets and remove the cloth.

18 With a sharp knife, make criss-cross slashes in the top of each loaf.

19 Put the loaves in the oven. Drop ice cubes into the roasting pan, then bake for 20 minutes.

20 Reduce to 375°F (190°C) and bake for another 20–25 minutes, until well browned.

21 Transfer to a wire rack. **STORE** These can be kept for 2–3 days, tightly wrapped in paper.

Sourdough Bread variations

Sourdough Rolls

These pretty rolls are perfect
for a picnic lunch.

MAKES 12	45–50 MINS	25–30 MINS	UP TO 8 WEEKS

Fermenting time
4–6 days

Rising and proofing time
2–2½ hrs

Ingredients
1 quantity sourdough bread dough,
see pages 452–453, steps 1–12

Method

1 Make the starter and the sponge; make
and knead the dough, and let it rise as
directed for Sourdough Bread (see page
452). Sprinkle 2 baking sheets with polenta.

2 Knock the air out of the dough, and let
rest as directed. Cut the dough in half. Roll
1 piece of dough into a cylinder about 2in
(5cm) in diameter. With a sharp knife, cut
the cylinder into 6 pieces. Repeat to shape
and divide the remaining dough.

3 Lightly flour a work surface. Cup a piece
of dough under the palm of your hand and
roll to form a smooth ball. Repeat to shape
the remaining dough. Set the rolls on the
prepared baking sheets. Cover, and let rise
in a warm place for about 30 minutes, until
doubled in size.

4 Preheat the oven to 400°F (200°C) and
heat the roasting pan as directed. Lightly
sprinkle each roll with flour, then, with a
scalpel, make an "x" in the center of each
roll. Bake as directed, until the rolls are
golden and sound hollow when tapped,
25–30 minutes.

STORE The rolls will keep for 2–3 days,
tightly wrapped in paper.

PREPARE AHEAD These rolls can be frozen at
the shaping stage, brought back to room
temperature, then glazed and baked.

Fruit and Nut Sourdough Loaf

Raisins and walnuts are a great addition to a tangy sourdough loaf. Once you've learned how to combine fruit and nuts into the dough, try experimenting with your own favorite combinations.

MAKES 2 LOAVES — **45–50 MINS** — **40–45 MINS** — **UP TO 8 WEEKS**

Fermenting time
4–6 days

Rising and proofing time
2–2½ hrs

Ingredients
1 quantity starter and sponge,
  see page 452, steps 1–7

For the dough
2 tsp dried yeast
1⅓ cups bread flour, plus extra for dusting
¾ cup rye flour
1 tbsp salt
¼ cup raisins
½ cup walnuts, chopped
vegetable oil, for greasing
polenta, for dusting

Method

1 Dissolve the yeast in 4 tablespoons lukewarm water. Leave for 5 minutes until frothy, then mix into the sponge. Combine the 2 types of flour and stir half the flour mix and all the salt into the sponge, mixing well to combine. Gradually add the remaining flour, mixing well, until the dough forms a soft, slightly sticky ball. Knead for 8–10 minutes, until very smooth and elastic. Flatten the dough into a rectangle, scatter over the raisins and walnuts, and bring together, kneading briefly to mix.

2 Place the dough in a large oiled bowl, cover with a damp kitchen towel, and let rise in a warm place until doubled in size; about 1–1½ hours. Line 2 x 8in (20cm) bowls with pieces of cloth, and sprinkle with flour. Knock back the dough on a floured surface, cut in half, and shape each half into a ball.

Place in the bowls, cover with dry kitchen towels, and let rise in a warm place until the bowls are full; about 1 hour.

3 Preheat the oven to 400°F (200°C) and place a roasting pan on the oven floor to heat up. Sprinkle 2 baking sheets with polenta. Turn the loaves, seam-side down, on to the sheets. With a sharp knife, make criss-cross slashes in the top of each loaf.

4 Put the loaves in the oven. Drop ice cubes into the hot roasting pan and return to the oven, then bake the bread for 20 minutes. Reduce the temperature to 375°F (190°C) and bake for another 20–25 minutes, until well browned. Transfer to a wire rack.

STORE The loaves will keep for 2–3 days, tightly wrapped in paper.

Pugliese

This classic Italian country loaf is flavored and preserved with olive oil. Do not worry if the dough seems wet at first, as the looser the dough, the larger the air pockets in the finished crumb.

MAKES 1 LOAF — **30 MINS** — **30–35 MINS** — **UP TO 4 WEEKS**

Fermenting time
12 hours or overnight

Rising and proofing time
up to 4 hours

Ingredients

For the biga
¼ tsp dried yeast
¾ cup bread flour
extra virgin olive oil, for greasing

For the dough
½ tsp dried yeast
1 tbsp extra virgin olive oil, plus extra for greasing
1⅔ cups bread flour, plus extra for dusting
1 tsp salt

Method

1 For the biga, dissolve the yeast in ½ cup warm water, whisking. Add the liquid to the flour and bring it together to form a dough. Place in an oiled bowl, cover with plastic, and put in a cool place to rise for at least 12 hours, or overnight.

2 For the dough, dissolve the yeast in ⅔ cup warm water, then add the oil. Put the biga, flour, and salt into a bowl. Add the liquid. Stir it to form a rough dough. Knead for 10 minutes on a well floured surface until smooth and elastic.

3 Put the dough in an oiled bowl, cover with plastic wrap, and leave to rise in a warm place for up to 2 hours, until doubled in size. Turn it out onto a floured surface. Gently knock it back and knead it into a shape; I like a rounded oblong.

4 Place the dough on a large baking sheet, cover with oiled plastic wrap and a kitchen towel, and leave in a warm place for up to 2 hours, until doubled in size. The bread is ready to bake when it is tight and well risen, and a finger gently poked into the dough leaves a dent that springs back quickly. Preheat the oven to 425°F (220°C).

5 Slash the the loaf in a slightly off-center line. This will allow the bread to continue to rise in the oven. Dust with flour, spray with water, and place on the middle rack. Bake for 30–35 minutes. For a crisper crust, spray with water every 10 minutes. Remove the bread from the oven and let cool.

STORE The loaf will keep for 2–3 days, tightly wrapped in paper.

Baguette

Master this basic recipe and you can shape it to produce baguettes, ficelles, or bâtards whenever you like.

MAKES 2 | **30 MINS** | **15–30 MINS** | **UP TO 4 WEEKS**

Fermenting time
12 hrs or overnight

Rising and proofing time
3½ hrs

Ingredients

For the sponge
⅛ tsp dried yeast
⅓ cup bread flour
1 tbsp rye flour
vegetable oil, for greasing

For the dough
1 tsp dried yeast
1⅔ cups bread flour, plus extra for dusting
½ tsp salt

1 Dissolve the yeast in ⅓ cup warm water and add to the 2 types of flour.

2 Form a sticky, loose dough and place in an oiled bowl, with room for it to expand.

3 Cover with plastic wrap and put in a cool place to rise for at least 12 hours, or overnight.

4 To make the dough, dissolve the yeast in ⅔ cup warm water, whisking to help it dissolve.

5 Put the risen sponge, flour, and salt into a large bowl and pour in the yeast liquid.

6 Stir it all together with a wooden spoon to form a soft dough.

7 Knead for 10 minutes on a floured surface, until smooth, soft, glossy, and elastic.

8 Place in oiled bowl, cover with plastic wrap, and let rise in a warm place for 2 hours.

9 Place it on a floured surface. Knock it back. Divide into 2 for baguettes or 3 for ficelles.

10 Knead briefly and shape each piece into a rectangle. Tuck one short edge into the center.

11 Press down firmly, fold over the other short edge, and press firmly again.

12 Shape the dough into a rounded oblong. Pinch to seal and turn seam-side down.

13 Shape into a long, thin log. A baguette is 1½in (4cm) wide, a ficelle ¾–1¼in (2–3cm).

FOR A BÂTARD LOAF Knead all the dough briefly and shape it into a rough rectangle.

Tuck the furthest edge into the center, press it, then do the same with the nearest edge.

Turn it over to tuck the seam underneath and gently shape it so it tapers at the ends.

14 Put loaves on baking sheets and cover with oiled plastic wrap and a kitchen towel.

15 Keep warm for 1½ hours until doubled. Preheat the oven to 425°F (220°C).

16 Slash the loaf deeply on the diagonal along the top, or crisscross for a bâtard.

17 Dust with a little flour, spray it with water, and place on the middle shelf of the oven.

18 Bake for 15 minutes for a ficelle, 20 for a baguette, and 25–30 for a bâtard. Let it cool.

BAGUETTE

Baguette variations

Pain d'épi

This attractive variation on the baguette gets its name from its resemblance to wheat ears, *épi* in French. The wheat-ear effect is not difficult to achieve and looks very decorative. Try to eat as soon as it cools.

MAKES 3 | 40–45 MINS | 25–30 MINS

Rising and proofing time
4–5 hrs

Ingredients
2½ tsp dried yeast
3 cups bread flour, plus extra for dusting
2 tsp salt
unsalted butter, for greasing

Method

1 In a small bowl, sprinkle the yeast over ¼ cup lukewarm water. Let stand for 5 minutes until dissolved, stirring once.

2 Put the flour onto a work surface with the salt. Make a large well in the center and add the dissolved yeast and 1½ cups lukewarm water. Gradually draw the flour into the liquid ingredients to form a smooth dough. It should be soft and slightly sticky.

3 On a floured surface, knead the dough for 5–7 minutes, until it is very smooth, elastic, and forms a ball. Brush a bowl with melted butter. Put the dough in the bowl, and flip it so the surface is lightly buttered. Cover with a damp kitchen towel and let rise in a warm place for 2–2 ½ hours, until tripled in size.

4 Turn the dough onto a lightly floured work surface and knock back. Return to the bowl, cover, and let rise in a warm place for 1–1½ hours, until doubled in size.

5 Sprinkle a cloth with flour. Turn the dough onto a floured work surface and knock back. With a sharp knife, cut the dough into 3 equal pieces. Cover 2 pieces while shaping the other. Flour your hands and pat 1 piece of dough into a 7 x 4in (18 x 10cm) rectangle.

6 Starting with a long side, roll the rectangle into a cylinder, pinching and sealing it with your fingers as you go. Roll the cylinder, stretching it until it is a stick shape, about 14in (35cm) long. Put on the cloth. Repeat with the remaining dough, pleating the cloth between the pieces of dough.

7 Cover with a dry kitchen towel, and let rise in a warm place for 1 hour, until doubled in size. Preheat the oven to 425°F (220°C). Set a roasting pan to heat on the floor of the oven. Sprinkle 2 baking sheets with flour. Roll 2 loaves onto 1 baking sheet, placing them 6in (15cm) apart. Roll the third loaf onto the other baking sheet.

8 Make a V-shaped cut halfway through 1 of the loaves, 2-3in (5-7cm) from the end. Pull the point to the left. Make a second cut 2-3in (5-7cm) from the first, pulling to the right. Continue to shape the remaining dough. Place the loaves in the oven. At once drop ice cubes into the hot roasting pan. Bake for 25–30 minutes, until browned. Turn them over and tap the bottoms with your knuckles. The bread should sound hollow. Let cool.

Whole Wheat Baguette

Try this healthier, high-fiber alternative to a white baguette.

| MAKES 2 | 20 MINS | 20–25 MINS | UP TO 4 WEEKS |

Fermenting time
12 hrs or overnight

Rising and proofing time
3½ hrs

Ingredients
1 quantity sponge, see page 458, steps 1–3, substituting whole wheat for the white bread flour

For the dough
½ tsp dried yeast
¾ cup whole wheat bread flour
1¼ cups bread flour, plus extra for dusting
½ tsp salt

Method

1 To make the dough, dissolve the yeast in ⅔ cup warm water. Put the risen sponge, 2 types of flour, and salt into a large bowl. Gradually pour in the dissolved yeast, stirring together to form a dough.

2 Knead for 10 minutes on a floured work surface, until smooth, glossy, and elastic. Put the dough in a lightly oiled bowl, cover loosely with plastic, and leave in a warm place for up to 1½ hours, until doubled.

3 Turn the dough out onto a floured surface and knock it back. Divide into 2 equal pieces. Knead each piece briefly and shape it into a rough rectangle. Use your hands to tuck the furthest edge of the dough into the center, pressing it down with your fingertips, then do the same with the nearest edge. Fold the dough in half to make a long, thin oblong and press down to seal the edges.

4 Turn the dough over so the seam is underneath and use your hands to gently stretch and roll it into a long, thin log shape, no more than 1¾in (4cm) wide. Be careful not to roll it out longer than the length of a baking sheet, and bear in mind that it will expand when rising.

5 Place the loaves on 2 large baking sheets and cover loosely with oiled plastic wrap and a kitchen towel. Leave in a warm place until well risen, and almost doubled in size. This could take up to 2 hours. The bread is ready to bake when it is tight and well risen, and a finger gently poked into the dough leaves a dent that springs back quickly. Preheat the oven to 450°F (230°C).

6 Take a sharp knife and slash the top of the loaves quite deeply diagonally all along the top. This will allow the bread to continue to rise in the oven. Dust the tops with a little flour and, if you like, spray with water. Place on the middle rack of the oven, and bake for 20–25 minutes. For a crisper crust, spray the loaves with water every 10 minutes during baking. Remove the bread from the oven and cool on a wire rack.

STORE The baguette can be stored, loosely wrapped in paper, overnight.

Artisan Rye Bread

Breads made with rye flour are very popular in central and eastern Europe. This version uses a starter.

MAKES 1 LOAF   **25 MINS**   **40–50 MINS**

Fermenting time
overnight

Rising and proofing time
1½ hrs

Ingredients

For the starter
1 cup rye flour
⅔ cup plain yogurt
1 tsp dried yeast
1 tbsp molasses
1 tsp caraway seeds, lightly crushed

For the dough
1 cup rye flour
1½ cups bread flour,
  plus extra for dusting
2 tsp salt
vegetable oil, for greasing
1 egg, beaten
1 tsp caraway seeds, to decorate

1 In a bowl, mix all the starter ingredients together with 1 cup tepid water.

2 Cover and leave overnight. When you look at it the next day, it should be bubbling.

3 For the dough, mix the flours together with the salt, then stir into the starter.

4 Mix to make a dough, adding a little extra water if required.

5 Turn out onto a floured surface and knead for 5–10 minutes, or until smooth and springy.

6 Shape into a ball, put into an oiled bowl, and cover loosely with oiled plastic wrap.

7 Leave in a warm place for 1 hour, or until doubled in size.

8 Flour a baking sheet. Lightly knead the dough again, then form into a football shape.

9 Lift onto the tray, re-cover it loosely, and leave to rise again for another 30 minutes.

10 Preheat the oven to 425°F (220°C). Brush the dough with the egg.

11 Immediately sprinkle evenly with the caraway seeds; they should stick to the egg.

12 Slash the loaf along its length. Bake for 20 minutes, then reduce to 400°F (200°C).

13 Bake for 20–30 minutes until dark golden. Cool on a wire rack. **STORE** Keeps well, wrapped, for 2–3 days. **ALSO TRY... Seeded Rye Bread** Knead in 4oz (100g) mixed seeds, such as pumpkin, sunflower, sesame, poppy seeds, and pine nuts, at the end of step 5.

Artisan Rye Bread variations

Hazelnut and Raisin Rye Bread

The hazelnuts and raisins in this version add a little sweetness and crunch to the bread. Try experimenting with different combinations of your own favorite nuts and dried fruit.

MAKES 1 LOAF — 25 MINS — 40–50 MINS — UP TO 8 WEEKS

Fermenting, rising, and proofing time
overnight, then 1½ hrs

Ingredients

For the starter
1 cup rye flour
⅔ cup plain yogurt
1 tsp dried yeast
1 tbsp molasses

For the dough
1 cup rye flour
1½ cups bread flour, plus extra for dusting
2 tsp salt
½ cup hazelnuts, toasted, and roughly chopped
¼ cup raisins
vegetable oil, for greasing
1 egg, beaten

Method

1 In a bowl, mix all the starter ingredients together with 1 cup lukewarm water. Cover and leave overnight. When you look at it the next day, it should be bubbling.

2 For the dough, mix the flours together with the salt, then stir into the starter. Mix to make a dough, adding extra water if required. Turn out onto a floured surface and knead for 5–10 minutes, or until smooth and springy.

3 Stretch out the dough to a rough rectangle, scatter the hazelnuts and raisins on top, fold it over, and knead gently to incorporate. Shape into a ball and place in an oiled bowl, covered with plastic wrap. Leave in a warm place for 1 hour, until doubled in size.

4 Flour a baking sheet. Lightly knead the dough again, then form it into a shape like a football. Lift onto the sheet, cover loosely with plastic wrap, and leave to rise again for another 30 minutes.

5 Preheat the oven to 425°F (220°C). Brush the loaf with egg and slash along its length. Bake for 20 minutes. Reduce to 400°F (200°C) and bake for 20–30 minutes, until dark golden. Leave to cool on a wire rack.

STORE This rye bread will keep, wrapped in paper, for 2–3 days.

BAKER'S TIP

Rye bread makes a healthy alternative to sandwich bread. It is denser in the crumb, so makes a more substantial bite. The addition of a variety of seeds, nuts, and fruit brings crunch, extra nutrition, and texture to the finished bread. It is especially delicious with roast beef and pickles, or with cheese.

Pumpernickel

The unlikely inclusion of cocoa and coffee powder add depth of flavor.

| MAKES 1 LOAF | 20 MINS | 30–40 MINS | UP TO 8 WEEKS |

Fermenting, rising, and proofing time
12 hrs or overnight, then 4½ hrs

Special equipment time
1 x 9 x 5in (1-liter) loaf pan

Ingredients

For the starter
½ tsp dried yeast
½ cup rye flour
2 tbsp plain yogurt

For the dough
½ tsp dried yeast
1 tsp coffee powder
1 tbsp sunflower or vegetable oil,
  plus extra for greasing
¾ cup whole wheat flour, plus extra for dusting
¼ cup rye flour
½ tbsp cocoa powder
1 tsp salt
½ tsp caraway seeds, lightly pounded

Method

1 To make the starter, dissolve the yeast in ½ cup warm water. Put the rye flour, yogurt, and yeasted liquid in a large china or glass bowl and stir well to combine. Cover with plastic wrap, and put in a cool place to rise for at least 12 hours, or overnight.

2 To make the dough, dissolve the yeast in 3–4 tablespoons warm water. Add the coffee powder and stir until dissolved. Add the oil. Put the starter, 2 types of flour, cocoa powder, salt, and caraway seeds into a large bowl. Add the liquid.

3 Stir the ingredients, and, when it seems a little stiff, use your hands to bring the dough together. Knead for 10 minutes on a floured work surface until smooth and elastic.

4 Put the dough in a lightly oiled bowl, cover loosely with plastic wrap, and leave to rise in a warm place for up to 2 hours, until doubled in size. Turn it out onto a lightly floured work surface and gently knock it back. Shape into a ball again, return to the bowl, and cover. Leave for another 1 hour while it rises again.

5 Turn it out onto a lightly floured work surface and knock it back again. Knead it briefly and shape it into an oblong shape. Put it into a 9 x 5in lightly oiled loaf pan, cover loosely with oiled plastic wrap and a kitchen towel, and leave it to rise in a warm place until well risen, and almost doubled in size. This could take another 1½ hours. It is ready to bake when it is tight and well risen, and a finger gently poked into the dough leaves a dent that springs back quickly. Preheat the oven to 400°F (200°C).

6 Bake in the center of the oven for 30–40 minutes until well risen and dark brown on top. Leave to cool on a wire rack.

STORE The pumpernickel keeps well, wrapped in paper, for 3 days.

Pane siciliano

This rustic semolina bread from Sicily toasts particularly well and makes deliciously crunchy bruschetta.

MAKES 1 LOAF | 20 MINS | 25–30 MINS | UP TO 4 WEEKS

Fermenting time
12 hrs or overnight

Rising and proofing time
2½ hrs

Ingredients

For the starter
¼ tsp dried yeast
½ cup fine semolina, or semolina flour
vegetable oil, for greasing

For the dough
1 tsp dried yeast
2 cups fine semolina, or semolina flour, plus extra for dusting
1 tsp fine salt
1 tbsp sesame seeds
1 egg, beaten, for glazing

Method

1 To make the starter, dissolve the yeast in ½ cup warm water. Add the liquid to the semolina and bring everything together to form a rough, loose dough. Place the dough in a large bowl, with plenty of room for it to expand, cover with plastic wrap, and put in a cool place to rise for at least 12 hours, or overnight.

2 To make the dough, dissolve the yeast in ¾ cup warm water. Put the risen starter, flour, and salt into a large bowl, or the bowl of an electric mixer fitted with a dough hook. Add the liquid.

3 Stir the ingredients. When it seems a little stiff use your hands to bring the dough together, or mix on a low speed. Knead by hand for up to 10 minutes, or 5–7 minutes in an electric mixer on medium speed, until smooth, glossy, and elastic.

4 Put the dough in a lightly oiled bowl, cover loosely with plastic wrap, and leave to rise in a warm place for up to 1½ hours, until doubled in size.

5 Turn the dough out onto a lightly floured work surface and gently knock it back. Knead it briefly and shape it into the desired shape; traditionally a tight boule shape. Place on a large baking sheet, cover loosely with oiled plastic wrap and a clean kitchen towel, and leave it to rise in a warm place until well risen and almost doubled in size. This could take another hour. The bread is ready to bake when it is tight and well risen, and a finger gently poked into the dough leaves a dent that springs back quickly.

6 Preheat the oven to 400°F (200°C). Brush the top of the bread with beaten egg, and scatter with the sesame seeds. Bake in the center of the preheated oven for 25–30 minutes until well risen and golden brown. Remove from the oven and transfer to a wire rack to cool for at least 30 minutes before serving.

STORE The bread can be stored, loosely wrapped in paper, for 2 days.

BAKER'S TIP
This bread can be made using either fine semolina or semolina flour. Semolina is made from durum wheat and therefore is not wheat free, but gives a deliciously rustic texture to the bread, similar to that of polenta or cornmeal. It is especially good on the side with an oil-rich tomato salad.

CLASSIC AND ARTISAN BREADS

Schiacciata di uva

This sweet Italian "squashed" bread is very similar to a sweetened focaccia, and can be served cold or while still warm.

MAKES 1 LOAF **25 MINS** **20–25 MINS**

Rising and proofing time
3 hrs

Special equipment
8 x 12in (20 x 30cm) jelly roll pan
electric mixer with dough hook (optional)

Ingredients

For the dough
3¾ cups bread flour, plus extra for dusting
1 tsp fine salt
2 tbsp sugar
1½ tsp dried yeast
1 tbsp extra virgin olive oil, plus extra for greasing

For the filling
1lb 2oz (500g) small red seedless grapes, washed
3 tbsp sugar
1 tbsp finely chopped rosemary (optional)

Method

1 Put the flour, salt, and sugar into a large bowl, or the bowl of an electric mixer fitted with a dough hook. Dissolve the dried yeast in 1⅔ cups warm water. Once it has dissolved, add the oil.

2 Gradually pour the liquid into the flour mixture, stirring it together, or mixing on a low speed, to form a soft dough. Knead by hand for 10 minutes on a floured work surface, or 5–7 minutes in an electric mixer on medium speed, until smooth, glossy, and elastic. This dough should remain soft.

3 Put the dough in a lightly oiled bowl, cover loosely with plastic wrap, and leave to rise in a warm place for up to 2 hours, until doubled in size. Turn it out onto a lightly floured work surface and gently knock it back. Knead it briefly and divide it into 2 pieces, with one-third and two-thirds of the dough in each piece. Lightly oil a 8 x 12in (20 x 30cm) jelly roll pan.

4 Take the largest piece and roll it out roughly to the size of the pan. Place it in the pan and stretch it out to fill the pan, using your fingers to mold it to the sides. Scatter two-thirds of the grapes over the surface, and sprinkle with 2 tablespoons of the sugar.

5 Now roll the smaller piece of dough out to fit on top of the grapes, stretching it with your hands if necessary. Scatter the remaining grapes on the surface of the dough, and the chopped rosemary, if using. Place the dough onto a large baking sheet, cover it loosely with lightly oiled plastic wrap and a clean kitchen towel, and leave it to rise in a warm place until well risen, and almost doubled in size. This could take up to 1 hour. Preheat the oven to 400°F (200°C).

6 Scatter the top of the risen dough with the remaining 1 tablespoon sugar, and bake for 20–25 minutes, until well risen and golden brown. Remove from the oven and leave to cool for at least 10 minutes before serving.

STORE This is best eaten the day it is made, but will store, wrapped in paper, overnight.

BAKER'S TIP

This unusual Italian flat bread is traditionally served to celebrate the grape harvest in the Tuscany region of Italy. It is best eaten the day it is made, and more or less sugar can be added to taste. It is great with cheese and, of course, with Italian red wines.

flat breads

Four Seasons Pizza

These pizzas have different toppings, arranged separately, to represent the four seasons. Start the day before.

MAKES 4 PIZZAS | 40 MINS | 40 MINS

Rising time
1–1½ hrs or overnight

Ingredients
2¾ cups bread flour
3 tsp dried yeast
½ tsp salt
2 tbsp extra virgin olive oil, plus extra
 for greasing

For the tomato sauce
2 tbsp unsalted butter
2 shallots, finely chopped

1 tbsp olive oil
1 bay leaf
3 garlic cloves, crushed
2¼lb (1kg) ripe plum tomatoes,
 seeded and chopped
2 tbsp tomato paste
1 tbsp sugar
sea salt
freshly ground black pepper
pinch of chili flakes (optional)

For the toppings
6oz (175g) mozzarella, thinly sliced
4oz (115g) mushrooms, thinly sliced
2 tbsp extra virgin olive oil
2 roasted red peppers, thinly sliced
8 anchovy fillets, halved lengthways
4oz (115g) pepperoni, thinly sliced
2 tbsp capers
8 artichoke hearts, halved
12 black olives

1 Put the flour in a mixing bowl, and stir in the yeast and salt.

2 Add the olive oil and 1½ cups lukewarm water, then mix to a dough.

3 Knead on a floured surface for 10 minutes, or until the dough is smooth and elastic.

4 Roll the dough into a ball, and place in an oiled bowl covered with oiled plastic wrap.

5 Leave in a warm place for 1–1½ hours, until doubled; or store in the refrigerator overnight.

6 For the sauce, put a saucepan over low heat. Add the butter, shallots, oil, bay leaf, and garlic.

7 Stir, cover, and sweat the ingredients together for 5–6 minutes, stirring occasionally.

8 Add the tomatoes, tomato paste, and sugar. Cook for 5 minutes, stirring.

9 Now pour in 1 cup water, bring to a boil, and reduce the heat to a simmer.

FLAT BREADS

10 Cook for 30 minutes, stirring, until reduced to a thick sauce. Season to taste.

11 Using a wooden spoon, press the sauce through a sieve. Cover and chill until needed.

12 To bake, preheat the oven to 400°F (200°C). Transfer the dough to a lightly floured surface.

13 Knead lightly, divide into 4, and roll or press out into 9in (23cm) rounds.

14 Grease 4 baking sheets, and carefully lift a pizza base on to each.

15 Spread the sauce over the bases, leaving a ¾in (2cm) border around the edge of each.

16 Place any leftover sauce in a small freezer-safe container and freeze for later use.

17 Top the pizzas with mozzarella, dividing it equally between the bases.

18 Arrange the mushroom slices on a quarter of each pizza and brush with the olive oil.

19 Pile the roasted pepper slices on another quarter with the anchovy fillets on top.

20 Use pepperoni and capers for the third and artichokes and olives for the fourth quarter.

21 Bake at the top of the oven, 2 at a time, for 20 minutes, or until golden brown. Serve hot.

FOUR SEASONS PIZZA

473

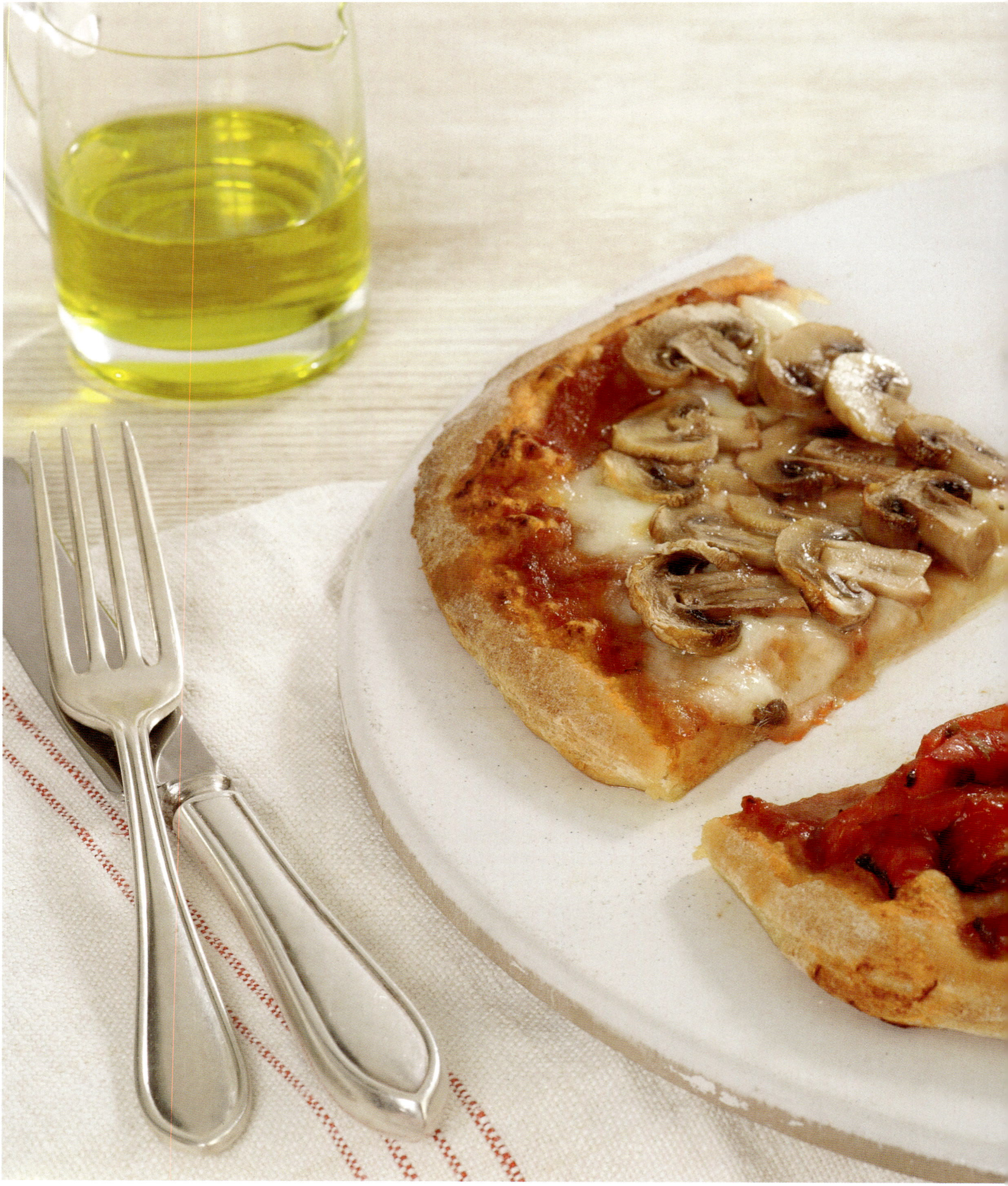

Pizza variations

Three Pepper Calzone with Cheese

"Calzone" means "trouser leg" in Italian, perhaps due to a resemblance or because this pizza turnover could be stuffed into a roomy trouser pocket!

MAKES 4 CALZONE | **25 MINS** | **15–20 MINS**

Rising and proofing time
1½–2 hrs

Ingredients
1 quantity pizza dough, see pages 472–473, steps 1–5
¼ cup extra virgin olive oil, plus extra to serve
2 onions, thinly sliced
2 red bell peppers, cut into strips
1 green bell pepper, cut into strips
1 yellow bell pepper, cut into strips
3 garlic cloves, finely chopped
1 small bunch of any herb, such as rosemary, thyme, basil, or parsley, or a mixture, leaves finely chopped
sea salt
cayenne pepper, to taste
6oz (175g) mozzarella, sliced
all-purpose flour, for dusting
1 egg, beaten

Method

1 Heat 1 tablespoon of oil in a frying pan, add the onions, and cook, stirring, for 2–3 minutes, until soft but not brown. Transfer to a bowl and set aside. Add the remaining oil to the pan, then the peppers, garlic, and half the herbs. Season with salt and cayenne. Sauté, stirring, for 7–10 minutes, until softened but not brown. Taste for seasoning: it should be quite spicy. Add to the onions, and let cool.

2 Divide the dough into 4 equal pieces. Roll and pull each piece into a square about ½in (1cm) thick. Spoon the pepper mixture onto a diagonal half of each square, leaving a 1in (2.5cm) border. Arrange the mozzarella slices on top. Moisten the edge of each square with water, and fold 1 corner over to meet the other, forming a triangle. Pinch the edges together to seal. Put the triangles on the floured baking sheet and let rise for 30 minutes. Preheat the oven to 450°F (230°C).

3 Whisk the egg with ½ teaspoon salt, and brush over the calzone. Bake for 15–20 minutes, until golden brown. Brush each with a little olive oil, and serve.

Chicago Deep-dish Pizza

A hearty pizza, dating back to 1940s Chicago.

SERVES 4 | **35–40 MINS** | **20–25 MINS**

Rising and proofing time
1 hr 20 mins–1 hr 50 mins

Special equipment
2 x 9in (23cm) cake pans

Ingredients

For the dough
2½ tsp dried yeast
2¾ cups bread flour, plus extra for dusting
2 tsp salt
3 tbsp extra virgin olive oil, plus more for greasing
2–3 tbsp polenta

For the sauce
13oz (375g) mild Italian sausage
1 tbsp extra virgin olive oil
3 garlic cloves, finely chopped
2 x 14oz (400g) cans chopped plum tomatoes
freshly ground black pepper
leaves from 7–10 flat-leaf parsley sprigs, chopped
6oz (175g) mozzarella, torn into chunks

Method

1 In a small bowl, sprinkle the yeast over ¼ cup lukewarm water. Let stand for 5 minutes, stirring once, until dissolved. Put the flour onto a work surface with the salt. Make a large well in the center and add the dissolved yeast, 1 cup lukewarm water, and the oil. Draw in the flour and work it into the other ingredients, to form a smooth dough. It should be soft and slightly sticky.

2 Lightly flour the work surface, and knead the dough for 5–7 minutes, until very smooth and elastic. Brush a large bowl with oil. Put the dough in the bowl and flip it so the surface is lightly oiled. Cover with a damp kitchen towel and let rise in a warm place for 1–1½ hours, until doubled in size.

3 Slit the side of each sausage and push out the meat, discarding the casing. Heat the oil in a sauté pan. Add the sausage and cook over medium-high heat, breaking up

the meat with the wooden spoon, for 5–7 minutes, until cooked. Reduce the heat to medium, remove the meat from the pan, and pour off all but 1 tablespoon of the fat.

4 Stir in the garlic and cook for about 30 seconds, until fragrant. Return the sausage and stir in the tomatoes, salt, pepper, and all but 1 tablespoon of the parsley. Cook, stirring occasionally, for 10–15 minutes, until thickened. Remove from the heat, taste for seasoning, and let cool completely.

5 Brush the pans with oil. Sprinkle the polenta in the pans, and turn it to coat the bottom and side, then turn upside down and tap to remove the excess. Turn the dough onto a lightly floured work surface and knock back. Shape the dough into 2 loose balls. With a rolling pin, roll the balls into rounds to fit your pans. Working carefully, wrap the dough around the rolling pin and drape it over the pans. With your hands, press the dough into the bottom of the pans, and 1in (2.5cm) up the side, to form a rim. Cover with a dry kitchen towel, and let rise for about 20 minutes. Preheat the oven to 450°F (230°C). Heat a baking sheet in the oven.

6 Spread the sauce over the dough, leaving a border. Sprinkle with the cheese and remaining parsley. Bake for 20–25 minutes, until crisp and golden.

Pizza Bianca

This version is made without tomato sauce, kept moist with olive oil instead, and packed with fresh Mediterranean flavors.

MAKES 4 PIZZAS   25 MINS   20 MINS

Rising time
1–1½ hrs

Ingredients
4 pizza bases, see pages 472–473, steps 1–5 and 12–14
¼ cup extra virgin Italian olive oil
5oz (140g) Gorgonzola cheese, crumbled
12 slices prosciutto, torn into strips
4 fresh figs, each cut into 8 wedges, and peeled
2 tomatoes, seeded and diced
4oz (115g) arugula leaves
freshly ground black pepper

Method
1 Preheat the oven to 400°F (200°C). Place the pizza bases on the greased baking sheets. Brush with half the olive oil and scatter over the Gorgonzola cheese.

2 Bake in the oven for 20 minutes, or until the bases are crisp and turning golden. Remove from the oven.

3 Arrange the prosciutto, figs, and tomatoes on top, and return to the oven for 8 minutes, or until the toppings are just warmed and the bases are golden brown.

4 Scatter over the arugula, season with plenty of black pepper, and serve at once, drizzled with the rest of the olive oil.

BAKER'S TIP
Pizzas are delicious with or without tomato sauce. However you prefer your pizza, always remember that the toppings should be spread evenly over the base, and enough moisture added—either from tomato sauce, cheese, or good-quality extra virgin olive oil—to ensure the topping remains lubricated and appetizing.

Pissaladière

This French version of the Italian pizza derives its name from *pissala*, a paste made from anchovies.

SERVES 4 | 20 MINS | 1 HOUR 25 MINS | UP TO 12 WEEKS

Rising time
1 hr

Special equipment
13 x 9in (32.5 x 23cm) jelly roll pan

Ingredients

For the base
1¼ cups bread flour, plus extra for dusting
sea salt
freshly ground black pepper

1 tsp brown sugar
1 tsp dried yeast
1 tbsp extra virgin olive oil, plus extra for greasing

For the topping
¼ cup extra virgin olive oil
2lb (900g) onions, finely sliced
3 garlic cloves
sprig of thyme
1 tsp herbes de Provence (dry mix of thyme, basil, rosemary, and oregano)
1 bay leaf
3½oz (140g) jar anchovies in oil
12 black pitted niçoise olives, or Italian olives

Method

1 For the base, combine the flour, 1 teaspoon salt, and black pepper to taste in a large bowl. Pour ⅔ cup lukewarm water into a separate bowl, and use a fork to whisk in the sugar, then the yeast. Set aside for 10 minutes to froth, then pour into the flour with the olive oil.

2 Mix to form a dough, adding another 2 tablespoons lukewarm water if the mixture looks too dry. Turn the dough out onto a floured board, and knead for 10 minutes, or until smooth and elastic. Shape the dough into a ball, return to a cleaned, oiled bowl, and cover with a kitchen towel. Leave in a warm place for 1 hour, or until doubled in size.

3 For the topping, put the oil in a saucepan over very low heat. Add the onions, garlic, herbs, and bay leaf. Cover and simmer gently, stirring occasionally, for 1 hour, or until the onions look like a stringy purée. Be careful not to let the onions catch; if they begin to stick, add a little water. Drain well, season with salt, and set aside, discarding the bay leaf.

4 Preheat the oven to 350°F (180°C). Knead the dough briefly on a floured surface. Roll it out so it is thin and large enough to fit the jelly roll pan. Prick all over with a fork.

5 Spread the onions over the base. Drain the anchovies, reserving 3 tablespoons oil, and slice the fillets in half lengthwise. Embed the olives in rows in the dough, and drape the anchovies in a criss-cross pattern on top of the onions. Drizzle with the reserved anchovy oil, and sprinkle with pepper.

6 Bake for 35 minutes, or until the crust is brown. The onions should not brown or dry out. Remove and serve warm, cut into rectangles, squares, or wedges, or allow to cool before serving.

BAKER'S TIP

All the elements of pissaladière are very simple, so it is imperative that you use the best-quality ingredients for the finest result. Take special care when selecting anchovies, and make sure they are packed in good-quality oil. When you can find them, smoked anchovies make an amazing substitution.

Pita Bread

This pocket bread is delicious stuffed with salad and other fillings, or cut up and eaten with dips.

MAKES 6 PITAS | **20–30 MINS** | **5 MINS** | **UP TO 8 WEEKS**

Rising and proofing time
1 hr–1 hr 50 mins

Ingredients
1 tsp dried yeast
⅓ cup whole wheat flour
1⅓ cups bread flour, plus extra
    for dusting
1 tsp salt
2 tsp cumin seeds
2 tsp extra virgin olive oil, plus extra
    for greasing

1 In a small bowl, mix the yeast with ¾ cup lukewarm water. Leave 5 minutes, then stir.

2 In a large bowl, mix together the two types of flour, salt, and cumin seeds.

3 Make a well and pour in the dissolved yeast, ¾ cup lukewarm water, and oil.

4 Combine the flour mix with the wet ingredients, mixing to form a soft, sticky dough.

5 Turn the dough onto a floured work surface and knead until very smooth and elastic.

6 Place the dough in a lightly greased bowl and cover with a damp kitchen towel.

7 Leave to rise in a warm place for 1–1½ hours, until doubled in size. Flour 2 baking sheets.

8 Turn the dough onto a lightly floured work surface, and knock back.

9 Shape the dough into a cylinder 2in (5cm) wide, then cut into 6 pieces.

10 Take 1 piece of dough and leave the rest covered with a kitchen towel as you work.

11 Shape the dough into a ball, then roll into an 8in (20cm) oval.

12 Transfer to a baking sheet. Repeat to shape the remaining pitas. Cover with a kitchen towel.

13 Leave to rise in a warm place for 20 minutes. Preheat the oven to 475°F (240°C).

14 Place another baking sheet in the oven. Once hot, transfer half the pitas to the sheet.

15 Bake for 5 minutes. Transfer to a wire rack and brush the tops lightly with water.

16 Bake the remaining rounds, transfer to the rack, and brush with water. **STORE** Best eaten warm from the oven, pitas can be stored overnight in an airtight container.

Pita variations

Spiced Lamb Pies

Snacks such as these are found all around the Middle East.

| MAKES
12 PIES | 40–45
MINS | 10–15
MINS |

Rising and proofing time
1 hr–1 hr 50 mins

Ingredients
1 quantity pita dough, see page 480,
  steps 1–8, omitting the cumin seeds
2 tbsp extra virgin olive oil
13oz (375g) ground lamb
sea salt
freshly ground black pepper
3 large garlic cloves, finely chopped
½in (1cm) piece of fresh ginger, finely chopped
1 onion, finely chopped
½ tsp ground coriander
¼ tsp ground cumin
¼ tsp ground turmeric
large pinch of cayenne pepper
2 tomatoes, peeled, seeded, and chopped
leaves from 5–7 cilantro sprigs, finely chopped

Method
1 Heat the oil in a sauté pan. Add the lamb, season with salt and pepper, and stir over medium-high heat, until evenly browned. With a slotted spoon, transfer to a bowl. Reduce the heat to medium, and pour off all but 2 tablespoons of the fat. Add the garlic and ginger and cook for 30 seconds. Add the onion and stir until soft. Add the ground coriander, cumin, turmeric, cayenne, lamb, and tomatoes. Cover and cook for 10 minutes, until thickened.

2 Remove the pan from the heat. Stir in the cilantro and taste for seasoning. Let the filling cool, then taste again: it should be well seasoned, so adjust if necessary.

3 Cut the dough in half. Shape 1 piece into a cylinder about 2in (5cm) in diameter. Cut into 6 pieces, and cover. Repeat with the remaining dough. Shape a piece of dough into a ball. With a rolling pin, roll into a 4in (10cm) round. Spoon some of the lamb into the center of the round, leaving a 1in (2.5cm) border. Lift the dough up and over the filling, to form a triangular parcel. Pinch

the edges with your fingers to seal. Place the pie on a baking sheet. Repeat to shape and fill the remaining dough.

4 Cover the pies with a kitchen towel, and let rise in a warm place until puffed, about 20 minutes. Preheat the oven to 450°F (230°C). Bake for 10–15 minutes until golden brown. Serve warm from the oven with a spoonful of Greek yogurt on the side, if you like.

STORE The pies will keep in an airtight container overnight.

PREPARE AHEAD The lamb filling can be prepared, covered, and refrigerated 1 day ahead.

Spiced Garbanzo Bean Pitas

These are good grilled, and best eaten on the day they are made.

MAKES 8 PITAS — **25 MINS** — **15 MINS**

Rising time
1 hr

Ingredients
1 tsp dried yeast
1½ tsp cumin seeds, plus more for sprinkling
1½ tsp ground coriander
3½ cups bread flour, plus extra for dusting
1 tsp salt
small bunch of cilantro, coarsely chopped
7oz (200g) can garbanzo beans,
  drained and crushed
⅔ cup plain yogurt
1 tbsp extra virgin olive oil, plus extra for greasing

Method
1 Sprinkle the yeast over 1¼ cups lukewarm water and allow to dissolve, stirring once. Toast the cumin and ground coriander in a dry pan for a minute. Mix the flour and salt in a bowl. Stir in the spices, cilantro, and garbanzo beans, then make a well in the middle. Pour in the yogurt, oil, and yeast liquid, and bring together to form a sticky dough. Set aside for 10 minutes.

2 Turn the dough out onto a floured surface, and knead it for 5 minutes, shaping it into a ball. Place the dough in an oiled bowl, cover it with oiled plastic wrap, and leave it to rise in a warm place for 1 hour, or until doubled in size.

3 Dust 2 baking sheets with flour. Preheat the oven to 425°F (220°C). Turn the dough out onto a floured surface. Cut into 8 pieces.

4 Using a rolling pin, flatten them out into ovals, each about ¼in (5mm) thick. Place them on the baking sheets, brush with oil, and scatter over cumin seeds. Bake for 15 minutes, or until golden and puffed up.

STORE The pitas will keep in an airtight container overnight.

Pita Chips

Serve these simple, homemade pita chips as part of a range of appetizers for a healthier alternative to potato chips.

SERVES 8 — **10 MINS** — **7–8 MINS**

Ingredients
6 pita breads, store-bought, or see pages 480–481
extra virgin olive oil, for greasing
cayenne pepper, for sprinkling
sea salt, for sprinkling

Method
1 Preheat the oven to 450°F (230°C). Divide the pita breads in half by separating the 2 layers of bread. Brush the pieces of bread on both sides with a little olive oil, then sprinkle them with salt and a scattering of cayenne pepper.

2 Stack the pieces of pita bread on top of each other in piles of 6, and cut them into large triangles. Lay the cut chips out onto several large baking sheets in a single layer, making sure they do not overlap.

3 Bake the chips in the top of the oven for 5 minutes, or until the bottoms are starting to brown. Turn over and continue to cook for another 2–3 minutes until they are browned and crisp all over. Watch them to make sure that they do not burn. Leave to cool on paper towels, and serve with dips such as baba ganoush or hummus.

STORE The chips will keep in an airtight container for 2 days.

BAKER'S TIP
These simple snacks go well with homemade dips and salsas, or even chili con carne. They are an inexpensive alternative to chips, and much healthier too! To make them even more nutritious, bake whole wheat pita chips instead.

Naan Bread

This familiar Indian flat bread is traditionally cooked in a tandoor oven, but this recipe uses a conventional oven.

MAKES 6 NAAN | **20 MINS** | **8 MINS** | **UP TO 12 WEEKS**

Rising time
1 hr

Ingredients

2¾ cups bread flour, plus extra for dusting
2 tsp dried yeast
1 tsp sugar
1 tsp salt
2 tsp black onion seeds
½ cup full-fat plain yogurt
4 tbsp ghee, or butter, melted

1 Heat the ghee or butter in a small saucepan until melted. Set aside.

2 In a large bowl, mix together the flour, yeast, sugar, salt, and onion seeds.

3 Make a well. Add ¾ cup lukewarm water, the yogurt, and the melted ghee.

4 Draw in the flour and mix gently with a wooden spoon to combine.

5 Keep mixing for 5 minutes, until it forms a rough dough.

6 Cover and keep warm until doubled; about 1 hour. Preheat the oven to 475°F (240°C).

7 Place 2 baking sheets in the oven. Knock back the dough.

8 Knead the dough on a floured surface until smooth. Divide into 4 equal pieces.

9 Roll each piece into an oval shape about 10in (24cm) long.

FLAT BREADS

10 Transfer the bread to the preheated sheets and bake for 6–7 minutes, until well puffed.

11 Preheat the broiler to its hottest setting. Transfer the breads to the broiler pan.

12 Cook the naans for 30–40 seconds on each side, or until they brown and blister.

13 When broiling, take care not to put the breads too close to the heat, to prevent burning. Transfer to a wire rack and serve warm.
ALSO TRY... Garlic and Cilantro Naan Add 2 crushed garlic cloves and 4 tablespoons finely chopped cilantro in step 2.

Naan variations

Feta, Chile, and Herb-stuffed Naan

Try stuffing a simple naan bread dough with this herby feta mix for an unusual picnic dish, which brings together flavors of the Mediterranean with those of India.

MAKES 6 NAAN · **15 MINS** · **6–7 MINS**

Rising time
1 hr

Ingredients
1 quantity naan bread dough, see page 484, steps 1–7
6oz (150g) feta cheese, crumbled
1 tbsp finely chopped red or jalapeño chile
3 tbsp chopped mint
3 tbsp chopped cilantro

Method

1 Make the naan dough up to the end of step 7 (see page 484). Make the stuffing by mixing together the feta, chile, and herbs. Preheat the oven to 475°F (240°C) and place 2 large baking sheets in the oven.

2 Divide the dough into 6, and roll each piece into a circle. Divide the filling into 6, and put 1 portion of the filling into the middle of each piece of dough. Pull the edges up around it to form a purse shape. Pinch the edges together to seal.

3 Turn the dough over and roll out carefully into an oval, taking care not to tear the dough or reveal any of the filling.

4 Carefully transfer the breads onto the preheated baking sheets and cook in the oven for 6–7 minutes, or until well puffed. Carefully transfer to a wire rack, and serve while still warm.

PREPARE AHEAD These can be stored overnight, wrapped in plastic wrap. To reheat (from fresh or frozen), scrunch up a piece of parchment paper and soak in water. Squeeze out the excess water, and use to wrap the naan. Place in a medium oven for 10 minutes until warm and soft.

Peshwari Naan

Children love these sweet, nutty stuffed naans, best eaten still warm from the pan, either as a dessert or a side dish to savory curry. Try substituting finely chopped apple for the raisins and adding some cinnamon. ▶

MAKES 6 NAAN · **15 MINS** · **6–7 MINS** · **UP TO 8 WEEKS**

Rising time
1 hr

Special equipment
food processor with blade attachment

Ingredients
1 quantity naan bread dough, see page 484, steps 1–7
2 tbsp raisins
2 tbsp unsalted pistachios
2 tbsp almonds
2 tbsp unsweetened coconut
1 tbsp sugar

Method

1 Make the naan dough up to the end of step 7 (see page 484). Make the stuffing by putting all the remaining ingredients in a food processor, and purée until finely chopped. Preheat the oven to 475°F (240°C) and place 2 large baking sheets in the oven.

2 Divide the dough into 6, and roll each piece into a circle. Divide the filling into 6. Put 1 portion of the filling into the middle of each piece of dough, and pull the edges up around it to form a purse shape. Pinch the edges together to seal.

3 Turn the dough over and roll out carefully into an oval, taking care not to tear the dough or reveal any of the filling.

4 Carefully transfer the breads onto the preheated baking sheets and cook in the oven for 6–7 minutes, or until well puffed. Carefully transfer to a wire rack, and serve while still warm.

PREPARE AHEAD These can be stored overnight, wrapped in plastic wrap. To reheat (from fresh or frozen), scrunch up a piece of parchment paper and soak in water. Squeeze out the excess water, and use to wrap the peshwari naan. Place them in a medium oven for 10 minutes until they are warm and soft.

BAKER'S TIP
Once you have mastered the art of stuffing naan dough, there's no end to the things you can fill it with. Here the naan is stuffed with a mixture of nuts and dried fruit, sweetened with shredded coconut. Try a spiced lamb filling as well, and serve with a minted yogurt dip.

Stuffed Paratha

These stuffed flat breads are quick and easy to make. Try doubling the quantities, then freezing half stacked between layers of wax paper.

MAKES 4   **20 MINS**   **15–20 MINS**   **UP TO 8 WEEKS**

Rising time
1 hr

Ingredients

For the dough
1½ cups chapatti flour
½ tsp fine salt
4 tbsp unsalted butter, melted and cooled

For the stuffing
9oz (250g) peeled and diced sweet potato
1 tbsp sunflower or vegetable oil, plus extra for brushing
½ red onion, finely chopped
2 garlic cloves, crushed
1 tbsp finely chopped red or jalapeño chile, or to taste
1 tbsp finely chopped fresh ginger
2 heaped tbsp chopped cilantro
½ tsp garam masala
sea salt

Method

1 To make the dough, sift the flour and salt together. Add the butter and ⅔ cup water and bring the mixture together to form a soft dough. Knead by hand for 10 minutes, or for 5 minutes in the electric mixer, then leave the dough to rest, covered, for 1 hour.

2 Boil the sweet potato for about 7 minutes, until tender. Drain well. In a frying pan, heat the sunflower oil over medium heat, and fry the red onion for 3–5 minutes, until soft, but not golden. Add the garlic, chile, and ginger and fry for 1–2 minutes.

3 Add the cooked onion mixture to the sweet potato and mash. You should not need any extra liquid. Add the chopped cilantro, garam masala, and salt and beat until smooth. Set aside to cool.

4 When the dough has rested, divide it into 4 equal pieces. Knead each piece a little and roll it out into a small circle, around 4in (10cm) in diameter. Put a quarter of the stuffing mixture into the middle of the dough and pull the edges up around it into the middle, forming a purse shape.

5 Pinch the edges together to seal in the stuffing, turn the dough over and roll out carefully into a circle about 7in (18cm) in diameter, taking care not to roll too hard. If the filling bursts out of the dough, pinch the dough together to reseal the paratha.

6 Heat a large cast iron frying pan over medium heat. Fry the parathas for 2 minutes on each side, turning occasionally to make sure they are well cooked and browning in places. Once they have cooked on each side once, brush the surface with a little sunflower oil before turning them again. Serve immediately alongside a curry, or as a light lunch dish with a green salad.

PREPARE AHEAD These can be stored overnight, wrapped in plastic wrap. To reheat (from fresh or frozen), scrunch up a piece of parchment paper and soak in water. Squeeze out the excess water, and use to wrap the parathas. Place them in a medium oven for 10 minutes until soft.

BAKER'S TIP

These Indian flat breads are made with traditional chapatti flour, but if you cannot find it easily, use whole wheat flour instead. Try stuffing them with a variety of fillings, including leftover vegetable curry, just make sure the ingredients are diced small so the stuffing is easily contained.

FLAT BREADS

Tortillas

These classic Mexican flat breads are simple to make and far tastier than any store-bought tortilla.

MAKES 8 | **10 MINS** | **15–20 MINS** | **UP TO 8 WEEKS**

Resting time
1 hr

Ingredients
1¾ cups all-purpose flour, plus extra
   for dusting
scant 1 tsp salt
½ tsp baking powder
4 tbsp lard or vegetable shortening,
   chilled and diced, plus extra
   for greasing

1 Put the flour, salt, and baking powder into a large bowl. Add the lard.

2 Rub the lard in with your hands until the mixture resembles fine crumbs.

3 Add ⅔ cup warm water. Bring the mixture together to form a rough, soft dough.

4 Turn it out onto a lightly floured work surface and knead for a few minutes until smooth.

5 Put the dough in a greased bowl. Cover with plastic wrap. Rest in a warm place for 1 hour.

6 Turn the dough out onto a floured work surface and divide it into 8 equal portions.

7 Take 1 piece and leave the others covered with plastic wrap to prevent them from drying.

8 Roll each piece of dough out thinly to a circle about 8-10in (20-25cm) in diameter.

9 Stack the rolled tortillas in a pile. Place a piece of parchment paper between each.

10 Heat a pan over medium heat. Take 1 tortilla and dry fry for 1 minute.

11 Turn it over and continue to fry until both sides are cooked and browned in places.

12 Transfer to a wire rack and repeat to cook all the remaining tortillas. Serve warm or cool.

PREPARE AHEAD Cooled tortillas can be stored overnight, wrapped in plastic wrap. To reheat from fresh or frozen, scrunch up wax paper and soak it in water. Squeeze out the excess, use to wrap the tortillas, and bake in a medium oven for 10 minutes.

Tortilla variations

FLAT BREADS

Quesadillas

Almost any filling works for quesadillas: try substituting chicken, ham, Gruyère cheese, or mushrooms.

MAKES 1 OF EACH | **5–10 MINS** | **30–35 MINS**

Ingredients

For the spiced beef and tomato filling
1 tbsp extra virgin olive oil
6oz (150g) good-quality ground beef
pinch of hot cayenne pepper
sea salt
freshly ground black pepper
small handful fresh flat-leaf parsley, chopped
2 tomatoes, diced
2oz (50g) Cheddar cheese

For the avocado, scallion, and chile filling
4 scallions, finely chopped
1–2 fresh jalapeño chiles, seeded and chopped
juice of ½ lime
½ avocado, sliced
2oz (50g) Cheddar cheese

For the tortillas
2 tbsp oil
4 tortillas, see pages 490–491

Method

1 For the beef filling, heat 1 tablespoon of the oil in a frying pan, then fry the beef with the cayenne pepper over medium heat for 5 minutes, or until no longer pink. Reduce the heat and loosen with a little hot water. Season, and cook for 10 minutes, until the beef is cooked through. Stir in the parsley.

2 For the avocado filling, place the scallion, chiles, and lime juice in a bowl. Season and mix. Set aside for 2 minutes.

3 Heat half the oil for the tortillas in a non-stick frying pan. Fry 1 tortilla for 1 minute, or until lightly golden. Spoon the beef mixture over. Scatter over the tomato and cheese, then top with the other tortilla, pressing it down with the back of a spatula to sandwich the two. Scoop the quesadilla up, carefully turn it over, and cook the other side for another minute, or until golden. Slice in halves or quarters, and serve.

4 Heat the remaining oil in the frying pan, then fry 1 tortilla for 1 minute, or until golden. Scatter over the avocado, leaving a little space around the edge, and spoon on the scallion mixture, and sprinkle with the cheese. Continue as in step 3.

Kids' Hot Tortilla Sandwiches

A quick alternative to a sandwich lunch that kids love.

SERVES 2 | **10 MINS** | **8 MINS**

Ingredients
4 tortillas, store-bought, or see pages 490–491
4 thin slices ham
ketchup, mild mustard, or chili sauce
2oz (50g) grated cheese, such as Cheddar
carrots, peeled and chopped, to serve (optional)
cucumber, chopped, to serve (optional)

Method

1 Place 2 of the tortillas on the work surface. Place 2 slices of ham on each tortilla, trying to ensure that the ham covers the whole tortilla. Tear it a little and spread it out if necessary.

2 Depending on your children's tastes, you could spread a little ketchup, mild mustard, or chili sauce over the top of the ham. Sprinkle the grated cheese evenly over both the tortillas, and top with a second tortilla to make a sandwich.

3 Heat a large frying pan (big enough to take the tortillas) to a medium heat. Fry the tortillas 1 at a time for 1 minute on each side. Turn them after each minute and continue to cook until both sides are cooked and browned in places.

4 Cut each tortilla into 8 segments, as you would a pizza, and serve immediately, with some chopped carrot and cucumber for a quick lunch.

Prawn and Guacamole Tortilla Stacks

These sophisticated Mexican-style canapés are simple to make.

MAKES 50   **15 MINS**   **5 MINS**

Special equipment
1¼in (3cm) pastry cutter
piping bag with small plain nozzle

Ingredients
5 tortillas, store-bought, or see pages 490–491
48oz sunflower or vegetable oil, for deep-frying
2 ripe avocados
1 lime
Tabasco sauce
¼ cup finely chopped cilantro
4 scallions, trimmed and finely chopped
sea salt
freshly ground black pepper
25 cooked king prawns, peeled and deveined

Method

1 Cut 100 disks out of the tortillas with the pastry cutter. Heat the oil in the largest saucepan you have. Drop the tortillas into the oil a handful at a time and deep-fry until golden. Do not overcrowd the pan, or the tortillas will not crisp properly. Remove and drain on paper towels. Cool.

2 Mash the avocado with the juice of half the lime, a few shakes of Tabasco, 3 tablespoons cilantro, the scallion, and salt and pepper to taste. Slice each prawn in half horizontally.

3 When there are 30 minutes left before serving, marinate the prawns with the juice of the other half of the lime and the remainder of the chopped cilantro.

4 Pipe a little guacamole on a tortilla, top it with another tortilla, pipe more guacamole on top, and finish with a curl of prawn. If it is too big, twist it on the diagonal and stand it up in the guacamole. Serve immediately.

PREPARE AHEAD The fried tortilla disks can be stored in an airtight container for 2 days.

quick breads & batters

Soda Bread

This has a light, cakelike texture. As an added bonus, it requires no kneading, so is a wonderfully effort-free loaf.

MAKES 1 LOAF | **10–15 MINS** | **35–40 MINS**

Ingredients

unsalted butter, for greasing
3 cups whole wheat flour,
  plus extra for dusting
1½ tsp baking soda
1½ tsp salt
2 cups buttermilk,
  plus extra if needed

1 Preheat the oven to 400°F (200°C). Grease a baking sheet with butter.

2 Sift the flour, baking soda, and salt into a large bowl, adding in any leftover bran.

3 Mix thoroughly to combine and make a well in the center.

4 Gradually pour the buttermilk into the center of the well.

5 With your hands, quickly draw in the flour to make a soft, slightly sticky dough.

6 Do not overwork the dough. Add a little more buttermilk if it seems dry.

7 Turn the dough out onto a floured surface, and quickly shape into a round loaf.

8 Put the loaf on the baking sheet and pat it down into a round, about 2in (5cm) high.

9 Make a cross ½in (1cm) deep in the top of the loaf with a very sharp knife or scalpel.

10 Bake the loaf in the preheated oven for 35–40 minutes, until brown.

11 Turn the loaf over and tap the bottom. The bread should sound hollow.

12 Transfer the bread to a wire rack and let it cool slightly.

13 Cut the bread into slices or wedges and serve warm, with plenty of butter. Soda bread also makes very good toast.
STORE This will keep, well wrapped in paper, for 2–3 days.

Soda Bread variations

Skillet Bread

In this version, the dough is cut in wedges and cooked in a heavy frying pan or skillet, and the addition of white flour makes it a little lighter.

MAKES 4 WEDGES | **5–10 MINS** | **30–40 MINS**

Special equipment
lidded cast-iron frying pan

Ingredients
2⅓ cups stone-ground whole wheat flour
¾ cup bread flour,
   plus extra for dusting
1½ tsp baking soda
1 tsp salt
1⅔ cups buttermilk
unsalted butter, melted,
   for greasing

Method
1 Put the 2 types of flour, the baking soda, and salt into a large bowl, and make a well in the center. Pour the buttermilk into the well. With your hand, quickly draw the flour into the buttermilk to make a soft dough. It should be slightly sticky.

2 Turn the dough onto a lightly floured work surface, and quickly shape it into a round loaf. Pat the dough with the palms of your hands to form a round, about 2in (5cm) high. With a chef's knife, cut the round into 4 wedges.

3 Heat a large cast-iron frying pan to medium-low. Brush the heated pan with melted butter. Put the dough into the pan, cover, and cook, turning the wedges frequently, for 15–20 minutes, until golden brown, puffed, and cooked through. Serve warm, spread with soft cheese or butter.

Griddle Cakes

These sweet cakes are crisp on the outside and moist in the center.

MAKES 20 CAKES | **5–10 MINS** | **10 MINS**

Special equipment
griddle or large cast-iron frying pan

Ingredients
1⅓ cups stone-ground whole wheat flour
1½ tsp baking soda
1½ tsp salt
1 cup rolled oats
3 tbsp brown sugar
2 cups buttermilk
unsalted butter, melted, for greasing

Method
1 Put the flour, baking soda, and salt into a large bowl. Stir in the oats and sugar, and make a well in the center. Pour the buttermilk into the well. Stir, gradually drawing in the dry ingredients to make a smooth batter.

2 Heat a griddle or a large cast-iron frying pan to medium-low. Brush the heated griddle with melted butter. Using a small ladle, drop about 2 tablespoons batter onto the hot surface. Repeat to make 5–6 cakes. Cook for about 5 minutes, until the undersides of the griddle cakes are golden brown and crisp. Turn and brown them on the other side for about 5 minutes longer.

3 Transfer to a platter, cover, and keep warm. Continue with the remaining batter, brushing the griddle with more butter as needed. Serve the cakes warm with plenty of butter and jam.

American Soda Bread

This classic sweet bread can be ready for an afternoon snack in no time.

MAKES 1 LOAF | **10–15 MINS** | **50–55 MINS** | **UP TO 8 WEEKS**

Ingredients

2¼ cups all-purpose flour, plus extra for dusting
1 tsp fine salt
2 tsp baking powder
¼ cup sugar
1 tsp caraway seeds (optional)
4 tbsp unsalted butter, chilled and diced
⅔ cup raisins
1 large egg
⅔ cup buttermilk

Method

1 Preheat the oven to 350°F (180°C). In a large bowl mix together the flour, salt, baking powder, sugar, and caraway seeds (if using). Rub in the butter until the mixture resembles fine crumbs. Add the raisins and mix well to combine.

2 Whisk together the egg and the buttermilk. Make a well in the center of the flour mixture and gradually pour in the buttermilk mixture, stirring until it is all incorporated. You will need to use your hands at the end to bring it all together to form a loose, soft dough.

3 Turn the dough out onto a lightly floured work surface and knead it briefly until smooth. Shape it into a round about 6in (15cm) in diameter, and slash the top with a cross to allow the bread to rise easily.

4 Place the dough onto a baking sheet lined with parchment paper, and cook in the middle of the preheated oven for 50–55 minutes, until well risen and golden brown. Transfer to a wire rack and allow to cool for at least 10 minutes before serving.

STORE This bread is best eaten the day it is baked, but will keep, well wrapped in paper, for 2 days.

Pumpkin Soda Bread

The use of grated pumpkin ensures this quick bread keeps moist for days. A perfect accompaniment for soup.

MAKES 1 LOAF | **20 MINS** | **50 MINS** | **UP TO 8 WEEKS**

Ingredients
1¾ cups all-purpose flour,
  plus extra for dusting
¾ cup whole wheat flour
1 tsp baking soda
½ tsp fine salt
⅓ cup pumpkin seeds
5oz (120g) pumpkin or butternut
  squash, roughly grated
1¼ cups buttermilk

1 Preheat the oven to 425°F (220°C). In a large bowl, mix the flour, baking soda, and salt.

2 Add the grated pumpkin and seeds, and stir well to combine so that no clumps remain.

3 Make a well in the center and pour in the buttermilk. Stir together to form a loose dough.

4 Use your hands to bring the mixture together into a ball, then turn out onto a floured surface.

5 Knead the dough for 2 minutes until it forms a smooth mass. You may need to add flour.

6 Shape the dough into a round 6in (15cm) in diameter. Place on a lined baking sheet.

7 Use a sharp knife to slash a cross into the top. This helps the bread to rise when baking.

8 Cook in the middle of the oven for 30 minutes, until risen. Reduce to 400°F (200°C).

9 Cook for a further 20 minutes. The base should sound hollow when tapped.

QUICK BREADS AND BATTERS

10 Transfer the bread to a wire rack and allow it to cool for at least 20 minutes before serving. Cut the bread into wedges or slices, and serve as an accompaniment to soups and stews. **STORE** This will keep, well wrapped in paper, for 3 days.

Vegetable Soda Bread variations

Sweet Potato and Rosemary Rolls

The gentle scent of rosemary makes these rolls something special.

| MAKES 8 ROLLS | 20 MINS | 20–25 MINS | UP TO 8 WEEKS |

Ingredients
1½ cups all-purpose flour, plus extra for dusting
¾ cup whole wheat flour
1 tsp baking soda
½ tsp fine salt
freshly ground black pepper
5oz (140g) sweet potato
1 tsp finely chopped rosemary
1 cup buttermilk

Method

1 Preheat the oven to 425°F (220°C). Line a baking sheet with parchment paper. In a bowl mix the all-purpose flour, whole wheat flour, baking soda, salt, and pepper. Peel and roughly grate the sweet potato, then chop it roughly to reduce the size of the shreds. Add it to the bowl with the rosemary, mixing well so that no clumps form.

2 Make a well in the center of the dry ingredients and gently stir in the buttermilk, bringing the mixture together to form a loose dough. Use your hands to bring the mixture together into a ball, then turn it out onto a floured surface and knead for 2 minutes until it forms a smooth dough. You may need to add a little flour at this stage.

3 Divide the dough into 8 equal pieces, and shape into tight rounds. Flatten the tops and cut a cross in the center of each roll to allow the dough to rise easily in the oven.

4 Place the rolls onto a baking sheet lined with parchment paper and cook them in the middle of the oven for 20-25 minutes, until well risen. Transfer to a wire rack and let cool for 10 minutes before serving. These are especially delicious eaten while warm.

STORE These rolls will keep, well wrapped in paper, for 3 days.

Zucchini and Hazelnut Bread

Hazelnuts add taste and texture to this quick and easy bread.

MAKES 1 LOAF | 20 MINS | 50 MINS | UP TO 8 WEEKS

Ingredients

1½ cups all-purpose flour, plus extra for dusting
1 cup whole wheat flour
1 tsp baking soda
½ tsp fine salt
⅓ cup hazelnuts, roughly chopped
6oz (150g) zucchini
1 cup buttermilk

Method

1 Preheat the oven to 425°F (220°C). Mix together the all-purpose flour, whole wheat flour, baking soda, salt, and hazelnuts. Coarsely grate the zucchini and add it to the bowl, mixing well so that no clumps form.

2 Make a well in the center of the dry ingredients and stir in the buttermilk to form a loose, ragged dough. Use your hands to bring the mixture together into a ball, then turn it out onto a lightly floured work surface and knead for 2 minutes until it forms a smooth dough. You may need to add a little extra flour at this stage, depending on the water content of your vegetables.

3 Shape the dough into a round about 6in (15cm) in diameter, and slash the top with a cross to allow the bread to rise when baking.

4 Place the dough onto a baking sheet lined with parchment paper, and cook in the middle of the oven for 30 minutes to create a good crust. Reduce the oven temperature to 400°F (200°C), and bake for a further 20 minutes until well risen, golden brown, and a skewer inserted into the middle emerges clean. Transfer the bread to a wire rack and allow it to cool for at least 20 minutes before serving.

STORE This bread will keep, well wrapped in paper, for 3 days.

Parsnip and Parmesan Bread

A perfect combination of flavors to serve with a bowl of warm soup on a cold winter's day.

MAKES 1 LOAF | 20 MINS | 50 MINS | UP TO 8 WEEKS

Ingredients

1½ cups all-purpose flour, plus extra for dusting
¾ cup whole wheat flour
1 tsp baking soda
½ tsp fine salt
freshly ground black pepper
2oz (50g) Parmesan cheese, finely grated
6oz (150g) parsnip
1¼ cups buttermilk

Method

1 Preheat the oven to 425°F (220°C). Mix together the all-purpose flour, whole wheat flour, baking soda, salt, pepper, and Parmesan. Grate the parsnip, then chop it roughly to reduce the size of the shreds. Add it to the bowl, mixing well so no clumps form.

2 Make a well in the center of the dry ingredients and stir in the buttermilk to form a loose, ragged dough. Use your hands to bring the mixture together into a ball, then turn it out onto a lightly floured work surface and knead it for 2 minutes until it forms a smooth dough. You may need to add a little extra flour at this stage, depending on the water content of your vegetables.

3 Shape the dough into a round about 6in (15cm) in diameter, and slash the top with a cross to allow the bread to rise when baking. Place the dough onto a baking sheet lined with parchment paper and cook in the middle of the oven for 30 minutes to create a good crust. Reduce the oven temperature to 400°F (200°C), and bake for a further 20 minutes until well risen, golden brown, and a skewer inserted into the middle emerges clean. Transfer the bread to a wire rack and let cool for at least 20 minutes before serving.

STORE This bread will keep, well wrapped in paper, for 3 days.

Cornbread

Cornbread is a traditional American loaf that makes a quick and easy accompaniment to soups and stews.

SERVES 8 | **15–20 MINS** | **20–25 MINS**

Special equipment
9in (23cm) flameproof cast-iron frying pan
loose-bottomed round cake pan

Ingredients
2 fresh corn cobs, about 7oz (200g) weight of kernels
4 tbsp unsalted butter or bacon dripping, melted and cooled, plus extra for greasing
1¼ cups fine yellow cornmeal or polenta
¾ cup bread flour
¼ cup sugar
1 tbsp baking powder
1 tsp salt
2 large eggs
1¼ cups milk

1 Preheat the oven to 425°F (220°C). Oil the pan with butter or bacon dripping. Place in oven.

2 Cut away the kernels from the cobs and scrape out the pulp with the back of the knife.

3 Sift the cornmeal, flour, sugar, baking powder, and salt into a bowl. Add the corn.

4 In a bowl, whisk together the eggs, melted butter or bacon dripping, and milk.

5 Pour three-quarters of the milk mixture into the flour mixture and stir.

6 Draw in the dry ingredients, adding the remaining milk mixture. Stir just until smooth.

7 Carefully take the hot pan out of the oven and pour in the batter; it should sizzle.

8 Quickly brush the top with butter or bacon dripping. Bake for 20–25 minutes.

9 The bread should shrink from the sides of the pan and a skewer should come out clean.

10 Let the cornbread cool slightly on a wire rack. Serve warm, with soup, chilli con carne, or fried chicken. The cornbread does not keep well but leftovers can be used as a stuffing for roast poultry.

Cornbread variations

Corn Muffins with Roasted Red Pepper

In the spirit of the American West, sweet red pepper is roasted, diced, and stirred into a corn batter. Baking the cornbread in muffin trays makes it easily portable for a picnic, packed lunch, or buffet.

MAKES 12 — 20 MINS — 15–20 MINS

Special equipment
12-hole muffin pan

Ingredients
1 large red bell pepper
1¼ cups fine yellow cornmeal
¾ cup all-purpose flour
1 tbsp sugar
1 tbsp baking powder
1 tsp salt
2 large eggs
4 tbsp unsalted butter or bacon dripping, plus extra for greasing
1¼ cups milk

Method

1 Heat the broiler on its highest setting. Set the pepper underneath and broil, turning as needed, until the skin blackens and blisters. Put the pepper in a plastic bag, close it, and let cool. Peel off the skin and out the core. Cut the pepper in half and scrape out the seeds and ribs. Dice the flesh finely.

2 Preheat the oven to 425°F (220°C). Generously grease the muffin pan and place it in the oven to heat up. Sift the cornmeal, flour, sugar, baking powder, and salt into a large bowl, and make a well in the center. In a bowl, whisk together the eggs, melted butter or bacon dripping, and milk. Pour three-quarters of the milk mixture into the well in the flour, and stir. Gradually draw in the dry ingredients, adding the remaining milk mixture, and stirring just until smooth. Stir in the diced pepper.

3 Carefully remove the hot pan from the oven and spoon the batter into the muffin holes. Bake in the oven for 15–20 minutes, until they start to shrink from the sides of the holes and a metal skewer inserted in the center of a muffin comes out clean. Unmold the muffins and let cool slightly.

PREPARE AHEAD Best served warm from the oven, these can be made 1 day ahead and kept tightly wrapped in paper. If possible, warm gently in the oven before serving.

Southern-style Cornbread

This quick cornbread is traditionally served as an accompaniment for a barbecue, soup, or stew. Some authentic Southern recipes omit the honey. ▶

SERVES 8 — 10–15 MINS — 25–35 MINS

Special equipment
8in (20cm) springform round cake pan or similar-sized flameproof cast-iron frying pan

Ingredients
1⅔ cup fine cornmeal or polenta, ideally white cornmeal if you can get it
2 tsp baking powder
½ tsp fine salt
2 large eggs
1 cup buttermilk
4 tbsp unsalted butter or bacon dripping, melted and cooled, plus extra for greasing
1 tbsp honey (optional)

Method

1 Preheat the oven to 425°F (220°C). Grease the cake pan or frying pan and place it in the oven to heat up. In a large bowl, mix together the cornmeal, baking powder, and salt. Whisk together the eggs and buttermilk.

2 Make a well in the center of the cornmeal mixture and gradually pour in the buttermilk mixture, slowly stirring until incorporated. Stir in the melted butter or bacon dripping, and honey, if using, and mix until smooth.

3 Carefully remove the hot pan from the oven and pour in the mixture. The pan should be hot enough to make the batter sizzle as it goes in; this is what gives the cornbread its distinctive crust.

4 Bake in the middle of the oven for 20–25 minutes until slightly risen and browning at the edges. Leave to cool for 5 minutes.

PREPARE AHEAD Best served warm from the oven, the bread can be made 1 day ahead and kept tightly wrapped in paper.

ALSO TRY...
Chile and Cilantro Cornbread
Add 1 red chile, deseeded and finely chopped, and 4 tablespoons finely chopped cilantro at the same time as the honey.

BAKER'S TIP
Southern cornbread gains a lot of its flavor from the use of melted bacon dripping in the batter, and a jar of collected leftover bacon grease is a common sight in kitchens across the Southern United States for this very reason—so start your own collection!

Blueberry Pancakes

Dropping the blueberries on top of the half-cooked pancakes stops the juice from leaking into the pan and burning.

MAKES 30   10 MINS   15–20 MINS

Ingredients

2 tbsp unsalted butter, plus extra
   for frying and to serve
2 large eggs
1½ cups all-purpose flour
1½ tsp baking powder

2 tbsp sugar
¼ teaspoon salt
1 cup milk
1 tsp pure vanilla extract
6oz (150g) blueberries
maple syrup, to serve

1 Melt the butter in a small saucepan and set aside to cool.

2 Crack the eggs into a small bowl and lightly beat with a fork until combined.

3 Sift the flour and baking powder into a bowl, lifting the sieve high above to aerate the flour.

4 Stir in the sugar and salt until evenly and thoroughly mixed with the flour.

5 In a large measuring cup, beat together the milk, eggs, and vanilla, until well blended.

6 With a spoon, form a well in the center of the dry ingredients.

7 Pour a little of the egg mixture into the well and start to whisk it in.

8 Wait until each addition of egg mixture has been incorporated before whisking in more.

9 Finally, whisk in the melted butter until the mixture is entirely smooth.

10 Melt a knob of butter in a large, non-stick frying pan over medium heat.

11 Pour 1 tablespoon of the batter into the pan, to form a round pancake.

12 Continue to add tablespoons of batter, leaving space between for them to spread.

13 As they begin to cook, sprinkle a few blueberries over the uncooked surface.

14 They are ready to turn when small bubbles appear and pop, leaving small holes.

15 Turn the pancakes over carefully with a metal spatula.

16 Continue to cook for a minute or two until golden brown on both sides and cooked.

17 Remove the pancakes from the pan, and drain briefly on paper towels.

18 Place the pancakes on a plate and transfer to a warm oven.

19 Wipe out the frying pan with paper towels, and add another knob of butter.

20 Repeat for all the batter and wipe between batches. The pan should not get too hot.

21 Remove the pancakes from the oven. Serve warm in stacks, with butter and maple syrup.

BLUEBERRY PANCAKES

Pancake variations

Cinnamon Pancakes

Transform any leftover pancakes with this quick topping.

MAKES 8 · 10 MINS · 5 MINS

Ingredients

1 tsp ground cinnamon
¼ cup sugar
8 leftover pancakes, see Blueberry Pancakes, pages 508–509
2 tbsp unsalted butter, melted

Method

1 Preheat the broiler. Mix the cinnamon and sugar together and pour onto a plate. Brush each pancake on both sides with melted butter and press each side into the sugar and cinnamon mix, shaking off the excess sugar.

2 Place the pancakes on a baking sheet and cook under the hot broiler until the sugar is bubbling and melted. Leave the sugar to set for 1 minute before turning them over and broiling on the other side. Serve immediately with Greek yogurt, or just plain as an afternoon snack.

BAKER'S TIP

American pancakes are a great standby, and the recipe is easy to remember once you have cooked it a few times. They can be served for breakfast or dessert, with strawberries, chocolate sauce, or banana and yogurt. Make the toppings as decadent, or as healthy, as you like.

Drop Scones

So-called because the batter is dropped onto a frying pan.

MAKES 12 · 10 MINS · 15 MINS · UP TO 4 WEEKS

Ingredients

1⅓ cup all-purpose flour
4 tsp baking powder
1 large egg
2 tsp corn syrup
¾ cup milk, plus extra if needed
vegetable oil

Method

1 Place a flat griddle pan or large frying pan over medium heat. Fold a kitchen towel in half and lay it on a baking sheet.

2 Sift the flour and baking powder into a bowl; make a well in the center, and add the egg, corn syrup, and milk. Whisk well to make a smooth batter the consistency of thick cream. If the mixture is too thick, beat in a little more milk.

3 Test that the griddle pan is hot enough by sprinkling a little flour onto the hot surface. If it burns, the pan is too hot. When the temperature is right, dust off the flour and rub a paper towel dipped in cooking oil lightly over the surface.

4 Lift out 1 tablespoon of batter. Drop the batter from the tip of the spoon onto the hot pan to make a nice round shape. Repeat, leaving enough room between the rounds for the pancakes to rise and spread.

5 Bubbles will appear on the surface of the pancakes. When they begin to burst, ease a spatula underneath the pancakes and flip to cook the other side. Place cooked pancakes inside the folded towel to keep them soft while you cook the rest of the batch.

6 Oil the hot pan after each batch and watch the heat. If the pancakes are pale and take a long time to cook, increase the heat. If they brown too quickly on the outside and are still raw in the middle, reduce the heat. These are best eaten freshly baked and warm.

Banana, Yogurt, and Honey Pancake Stack

Try stacking pancakes for a luxurious breakfast treat. ▶

SERVES 6 · 10 MINS · 15–20 MINS

Ingredients

1 cup all-purpose flour
1 tsp baking powder
¼ cup sugar
1 cup whole milk
2 large eggs, beaten
½ tsp pure vanilla extract
2 tbsp unsalted butter, melted and cooled, plus extra for cooking
1 large banana
7oz (200g) Greek yogurt
honey, to serve

Method

1 Sift the flour and baking powder into a large bowl. Add the sugar. In a large measuring cup or pitcher whisk together the milk, eggs, and vanilla. Make a well in the center of the flour mixture and whisk in the milk mixture, a little at a time. Whisk in the butter until the mixture is entirely smooth.

2 Melt a tablespoon of butter in a large, non-stick frying pan. Pour tablespoons of the pancake batter into the pan, leaving space between them for the pancakes to spread. The pancakes should spread to be approximately 3¼-4in (8-10cm) in diameter. Cook the pancakes over medium heat. Turn the pancakes when small bubbles begin to appear on the surface and pop. Cook for another minute or 2 until golden brown on both sides and cooked through.

3 Slice the banana diagonally to produce 2in (5cm) long strips. Place 1 warm pancake on a plate. Top with a spoonful of Greek yogurt and some slices of banana. Top with another pancake, more yogurt, and honey. Finish the stack with a third pancake, topped with a spoonful of yogurt and drizzled generously with honey.

Buttermilk Biscuits

A favorite dish in the South, where biscuits are eaten for breakfast spread with something sweet or to accompany sausage gravy.

MAKES 12 · **10 MINS** · **15 MINS** · **UP TO 4 WEEKS**

Special equipment
2½in (6cm) pastry cutter

Ingredients

1⅓ cups self-rising flour
1 tsp baking powder
½ tsp fine salt
7 tbsp unsalted butter, softened
1½ cups buttermilk, plus extra for brushing
1 tbsp honey

Method

1 Preheat the oven to 400°F (200°C). Sift the flour and baking powder into a bowl and add the salt. With your fingertips, rub the butter into the dry ingredients until the mixture resembles fine crumbs.

2 Make a well in the center and pour in the buttermilk and honey. Work the mixture together to form a rough dough, then turn it out onto a lightly floured work surface and bring it together into a smooth ball. Do not over handle it or the biscuits may harden (see Baker's Tip).

3 Roll out the dough to a thickness of ¾in (2cm) and cut 2½in (6cm) biscuits out of it with the pastry cutter. Gather up the remaining dough, re-roll it, and cut out biscuits until all the dough is used up.

4 Place the biscuits on a non-stick baking sheet and brush the tops with buttermilk, to give them a golden finish. Bake in the top third of the oven for 15 minutes until golden brown and well risen. Remove from the oven and cool for 5 minutes on a wire rack before serving, still warm.

STORE The biscuits can be kept in an airtight container for 1 day and warmed up again in the oven before serving.

BAKER'S TIP

Buttermilk biscuits have a tendency to harden and taste tough if overhandled. To avoid this, bring the mix together gently and stop as soon as it forms a dough. When rolling gently, try to cut out as many biscuits from the first rolling as possible, as biscuits from subsequent rollings will be tougher.

Crumpets

Eaten for breakfast or as an afternoon snack, toasted crumpets are great with both sweet and savory toppings.

MAKES 8 | **10 MINS** | **20–26 MINS** | **UP TO 4 WEEKS**

Special equipment
4 crumpet rings, or 4in (10cm) metal pastry cutters

Ingredients
1 cup all-purpose flour
¾ cup bread flour
½ tsp dried yeast
⅔ cup tepid milk
½ tsp salt
½ tsp baking soda
vegetable oil, for greasing

Method

1 Mix together the flours and yeast. Stir in the milk and ⅔ cup tepid water, and leave for 2 hours, or until the bubbles have risen and then started to fall again. Mix the salt and baking soda into 2 tablespoons lukewarm water and whisk in. Set aside for 5 minutes.

2 Oil the crumpet rings or pastry cutters. Lightly oil a large, heavy frying pan and place the rings in the pan.

3 Pour the batter into a large measuring cup or pitcher. Heat the pan over a medium heat and pour batter into each ring to a depth of ½–¾in (1-2cm). Cook the crumpets for 8–10 minutes, or until the batter has set all the way through and the top is covered in holes. If no bubbles appear, the mixture is too dry, so stir a little water into the remaining batter.

4 Lift the rings off the crumpets, turn them over, and cook for another 2–3 minutes, or until just golden. Repeat with the remaining batter. Serve the freshly cooked crumpets warm and buttered, or toast to reheat if serving them later.

BAKER'S TIP
The holes on top of crumpets are their unique selling point, making them the perfect repository for butter, jam, or marmalade. The leavening creates bubbles as they cook, which burst to produce these holes. Homemade crumpets tend to have fewer holes, but are no less tasty or absorbent for it.

Crêpes Suzette

In this most classic of French desserts, crêpes are flambéd just before serving. A sure way to create culinary drama.

SERVES 6   **40–50 MINS**   **45–60 MINS**

Standing time
30 mins

Ingredients

For the crêpes
1 cup all-purpose flour, sifted
1 tbsp sugar
½ tsp salt
4 large eggs, at room temperature
1½ cups milk, plus extra if needed
6 tbsp unsalted butter, melted and cooled, plus extra if needed

For the orange butter
1 stick, plus 4 tbsp unsalted butter, at room temperature
⅓ cup confectioner's sugar
3 large oranges, 2 finely grated and 1 peeled with a vegetable peeler then cut into julienne strips
1 tbsp Grand Marnier

For flaming
⅓ cup brandy
⅓ cup Grand Marnier

1 Mix the flour, sugar, and salt. Make a well in the center, and add the eggs and half the milk.

2 Whisk, drawing in the flour, to make a batter. Whisk in half the butter, until smooth.

3 Add milk to give the batter the consistency of half-and-half. Cover and leave for 30 minutes.

4 For the orange butter, cream the butter and confectioner's sugar with a hand mixer.

5 With a sharp knife, cut the pith and skin from all 3 oranges.

6 Slide the knife down both sides of each segment to cut it free. Set aside.

7 Add the zest and 2 tablespoons juice to the butter with the Grand Marnier. Whisk well.

8 Add the julienned orange to a saucepan of boiling water; simmer for 2 minutes. Drain.

9 Add a little melted butter to a small frying pan and heat over medium-high heat.

10 Ladle 2–3 tablespoons of the batter into the pan, tilting the pan so the base is covered.

11 Fry for 1 minute. Gently loosen with a palette knife. Turn and cook for 30–60 seconds.

12 Repeat, adding butter only when the crêpes start to stick, making 12 crêpes.

13 Spread the orange butter over 1 side of each crêpe. Heat the pan over medium heat.

14 Add 1 crêpe at a time, butter-side down. Cook for 1 minute and fold into quarters.

15 Arrange the crêpes in the hot frying pan. Heat the alcohol, then pour over the crêpes.

16 Stand back. Hold a lighted match to the side of the pan. Baste until the flames die down.

17 Divide the crêpes among warmed plates, and spoon the sauce from the pan over them.

18 Decorate with orange segments and strips, and serve. **PREPARE AHEAD** The plain crêpes can be made 3 days ahead, layered with parchment, and stored, wrapped, in the refrigerator.

Crêpe variations

Buckwheat Galettes

These savory pancakes are popular in the Brittany region of France, where the local cuisine is defined by rich, rustic flavors.

SERVES 4 | 25 MINS | 25–30 MINS | 12 WEEKS, UNFILLED

Resting time
2 hrs

Ingredients

For the galettes
½ cup buckwheat flour
½ cup all-purpose flour
2 large eggs, beaten
1 cup milk
sunflower or vegetable oil, for greasing

For the filling
2 tbsp sunflower or vegetable oil
2 red onions, peeled and thinly sliced
7oz (200g) smoked ham, chopped
1 tsp thyme leaves
4oz (115g) Brie cheese, cut into small pieces
½ cup crème fraîche

Method

1 Sift the flours into a large mixing bowl, make a well in the center, and add the eggs. Gradually beat the eggs into the flour using a wooden spoon, then add the milk and ½ cup water to make a smooth batter. Cover and let stand for 2 hours.

2 Heat the oil for the filling in a small frying pan, add the onions, and cook gently until softened. Add the ham and thyme, then remove from the heat and set aside.

3 Preheat the oven to 300°F (150°C). Heat the crêpe pan and grease lightly. Spoon in 2 tablespoons of batter and swirl so it coats the base of the pan. Cook for 1 minute, or until lightly browned underneath, then flip over and cook for another 1 minute, or until browned on the other side. Make 7 more crêpes, re-greasing the pan as necessary.

4 Stir the Brie and crème fraîche into the filling and divide between the pancakes. Roll or fold up the filled pancakes and place on a baking sheet. Heat through in the oven for 10 minutes before serving.

PREPARE AHEAD Make the batter a few hours in advance and leave to stand until ready to cook. If it thickens too much, stir in a little water before using.

Spinach, Pancetta, and Ricotta Pancake Bake

Try making with store-bought pancakes for a speedy supper.

SERVES 4 | 30 MINS | 35 MINS | 12 WEEKS, UNBAKED

Special equipment
9 x 13in (23 x 33cm) shallow ovenproof dish

Ingredients

For the batter
1¼ cups all-purpose flour
½ tsp fine salt
1 cup whole milk, plus extra if needed
4 large eggs
4 tbsp unsalted butter, melted and cooled, plus extra for cooking and greasing

For the filling
½ cup pine nuts
2 tsp extra virgin olive oil, plus extra for greasing
1 red onion, finely chopped
4oz (100g) diced pancetta
2 garlic cloves, crushed
10oz (300g) baby spinach, washed and dried
9oz (250g) ricotta
3–4 tbsp heavy cream
sea salt
freshly ground black pepper

For the cheese sauce
1½ cups heavy cream
2oz (60g) Parmesan cheese, finely grated

Method

1 Mix the flour and salt in a large bowl. Separately whisk together the milk and eggs. Make a well in the center of the flour mixture and whisk in the milk mixture, a little at a time, until it is all incorporated. Add the butter and whisk until entirely smooth. The mixture should be the consistency of pouring cream. Add extra milk if needed. Transfer to a large measuring cup or pitcher, cover with plastic wrap, and leave to rest for 30 minutes.

2 To make the filling, dry fry the pine nuts in a large sauté pan for 2 minutes over medium heat, turning often until they turn golden brown in places. Set aside.

3 Add the olive oil to the pan and sauté the onion for 3 minutes until softened, but not brown. Add the pancetta and cook it over medium heat for another 5 minutes, until golden brown and crispy. Add the garlic and cook for another minute. Add the baby spinach in handfuls; it will wilt down very quickly. Cook the spinach only until it begins to wilt, then take the pan from the heat.

4 Place the spinach mixture into a sieve, and press down with the back of a spoon to remove excess water. Transfer to a bowl, add the pine nuts, and mix with the ricotta and the cream. Season well and set aside.

5 Melt a tablespoon of butter in a large, non-stick frying pan, and when it begins to sizzle wipe away any excess with a piece of paper towel. Pour a couple of tablespoonfuls of the pancake mixture into the frying pan, and then tip the pan to cover with a thin layer of the batter. Cook for a couple of minutes on each side, turning them when the first side is golden brown. Set the cooked pancakes aside and continue until all the batter has been used up, adding a tablespoon more butter when necessary. This should give you approximately 10 pancakes.

6 Preheat the oven to 400°F (200°C). Lay a pancake out flat. Put 2 tablespoons of filling into the middle of the pancake. Use the back of the spoon to spread it out into a thick line, then roll the pancake up around it. Grease the dish and lay the pancakes side by side in the dish.

7 For the sauce, heat the heavy cream until nearly boiling. Add nearly all the Parmesan. Whisk until the cheese melts, then bring to a boil and simmer for 2 minutes until it thickens slightly. Season to taste and pour over the pancakes. Top with the reserved cheese.

8 Bake at the top of the oven for 20 minutes until golden and bubbling in places. Remove and serve immediately with a green salad.

PREPARE AHEAD This can be made up to the end of step 6, covered, and refrigerated for up to 2 days, before finishing with the sauce and baking as described.

Swedish Pancake Stack Cake

Make sure you use only the thinnest of crêpes for this sumptuous dessert. A perfect summer birthday cake and a children's favorite.

SERVES 6–8	10 MINS	15 MINS

Ingredients
6 pancakes, made using ½ quantity crêpe batter, see pages 518–519, steps 1–3 and 10–12
¾ cup heavy cream
1 cup crème fraîche
3 tbsp sugar
¼ tsp pure vanilla extract
9oz (250g) raspberries
confectioner's sugar, to serve

Method
1 Whip the cream into stiff peaks. Combine the whipped cream, crème fraîche, sugar, and vanilla, and whisk until well mixed. Set aside ¼ cup to decorate the top of the cake.

2 Reserve a good handful of the raspberries. Lightly crush the remaining fruit with a fork and add them to the remaining cream mixture, folding them through roughly to create a rippled effect.

3 Place the first pancake on a serving platter, and spread one-fifth of the raspberry and cream mixture over the surface. Continue to layer until all the pancakes and cream are used up.

4 Top with the reserved cream mixture and the remaining raspberries. Dust with confectioner's sugar, and serve.

BAKER'S TIP
This stack cake is extremely versatile. You can try using chopped strawberries or blueberries, which will make an equally delicious cake. In Sweden, lingonberry jam (similar to sweet cranberry sauce) is often used as a substitute for the fresh fruit. You can find the jam in Scandinavian delicatessens.

Staffordshire Oatcakes

These oat pancakes can have sweet or savory fillings, can be folded in half, rolled up, or cooked on top of each other, then sliced in quarters.

MAKES 10 **10 MINS** **15 MINS**

Resting time
1–2 hrs

Ingredients
1 cup oat bran
1 cup whole wheat flour
1 cup all-purpose flour
½ tsp fine salt
2 tsp dried yeast
1¼ cups milk
unsalted butter, for frying

For the filling
9oz (250g) cheese, such as Cheddar
  or red Leicester, grated
20 slices bacon

Method

1 Sift together the oat bran, whole wheat flour, all-purpose flour, and salt. Add the dried yeast to 1¾ cups warm water and whisk well until it is completely dissolved. Add the milk. Make a well in the center of the dry ingredients and stir in the milk and water mixture.

2 Whisk the mixture together until the batter is completely smooth. Cover and set aside for 1–2 hours, until small bubbles start to appear on the surface of the batter.

3 Melt a knob of butter in a large, non-stick frying pan and, when it begins to sizzle, wipe any excess away quickly with a piece of paper towel.

4 Pour a ladleful of the oatcake mixture into the center of the frying pan, and then tip the pan to allow the batter to spread all around. The idea is to cover the surface of the pan very quickly with a thin layer of the batter.

5 Cook the oatcakes for a couple of minutes on each side, turning them when the edges are cooked through and the first side is golden brown. Set the cooked oatcakes aside in a warm place and continue until all the batter has been used up.

6 Meanwhile, preheat the broiler on its highest setting, and broil the bacon. Sprinkle a handful of grated cheese all over the surface of an oatcake.

7 Place it under the broiler for a couple of minutes until the cheese has completely melted. Place 2 slices of bacon on top of the melted cheese to 1 side of the oatcake, and roll it up before serving.

BAKER'S TIP
These traditional oatcakes are really savory pancakes, though a little more wholesome, and make a fantastic breakfast treat every once in a while. For an even quicker breakfast, the batter can be made the night before and stored, covered, in the refrigerator overnight.

Blinis

These buckwheat-based pancakes originated in Russia. Try serving them as canapés, or larger topped with smoked fish and crème fraîche for lunch.

MAKES 48 BLINIS | 20 MINS | 15 MINS | UP TO 8 WEEKS

Resting time
2 hrs

Ingredients
½ tsp dried yeast
¾ cup warm milk
½ cup sour cream
1 cup buckwheat flour
1 cup bread flour
½ tsp fine salt
2 large eggs, separated
4 tbsp butter, melted and cooled,
  plus extra for cooking

Method

1 Mix the yeast with the warm milk and whisk until the yeast dissolves. Whisk in the sour cream and set aside.

2 In a large bowl, mix together the 2 types of flour and the salt. Make a well in the center of the flour mixture and gradually whisk in the milk and sour cream. Add the egg yolks and continue to whisk. Finally add the butter and whisk until smooth.

3 Cover the bowl with plastic wrap and set aside in a warm place for at least 1 hour, until bubbles appear all over the surface.

4 In a clean bowl whisk the egg whites to soft peaks. Add the egg whites to the batter and gently fold them in using a metal spoon or spatula, until they are well combined and there are no lumps of egg white. Transfer the batter to a large measuring cup or pitcher.

5 Heat a tablespoon of butter in a large, non-stick frying pan. Pour 1 tablespoon of the batter at a time into the pan to form small blinis approximately 2½in (6cm) in

diameter. Cook the blinis for a minute or 2 over medium heat until bubbles start to appear on the surface. When the bubbles begin to pop, turn and cook for a minute on the second side. Remove the blinis to a warm plate, cover with a clean kitchen towel, and continue to cook until all the batter is used up.

6 Serve the blinis still warm, with sour cream and smoked salmon for a delicious canapé. They can also be wrapped in foil and gently reheated in a warm oven for 10 minutes before serving.

PREPARE AHEAD The blinis will keep in an airtight container in the refrigerator for up to 3 days. Reheat them (from fresh or frozen) as in step 6.

BAKER'S TIP
Blinis are simple to make, but can be difficult to get perfectly circular, and small enough to serve as a canapé. Remember to pour the batter directly into the center of the blini, and use a spoon to catch any drips from the pitcher as you finish pouring.

QUICK BREADS AND BATTERS

Cherry Clafoutis

This French favorite can be enjoyed warm or at room temperature.

SERVES 6 | 12 MINS | 35–45 MINS

Resting time
30 mins

Special equipment
10in (25cm) tart pan or shallow
  ovenproof dish

Ingredients
1lb 10oz (750g) cherries
3 tbsp Kirsch
⅓ cup sugar
unsalted butter, for greasing

4 large eggs, at room temperature
1 vanilla pod, split, seeds scraped
  out and reserved (optional)
¾ cup all-purpose flour
1¼ cups milk
pinch of salt

1 Toss the cherries with the Kirsch and 2 tablespoons sugar. Leave for 30 minutes.

2 Preheat the oven to 400°F (200°C). Butter the tart pan, and set aside.

3 Strain the liquid from the cherries into a large bowl. Set the cherries aside.

4 Beat the eggs into the Kirsch mixture, until very well amalgamated.

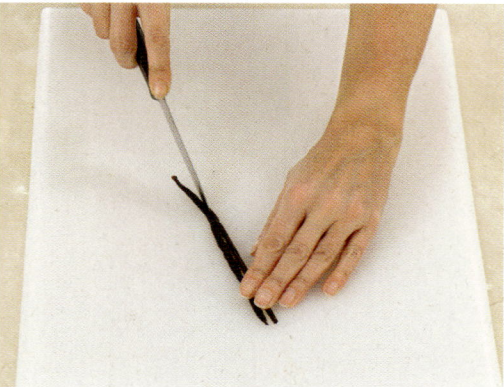

5 With a sharp knife, split the vanilla pod (if using) vertically down the middle.

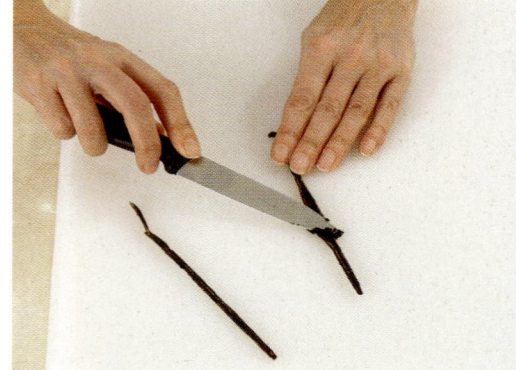

6 Run the tip of the knife down the middle of each half to scrape out all the seeds.

7 Add the seeds to the egg and Kirsch mixture and mix well to distribute.

8 Add the remaining sugar and beat well to combine.

9 Sift the flour into a large bowl, lifting the sieve high to aerate the flour as it floats down.

10 Beat the flour into the egg mixture, whisking after each addition, to make a smooth paste.

11 Pour in the milk, add the salt, and whisk until it makes a smooth batter.

12 Arrange the cherries in 1 layer in the tart dish. They should fill the dish.

13 Slowly pour the batter over the top of the cherries, trying not to displace the cherries.

14 Bake for 35–45 minutes, or until the top is browned and the center is firm to the touch.

15 Allow to cool on a wire rack. Remove from the pan and dust with confectioner's sugar.

16 Serve warm or at room temperature, with plenty of thick cream or crème fraîche for spooning over, or with vanilla ice cream.

CHERRY CLAFOUTIS

Clafoutis variations

Toad in the Hole

This classic British version of clafoutis is perfect comfort food.

SERVES 4 | 20 MINS | 35–40 MINS

Standing time
30 mins

Special equipment
roasting pan or shallow ovenproof dish

Ingredients
1 cup all-purpose flour
pinch of salt
2 large eggs
1¼ cups milk
2 tbsp vegetable oil
8 Toulouse or Italian sausages

Method

1 To make the batter, put the flour into a bowl with the salt, make a well in the center, and add the eggs with a little of the milk. Whisk together, gradually incorporating the flour. Add the remaining milk and whisk to make a smooth batter. Leave to rest for at least 30 minutes.

2 Preheat the oven to 425°F (220°C). Heat the oil in a roasting pan or shallow ovenproof dish. Add the sausages and toss them in the hot oil. Bake for 5–10 minutes, or until the sausages are just colored and the fat is very hot.

3 Reduce the oven temperature to 400°F (200°C). Carefully pour the batter around the sausages and return to the oven for a further 30 minutes, until the batter is risen, golden, and crisp. Serve immediately, with onion gravy, green vegetables, and mustard.

PREPARE AHEAD The batter can be made 24 hours in advance. Keep chilled and whisk briefly just before using.

Apricot Clafoutis

This French favorite can be enjoyed warm or at room temperature. Canned apricots taste just fine, when fresh are out of season.

SERVES 4 | 10 MINS | 35 MINS

Special equipment
shallow ovenproof dish

Ingredients
unsalted butter, for greasing
1 can of apricot halves, drained, or 9oz (250g) fresh ripe apricots, halved and pitted
1 large egg, plus 1 large egg yolk
2 tbsp all-purpose flour
¼ cup sugar
⅔ cup heavy cream
¼ tsp pure vanilla extract

Method

1 Preheat the oven to 400°F (200°C). Lightly grease the dish; it should be big enough to fit the apricots in a single layer. Place the apricots cut side down in a single layer in the dish; there should be spaces between them.

2 In a bowl whisk together the egg and egg yolk and the flour. Whisk in the sugar. Finally add the cream and vanilla extract and whisk thoroughly to a smooth custard.

3 Pour the custard around the apricots. The tops of the apricots should be just visible here and there above the custard.

4 Bake at the top of the preheated oven for 35 minutes until puffed up and golden brown in places. Remove from the oven and allow to cool for at least 15 minutes. This clafoutis is best served warm with thick cream or crème fraîche.

PREPARE AHEAD This dessert is best freshly baked and served warm, but can also be cooked up to 6 hours ahead and served at room temperature.

Plum and Marzipan Clafoutis

This stunning version is equally good made with plums or cherries, but instead of putting the marzipan in the fruit cavities, dot little pieces between each fruit.

SERVES 6   **30 MINS**   **50 MINS**

Special equipment
shallow ovenproof dish

Ingredients

For the marzipan
1 cup ground almonds
½ cup sugar
½ cup confectioner's sugar, plus extra for dusting
a few drops of almond extract
½ tsp lemon juice
1 large egg white, lightly beaten

For the clafoutis
1½lb (675g) plums, halved and pitted
5 tbsp butter
4 large eggs and 1 egg yolk
½ cup sugar
⅓ cup all-purpose flour, sifted
2 cups milk
⅔ cup half-and-half

Method

1 Preheat the oven to 375°F (190°C). Mix the marzipan ingredients together with enough of the egg white to form a stiff paste. Push a tiny piece of the paste into the cavity in each of the plum halves.

2 Grease a shallow, ovenproof dish, large enough to hold the plums in a single layer, with 1 tablespoon of the butter. Arrange the plums cut-side down in the dish, with the marzipan underneath. Melt the remaining butter and leave to cool.

3 Add any leftover egg white from the marzipan to the eggs and egg yolk. Add the sugar and whisk until thick and pale. Whisk in the melted butter, flour, milk, and half-and-half to form a batter. Pour over the plums and bake in the oven for about 50 minutes until golden and just set. Serve warm, dusted with confectioner's sugar.

PREPARE AHEAD The clafoutis is best freshly baked and served warm, but can be cooked up to 6 hours ahead and served at room temperature.

> **BAKER'S TIP**
> Clafoutis is basically a sweetened custard, baked around any type of seasonal fruit. As a pantry standby, try the classic version with canned apricots, but in season, you can use cherries, blackberries, plums, and black, white, or red currants.

Plum Clafoutis

This is a satisfying fall dessert to make, when the plums are at their peak. You can substitute plum or ordinary brandy for the Kirsch, if preferred. **PICTURED OVERLEAF**

SERVES 6–8   **20–25 MINS**   **30–35 MINS**

Special equipment
shallow ovenproof dish

Ingredients
unsalted butter, for greasing
½ cup sugar, plus extra for baking dish
1lb 6oz (625g) small plums, halved and pitted
2 tbsp all-purpose flour
salt
⅔ cup milk
⅓ cup heavy cream
4 large eggs, plus 2 large egg yolks
3 tbsp Kirsch
2 tbsp confectioner's sugar

Method

1 Preheat the oven to 350°F (180°C). Grease the baking dish with the butter. Sprinkle some sugar into the dish. Turn the dish around and shake it to coat the bottom and side evenly. Tap out any excess. Spread the plums, cut side up, evenly in the dish.

2 Sift the flour and a pinch of salt into a bowl and make a well in the center. Pour in the milk and cream and whisk, drawing in the flour, to make a smooth paste. Add the eggs, egg yolks, and sugar, and whisk to make a smooth batter.

3 Just before baking, ladle the batter over the plums, then spoon over the Kirsch. Bake the clafoutis in the oven for 30–35 minutes, until puffed up and beginning to brown. Just before serving, sift over the confectioner's sugar. Serve warm or at room temperature, with whipped cream.

PREPARE AHEAD The clafoutis is best freshly baked and served warm, but can be cooked up to 6 hours ahead and served at room temperature.

Waffles

These easy-to-make and versatile waffles are perfect for breakfast, a light snack, or dessert.

MAKES 6–8 **10 MINS** **20–25 MINS** **UP TO 4 WEEKS**

Special equipment
waffle maker or waffle iron

Ingredients
1 cup all-purpose flour
1 tsp baking powder
2 tbsp sugar
1¼ cups milk
5 tbsp unsalted butter, melted
1 tsp pure vanilla extract
2 large eggs, separated
maple syrup, jam, fresh fruit, sweetened cream,
  or ice cream, to serve (optional)

Method

1 Place the flour, baking powder, and sugar in a bowl, make a well in the center, and pour in the milk, butter, vanilla extract, and egg yolks. Gradually whisk in the flour.

2 Preheat the waffle maker or iron. In a clean large bowl, whisk the egg whites until standing in soft peaks. Fold into the batter with a metal spoon.

3 Preheat the oven to 250°F (130°C). Spoon a small ladleful of the batter onto the hot iron (or the amount recommended by the waffle maker manufacturer) and spread almost to the edge. Close the lid and bake until golden.

4 Serve immediately, with maple syrup, jam, fresh fruit, sweetened cream, or ice cream, or keep warm in a single layer in the oven until all are ready.

PREPARE AHEAD Although best eaten as fresh as possible, you can make waffles 24 hours in advance and reheat in a toaster.

BAKER'S TIP

Whenever a recipe calls for the addition of melted butter, as here, make sure it is completely cooled before adding to a batter. Warm—or worse, hot—butter, can curdle a mixture, starting to cook it before time, or forming lumps of cooked eggs. So do not skip the vital step of cooling melted butter.

Index

INDEX

About the author

After spending years as an international model, Caroline Bretherton dedicated herself to her passion for food, founding her company, Manna Food, in 1996.

Her fresh, light, and stylish cooking soon developed a stylish following to match, with a catering clientele that included celebrities, art galleries, theaters, and fashion magazines, as well as cutting edge businesses. She later expanded the company to include an all-day eatery called Manna Café on Portobello Road, in the heart of London's Notting Hill.

A move into the media has seen her working consistently in television over the years, appearing as a guest on and presenting a wide range of food programs for local and cable broadcasters.

More recently Caroline has worked increasingly in print, becoming a regular contributor to *The Times on Saturday*, and writing her first book *The Kitchen Garden Cookbook*.

In her spare time, Caroline tends her beloved community garden near her home in London, growing a variety of fruits, vegetables, and herbs. When she can, she indulges her passion for wild food foraging, both in the city and the country.

She is married to Luke, an academic, and has two boys, Gabriel and Isaac, who were more than happy to test the recipes for this book.

Acknowledgments

The author would like to thank
Mary-Clare, Dawn, and Alastair at Dorling Kindersley for their help and encouragement with this massive task, as well as Borra Garson and all at Deborah McKenna for all their work on my behalf. Lastly I would like to thank all my family and friends for their tremendous encouragement and appetites!

Dorling Kindersley would like to thank
The following people for their work on the photoshoot:

Art Directors
Nicky Collings, Miranda Harvey, Luis Peral, Lisa Pettibone

Props Stylist
Wei Tang

Food Stylists
Kate Blinman, Lauren Owen, Denise Smart

Home Economist Assistant
Emily Jonzen

Baking equipment used in the step-by-step photography kindly donated by Lakeland. www.lakeland.co.uk; 011 44 15394 88100.

Caroline de Souza for art direction and setting the style of the videos and presentation stills photography.

Dorothy Kikon for editorial assistance and Anamica Roy for design assistance.

Jane Ellis for proofreading and Susan Bosanko for indexing.

Thanks to the following people for their work on the US edition:

Consultant
Kate Curnes

Americanizers
Nichole Morford and Jenny Siklós

Thanks also to Steve Crozier for retouching.

Useful Information

Oven temperature equivalents

For a fan-assisted oven, reduce the temperature by at least 25°F/10°C.

FAHRENHEIT	CELSIUS	DESCRIPTION
225°F	110°C	Cool
250°F	130°C	Cool
275°F	140°C	Very low
300°F	150°C	Very low
325°F	160°C	Low
350°F	180°C	Moderate
375°F	190°C	Moderately hot
400°F	200°C	Hot
425°F	220°C	Hot
450°F	230°C	Very hot
475°F	240°C	Very hot

Volume equivalents

Note that 1 teaspoon measures 5ml and 1 tbsp measures 15ml.

IMPERIAL	METRIC	IMPERIAL	METRIC
1fl oz	30ml	15fl oz	450ml
2fl oz	60ml	16fl oz	500ml
2½fl oz	75ml	1 pint	600ml
3½fl oz	100ml	1¼ pints	750ml
4fl oz	120ml	1½ pints	900ml
5fl oz (¼ pint)	150ml	1¾ pints	1 liter
6fl oz	175ml	2 pints	1.2 liters
7fl oz (⅓ pint)	200ml	2½ pints	1.4 liters
8fl oz	240ml	2¾ pints	1.5 liters
10fl oz (½ pint)	300ml	3 pints	1.7 liters
12fl oz	350ml	3½ pints	2 liters
14fl oz	400ml	5¼ pints	3 liters

Butter equivalent

1 stick of butter = 8 tablespoons